# Chinese Connections

# Chinese Connections

*Critical Perspectives on Film, Identity, and Diaspora*

*Edited by*

Tan See-Kam, Peter X Feng, and Gina Marchetti

TEMPLE UNIVERSITY PRESS
Philadelphia

Publication of this book is made possible through the generous support of the Chiang Ching-Kuo Foundation for International Scholarly Exchange.

**Temple University Press**
1601 North Broad Street
Philadelphia PA 19122
*www.temple.edu/tempress*


Published 2009
Printed in the United States of America

Text design by Kate Nichols

♾ The paper used in this publication meets the requirements of the American National Standard for Information Sciences—Permanence of Paper for Printed Library Materials, ANSI Z39.48-1992

Library of Congress Cataloging-in-Publication Data

See Kam, Tan, 1958–
Chinese connections : critical perspectives on film, identity and diaspora / Tan See-Kam, Peter X Feng, and Gina Marchetti.
p. cm.
Includes bibliographical references and index.
ISBN 978-1-59213-267-6 (cloth : alk. paper)—ISBN 978-1-59213-268-3 (pbk. : alk. paper) 1. Motion pictures—China. 2. Motion pictures, Chinese—United States.
I. Feng, Peter X, 1966– II. Marchetti, Gina. III. Title.
PN1993.5.C4S28 2008
791.430951—dc22 2008012714

2 4 6 8 9 7 5 3 1

# Contents

## PART II Questions of Gender



## PART III At the Millennium and Beyond

# Acknowledgments

This anthology would not have been possible without the support of John Hess, Chuck Kleinhans, Julia Lesage, and other members of the editorial board for *Jump Cut: A Review of Contemporary Media.* Their commitment to Chinese-language and Chinese-diaspora cinema and their vision of the place of media and film history, theory, and criticism within the social and political sphere have been a major source of inspiration. We would like to thank the editors at the *Asian Journal of Communication*, especially Indrajit Banerjee of the Asian Media Information and Communication Centre (or AMIC, Singapore). We owe a debt of gratitude to the editors at *Asian Cinema, Film International, SITES: The Journal of Contemporary French and Francophone Studies, Jump Cut: A Review of Contemporary Media*, and *Bright Lights Film Journal*, as well as to Pluto Press, publishers of the book *Aliens R Us: The Other in Science Fiction Cinema*, for allowing us to reprint particular essays in this book. We also thank Eric and Jacqueline Khoo of Zhao Wei Films (Singapore) for granting reproduction permission for stills culled from *Mee Pok Man* (1995), *12 Storeys* (1997), and *Be With Me* (2005).

We would particularly like to thank all those who helped bring this book to press, including Elisabela Larrea (University of Macau) and Amy Lee (University of California, Berkeley) for helping compile the anthology's Chinese glossaries and filmography. We are grateful to Hao Youfan (University of Macau), Kam Louie (Hong Kong University), and Tim Simpson (University of Macau) for their kind support. We are likewise grateful to have the support of the Chiang Ching-Koo (CCK) Foundation and we applaud its commitment to scholarship on the cultures of the Chinese diaspora.

Last but not least, we would like to express our gratitude to those who helped at Temple University Press, especially Micah Kleit and David A. Pausch, whose vision brought this book to completion. We are forever grateful for their commitment to Chinese cinema, Asian American culture, and this project which comprises original essays, reprints and reworked versions of earlier publications.

# Introduction: Chinese Connections

## *Critical Perspectives on Film, Identity, and Diaspora*

Tan See-Kam, Peter X Feng, and Gina Marchetti

In a scene from Peter Wang's film *A Great Wall* (1985), a Chinese student demonstrates his command of English by haltingly reciting the Gettysburg Address; his reward for completing his college entrance exams is a bottle of Coca-Cola. Wang's film follows a Chinese American family's trip to China to visit their relatives, but the expected "culture clash" is mediated by the realization that aspects of American culture have already been assimilated into Chinese society. As Lisa Lowe points out, "the Great Wall of China, from which the film takes its title, is a monument to the historical condition that not even ancient China was 'pure' but coexisted with 'foreign barbarians' against which the Middle Kingdom erected such barriers."[1] Just as the wall begs the question of cultural cross-contamination, so do the Chinese diaspora and the globalization of the economy beg the question of the influence of Chinese culture generally, and Chinese cinema specifically, on the rest of the world (and vice versa). Cinema is like the Great Wall, a symbolic system that shapes our perception of reality, a transnational product that serves to bring China and the world together even as it defines the difference between China and the world.

*Chinese Connections: Critical Perspectives on Film, Identity, and Diaspora* brings together scholarship written in English on the cinema of China, the Chinese diaspora, and the cross-fertilization between Chinese film and global film culture. This volume primarily deals with "connections" within transnational, diasporic, migrant, historical, cultural, and political contexts. Previous collections have initiated comparative approaches, but even such significant contributions as Chris Berry's *Perspectives on Chinese Cinema* (1985),[2] Nick Browne et al.'s *New Chinese Cinemas* (1994),[3] Sheldon Hsiao-peng Lu's *Transnational Chinese Cinemas* (1997),[4] and Lu and Emilie Yueh-yu Yeh's *Chinese-Language Film* (2005)[5] have not extended their reach much beyond the so-called "three Chinas": the People's Republic of China (PRC), Taiwan, and Hong Kong. *Chinese Connections* brings Chinese American cinema, ethnic Chinese filmmakers in Hollywood, French and U.S. discourses about Hong Kong and PRC film, and more into the mix, highlighting the connections between Chinese-language cinema and global films with Chinese input but made in languages other than Chinese.

The flow of talent and filmmaking resources from East to West, and vice versa, has not diminished global Hollywood's continuing grip on the transnational film economy. But it is clear that, since the 1980s, Chinese-language films have slowly but surely burned a visible trail on the world-cinema map, making their mark on the global distribution and consumption film circuits, from Cannes to Hollywood and the video and digital video disc (DVD) stores in between. The global highway and byway for the film traffic, channeled by economic policies that range from protectionist legislation to international copyright laws, will without a doubt continue to be a hotly contested arena for years to come. It remains to be seen if the playing ground for this traffic will eventually even out significantly.

The intellectual enterprise of Chinese film scholarship in English, including Asian American studies with a focus on the complexity of Asian American studies identity formations, parallels the Chinese-language films' ride to the global arena. *Chinese Connections* partakes in this endeavor by exploring the film cultures of what we would call "transnational China." Separated yet connected to mainland China, "transnational Chinese" film cultures constitute a useful category for grouping diverse works by "Chinese" filmmakers variously associated with the PRC, Taiwan, Hong Kong, and Singapore, as well as Chinese American and Chinese Canadian filmmaking communities in the Western hemisphere. It encompasses audiences that make up the consumer base for Chinese-language films, from the Antipodes to the American continents, from the Middle East to the PRC, from Africa to India, from France to Singapore. This book also makes connections with films and filmmakers in conversation with Chinese film culture that range from Olivier Assayas to the Wachowski Brothers.

When taken together, *Chinese Connections* brings to focus hot topics in transnational Chinese and Chinese diasporic cinemas, including issues of national politics, gender, sexuality, immigration, class, race, and economic displacement. The original impetus for this anthology came from a series of special issues that the film-and-media journal *Jump Cut: A Review of Contemporary Media* devoted to the topic of transnational and diasporic Chinese cinemas. All of these fine articles are now available online at http://www.ejumpcut.org/home.html. Although we are not able to reprint them here, we strongly urge you to use this volume in conjunction with the *Jump Cut* material, especially issues number 42 (Winter 1998), 46 (Summer 2003,) and 49 (Spring 2007). This collection bears the imprint of *Jump Cut*'s emphasis on a radical critique of the global media, highlighting issues of class, race, and sexual politics. In addition, several essays reprinted here come from a special issue of the *Asian Journal of Communication* devoted to critical perspectives on gender and sexuality in Asian cinema. The previously unpublished essays solicited for the volume were chosen to reflect this editorial perspective. Across the broad range of subject matter, the focus remains on ideology and cultural and political critique, and this is what makes this volume unique.

## The Structure of Chinese Connections

This anthology consists of three sections, with each exploring various aspects of "transnational Chinese" film cultures. The first section, "Global Connections," revolves around the evolving interaction among American, European, and Chinese cultures in the cinema. In addition to exploring the impact that the influx of Hong Kong's talent into Hollywood has had on the imagination of the postmodern condition in films like *The Matrix* (1999), *Lethal Weapon 4* (1998), and *Rush Hour* (1998), this section includes an examination of the intersection of Hong Kong action films and African American hip-hop, the use of American music in Taiwan's New Wave cinema, an account of the reception of Hong Kong popular film in France, a contrasting account of the Chinese reception of Hollywood films, a study of Hong Kong cinema in the context of the global film market, and a case study of *Hulk* (2003), a Hollywood film by Taiwan-born filmmaker Ang Lee, and its relationship to Chinese culture and Asian American politics.

The second section, "Questions of Gender," explores the representation of masculinity, femininity, sexuality, and queer issues in PRC and Hong Kong films from the postwar years onward. Although separated by different histories apropos to Chinese socialism and British colonialism, the postwar films of these two culturally connected geopolitical entities share a fascination and obsession for supposedly gender-neutral, or neutered, figures. By around 1997, such figures are memories of the past, but political tensions arising from Hong Kong's impending return to the "motherland" result in the imagining of the parent and child's relationship in the metaphorical terms of failed romances and unrequited love affairs that likewise question male potency or "authentic" femininity. Hence the essays collected here chart the changing representation of Chinese women *and* men from de-gendered socialist figures to sexually liberated ones, from seemingly sexless cross-gender actresses to sexy powerful vamps, from effete romantic heroes to *kung fu* boxer-dancers, in an assortment of youth films, action comedies, "failed gay texts," and Category III films (soft porn).

The chapters in this section show that gender roles in Chinese films do not depict a stable universality, but embody a contested area rife with contradictions and negotiations, variously and concurrently demonstrating that

> [Women in films] . . . have been allegorized . . . as the beleaguered representative of a nation, race, ethnicity or class . . . as the embodiment of the contradictions surrounding nationalism, tradition, and modernity. As the clearest figure that has the most to gain and the least to lose from the loosening of feudal, patriarchal strictures against female mobility and autonomy, women have also served as symbols of rewards and dangers of the modern era in [films] that show them struggling against the vestiges of colonialism and poverty within . . . decaying traditional [Chinese patriarchies].[6]

Women in these films, as well as men, thus analogously come to represent "the 'new' Asian (that is, cosmopolitan, flexible, polyglot, competent, and competitive, but often cold, threatening, deracinated, and unappealing)"[7] inside and outside "transnational China," fostering the Chinese connections therein. Gender identities are not static, but perennially constituted and reconstituted in dynamic ways, variously serving as metaphors for the signs of changing times, including economic, political, national, ethnic, cultural, and other areas of dramatic transformation. For film scholars globally, then, the configurations of shifting genders within the cinemas of "transnational China" present a tremendous challenge because they throw issues of spectatorship, representation, national cinema, and genre as well as gender into a state of crisis.

The concluding section, "At the Millennium and Beyond," features chapters on the current state of Chinese-language and Chinese diasporic filmmaking. It deals with current films by Hong Kong directors, new Taiwanese filmmakers like Tsai Ming-Liang, contemporary Singaporean films (Eric Khoo), and the Chinese Sixth Generation. The volume concludes with a critical look at how China's Fifth Generation filmmakers like Zhang Yimou have approached the new millennium.

This anthology brings these essays together to underscore common ground and expand the range of connections made among Chinese-language cinemas, films from the Chinese diaspora, and films made outside of the Chinese-speaking world dealing with Chinese themes. Taken together, the essays make a compelling case for exploring broader connections involving ethnicity and culture across national and linguistic borders. As transnational productions become more common, questions of politics and nationalism, particularly involving Hong Kong and Taiwan, continue to strain against a facile leap to an imagined "Greater China." However, the common experiences of the Chinese diaspora and the global links among various Chinese communities must not be dismissed—particularly for those who traditionally may be at odds with a conservative Chinese patriarchy, such as heterosexual women, lesbians, and gay men, and who have the ability to cross borders and to participate in a wider, global sphere that transcends ethnic and cultural ties. The contradictions surrounding the label of "Chinese cinema" call for a truly dialectical film criticism. These chapters provide excellent examples of critical thinkers engaging these political, social, and cultural complexities. We anticipate this book will form a basis for conducting ongoing conversations and debates: by serving as a bridge to future scholarship, we hope this volume serves to foster continuing engagement with *Chinese Connections*.

## Notes

1. Lisa Lowe, *Immigrant Acts: On Asian American Cultural Politics* (Durham, NC: Duke University Press, 1996), 80.
2. Chris Berry, ed., *Perspectives on Chinese Cinema* (Ithaca: Cornell East Asia Papers, 1985); reprinted, London: British Film Institute, 1991.
3. Nick Browne, Paul G. Pickowicz, Vivian Sobchack, and Esther Yau, eds., *New Chinese Cinemas: Forms, Identities, Politics* (NY: Cambridge University Press, 1994).
4. Sheldon Hsiao-peng Lu, ed., *Transnational Chinese Cinemas: Identity, Nationhood, Gender* (Honolulu: University of Hawaii Press, 1997).
5. Sheldon Hsiao-peng Lu and Emilie Yueh-yu Yeh, eds., *Chinese-Language Film: Historiography, Poetics, Politics* (Honolulu: University of Hawaii Press, 2005).
6. Tan See-Kam and Gina Marchetti, "Foreword," *Asian Journal of Communication* 11.2 (2001), vii.
7. Ibid., ix.

PART I

# Global Connections

# 1

# False Consciousness and Double Consciousness

## *Race, Virtual Reality, and the Assimilation of Hong Kong Action Cinema in* The Matrix

PETER X FENG

In a seminal 1975 essay, Jean-Louis Baudry examines the power of the "reality effect" of cinema on the spectator, or, more precisely, on what he called *"le ciné-sujet,"* or the cine-subject—the subject as constituted by cinema.[1] Baudry draws an analogy between cinema and Plato's cave, from which the philosopher emerges (temporarily blinded by the light of day) to report of prisoners who are captivated by representations of reality. Noting that the prisoners would not leave the cave even if their chains were broken, Baudry asks why the cine-subject finds the cinema so appealing. He turns to Freudian psychoanalysis for an answer, stating, "Cave, grotto, 'sort of a cavernous underground,' people have not failed to see in it a representation of the maternal womb, of the matrix into which we are supposed to wish to return."[2] Unable to return to the womb, we instead enter the movie theater's matrix: if someone were to refuse ever to leave the theater, we would consider her or him to be mentally ill, but we would understand the impulse.

Larry and Andy Wachowski's film *The Matrix* (1999) offers a parable of the cinematic apparatus. Laurence Fishburne's Morpheus has emerged from the cave and seeks to liberate the prisoners but does not realize that Joe Pantoliano's Cypher resents being unchained and wants to return to the bliss of the cave. Morpheus pins his hopes on Keanu Reeves's Neo and sets about

From *Aliens R Us: The Other in Science Fiction Cinema*, Ziauddin Sardar and Sean Cubitt, eds. (London; Sterling, VA: Pluto Press, 2002), 149–163. Reprinted with permission.

reprogramming him: as in the 1995 film adaptation of William Gibson's *Johnny Mnemonic*, Reeves's passivity and wooden demeanor make him the über-cybermovie hero.[3] Reeves's charisma emerges precisely from his lack of presence, a quality that Gus Van Sant found enigmatic in *My Own Private Idaho* (1991) and that Jan DeBont found heroic in *Speed* (1994). As Bey Logan observes, *The Matrix* cannily draws on both sides of Reeves's coin: "*The Matrix* seems to redefine the two sides of his nature. It's too out there for Hollywood, too expensive to be a true independent."[4] If *The Matrix* is Reeves's vehicle, then Reeves is *The Matrix*'s vessel. His star persona (what Logan might call his hybrid indie-Hollywood appeal) is uniquely suited to a story in which characters' abilities change according to their surroundings, and in this we come back to Baudry's cine-subject: spectators imbue their favorite stars with their own personalities and thereby endow themselves with cinematic qualities. In short, while Reeves's Neo jacks into the Matrix, spectators of *The Matrix* are jacking into Reeves.[5]

In this chapter, I offer a series of allegorical readings of *The Matrix*, exploring the film in relation to cyberpunk and other fantasies of swapping one's consciousness from body to body, discussing the film's casting, and musing on its production by the new transnational Hollywood. Each reading could also be described as an attempt to explain how characters pass from one level of consciousness to another through a series of nested diegeses within the film. By "nested diegeses," I mean the worlds within worlds in the film's narrative: "the Matrix" is a virtual-reality simulation that resembles a North American city in 1999, a world within a world. Within the Matrix, Neo is the hacker alter ego of Thomas Anderson, a white-collar drone. When he meets Morpheus, Neo discovers that humanity has been enslaved by machines following a war between humanity and Artificial Intelligence (AI). The machines created the Matrix to occupy and pacify human minds while the energy produced by their bodies is being harvested. Human resistance fighters hack into the Matrix, where they are able to perform superhuman feats since they possess awareness of their potential to transcend physical laws that are, after all, only simulated. Morpheus has been searching for a human with the potential to defeat the Agents (sentient programs who appear in the Matrix as men-in-black), and Neo turns out to be "the One."

The Resistance operates in submarine-like hovercraft such as Morpheus's ship, the *Nebuchadnezzar*. The *Nebuchadnezzar* is thus the film's "reality," or its primary diegesis. The Matrix itself is a virtual world built by the machines: insofar as it is another reality within the film, it is a diegetic world nested within the film's primary diegesis, a diegesis that I will name Inner Diegesis$_1$. There is another virtual space built by the resistance, where the humans plug in so they can train, debrief, and arm themselves: the Construct, or Inner Diegesis$_2$, is of a lower order than the Matrix, since as a training ground there are no real consequences (demonstrated when

Neo falls off a skyscraper and bounces off the ground). In the Matrix, however, if your virtual body is killed, you die. And in the primary diegesis, if your body is disconnected from the Matrix while your consciousness is inside it, both you and your virtual body die.

The Matrix (Inner Diegesis$_1$) is populated by prisoners whom the resistance fighters contemptuously call "copper-tops," mere batteries unaware of their enslavement. From the resistance perspective, copper-tops are trapped in false consciousness whereas the resistance fighters possess double consciousness. I am borrowing the term "false consciousness" from Marxism, where it describes "those who live their relation to economic life exclusively within its categories of thought and experience."[6] Copper-tops misunderstand the nature of their relationships with each other and to the Matrix.[7] "Double consciousness" is of course W.E.B. DuBois's famous formulation, the phenomenon of the racialized subject's awareness of both how he sees himself and how he is seen by others.[8] While racialized ideologies often cast double consciousness as a tragic handicap,[9] we might also conceive of double consciousness as a potential advantage in negotiating complicated hegemonic formations with their competing interpellations. Here, I am suggesting that the agility of Neo and the other resistance fighters, when they are jacked into the Matrix, derives from their awareness of themselves as existing simultaneously in two worlds.

I began this essay by suggesting that Keanu Reeves's blank visage allows spectators to jack into him. Surely a great deal of *The Matrix*'s audience appeal is attributable to spectatorial fantasies of being able to execute Neo's superhuman martial-arts moves (and the fact that Neo was able to learn those moves effortlessly marks it as doubly fantastic). Like Baudry, Christian Metz argues that spectatorial involvement arises from the way that cinema turns the spectator into a subject who exists to see and perceive, and that this is accomplished through identification with the camera.[10] The celebrated visual effects of *The Matrix* do not just engage the spectator's passion for perceiving (as when the camera swoops around the action, which Metz would note marks the spectator's identification with the camera as "a transcendental, not an empirical subject"[11]); the slow-motion effects allow the spectator to perceive the Matrix as Neo does. Visual effects sell us (consumers) on *The Matrix*, but they do not merely bring us into the theaters—they actually encourage us to enter the Matrix itself. Let us take a moment and contemplate the visual effects of *The Matrix*, for it is through analysis of this mode of perception that I find my own points of entry into the film.

It is a banal irony that this film that supposedly celebrates the human spirit's triumph over machines could not have been achieved without computer technology. For example, in the film's advanced form of Flow-Motion—dubbed "bullet time"—the effect of a moving camera shooting up to 12,000 frames per second is simulated. This effect was achieved with an array of still cameras with 1/1000th-of-a-second shutters. The placement of these cameras was determined after a computer graphic (CG) "visualization" plotted their exact positions; each camera was then aligned using a laser-guided tracking system.[12] In short, a computer model determined the contours of the profilmic space. A computer program then created images to fill "in between" the still shots: this process of creating images attributable to virtual cameras is called interpolation (and here I might note that "interpellation" is what happens when a computer visualization tells you where to stand, whereas "interpolation" is what happens when a computer extrapolates and simulates bodily movements that the cameras were unable to capture or that you were unable to perform). The backgrounds were rendered using a virtual cinematographic process that converted as few as a dozen stills of the set into a 3-D environment. Lighting levels were adjusted so that the background matched the foreground.

This irony of computer-constructed film sequences that are supposed to depict humanity's ability to transcend AI is, as I noted, somewhat obvious. I mention it because I want to take an almost incidental technical aside as my way into the film, jacking into *The Matrix* through an unguarded back door, as it were. Bullet-time technician[13] Dan Piponi explains that the still cameras in the rig were not perfectly aligned and therefore captured images with slight but noticeable variations in exposure. In his words, "We had to bring that pixel into alignment, plus create software needed to color-correct the still images so they could be blended together."[14] Transcendent "humanity" is only visualizable in a world in which representations of humans are carefully manipulated via color correction.[15] *The Matrix* depends on the elision of racial difference.

## Racial Drag in Virtual Reality

When Morpheus is captured by the Agents, he is told that the Matrix was originally a Utopic virtual reality that was not convincing enough to keep humanity enslaved. (If the first version of the Matrix were a diegesis, then it would fit Jean-Louis Comolli and Jean Narboni's category 5, a narrative seemingly fully within the dominant ideology but cracking apart at the seams.[16]) The Matrix version 2.0 is more convincing because it is less perfect, and as such is better able to suspend humans in "false consciousness." One example of *The Matrix*'s imperfection is its reliance on stale racial archetypes. The leader of the resistance cell is Morpheus, equal parts spiritual guide and rebellious slave. Of course Morpheus is Black, and the camera lingers on his tortured body. The Oracle is a folksy Black earth mother who runs a virtual day-care center populated with precocious children. In the Matrix, race functions as a narrative shorthand, not surprising given that the machines desire human consciousness and virtual performance to be strictly correlated—a textbook definition of essentialism.

The resistance fighters strut through the Matrix secure in their beautiful bodies, manifestations of their idealized self-images.[17] Their ability to perform incredible feats of martial arts prowess reminds me of nothing so much as Nintendo's *Street Fighter II*, a video game in which players choose to manipulate racially marked characters such as the Japanese Ryu, the Chinese Chun Li, and the Indian Dhalsim.[18] In his essay "cyborg identity/metamorphosis/skin," Quentin Lee connects *Street Fighter II* with Michael Jackson's bodily transformations through plastic surgery and *Thriller*'s lycanthropy: Jackson's body is a conflicted, contradictory, and contested terrain of racial and sexual discourses. Lee compares desire for Michael Jackson with choosing (to be? to control?) a character in *Street Fighter II*. The link between desire for and identification with a screen character is at the center of theories of cinematic spectatorship.[19] Freud's 1919 paper "A Child Is Being Beaten" is a useful touchstone for such investigations since Freud attempts to account for how children shift from observer to participant as they narrate scenes of punishment. Fantasies of bodily transformation thus go hand in hand with spectacles of physical violence.[20]

The Internet and the cinematic cyberpunk narratives it has inspired offer a space in which users can perform racial drag, suggesting that jacking into virtual spaces occasions fantasies of passing (in terms of race, gender, age, and so forth). The game *Street Fighter II* permits racial drag only within the highly circumscribed limits of its narrative setting, but the Internet theoretically allows users to inhabit gendered and raced profiles indefinitely, limited only by the user's successful deployment of textual signifiers of identity. The narrative of *The Matrix* is structured by the consequences of failed passing: if a hacker unplugs from the Matrix, the hacker's body dies and the virtual persona disintegrates. In specifying that hackers cannot transcend their bodies upon pain of death, *The Matrix* insists on the coherent materiality of the bodies that inhabit its primary diegesis. *The Matrix* thus rejects a narrative resolution common to cyberpunk, wherein consciousness separates from the body and lives on in cyberspace,[21] instead evincing Judith Butler's distinction between performance and performativity, wherein "performance" describes Internet users in drag while "performativity" describes the process of citation by which the body's materiality is continually reinscribed. This is a welcome corrective to Jean Baudrillard's celebration of cyberpunk as a means to transcend bodily materiality and deny mortality, a desire that Vivian Sobchack scathingly labels "beating the meat" (with deliberate masturbatory connotations: autoerotic orgasm as transcendence). Sobchack observes that "the increasing transparency of one's lived-flesh enabled by new technologies . . . leads to euphoria and a sense of the limitless extension of being beyond its materiality and mortality. This, however, is 'false' consciousness—for it has 'lost touch' with the very material and mortal body that grounds its imagination and imagery of transcendence."[22] The imagery of the Matrix—its deployment of racial archetypes of Blackness and men-in-blackness (which is to say, Will Smith notwithstanding, whiteness)—is reliant on the world we live in: *The Matrix* is thoroughly implicated in our bodily materiality.[23]

## Typecasting and Multiracial Actors

Earlier I read an intimation of race in Piponi's apparently innocent reference to "color correction." I now want to return to that quotation to highlight another racial intimation: "We had to . . . create software . . . to color-correct the still images so they could be blended together." Color correction is the means; blending is the eventual goal. To be precise, racial difference is not elided, but put in service of a miscegenated aesthetic.

Tank is the name of a crucial member of Morpheus's resistance cell. Born in the space of the primary diegesis, Tank has never entered virtual reality himself. Instead, he runs the *Nebuchadnezzar*'s computers and hacks into the Matrix. Shot by Cypher, Tank survives the blast and kills Cypher before he can unplug Neo, permitting Neo to return to the primary diegesis, where he comes to comprehend the Oracle's prophesy. In a sense, Tank rises from the dead before Neo does, establishing a narrative structure in which resurrection of the material body in the film's primary diegesis allows Neo to make the quantum leaps in consciousness that attend his transitions in and out of the Matrix. By operating the machinery that permits the resistance fighters to hack into the Matrix, and by embodying the hope for a future humanity born and not harvested by the machines, Tank crosses the borders that define humanity and shows the way to the future. This transitional figure is portrayed by Marcus Chong, an actor of mixed African and Chinese ancestry.[24]

The multiracial typecasting does not end with Marcus Chong. As many Asian Pacific filmgoers know, Keanu Reeves has an English mother and a Chinese Hawaiian father. While Reeves reportedly describes himself as white, Asian American spectators frequently label Reeves as Asian Pacific passing as white. Neo's passing from one diegesis to another occasions leaps in consciousness; Reeves's passing for white implies the heightened awareness of double consciousness.

The term "passing" is highly problematic: I want to embrace its complexities and ambivalences, its complicity and duplicity, in the context of performance and spectatorship, for passing is not necessarily an act but may be a spectatorial perception. Following Ari Rosner, Teresa Kay Williams draws a distinction between active and passive passing, implying that passing is not necessarily something that Reeves does but rather a way that he is read. Williams asks rhetorically, "Can a multiracial individual pass for what he or she is *not*? Can a multiracial individual pass for what he or she is? Does passing for what you are count as really passing?"[25] To judge a multiracial individual for "passive passing" is to assume that the individual has control over how he or she is read or misread by others.

I am attributing the problem of passing to Asian American spectators in order to emphasize that passing is a triangular narrative structure: it requires not just the purportedly passing figure, but a dupe who does not recognize the pass and an insider who registers that the dupe has failed to read the passer "correctly." Reeves can be passing only if an audience of insiders judges that another audience (presumably white) has been duped. The insiders believe that there is a true Asian Pacific identity behind the appearance. (Ironically, the insiders might be presuming that the duped audience is unproblematically white.)[26] Elaine K. Ginsberg notes, "One of the assumed effects of a racist society is the internalization, by members of the oppressed race, of the dominant culture's definitions and characterizations. This is the context in which the literature of race passing has most often been read."[27] In this context, people of color temper their impulse to judge putative passers with their sympathy for the complicated manner in which the passer negotiates a racist society. Ginsberg quotes Nella Larsen's *Passing*, in which a character observes, "We disapprove of it and at the same time condone it."[28]

If we conceive of Reeves's passing for white not as something that he does but as something that others perceive, then passing may involve Reeves's awareness of how he is seen by others; passing is therefore double consciousness turned upside down, for the mainstream sees the multiracial movie star not as different, but as white. Reeves's ancestry usually escapes commentary in the mainstream press. In researching *The Matrix*, I found only one magazine article that made note of Reeves's multiracial ancestry: the U.K.-based action-movie magazine *Impact* floridly remarks, "What Chinese blood flows in the veins of Keanu Reeves must have sung as he finally found a role that played to his mixed ancestry."[29] Reeves's Chinese blood (and Canadian nationality) is shared with Chong, and Black Asian Tank links Asian white Neo to Black Morpheus, perhaps via an intertextual allusion to Melvin and Mario van Peebles's film *Panther* (1995), in which Chong played Huey Newton.[30]

## Industrial Assimilation

The 1997 Hong Kong handover precipitated an exodus of the island's action filmmakers. *Matrix* directors Larry and Andy Wachowski tapped the director and fight choreographer of *Fist of Legend* (1994), Yuen Wo Ping, to train the actors, stage their scenes, and oversee the wire work. The absorption of Hong Kong style into Hollywood's melting pot was noted by many commentators. For example, Roald Rynning has observed that the film introduces "the Asian cinematic technique of wire-fighting into an American action film."[31] Multiracial Keanu Reeves becomes the primary conduit for *The Matrix*'s assimilation of Hong Kong action filmmaking.

I see a metaphor for the assimilation of Hong Kong action cinema in the film's nested diegeses. The film's primary diegesis is a science-fiction world, but one in which humans have soft bodies that are flabby from underuse. The fantasy of this diegesis is that the knowledge necessary to overthrow the machines can be downloaded instantaneously and that bodies can be reconstructed using high-tech acupuncture. Similarly, Hollywood filmmaking turns to Hong Kong to recondition actors' bodies and to train them in the physical and mental skills of martial-arts filmmaking. (One wonders if the AI machines should have constructed the Matrix to resemble North America before the 1997 handover, thereby forestalling the introduction of martial-arts know-how into the programming.)

Neo trains in the Construct (Inner $\text{Diegesis}_2$). The poses that Keanu Reeves adopts throughout the dojo sequence are patterned on the style of Jet Li, whose *Black Mask* (1996) was Yuen Wo Ping's last film in Hong Kong.[32] In the Construct, everyone knows kung fu—like *Street Fighter II*, the Construct is a fantasy world in which flabby-bodied users jack into idealized bodies. (Like a video game, the Construct is deployed as a series of "levels" through which the user advances.)

Between these two poles—a diegesis of flabby bodies and a diegesis of superhuman bodies—lies the Matrix (Inner $\text{Diegesis}_1$). In the Matrix, the majority of the inhabitants do not know kung fu and only a select few can perform superhuman feats. The superiority of our protagonists can best be displayed within the Matrix, which lies between the Hollywood world of the *Nebuchadnezzar* and the Hong Kong world of the Construct. Inner $\text{Diegesis}_1$ represents Hong Kong action cinema assimilated into Hollywood. Neo, the Chosen One, prevails by grace of his double consciousness, that is, his awareness of his existence in both Inner $\text{Diegesis}_1$ and Inner $\text{Diegesis}_2$. The successful postmodern subject is an Asian passing for white, a resistance fighter passing as a drone, a martial artist hiding not behind Jet Li's black mask but behind Keanu Reeves's blank mask.

When initial plans to shoot *The Matrix* in Chicago and Los Angeles were scrapped in favor of an Australian location with a favorable exchange rate, the Wachowskis modified the Matrix into a nondescript American city, permitting Sydney to be used for select exterior shots.[33] If the imperatives of transnational capital compelled the producers to relocate to Sydney, the location of Rupert Murdoch's Fox Studios marks Hollywood's foray into the Pacific Rim.[34]

## "A World Without Rules and Controls, Without Borders or Boundaries"

Late capitalism's shift into a transnational phase makes it more difficult but more imperative to update Marx's theories of culture and ideology.

What is the relationship between the superstructure of cinematic fantasy and the base of transnational capitalism? What is the nature of false consciousness in a global economy? Reading *The Matrix* as an allegory of transnational capitalism suggests that false consciousness consists of thinking locally and not globally (in Stuart Hall's terms, functioning with only the local as "category of thought and experience").[35] For the copper-tops in the Matrix, false consciousness consists of not being aware of their actual function in the AI economy. In the contemporary world, the flow of transnational capital is in the process of restructuring local and global economies: Rupert Murdoch's media empire provides the circuit for Hollywood to exploit Australia's film industry[36] and Hong Kong cinema expertise.

In his book *Asian/American: Historical Crossings of a Racial Frontier*, David Palumbo-Liu argues that the United States' vision of its role in the global system

> is inseparable from historical occasions of real contact between and interpenetration of Asia and America, in and across the Pacific Ocean. The defining mythos of America, its "manifest destiny," was, after all, to form a bridge westward from the Old World, *not just* to the western coast of the North American content, but from there to the trans-Pacific regions of Asia.[37]

Palumbo-Liu shows that for most of the twentieth century American modernity was marked by its efforts to modify Asian bodies and psyches to serve the United States. As the Pacific Century dawns, American anxieties about Asian investment in Monterey Park, California (birthplace of the English-only movement) and other West Coast sites reveal a fear that Asians are superior transnational subjects.[38] The arrival of Asian money, characterized as neo-Confucian, forces the United States to adapt somatically and psychically.

In the words of *The Matrix*'s visual-effects supervisor, John Gaeta, I found a startling echo of David Palumbo-Liu's thesis. In referring to "bullet time" and other visual effects, Gaeta observes, "All of these techniques and alterations in time created new physiological and psychological moments for the audience."[39] While American business fears neo-Confucianism, Hollywood is engaged in assimilating Neo's martial arts.

## Notes

1. Jean-Louis Baudry, "Le Dispositif: Approches Métapsychologiques de L'impression de Réalité," *Communications* 23 (1975): 56–72, here 62. Quotations in French are taken from this essay. Quotations in English are taken from Jean-Louis Baudry, "The Apparatus: Metapyschological Approaches to the Impression of Reality in Cinema," trans. Jean Andrews and Bernard Augst, in Leo Braudy and Marshall Cohen, eds., *Film Theory and Criticism: Introductory Readings*, 5th ed. (New York: Oxford University Press, 1999), 760–777; originally published in *Camera Obscura* 1.

2. Jean-Louis Baudry, "The Apparatus," 767. In French: "La caverne, la grotte, 'sorte de demeure souterraine,' on n'a pas manqué d'y voir une représentation du ventre maternel, de la matrice dans laquelle nous aspirerions à retourner" (Baudry, "Le Dispositif," 62).

3. Keanu and Neo almost rhyme. Thanks to my colleagues from UC-Irvine, Anne Friedberg and Sheila Murphy, for pointing out that Reeves is the ultimate cyberhero.

4. Bey Logan, "The Light Fantastic," *Impact* 90 (June 1999): 19.

5. This is of course attributable in part to Neo's function in the narrative: since we learn about the Matrix as he does, he is our touchstone, just as we cling to Alice when we follow her into the rabbit hole. Here I might observe that the rabbit hole is a subterranean space perhaps analogous to Baudry's and Plato's caves.

6. Stuart Hall, "The Problem of Ideology: Marxism Without Guarantees," in David Morley and Kuan-Hsing Chen, eds., *Stuart Hall: Critical Dialogues in Cultural Studies* (London: Routledge, 1996), 36.

7. This formulation of false consciousness is drawn from Stuart Hall's 1983 discussion in "The Problem of Ideology." Hall attempts to recuperate the term, since "false" suggests that the philosopher has a "true" consciousness and that people living within a distorted ideology have a "false" or incorrect understanding of their situation. Hall suggests that those who live within capitalist ideology do not have a false or distorted understanding, but a partial and inadequate one (Hall, 36–37). The question of "false consciousness" is crucial in understanding ideology: if consciousness were merely "false," then education should lead to revolution; instead, efforts should be focused on understanding people's investment (in multiple senses) in the system that exploits them.

8. DuBois is specifically describing Negro men in the United States. However, I would argue that DuBois allows us to extend the concept to all races and to women as well. While he seems at first to distinguish the Negro from six other races, he attributes the gift of double consciousness not to essence but to location, to being a minority, to "being a problem": "After the Egyptian and Indian, the Greek and Roman, the Teuton and Mongolian, the Negro is a sort of seventh son, born with a veil, and gifted with second-sight *in this American world*—a world which yields him no true self-consciousness, but only lets him see himself through the revelation of the other world. It is a peculiar sensation, this double-consciousness, this sense of always looking at one's self through the eyes of others . . . . One ever feels his twoness . . . ." (W.E.B. Dubois, *The Souls of Black Folk* [New York: Bantam Books, 1989; first pub. 1903], 45. Emphasis added.)

9. David Palumbo-Liu argues that assimilationist discourse employs the metaphor of schizophrenia to describe the minority subject's inability to accede fully to the nation's "invented hegemonic memory" (12)—a failure to link one's present self to the sanctioned version of the past—thereby pathologizing DuBois's "double consciousness" by casting "the psychic instability of the subject [as] a product of his or her own inability to make cultural choices" (300). See David Palumbo-Liu, *Asian/American: Historical Crossings of a Racial Frontier* (Stanford: Stanford University Press, 1999).

10. Christian Metz, "From *The Imaginary Signifier*," in Braudy and Cohen, *Film Theory and Criticism*, 803–804.

11. Ibid., 804.

12. Kevin H. Martin, "Jacking Into *The Matrix*," *Cinefex* 79 (October 1999): 70, 72.

13. Piponi's official title is science officer with Manex Special Effects.

14. Kevin H. Martin, "Jacking Into *The Matrix,*" 72.

15. This pun was inspired by the example of Marlon Riggs's *Color Adjustment* (1991).

16. Jean-Luc Comolli and Jean Narboni, "Cinema/Ideology/Criticism," in Leo Braudy and Marshall Cohen, eds., *Film Theory and Criticism: Introductory Readings*, 5th ed. (New York: Oxford University Press, 1999), 757.

17. Morpheus terms appearance within the Matrix or the Construct as "residual self-image," but he does not explain where this residue originated. Insofar as these idealized representations cannot be located in material experience, they might be attributed to the Lacanian Imaginary. However, the gendered and racial specificity of these representations suggests that self-image emerges from the Symbolic: if these representations do not correspond with awareness of real bodies, then physical appearance in the Matrix and the Construct is determined by consciousness. Rather than bodily materiality shaping consciousness, we have the reverse (cf. Judith Butler, *Bodies that Matter* [New York: Routledge, 1993]), indicative of *The Matrix*'s foundering on the shoals of essentialized identities.

18. Quentin Lee, "cyborg identity/metamorphosis/skin," *Critical Mass* 1.2 (Spring 1994): 114.

19. For a deft survey of theories of spectatorship, see Judith Mayne's *Cinema and Spectatorship* (London: Routledge, 1993).

20. *Street Fighter* was adapted into a 1994 movie with a racially diverse cast including Jean-Claude Van Damme, Raul Julia, Ming-Na Wen, Kylie Minogue, Roshan Seth, and Wes Studi. Its narrative, however, was firmly set within one diegesis, which is to say that the film took the characters for granted and did not narrativize their deployment by players or spectators. Likewise, the 1995 film of *Mortal Kombat* (whose cast included prominent white and Asian characters but no Black faces), the 1995–1996 television show *Mortal Kombat: The Animated Series*, the theatrical sequel *Mortal Kombat: Annihilation* (1997), and the 1998–1999 syndicated television show *Mortal Kombat: Conquest* did not acknowledge their genesis as a video game within their narrative diegeses, even as these diegeses necessarily differed in detail between incarnations. The racially diverse casts of these movies and shows thus do not invoke the possibility of cross-racial identification so much as the hyperpluralism of the martial-tournament genre, the cinematic touchstone of which remains *Enter the Dragon* (1973) but that continues through *The Quest* (1996) and *Space Jam* (1996). The last, in which NBA players team with animated characters, reveals that the inspiration behind the diverse casts is not a vision of interracial unity so much as the synergy of cross-market platforming of "properties" owned by various entertainment conglomerates; Michael Jordan's announcement that he is giving up endorsements suggests that he has realized that his paycheck does not compensate him adequately for becoming corporate property.

21. See the "Terminal Flesh" chapter of Scott Bukatman's *Terminal Identity* (Durham: Duke University Press, 1993), pp. 241-98.

22. Vivian Sobchack, "Beating the Meat/Surviving the Text, or How to Get Out of This Century Alive," in Paula A. Treichler, Lisa Cartwright, and Constance Penley, eds., *The Visible Woman: Imaging Technologies, Gender, and Science* (New York: New York University Press, 1998), 317. Sobchack's argument develops from Baudrillard's reading of the erotics of cyborg prosthetics in J. G. Ballard's *Crash*; along the way she critiques readers of "A Manifesto for Cyborgs" who miss Donna Haraway's irony (Sobchack, 314). See also Greta Ai-Yu Niu, *People of the Pagus: Orientalized Bodies and Migration in an Asian Pacific Rim*. Diss., Duke University (Ann Arbor: UMI, 1998), AAT 9829659. Greta Niu offers an interpretation of the manifesto that examines Haraway's deployment of Asian women as cyborgs (27–31).

23. By contrast, *The Thirteenth Floor* (released almost simultaneously with *The Matrix*) reveals even uglier implications. In that film, based on Daniel Galouye's novel *Simulacron-3* (New York: Bantam, 1964), a world that looks like ours has built a simulation of 1937 Los Angeles. Users jack into characters who are modeled after their physical appearance, temporarily displacing the character's constructed personality. If a character is killed while a user is jacked in, the user's consciousness is terminated and the user's body awakens with the consciousness of the simulation's character. *The Thirteenth Floor* thus posits mortality as the limit of the simulation, but supposes that simulated consciousness can be downloaded into a user's body. The turning point for the film is the revelation that 1999 is itself a simulation created in the twenty-first century; thus, *The Thirteenth Floor* goes *The Matrix* one better by nesting a diegesis within a diegesis within a diegesis. The final plot twist implies that the twenty-first-century character played by Gretchen Mol has manipulated her husband into jacking into the 1999 simulation so that he can be killed; she can return to her world with a husband who has a personality upgrade. The sunshine and sea breeze at the film's end cannot fully dispel the image of Mol as femme fatale.

24. Some sources state that Marcus Chong is Tommy Chong's son, some his godson or nephew, which would make him Rae Dawn Chong's brother, half-brother, or cousin.

25. Teresa Kay Williams, "Race-ing and Being Raced: The Critical Interrogation of 'Passing,'" *Amerasia Journal* 23.1 (1997): 62–63.

26. Samira Kawash, *Dislocating the Color Line: Identity, Hybridity, and Singularity in African-American Literature* (Stanford: Stanford University Press, 1997), 234, n. 39. Kawash discusses the triangular structure of passing with reference to Amy Robinson's "drama of the pass" in "It Takes One to Know One: Passing and Communities of Common Interest," *Critical Inquiry* 20:4 (1994), 715–736.

27. Elaine K. Ginsberg, "Introduction: The Politics of Passing," *Passing and the Fictions of Identity* (Durham: Duke University Press, 1996), 9.

28. Deborah McDowell, ed. and intro., *Quicksand and Passing* (New Brunswick: Rutgers University Press, 1986), 185–186; cited in Ginsberg.

29. Bey Logan, "The Light Fantastic," 18. In evaluating this magazine's fetishes, consider that the same issue includes an article on Thailand as "another bastion of Asian action cinema" alongside the third installment in an assessment of Rambo as "the century's most misunderstood movie hero" (*Impact* 90, 3).

30. Chong also portrayed Amerasian gang leader Fu Qua Johnson in the *Vanishing Son* television movies (1994). Nishime reads Neo as multiracial child fathered by Morpheus and reanimated by Trinity. She also points out that his removal from the Matrix mimics birth: he emerges from an amniotic sac, the umbilical cord detaches, and he travels down a birth canal. Recall that Baudry compared the cinema and the cave to the womb. LeiLani Nishime, "Is Keanu Reeves a Cyborg?: APA's in Science Fiction." Conference Presentation. Association for Asian American Studies. Scottsdale, Arizona, 25 May 2000.

31. Roald Rynning, "Magic 'Trix," *Film Review* 583 (July 1999): 54.

32. Arakawa points out that Reeves also performs one of Bruce Lee's signature moves, flicking his own nose with his thumb. Suzanne K. Arakawa. "To Whit, (Still) Too White?: How Millenium-End Sci-fi films Use 'Asian-ness' in the Struggle to Imagine and Reconfigure Race Relations in the U.S." Conference Presentation. Society for Cinema Studies. Chicago, Illinois, 11 March 2000.

33. Dennis Fischer, "*Matrix* Star Keanu Reeves Battles the Evils of Cyberspace Slavery," *Cinefantastique* 31.4 (April 1999): 20.

34. Gerald L. Houseman defines the Pacific Rim in terms of U.S. interests in the economy, security, and diplomacy (*America and the Pacific Rim: Coming to Terms*

*with New Realities* [Lanham, MD: Rowman and Littlefield Publishers, 1995], 3; cited in Niu, 10).

35. Stuart Hall, "The Problem of Ideology," 36.

36. Actor Hugo Weaving expresses his misgivings about the future of Australian national cinema in the shadow of Hollywood (Fischer, 20). Meaghan Morris discusses the economic context for Australian film production in the 1980s in her prescient essay "Tooth and Claw: Tales of Survival, and *Crocodile Dundee*," in Meaghan Morris, *The Pirate's Fiancée*, pp. 241–269 (London: Verso, 1988).

37. David Palumbo-Liu, *Asian/American: Historical Crossings of a Racial Frontier* (Stanford: Stanford University Press, 1999), 2.

38. In his closing chapters, Palumbo-Liu analyzes how anxieties about Asian economic power are manifested in science fiction by Philip K. Dick and William Gibson. Space precludes me from exploring in detail why author Neal Stephenson should be added to this list, but I will make a few suggestive comments. The hacker protagonist of *Snow Crash* (1992) is the multiracial offspring of a Korean woman and an African American soldier who met while he was stationed in Japan. *The Diamond Age* (1996) updates the yellow-peril-horde theme by imagining an army of Chinese girls abandoned by parents desperate for sons. *Cryptonomicon* (1999) links genocide in World War II to the creation of a present-day "data haven" in Southeast Asia. In these works, Asians are presented as the future and the past, saviors and threats—Asians are economic creatures. (Neal Stephenson, *Cryptonomicon* [New York: Avon, 1999]; *The Diamond Age* [New York: Bantam, 1996]; and *Snow Crash* [New York: Bantam, 1992]).

39. Martin, "Jacking Into *The Matrix*," 69.

# 2

# The Par-asian Cinematic Imaginary in Olivier Assayas's *Irma Vep*

Grace An

Olivier Assayas's 1996 film *Irma Vep* confronts the viewer with conflicting attitudes about French cinema at the end of the twentieth century and on the edge of a future that promises cultural and artistic uncertainty. These tensions are expressed through the staging of a remake of the 1915 movie *Les Vampires* (directed by Louis Feuillade), a project designed to rejuvenate a faltering French film industry. Played by the actress Musidora in the original film, the character Irma Vep is the leader of a band of male thieves who identify themselves as "les vampires."[1] Assayas capitalizes on this role to address urgent problems destabilizing French cinema, particularly in regard to the configuration and projection of markers of Frenchness in French movies. Even the film's title and the character's name, "Irma Vep," represents a deconstruction of Frenchness since, as an anagram of "vampire," it introduces an exotic element into the word it has rearranged, making it culturally and linguistically difficult to place. Near the opening of the film, the director of the remake, René Vidal (played by Jean-Pierre Léaud, the well-known star of François Truffaut's films) explains that Irma Vep is not a vampire but "the woman who inspires vampires." The viewer also learns that Irma Vep represents both the glorious past of French cinema and the "modern French woman." René

---

Originally published under the title "Par-Asian Screen Women and Film Identities: Irma Vep," *SITES: The Journal of Contemporary French and Francophone Studies* 4.2 (Fall 2000), 398–415. Reprinted with permission.

Figure 2.1 *Irma Vep*. Dir. Olivier Assayas. Dacia Films, 1996. Courtesy of Zeitgeist Films.

determines, however, that no French actress can play her. So whom do they hire to play the modern French woman and revive French cinema? Maggie Cheung, a Hong Kong action-movie star who plays herself in the leading role of the film and the film-within-the-film.[2]

The year *Irma Vep* appeared in theaters is significant, for 1996 marked the centennial of French cinema. The video release of *Les Vampires* just before the appearance of *Irma Vep* on the cinematic screen was just one component of the nostalgia that grew out of France's celebration of the first 100 years of film. It is suggestive, then, that the film-within-the-film is a remake of a vampire movie and thus brings into focus the tension that surrounds a wavering cinema trying to draw cultural and artistic sustenance from better-thriving art forms. Between the legacy of Feuillade's *Les Vampires* and the star presence of Maggie Cheung, *Irma Vep* remaps France's seventh art, taking it from the center to the periphery. Its self-referential structure highlights everything from film production on the set of the remake to the circulation of French movies and Frenchness in the larger international film market. Presenting itself almost as a faux documentary on the state of French cinema, the film reads as a French search for claims that the French might make in cinema, especially in relation to competition from other centers such as Hollywood and Hong Kong.

Might *Irma Vep* claim a privileged status in the history of the cinematic vampire by asserting the precedence of Feuillade's 1915 *Vampires* over, say, Germany's 1922 *Nosferatu* by F.W. Murnau? Might it stand as the French answer to other successful vampire flicks of the time, such as *Interview With a Vampire* (Neil Jordan, 1994) or *Bram Stoker's Dracula* (Francis Ford Coppola, 1992)? Or might the assignment of Maggie's face to the French vampire of the future (as opposed to the face of Catherine Deneuve, the French vampire in the 1983 film *The Hunger*) acknowledge the need to reckon with the cinemas emerging from East Asia, which were becoming increasingly popular in France in 1996? How will Maggie screen the intersections between these diverse cinemas?

Given the intertextuality it shares with the films mentioned above, *Irma Vep* may belong more to the genre of the vampire movie than to the category of "French national cinema." This classification might free us from the contradictions inherent in its status as a "French film." For example, even though the director and the original film (*Les Vampires*) are French, English is the dominant language of *Irma Vep*, and the female star signifies Hong Kong, Chinese cinema, martial arts, and other forms of non-French cultural production. The intersection of French, East Asian, and American visuals in this film occasions a countercurrent of panic, anxiety, and nostalgia for a time when markers of Frenchness alone could sustain the French film industry. What Steven Neale calls "generic verisimilitude" (the expectations for certain narrative and cinematographic elements that characterize the genre of the vampire movie) comes into direct conflict with "cultural regimes of verisimilitude," determined by the dominant "public opinion" in regard to the "cultural expression" that one expects from its movies.[3] Maggie's presence cannot but disrupt established French preconceptions about the French female vampire. Even if a seasoned cinephile will easily remember the importance of, say, American cinema for the directors of the French New Wave or the long-standing imperative to study and know world cinema *à la Henri Langlois* and the Cinemathèque that he founded in 1936, the fear of France's diminishing presence on the international screen fuels the nostalgic turn to a past that is exemplified by *Les Vampires*.

It becomes equally necessary to examine how the French interest in East Asia is structured and held up to the mirror during this moment of nostalgia for a certain kind of France. The Asian "otherness" in this film is not fully circumscribed by a discrete frame of geocultural reference. Therefore the turn to the foreign ricochets back on to the French center in a way that catalyzes self-critique and self-flagellation. This film represents a French subjectivity coming to grips with an alterity that no longer waits at the periphery but has taken root in the *métropole*. Emerging from this encounter is an awareness, or imagination, of a *Par-asian* cinema, morphing *Parisian* and *Asian* elements into a filmic culture whose way into the future may unfold *par l'Asie*, through Asia. Through the dramatization of efforts to exploit the caché imported from Hong Kong in order to claim precedence in the vampire genre, *Irma Vep* tackles France's local struggles with global remappings of cultural and generic forces. A subsequent challenge for the French, then, is to recognize themselves in a redefined manner—and perhaps necessarily through a site occupied by the Asian other. What kind of representational intensity does Maggie Cheung bring to this identity crisis? Is she a muse for French cinema, its entry into the future?

## Par-asian Mismatches, Misrecognitions, and Missed Encounters

From the opening scene of *Irma Vep*, the encounter between Maggie Cheung and French cinema seems headed for disaster. She arrives in Paris three days late, has to find her own way to the production set when stranded at the airport, and walks in on a tense phone conversation during which a producer furiously negotiates budgetary crises hampering the film. René, the director, is nowhere to be found, personality conflicts abound, and no one knows what to do with Maggie once she's there. Here, the "Frenchness" of the French production crew is hardly explicit. The Parisian location of the remake of *Les Vampires* is hardly signified by a nondescript office space where presumably north- and sub-Saharan-African transnationals manage the activity behind the screen. Spoken French is heard through voice-over, but soon enough it is replaced by English, the dominant language in this French film. By opening *Irma Vep* in the generic international space of film production, Assayas acknowledges the marginality of Frenchness in French cinema during the first thirty seconds of the film. Maggie enters not a very French space, but a transnational one, providing an apt setting for a missed encounter between the Hong Kong and French film industries.

With a language barrier preventing the Anglophone Hong Kong actress from conversing with her French co-workers, the tracking movement of the camera alone keeps this new portrait of French cinema together. Amid the chaotic studio rush around the remake, the camera fetishizes Maggie as it tracks her movement in and out of the whirlwind of conflicts on the set. Bumped around by the anxious crew members, Maggie maintains a relationship with the camera that constitutes her sole connection to the spectator. Also resisting integration is Maggie's Hong Kong film history, since her immediate French interlocutors fail to understand her latest film. When asked to explain it, she uncomfortably provides a summary to the crew, who listen intently to her definition of an action movie. Confronted with bemused faces, she offers, "You know, action? Fighting?" When she is met only with frustration, she concludes, "It's complicated, it's boring." Once the French begin to exhibit signs of comprehension, however, she resumes her narration but then immediately has to pause while one of the crew members translates "Frogmen" into French for the ones who do not understand English.

On the one hand, the first scene of *Irma Vep* displays an interrupted narrative of passing, that of Asian Maggie into French cinema. On the other, it foretells the eventual failure of the French to either assimilate an Asian other or exploit the tremendous cultural and artistic capital that Maggie Cheung's celebrity can offer their film project. The spectator observes the inability of the French to understand what they have forced Maggie to explain, not to mention the international idiom in which she speaks, the English language. What is put into question, then, are French cultural and linguistic competencies in an increasingly global cinematic marketplace.

Emerging from this intercultural disarray is the realization that the invitation extended to Maggie to play Irma Vep was motivated by a wish based on misrecognition, itself resulting from a shifting relationship to her images, which have been distributed to markets outside Hong Kong. For example, the viewer sees a clip from Maggie's film *The Heroic Trio* (Johnny To, 1993), a thrilling martial-arts scene with bullets, weapons, and humans flying through the blue-tinted air. The film then cuts to a rendezvous with her new director, René Vidal—or rather, the film cuts directly to a shot of René's hand on the remote control, bringing the action scene to a stop and visually reinforcing the power of his hand to control the images to his liking. The position of René's hand on the remote control demonstrates his insistence on occupying the viewer's gaze.

René has no difficulty interpreting the performance he has just shown to the performer herself, in contrast to Maggie's inability to translate her last film to the crew in the preceding scene. The viewer understands, however, that René does not address the film. Ignoring the martial-art acrobatics, the exaggerated cries, and the special effects of bullets and spears hurtling toward Maggie, he romanticizes and conjures up an incorrect portrait of "grace," "mysterious beauty," and "magic," all supposedly belonging to the woman who will be his modern Irma Vep. Self-effacingly, Maggie replies, "It was all stunts," but René is too absorbed in his misreading of her cinematic work to hear her. Failing to realize that importing (the body of) Maggie Cheung does not successfully follow from importing images of Maggie Cheung, René disavows the difficulty with which he appropriates her screen presence in order to revive the French female vampire.

After her meeting with René, Maggie is immediately shown with her costume designer, Zoé, who dresses the actress in a latex catsuit. This scene invites the spectator to consider how Maggie will "inspire" this particular vampire (remember that René explains that Irma Vep is not a vampire but a woman who inspires vampires): Zoe is a bisexual woman who threatens to emerge from her behind-the-scenes position as costume designer and occupy the gaze that has been anchored in René. Zoé is in the shop to dress Maggie in the "S-M bondage" suit that René has ordered. When Maggie asks if this is what René wants, Zoe proclaims, "If he says hooker, I say hooker." Zoé's role as René's interpreter, enactor, and even double displaces her own desire for the same woman René wants. In fact, her desire for Maggie is always read in relation to René's. Zoé's interest in Maggie becomes the story that intrigues her gossipy co-workers, while René's more insidious misappropriation of Maggie's image becomes dissimulated and de-incriminated. To a certain extent, Zoé screens a certain heteronormative panic that emerges alongside the imperative to remap French cinema.

Constantly worried about René's knowledge of her desire for Maggie, Zoé understands that her relationship with Maggie is vulnerable to the predatory grapevine of the crew. Later, she recounts the costume-fitting masquerade to the wife of a co-worker who, titillated by the possibility of a lesbian encounter, urges Zoé to hunt Maggie down, to go for the kill, blurting, "*Si elle t'a demandé le costume, ça veut dire que tu peux aller*!" ["If she wants the costume, go for it!"]. Thus, in her friend's fantasy of lesbian lust, Zoé is made to occupy a vampiric role that will seize Maggie—in an S-M latex costume, no less—as her prey. It is equally important to note that just as Zoé opens up the costume-fitting scene following René's definition of a vampire, Zoé also closes the scene by putting the vampire mask on herself and looking into the mirror. Specularized as vampiric, Zoé is pushed into the vampiric corner by other women, including Maïté, René's assistant, and her co-worker's wife. To a certain extent, the *vampire* role that Maggie is to play becomes entangled with the *vampiric* or *altered* role that Zoé is made to assume in the eyes of the crew and her friends. Maggie may give the vampire character a face, but it is Zoé who represents what Ellis Hanson calls a "vampire persona," which he describes as "an altered state of feeling . . . an identification with the position of abjection . . . a different way of looking" because of how she is treated and punished by the crew.[4]

The vampire persona and the vampiric do not index a cinematic genre as much they index a cinematic condition that gnaws at the boundaries of identity that insist on cultural purities. They also bring to the foreground crises around identification and self-recognition that seem to prey on Maggie's image and cultural symbolism. Zoé helps dress up and materialize the modern Par-asian female vampire, but she also occupies the vampiric position insofar as she is made to reinterpret and re-present cultural problems. Her lesbian desire for Maggie may be displaced as a bad copy of René's heterosexual lust for the same woman. Whether in regard to French film history, French femininity, lesbian sexuality, or a French desire for Asia, Zoé-as-bisexual-woman and Maggie-as-foreign-actress both function as vampiric screens of a heteronormative and xenophobic panic that is not their own but projected onto them.

My use of the "vampiric," then, brings these issues to the fore. "Vampiric" may serve as a term to identify and describe the cultural undertow eroding rules and established parameters of identity construction. Nonetheless, sites of the vampiric can also function as sites of resistance to such change. The vampiric in Assayas's *Irma Vep* might best recapture the power of the original Feuillade film, since the character Irma Vep, as originally played by the silent movie actress Musidora, also stood for what Kristine Butler calls a "zone of anxiety."[5] As an index to the cultural and generic transformations of Irma Vep, the vampiric also reveals the discontinuities that were disavowed in the process of enacting and sustaining the fantasy of a female vampire character that could, in its function as muse, reinvent French cinema. The extensive amount of attention paid to the labor behind the scenes already signals the film's inevitable failure to fulfill this fantasy. How can the cinematic illusion of a renascent Irma Vep fool, enchant, and stun spectators if they are made to sit through the tedious dysfunctionality of a crew who themselves do not believe in this Par-asian project? The narrative does not even give spectators the opportunity to believe in "the idea of Irma Vep," since the film demystifies the reinvention of the French female vampire muse by deconstructing her cinematic construction.

For instance, when Maggie asks, "Are you sure that's what René wants?" during the fitting of the S-M bondage suit, Zoé explains, "Look at the photo, this is the idea of Irma Vep," pointing to a photo of Catwoman, played by Michelle Pfeiffer in *Batman Returns* (Tim Burton, 1992). This still publicity photo supplements the "idea of Irma Vep," which René already visually accounted for through clips from Maggie's Hong Kong films. The "idea of Irma Vep" is thus exposed as a composite of multinational fragments brought together—in other words, a composite image that maps the globalized political economy of cinema onto a globalized character and icon whose national cinematic heritage has been surpassed.

Later, when René calls Maggie to his apartment after a domestic brawl, he acknowledges the impending failure of the project and laments that Irma Vep is "just images. Without soul. My fault. Just images of images. Doesn't mean anything." As if in a confessional, he admits his misfired fantasy, revealing to her, "I am interested in you more than the character. I thought of you in this role, in this costume—it was very exciting." He then explains, "You think you're at the core but really you're at the surface." What René has just indirectly confessed is the process by which he was taken in by images whose powers he had overestimated precisely because of the space of misrecognition between them and their user (that being René), only later to leave him disaffected after realizing his originary illusion. His confession further avows the discontinuities between the woman projected on the screen and her composite construction. Maggie tries to protect herself against disaster by attempting to legitimize her soon-to-be-confiscated role, and by extension, her director's conception of the film. This effort bemuses the viewer, who has already heard the rest of René's crew speak against the casting of the Hong Kong actress. In the meantime, the role of Irma Vep itself fades into the gaps between the Feuillade original, Hong Kong action flicks, and clipped photos of Catwoman. As Maggie tries to defend the integrity of a role that no longer makes sense even to the director, the role itself is emptied into being a false signifier for a failed fantasy. Nevertheless, one has to wonder if Maggie takes fantasy into her own hands during her memorable hotel escapade in the following scene.

After a camera sweep of magazines, clothes, and other items scattered around her hotel room, Maggie appears before the camera, restless and trapped in her hotel room. For once, the camera can hardly keep up with an elusive Maggie, until it catches her taking a long look at herself in the mirror and stealthily venturing out of her room into the hotel. The music of Sonic Youth has dominated the scene so far, but it comes to an abrupt halt as Maggie steals looks into other people's hotel rooms through open windows, sneaks up the fancy hotel staircase, and hides behind columns and walls as other hotel clients pass by. Note the absence of the dysfunctional film crew and of a male director. For the first time in the film, the fantasy of Irma Vep plays itself out, and perhaps it is precisely because the spectator is left alone, unburdened by the presence of the crew and ready to make sense of Maggie's presence in his or her own way. Maggie eventually enters the room of a naked woman (played by Arisinée Khanjian, a French-Canadian actress mostly known for her roles in films by husband-director Atom Egoyan), who argues on the phone with a male lover who has stood her up in Paris.

What is fascinating about this scene is how Maggie seizes the gaze and embodies the camera for the first and only time during the entire film. Maggie spots some jewels on the bathroom sink and steals them from the naked woman, who is heard through voice-over in the other room. A shot-reverse-shot between Maggie and the jewels on the bathroom counter attributes the point of view to Maggie and signals her theft of both the jewels and the camera shooting her. However brief and insignificant this moment may initially appear, the camera's patient and deliberate zoom on the jewels (which contrasts significantly with the normally rapid camerawork in the film) creates a pull, a sense of Maggie's absorption of the jewels, her own desire, her visual power and pleasure. What is also drawn into the scene is the spectator, captivated by Maggie's screen presence and liberated from the visual and narrative interference of the film crew. How do we interpret her seizure of another woman's jewels—a woman who is white and therefore visually and ethnically antithetical to Maggie but speaks with a heavy accent, and whose hotel surroundings frame her in a modern harem setting? Might we argue that she is Orientalized during the same moment when Maggie finally gets to inhabit the role of the French female vampire?

Freed from her containment within the camera frame (where she has been kept since the beginning of the film), Maggie is also liberated from her

Asian otherness and her exclusive positioning as spectacle. Tom Conley notes that "the staging of her gaze cast upon the integrally naked woman . . . brings forward a reversal of Laura Mulvey's famous theory of narrative desire, which aligns the pleasure gained from suspending disbelief in a story with male scopophilia."[6] Conley here rearticulates what Ellis Hanson referred to earlier as a "vampire persona" in order to identify a "different way of looking." What is more interesting to me is how Maggie's Asian otherness appears to have been instantly neutralized in the face of the heightened otherness of the naked woman, now vulnerable, exposed, and trapped in her Orientalized boudoir. Maggie then escapes from that hotel room, runs through the hallway and onto the balcony overlooking Parisian rooftops, and watches the glistening jewels fall in the heavy nightly rain. One of the most enigmatic moments of the film, this scene supplants a certain kind of fantasy that may have just been announced as terminated by René, and materializes a different one without him.

How does the spectator explain the cut from this strange nighttime episode of thievery and masquerade to the next morning when Maggie, still in costume, is forced awake by Zoé, who informs her that they are already late for that day's shoot? Was this scene a dream? A moment Maggie may have enjoyed in complete isolation? Immediately after Maggie's fantasy moment in the hotel, we return to the film-within-the-film on set, where one of Maggie's stunt-doubles acts out the character Irma Vep, sneaking up fire escapes, performing acrobatic feats, and running along the rooftops of Paris in the background, visually echoing what we have just seen Maggie do. Only her double does so awkwardly, eliciting the cameraman's comment that it was "too calculated" and that it needed to be "more feline, more feminine."

Once again, Assayas presents the two sides of the screen: on the one hand, the fantasy enacted for the spectator (that is, Maggie's fantasy moment in the hotel) and, on the other, the labor and artifice of production. Once the modern Irma Vep is realized by Maggie, the character finds itself immediately demystified and emptied out by the subsequent presentation of imperfect artifice. This dialectic does not negate the power of the artificial, for the spectator cannot forget the intriguing hotel escapade (en)acted by Maggie alone. The viewer is set up for disappointment in the French double who cannot replace or copy her, who cannot enact this cinematic fantasy with or of Maggie, who remains misunderstood and misused.

## Back to Hong Kong, Back to the Other Continent

I suggest that Maggie Cheung is portrayed as "misused" because the film-within-the-film reduces her to stereotypes, putting her artistic capital to waste. Let us recall her tremendous filmography, her 100 films in sixteen years: her start in martial-arts films (mostly in association with Jackie Chan), her extensive subsequent work in *auteur* cinema, including four films under the direction of Wong Kar-wai,[7] as well as her leading role in *Centre Stage* (Stanley Kwan, 1992), a film about the silent Hong Kong movie star Ruan Lingyu (1910–1935). Many parallels can be drawn between *Centre Stage* and *Irma Vep*: they are films about silent cinema, the modern woman, the treatment of actresses. They both also feature interviews of Maggie Cheung, who is asked to reflect on histories of cinemas. Given Assayas's interest in Asian cinema,[8] the exclusion of this particular history remains curious insofar as *Irma Vep* does not use narrative form to mine the potential for cross-fertilization between French and Asian cinemas. Instead, nostalgia for early French cinema gives way to panic about the increasing visibility of the Asian continent and Asian films.

After the exhilarating hotel scene in which the film finally shows Maggie in full vampiric force, the film quickly sews up its opening to fantasy and resists creative change. The camera resumes its tracking of Maggie; she is placed back in her frontal shots as well as in her Irma Vep costume with the requisite make-up, particularly during the interview scene when the French interviewer interrogates her about her opinions on French cinema. This scene presents Assayas's most severe and unsympathetic portrayal of French self-deprecation about French cinema, as well as a parodying critique of the tendency to essentialize the cultures that are represented by the cinemas they produce and disseminate.

The interview begins with Maggie's description of her work with Jackie Chan. When she tries to discuss other issues, such as gender problems in John Woo's "masculine" work, the French interviewer wants to hear only confirmations of his own stereotypical understanding of Hong Kong cinema. He constantly inserts the term "kung fu" in his questions, and mockingly describes gunfight scenes "like ballet, like choreography of extreme violence, *non*?" The exaggerated French accent and hyperbolic claims should alert the viewer to the film's mockery of the "exoticization" of Maggie. She is already being spoken for, since the interviewer draws answers on her behalf to his own questions, and yet she becomes an instrument of French self-flagellation when he poses the menacing question, "And what do you think of French cinema?" He seems to anticipate the painful truth when she answers that "French films don't really come to Hong Kong" (in contrast to her widely distributed films, to places including Marrakech, where René supposedly spotted her). Then he assaults her with his own frustration about French cinema being "*nombrilistique* [navel-gazing]—only to please yourself" (all the while insistently pointing to his own navel) since "France giv[es] France money to make films nobody ever sees." Figures like Arnold Schwarzenegger and Jean-Claude Van Damme become the surrogate ideals against which he trashes his national culture. The interview ends with the question, "Don't you think that the intellectuals have

Figure 2.2 *Irma Vep*. Dir. Olivier Assayas. Dacia Films, 1996. Courtesy of Zeitgeist Films.

killed the industry?" while the film immediately cuts to a shot of the actors at the precise moment they receive news of Rene's abandonment of the *Irma Vep* project.

While the camera is fixed on Maggie's face, the voice-over questions come hurling at her from the space beyond the frame (Figure 2.2). At this moment, the issue of point of view arises, since the camera is not a disembodied one. It carries the point of view of the interviewer who tries to make Maggie speak that malaise, as if she were a spokeswoman ready to recite a script. This scene becomes less an interview of Maggie Cheung than a projection of French self-deprecation onto her facial image. In fact, Maggie's awkward presence in the entire film embodies the ambivalence that the French in the film feel about her and about themselves. The black latex suit may neutralize national encodings on her body, but it is precisely that nondefinition that creates uncertainty and fear. She is the imported object that comes to show on screen the side of French identity that is uncertainty, that is resentment and wounds; she becomes the site onto which a certain French masochism is displaced.

Toward the end of the film, the viewer is privy to a conversation between Laure, Maggie's stunt-double, and José Murano, the welfare recipient who is asked to replace René as director. This moment most explicitly is an emblem of the limits of the cultural expediency of imported images and subjectivities. José offers his own interpretation of Irma Vep, claiming, *"Irma Vep, c'est les bas-fonds de Paris, c'est le Paris populaire, c'est Arletty"* ["Irma Vep is Paris. She's the Paris Underworld, she's working-class Paris, she's Arletty"]. Note the repetition of "Paris," the insistence on Paris and Parisian—not Par-asian—cinema. *"Les Vampires, ce n'est pas Fu Manchu!"* ["*The Vampires*, it ain't *Fu Manchu*!"] Images may just be images, as René suggests earlier in the film, but José insists on defending French territory from miscegenation and falls into the trap of a facile cultural reference point when he reduces Hong Kong cinema to *Fu Manchu*. José's agenda as the second director of the film-within-the-film—the reclaiming of French cinema in purely French terms—completely reverses René's desire to attract a successful Hong Kong actress in order to revive the very cinema that José wants to keep for the French. Let us not forget, however, the irony of José's non-French name, perhaps a reference to the German director of *Nosferatu,* F.W. Murnau. Hardly mentioning Maggie's name and constantly referring to her instead as *"la chinoise,"* José expects that the recently fired Irma Vep "will go back to Hong Kong," revealing his limited and misleading view that Maggie's appeal is restricted to her supposed place of origin. Amusingly, she leaves Paris for New York and Los Angeles, with a bigger fish, namely Ridley Scott, to fry.

Maggie is replaced by Laure, the self-effacing, giggly, hesitatingly ambitious, passive but maneuvering French actress who served as her double. The new director can project his desire for the character Irma Vep onto Laure. The new French woman steals the role—remember that Irma Vep and *les vampires* in the Feuillade original are thieves—and this replacement of one "French woman" for another is yet another structure in the film that operates according to male heterosexual desire. This time it demonstrates the process by which José attempts to map out the sexual and cultural terrain by clearly designating where everyone unequivocally belongs. Additionally, he seeks to return to the pure French female vampire, and reinstate cultural and generic verisimilitude in nationalistic and xenophobic terms.

The multiple interfaces in this film—and Maggie Cheung in particular—carry not only the narrativization of foreign encroachment upon French cinematic territory, but simultaneously, the tensions of different kinds of desire. Different forms of desire are seen to cover, screen, frame, and feed on each other, as well as on their objects of desire, in what I have attempted to define as a *vampiric* space. The points of the Par-asian encounter in *Irma Vep* bring us to a new stage where "Orientalism" may be reconsidered in a globalized marketplace. In fact, one could trace the path from Edward Said's fervent effort to prove Orientalism a dominant discourse[9] all the way to Rey Chow's demand that one think of and use one's analysis of Orientalism as a cultural critique by means of exhibitionism.

In her book *Primitive Passions*, Chow is concerned specifically with Chinese films that have often adopted a Western point of view in their own self-representation precisely to ensure their circulation by satisfying Western expectations of "China" and "Chineseness." Nevertheless, Chow locates a path of resistance in the Chinese performative critique of Orientalism, which she refers to as "the Oriental's Orientalism":

> This self-exhibitionism . . . turns the remnants of Orientalism into elements of a new ethnography . . . [that] accepts the historical fact of Orientalism and performs a critique (i.e., evaluation) of it by staging and parodying Orientalism's politics of visuality. In its

> self-subalternizing, self-exoticizing visual gestures, the Oriental's Orientalism is first and foremost a demonstration—the display of a tactic.[10]

Chow suggests that we marshal Orientalism as a critical framework—in the form of parodies of Orientalist tactics—to reveal the agendas and ideologies informing systematized understandings and misunderstandings of China.

In this vein, Assayas provides a *mise-en-scène* of Orientalism that demonstrates how a reflection on the signification of East Asia for the French becomes crucial for an account of French cinema. This kind of Orientalism becomes identifiable as a structure that has enabled France, in its literature and cinema, to negotiate its image on displaced sites and bodies. What distinguishes the vision of a Par-asian cinematic imaginary from Orientalism, however, is its desire for a genuine encounter between Paris and Asia, for the potential cross-fertilization between these geocultural entities and their cinemas, for an acknowledgement that what is "Parisian" or "Asian" relies on a derivative understanding of these notions through and against each other. In fact, René's positioning stands for the virtual notion of a Par-asian cinema that is recombinant and reflective of the globalized political economy of film culture, whereas José gives expression to an Orientalizing retreat back toward the essentialization of French and foreign presences and the restrictions on the meanings they carry. And yet, in this film, what "Asia" signifies to the French is much less at stake than what "France" means to everyone else—that is, *if* it continues to do so on the international cinematic screen.

The film closes with a showing of René's editings of rushes of Maggie as Irma Vep. He has already abandoned the project, and the crew is about to resume work with their new director, José. The editing of the images of Maggie, appearing through an array of geographic shapes and markings freely circulating around and over her face, seem to scratch and wipe and poke at her surface and eventually leave the viewer in a state of suspense about the residual traces of her contribution to French cinematic artistry. Her Asian body is flashed against a backdrop of penciled images of Paris. A discernible illustration of Notre Dame de Paris along with aerial shots of Paris rooftops (taken from clips of the film-within-the-film) mark the flashing movements of the Asian body through both the visualized metropolitan city (Figure 2.3) *and* the medium that patches together this bizarre but inventive piece of visual art. It is important to return to René's confessional, particularly the moment when he tells Maggie, "You think you're at the core but really you're at the surface." To a certain extent, this visual display flattens Maggie Cheung's cultural and cinematic identity to a manipulated and mutated visual form. A vision for a Par-asian cinema is reduced to an ephemeral moment, like that of the evaporating jewels that Maggie

Figure 2.3 *Irma Vep*. Dir. Olivier Assayas. Dacia Films, 1996. Courtesy of Zeitgeist Films.

captured but let fall through the rooftops and into the folds of a Parisian nightscape.

At the end of the first 100 years of French cinema, we are brought back to the surface and left in a state of ambivalence about its cultural and artistic future. *Irma Vep* points us to a phenomenon of the French looking at themselves as they try to look at an Asian other. Yet, given the misrecognitions and displacements discussed in this chapter, it comes down to the French, at least in this film, seeing themselves seeing something yet to be rendered discrete and identifiable beyond the surface. The question of surfaces opens to an exploration of interfaces that carry the ambivalence of intercultural encounters and *rapprochements*. These interfaces ask us to consider different ways to code "otherness," to discern and understand "different ways of looking," and to reflect on the consequences of the relationship between cultural centers and their margins, to be redefined and remapped in an awareness of the transnational cinematic imaginary that is, or could be, the Par-asian one.

## Notes

1. In this essay, all quotations from the film will be cited in their original language. If the original quote is in French, an English translation will follow in brackets.

2. Since Maggie Cheung plays herself in the film, it is necessary to be precise in the ways I will address her doubled presence in this chapter. When I write "Maggie Cheung," I am discussing the actress Maggie Cheung. When I refer to her as "Maggie," I am referring to the character Maggie Cheung in *Irma Vep*.

3. Steven Neale, "Questions of Genre," originally published in *Screen* 31.1 (1990), and republished in Robert Stam and Toby Miller, eds., *Film and Theory* (Malden, MA: Blackwell Publishers, 2000), 157–178. The quotes on this page are taken from the latter source, 158–159.

4. Ellis Hanson, "Lesbians Who Bite," Ellis Hanson, ed., *Out Takes* (Durham: Duke University Press, 1999), 196.

5. Kristine Butler, "*Irma Vep*, Vamp in the City: Mapping the Criminal Feminine in Early French Serials," Jennifer M. Bean and Diane Negra, eds., *A Feminist Reader in Early Cinema.* (Durham: Duke University Press, 2002), 204.

6. Tom Conley, "Revamping Irma: Immodest Reflections on French Cinema and Globalization," *Sites: The Journal of 20th Century Contemporary French Studies* 4.2 (Fall 2000): 417–434.

7. *As Tears Go By* (1988), *Days of Being Wild* (1990), *Ashes of Time* (1994), *In the Mood for Love* (2000), and *2046* (2006).

8. Assayas was the producer and interviewer for the documentary *A Portrait of Hou Hsiao-Hsien* (1997), which features this very successful and prominent director, known for films such as *Flowers of Shanghai* (1998) and *The Puppetmaster* (1993).

9. Edward Said, *Orientalism* (New York: Vintage, 1979).

10. Rey Chow, *Primitive Passions: Visuality, Sexuality, Ethnography, and Contemporary Chinese Cinema* (New York: Columbia University Press), 171.

# 3
# The *HK* Venture

## *The Francophone Cine-logocentric Nexus*

AARON HAN JOON MAGNAN-PARK

The reception of Hong Kong cinema in France provides a case study in transnational film culture, one that reveals France to be insufficient as a source of either all-encompassing cultural enrichment or cultural self-authentication, thereby challenging conventional film historiography and its reliance on national categories. On the cultural level, the trope of the nation has worked only from within a myopic and isolated ideological utopia. Despite the idealized formulation of the nation as a self-sufficient, self-encompassing, and self-generating entity, the national framework falls short in creating a mono-culture exclusively by itself, of itself, and for itself. A transnational perspective dispels this national hubris by revealing the nation as just one form of communal identification within a larger and expansive communal continuum. In fact, French cinematic culture is undergoing a dynamic process of cultural reinvigoration, with Hong Kong action cinema as a key participant.

The *HK* venture is the cine-logocentric nexus in the Francophone world that cultivated a constellated transnational community unwilling to limit itself to just what its national cinema creates and imagines for its self-appointed "community." Starting in 1996, the *HK* venture ruptured the ethnolinguistic exclusivism under which Hong Kong action cinema

---

Extract from *Cinescapes of the "Yet-to-be-Fully-National": Hong Kong Action Cinema's Transnational Engagement* (Ph.D. Dissertation, University of Iowa, 2002, 288 pages; AAT 3050821).

existed within France as part of a ghettoized geographic and linguistic circuit. It was ghettoized geographically in the thirteenth *arrondissement*, Paris' historical *huaqiao* (overseas ethnic Chinese) epicenter. It was further ghettoized linguistically because the available dialogues for these films featured Mandarin, Cantonese, and Vietnamese while the subtitles favored *fantizi* (traditional Chinese characters), *jiantizi* (simplified Chinese characters), Vietnamese, and English.[1] Notably absent was French.

To end this double constraint, the *HK* venture pursued a two-pronged strategy of translating the films into French and creating a Franco-friendly voice for Hong Kong action cinema in which *HK Video* handled video sales while *HK Orient Extreme Cinema* served as its critical publication arm. By combining visual capitalism with print capitalism, the *HK* venture pursued a cultural and linguistic embrace through which the larger Francophone society could be infused by means of its engagement with an imbedded "other"—the Hong Kong action cinema. Thus the French-initiated *HK* venture's cultural and linguistic embrace demonstrates how Hong Kong action cinema in particular, and Asian popular cinema in general, does not necessarily "belong" just within primordial ethnic enclaves of cultural and linguistic exclusivism but rather is part and parcel of a larger transnational imagining community[2] that comes into being through its cultural engagements.

## French Precursors to *HK*

In the 1970s, French demand for the *gongfupian* (kung fu films) became its own *vague* (wave). In this respect, France joined the United States and the rest of the world in what David Desser anoints as "the kung fu craze."[3] The demand was so high that unscrupulous distributors and exhibitors screened substandard, poorly dubbed prints, often truncated to maximize daily double billings. Still, French audiences endured even these compromises and claimed these films as part of their own dynamically evolving transnational cinematic culture.

Sustained coverage of this phenomenon did not occur in France until September 1984, when *Cahiers du cinéma* published a special double issue titled "Made in Hong-Kong."[4] At 128 pages, this publication served as an intense and condensed introduction to Hong Kong cinema's multiple dimensions. It was the first French publication to cover the Hong Kong film industry in depth. It oriented the Francophone world and, by extension, all of global film culture to this hitherto critically unaddressed film industry. It focused on Hong Kong's *auteurs*, studio system, and *Nouvelle Vague* with special attention placed on Hong Kong cinema's highly developed and diverse martial-arts tradition.

Unique to *Cahiers*' coverage is a two-page section documenting Hong Kong action cinema's entry into, circulation within, and invigoration of

French film culture, focusing on six key events concentrated in Paris: 1) André Koob and the discovery of Bruce Le;[5] 2) René Chateau's successful commercialization of the Bruce Lee cult; 3) new dubbing practices for *la version française*; 4) the rise of Chinese video outlets;[6] 5) the Hong Kong *kung fu vague*'s increasing popularity and financial prosperity outside of Le Hollywood Boulevard's Bruce Lee retrospectives;[7] and 6) Quach Thoai Huan's success in running a Chinese Vietnamese chain of theaters and video stores. This six-part coverage revealed an evolving situation in which parallel markets existed, separated by ethnicity and language. Clearly a historical *huaqiao* market operated almost independently within an ethnic enclave that serviced an Asian clientele. However, what is new is the fervor under which the *kung fu vague* (the kung fu wave) rapidly rose in popularity throughout France outside of traditional *huaqiao* confines. This cine-cultural explosion was initiated, sustained, and disseminated across a Francophone clientele by the French themselves.

René Chateau[8] single-handedly nurtured the cult of Bruce Lee in France by purchasing the French distribution rights to Lee's first two films. These were then screened at Le Hollywood Boulevard, a second-run theater of seven hundred seats near the Grand Rex Theatre in Paris, located on 4 Boulevard Montmartre.[9] Critical of fly-by-night film importers who purchased French distribution rights for Hong Kong films by the kilo, Chateau spearheaded a masterful marketing campaign to forward a non-dismissive approach to these martial-arts classics. He accomplished this in part by cowriting the best sellers *Bruce Lee: La Légende du petit dragon* (1975) and *Bruce Lee: Inédit* (1975). He also oversaw the publication of *Bruce Lee: La Vie et la mort tragique de Bruce Lee par sa femme Linda* (1976).[10] In this respect, Chateau pursued a similar two-pronged strategy that the *HK* venture would adopt a good two decades later: releasing *la version française* and utilizing print capitalism. Even as late as 1984, Lee's films could still attract around two thousand Parisian spectators per week.[11]

However, the tragic early death of Bruce Lee in 1973 led to the quick demise of the *kung fu vague* as a sustainable crossover genre. By 1975, the *kung fu vague* returned to its traditional *huaqiao* circuit and the ethnolinguistic exclusivism of these films again became the norm. Quach Thoai Huan was the owner of the sole Chinese Vietnamese cinema chain in France. Quach arrived in France in 1976, at the tail end of the *kung fu vague*, and owned a total of three cinemas, all concentrated in the thirteenth *arrondissement*, plus a chain of video stores that offered original-language videos of Hong Kong's Asia Television (ATV) broadcasts but not of feature films. Quach distributed about fifty-two films annually, with the Shaw Brothers accounting for twenty titles.[12] In his own estimation, his clientele broke into the following categories: 70 percent Southeast Asian, 25 percent Chinese, and 5 percent other.[13] With 95 percent of his clientele of Asian descent, Quach clearly operated within an ethnic enclave, and the only linguistic concession involved Vietnamese subtitles.

In 1988, François and Max Armanet addressed Hong Kong action cinema's continued presence within French film culture by authoring *Ciné Kung Fu*. Unlike *Cahiers*, *Ciné Kung Fu* devoted itself exclusively to the Hong Kong context and how permutations in the martial arts world distinguished its cinema. The Armanets promoted a *wushu* legacy, since it is the "*ingrédient clé*" in unlocking the secrets of Chinese culture and Hong Kong cinema.[14] They periodized Hong Kong action cinema as the Golden Age of *cape et d'épée* (1965–1971), the era of kung fu (1971–1975), and the Hong Kong *Nouvelles Vagues* (1975–1985).

After 1988, Hong Kong's cinema remained largely unaddressed in France until *HK*'s arrival in 1996. Based on this legacy, the members of *HK* viewed themselves as carrying the torch already established by their predecessors. Driving their venture was a conviction that Hong Kong cinema, and Asian popular cinema in general, deserved a more frequent and sustained coverage for an otherwise excluded Francophone audience.

## Mediating Communities: Seven/7 and the *HK* Venture

Culture does not circulate independently of the mediating communities that serve as a conduit and enable its transnational circulation. A split similar to that of the *kung fu vague* existed in the 1990s in terms of Asian cinema within France. The split but parallel network for the dissemination of popular Asian cinema within France is still marked today by ethnolinguistic exclusivism and complicated by a film exhibition practice that favors only a select few Asian *auteurs* of film festival fame.

Within this context, *HK* undertook efforts at disseminating these films for the general French-speaking public. *HK* operates as an extension of Seven/7, which is aligned with Metropolitan Film Distribution.[15] Historically, Metropolitan specialized in importing and distributing Hollywood action and B films. Under the Metropolitan umbrella, Seven/7 concentrates on videocassette sales. The *HK* venture became the transcultural nexus for the promulgation of popular Asian cinema for the Francophone world.

Launched in October 1996, the *HK* venture was divided into two components: *HK Video,* which covered videocassette sales, and *HK Orient Extrême Cinema,* which provided articles expounding on the cultural and cinematic dimensions of these films. The centrality of Hong Kong as the epitome of Asian popular cinema is acknowledged by the venture's adoption of Hong Kong's initials in its name.

As *directeur de la rédaction*, Christophe Gans[16] brought together other like-minded French cinephiles of Asian popular cinema and organized this group into the core membership of *HK*'s staff. Like Gans, the core membership was composed of individuals of European descent.[17] The *HK* triumvirate under Gans included David Martinez as *rédacteur en chef*, Léonard Haddad as *secrétaire de rédaction*, and Philippe Christin, who was in charge of public relations, promotions, and mail-order operations.

*HK* is not a subsidiary of an Asian film company. It started and continues to remain a French-initiated project. It is a group of French individuals enraptured by Asian popular cinema who find themselves disengaged with both French and Hollywood cinema. Reflecting this genesis, the magazine *HK Orient Extreme Cinema*'s premiere editorial encapsulated the prevailing condition of Asian popular cinema in the context of French national film culture.

> First of all, let us begin by stating the facts: in France, Asian cinema has never had the place it deserves. Cinemas as fundamental and essential as Hong Kong [or] Japan have always been odiously underrepresented on our screens. To give only a few of the poor reasons put forward: latent racism, American "imperialism," a lack of curiosity, cultural barriers, etc. Nevertheless, a tangible demand does exist. As proof, Japanese cinema, thanks to a few renowned *auteurs*, has always found a receptive public. The same is true for Hong Kong cinema. Bruce Lee, Jackie Chan and more recently John Woo have aroused enthusiasm and demonstrated that the popular cinema of the Far East could compete with and even infiltrate Hollywood.[18]

This *HK* editorial gives voice to a willingness and necessity to engage with these films because of their popular status.

## *HK Video*

Under the label of *HK Video*, the creation of a critical viewing space for Asian popular cinema in France first involved a collection of videos that encompassed *polar*, *kung fu*, *chambara*, and *anime*. Via videocassettes, *HK* bypassed the barriers to film distribution and exhibition for the big screen in favor of *le petit écran*. *HK Video*'s first videocassette series featured Jet Li, Tsui Hark, John Woo, and *chambara* films. The four titles were *Shaolin Temple*, *Zu: Warriors from the Magic Mountain*, *The Killer*, and *Shogun's Shadow*, respectively. Keeping with its *HK Video*'s cinephile sentiments, these videocassette releases matched the specifications established by the cable broadcasting industry and preserved the original release edits, provided new French subtitles and dubbings (retaining denotative and connotative aspects of the original dialogues), and respected the original aspect ratios.[19]

On average, *HK Video* releases two new titles every three months. By July 2000, its initial list of four videocassette titles had expanded to a total of seventy-nine titles plus eleven complementary titles. These videocassettes, along with the number of titles in each collection, were allocated into fourteen categories: Tsui Hark (seventeen), *kaiju* (featuring nine Godzilla titles), John Woo (seven), fantasy (seven), *polar* Hong Kong (six), Jet Li (six), Samo Hung (five), "Beat" Takeshi Kitano (five), Jackie Chan (four), superheroes (four), Yuen Woo Ping (three), ghouls and ghosts (three), *anime* (two), and *samurai* (one). Within these categories, films featuring martial arts were the best sellers. This categorization strategy is important because if customers enjoyed one title in a category, they were then more inclined to purchase the entire set. By July 2000, *HK Video* generated sales amounting to more than 20,000 videocassettes.[20] *HK Video* also distributes Asian videocassette titles for Canal+ and Pathé. Furthermore, its titles are distributed by the French television channel TF1. This later relationship opened up extensive, prominent, and national distribution opportunities with France's large-scale retail operations such as FNAC and Virgin.

The existence of transnational imagining communities within nationalized imagined communities is enhanced by the intervention of print capitalism. While the film journal *HK Orient Extreme Cinéma* is a money-losing venture, it nevertheless greatly promotes and enhances the sale of *HK*'s videocassette collection. *HK* thereby avoided repeating the mistake Polygram[21] and TF1 made of selling only videocassettes of Hong Kong action films without the aid of print capitalism. In fact, *HK* could not attain its commercial viability without its film journal.[22]

## *HK Orient Extreme Cinema*

*HK Orient Extreme Cinema* undertook the role of becoming the sustainable Francophone voice for this formerly unorganized, unrecognized, and unaddressed community. As a quarterly publication, *HK Orient Extreme Cinema* created a critical discursive space for Asian popular cinema and boasted an industry-setting standard. With close to one hundred pages per issue, it provides in-depth written coverage on their featured videocassette collection along with news concerning Asian cinema. It features "a team of passionate journalists that had long wished to put together its own specialized medium."[23] To counter the critical dismissal of these films as "trash" by the more established critical film community, the journal pursued relationships with film critics rather than video critics. This approach in critical media differentiation is significant because the former allows a more intense research mode to film criticism along with its associated cultural uplift.

Because *HK Orient Extreme Cinema* is the only Francophone magazine on the market that deals exclusively with the subject of Asian popular cinema, it was in *HK*'s best interests to target the largest possible audience right from its inception. The first issue is professional, thorough, and even glamorous; the outstanding quality of its images is matched by a slick yet sober cover design featuring a mesmerizing computer-enhanced still photograph that draws attention to the issue's featured coverage. Within its covers, *HK Orient Extreme Cinema* contains an opening editorial, an "Asia Report" news brief, and numerous articles and dossiers. These are accompanied by crisp color and black-and-white photographs that are of a caliber superior to those in similar journals dedicated to Hong Kong and Asian popular cinema. Through these means, it does "promote a certain idea of Asian cinema, away from the exoticism and the elitism which have thus far prevented it from being understood."[24]

With *HK Orient Extreme Cinema*'s origins as a project founded by cinephiles, the writing follows strict criteria that meet the horizon of expectations of neophytes, well-versed fans, and scholars. Thus, a prior knowledge of Asian cinema or Asian culture is not required to gain full access to these texts. For instance, culturally specific concepts such as *fengshui* (Chinese geomancy) are briefly explained within a set of parenthesis immediately following the first use of the term.[25] Since *HK Orient Extreme Cinema* deals not only with the Hong Kong cinema but also with mainland Chinese, Taiwanese, and Japanese film industries, the explanation of foreign terms is necessary. These cultural and linguistic explanations are also extended to English terms.

When it comes to their style and tone, the dossiers and articles are marked by their passionate cinephile engagement, complete with humor (a mix of tongue-in-cheek allusions and borderline geeky puns), insight, and journalistic thoroughness, if not complete objectivity since they are passionately partial to these films. An example of their humor occurs in an article addressing Samo Hung's contribution to kung fu comedy. Hervé Dante asserts, "Samo Hung *s'est fait la main sur deux films d'art martiaux survoltés,* The Iron-fisted Monk *et* Warriors Two, *dans lesquels les tartes étaient plus souvent dans la gueule qu'à la crème.*" [Sammo Hung got his hands wet in the action packed martial arts films *The Iron-Fisted Monk* and *Warriors Two*, in which the slapstick comedy involved a great deal of actual slaps in the face.] Dante places a pun on the word "*tarte,*" which in French means both "tart" of the edible kind as well as a "slap." Hence, "*tarte à la crème*" can translate to cream tart or slapstick comedy. Bringing Samo Hung back into the humor, Dante noticed that Hung's engagement with kung fu comedy gravitates towards the violent "slap" rather than the burlesque.[26] Furthermore, Dante continues to even locate Hung's helmet-like hairstyle as one that is replicated within a Francophone milieu by Mireille Matthieu. Ergo, Dante observes, "*Sa coupe de cheveux style 'Mireille Matthieu'*"[27]

Moreover, because the *HK* venture emerged at a time when Asian films in general were resurfacing in France and around the globe, the *HK* venture took upon itself a tacit pedagogical mission by pursuing an unofficial archival agenda. *HK Orient Extreme Cinema*'s coverage of Asian cinema provided in-depth analyses that accounted for various threads in Asian history, politics, and culture as they ran through the cinema. Their coverage is fueled by questions that ask who does what, how, and why. They are not unified by a strict adherence to a single theoretical school of thought. Instead, an exhaustive unleashing of facts, explanations, and insights derived from critical viewings, readings, and research unifies the journal's approach.

The intensity of their research and their desire to create an encyclopaedic database is reflected by the inclusion of a one- to two-page index at the end of each issue that provides cross-referenced citations based on individual names and film titles in French, English, and romanizations of Chinese characters. In contrast, most other fanzines are marked by an enthusiasm that is usually aligned with lower research protocols and a "must-see" rhetoric of personal preferences. Departing from the usual herd mentality, *HK Orient Extreme Cinema* eschews fanzine features such as a five- star rating system, top-ten lists, limited space for written texts, and a rhetoric of marginalized exceptionalism that is dismissive of cinema's critical legacy. Breaking from the pack, their aim is to extend an invitation to consume these films and arrive at one's own individual critical assessment of them rather than blindly accepting the magazine's chosen favorites as sacrosanct.

To minimize the dangers of such an enterprise becoming commercially co-opted, the magazine's journalistic team is governed by the following principle: "The films carrying the '*HK*' label will de facto be the works we have always dreamed of seeing released in France."[28] In deciding on the films to address, the staff searches for "Asian content" that would otherwise not be circulated via the usual routes of distribution and exhibition in France.

Ultimately, the *HK* venture gauges its success by advancing the following mission statement:

> Our objectives are the following: to grant the important Asian filmmakers as well as the larger Asian film industry their long deserved legitimate stature which has so far too often been considered as minor if not completely dismissed outright. This will constitute the *cinéphilique* part of our task mainly because there are so many stars yet to be discovered, so many films to catch up with, and so many connections to make. This is the mission we are undertaking with all the more confidence that we will perform it at last with the films themselves speaking as our evidence.[29]

These principles distinguish the *HK* venture as a means to reinvigorate French film culture by systematically disseminating Asian popular films for a French-speaking public.

Following these self-imposed guidelines, in less than two years the *HK* venture secured a prominent retail presence. By March 1998, *HK*'s journal and videocassettes were available at kiosks throughout France, Belgium, and Switzerland. In France alone, *HK*'s offerings were available at 164 retail outlets spread across fifty-three of France's ninety-five *départements*.[30] In Belgium, *HK*'s products were available in seven geographical zones at eleven retail sites. In French-speaking Switzerland, four stores in two cities featured *HK*'s products. Along with its access to France's leading multimedia superstores, the *HK* venture also secured cooperative agreements with smaller retail outlets specializing in videocassettes, books, comics, Asian publications, and computer games. In Paris these included Budostore, Ciné Reflet, Evil Zone, Junko, and You Feng. Through these arrangements, the *HK* venture secured its retail prominence.[31]

*HK* also circulated its film journal and videocassettes outside of retail operations, via mail-order and subscription sales. According to Philippe Christin, by June 2000 the customer base of *HK*'s publication arm, *HK Orient Extreme Cinema*, had risen to 7,384 members.[32] The vast majority of this number was male. Only thirty customers, or 0.4 percent, were female (identified solely on the basis of their first names).[33] Despite this gender difference, *HK*'s customer base was and is otherwise diverse and representative of a wide range of French society (including university professors). Notably absent in their client base is the thirteenth *arrondissement*. Nevertheless, while Chinese clients may be sparse, other Asian communities representing France's former Southeast Asian colonies are represented. The deaf community represents another important segment of *HK*'s clientele since they desire French subtitles. On June 2000, *HK*'s customer base totaled around fifteen thousand individuals, including *HK Orient Extreme Cinema*'s subscription base of 7,384 customers.[34] The economics of *HK*'s dual-focus approach—videocassettes plus film journal—takes advantage of French commercial tax laws that provide a tax reduction for videocassette distributors that incorporate a film journal in their operation. Consequently, the *HK* venture initiated the inclusion of a complementary videocassette with each issue of *HK Orient Extreme Cinema*. This practice started with the fourth issue in October 1997.[35] Since October 1996, *HK Orient Extreme Cinema*'s features and accompanying videocassettes have reinforced the centrality of Hong Kong in the *HK* venture's mind frame, with twelve of fifteen issues and all of the complementary videocassettes addressing an aspect of Hong Kong cinema.[36] The addition of a complementary videocassette to the film journal allowed *HK* to increase the journal's cover price by almost a third, from 60 FF to 79 FF, while simultaneously expanding its presence and share of the market.

*HK*'s financial viability is enhanced by France's general preference for buying rather than renting videocassettes. France's videocassette market is dominated by sell-throughs that command 81 percent of the market. In contrast, videocassette rentals hold a minor presence at 19 percent. This is almost the reverse of the videocassette market in the United States. Through *HK*'s mail-order operations alone, on average, each customer in France purchased about 400 FF in videos, journals, and related *HK* merchandise per month in 2000.

Finally, true to its cinephile roots, the *HK* venture has also sponsored film retrospectives in Paris, such as the John Woo retrospective of twelve films held in UGC Ciné Cité Les Halles and Le Balzac during the summer of 1999.[37] A twenty-page feature in the June 1999 issue of *HK Orient Extreme Cinema* accompanied the retrospective. At the retrospective itself, a thirty-four-page program accompanied the screenings. As a result, the retrospective served as a mini-film-festival devoted to John Woo's *auteur* status, with print capitalism serving to enhance and inform the viewing public.[38]

## Conclusion

The *HK* venture's celebration of Hong Kong cinema's success in breaking Hollywood's monopoly over the action cinema, along with its transnational Francophone engagement with an otherwise "foreign" film culture, attests to the existence of proactive transnational imagining communities within preexisting national imagined communities in which ethnicity and language do not necessarily coincide. *HK Orient Extreme Cinema*'s holds true to the idea that "the cinema doesn't belong to anyone. It belongs to everyone."[39] Hong Kong's *Nouvelle Vague* director Allen Fong amplifies this sentiment by holding that "The film industry is a world which has to ignore boundaries. All filmmakers belong to the same race. My nationality is that of the cinema."[40]

Stepping out of the Francophone microcosm, the transnationality of Hong Kong action cinema promotes a move away from the strictly national and its self-serving agenda of repressing the transnational. Placing into the foreground the return of the transnationally repressed makes it possible to acknowledge a situation in which one's given nationality does not preclude or exclude the possibility and the opportunity to form transnational communal attachments that provide deeper satisfactions than what is currently available within one's own immediate and limiting national horizons.[41]

## Notes

The author wishes to thank Philippe Christin and the *HK* venture for their generosity in sharing their publications and videocassette releases in the preparation of this chapter. Special thanks are also extended to Anne Magnan-Park, Bruce Heppner-Elgin, Greg Beatty, Lauren Rabinovitz, and the editors of this anthology for their wise counsel and support.

1. English subtitles were included in all Hong Kong film releases as a regular practice for the domestic and *huaqiao* circuits as a legacy of Hong Kong's geopolitical status as a member of the British Empire. Efforts to minimize error-prone "Chinglish" (Chinese-inflected English) were a minor concern.

2. My idea of a "*trans*nationalized imagin*ing* community" is a modification of Benedict Anderson's nation-centric formulation of the "imagin*ed* community." Benedict Anderson, *Imagined Communities: Reflections on the Origin and Spread of Nationalism* (London: Verso, 1991).

3. David Desser, "The Kung Fu Craze: Hong Kong Cinema's First American Reception," *The Cinema of Hong Kong: History, Arts, Identity*, Poshek Fu and David Desser, eds. (Cambridge: Cambridge University Press, 2000), 19–43.

4. The publication date coincided with the September 26, 1984 Sino-Anglo Joint Declaration on Hong Kong, which established July 1, 1997 as the official transfer date when Hong Kong would then become a Special Administrative Region of the People's Republic of China.

5. Bruce Le should not be mistaken for Bruce Lee. Koob discovered Le, a former Shaw Brothers actor, and directed him in *Bruce Contre Attaque*, the first *gongfupian* directed by a Frenchman and set in Paris, Rome, and Hong Kong. Coproduced for 800,000 to 900,000 FF, Koob obtained quite a personal fortune by having a share in this film's Francophone distribution. Koob coproduced two more films featuring Le, *Contrat pour la Mort* and *Combats de Rue*. See "André Koob: Il a lancé Bruce Le!" [Made in Hong Kong], *Cahiers du cinéma* 360–361 (September 1984): 116.

6. The large Indo-Chinese population in the thirteenth *arrondissement* created a demand for videocassette versions of films and television programs that could not be adequately met by France's only Chinese Vietnamese film theater, L'Orient-Ciné. These video stores catered to a population that spoke Mandarin, Cantonese, Vietnamese, or all three, so French subtitles rarely appeared. Cogeda (Comptoir Général d'Asie) was the market leader, with France Asia its main competitor. See "Vidéo-Clubs Chinois," [Made in Hong Kong], *Cahiers du cinéma* 360–361 (September 1984): 116–117.

7. Outside of Le Hollywood Boulevard's Bruce Lee retrospectives, two other Parisian film theater chains monopolized the Hong Kong *kung fu vague*. René Lévy-Balensi owned one of these chains. Of four theaters, Lévy-Balensi's two main exhibition sites for the *kung fu vague* were the Trianon and the Cigale. Both were located in Pigalle, Paris' historic red-light district. The other two Lévy-Balensi theaters were Montmartre Ciné and Concordia. Lévy-Balensi's first three theaters were elegantly designed in the neobaroque style. Concordia, located near the offices of *Cahiers du cinéma*, did not share this architectural feature. The height of the *kung fu vague* in France occurred between 1973 and 1978. The weekly attendance figures for *Fist of Fury/Chinese Connection* serve as one marker. The Trianon received sixteen thousand spectators per week and the Cigale received eleven thousand. The Trianon's high attendance rate is in part explained by its distinction as France's least expensive cinema, running double features for only 9 FF. At the Trianon, regular double features ran from 10 A.M. until midnight, averaging a high of nine thousand to ten thousand spectators per week. During the same period, the Cigale averaged a high of seven thousand to eight thousand spectators. Lévy-Balensi circulated his Hong Kong titles among these four theaters. Audience loyalty revolved around stars and particular subgenres. Any films with "Shaolin" or "*hommes de bronze*" insured exceptional box-office successes.

Gaston Douvin owned the other major exhibition circuit, a distinction he arrived at haphazardly. Douvin was the first to release Hong Kong films in France, with *La*

*Dialectique* released in March 1972 at the Grands Augustins cinema, where it ran for eight continuous weeks. Witnessing the phenomenal box-office successes of some Hong Kong films in Africa, he decided to take a risk by obtaining the distribution rights for a collection of thirty Hong Kong films. According to Douvin, the height of the *kung fu vague* in France peaked between 1974 and 1975. Gaston circulated his films among three theaters: La Gaîté Rochechouart with seven hundred and fifty seats, Le Gaîté Boulevards with two hundred and sixty seats, and Le Paris-Ciné with two hundred seats. All three screened double features. At the height of the *kung fu vague*, more than ten thousand viewers per week frequented La Gaîté Rochechouart. By the mid-1980s, these weekly figures had dwindled to six thousand. Douvin attributes this decline to the lack of quality controls implemented by the distributors of Hong Kong films, which caused many technical problems during their screenings in France. See "Les Derniers Temples" [Made in Hong Kong], *Cahiers du cinéma* 360–361 (September 1984): 117.

8. Réné Chateau is best known for producing films starring Jean-Paul Belmondo, France's only action star who performs his own stunts. Belmondo is also the lead actor in Jean-Luc Godard's *À Bout de Souffle* (1959).

9. This same venue would later host the first homage to Bruce Lee between July 31 and August 13, 1974 with *Big Boss*, *La Fureur de Vaincre*, and *Opération Dragon*. "Réné Chateau : Le Culte Bruce Lee" [Made in Hong Kong], *Cahiers du cinéma* 360–361 (September 1984): 116.

10. Originally Linda Lee's *Bruce Lee: The Man Only I Knew* (New York: Warner Paperback Library, 1975).

11. "Réné Chateau," 116.

12. "M. Quach, L'Unique Exploitant Sino-Vietnamien en France" [Made in Hong Kong], *Cahiers du cinéma* 360–361 (September 1984): 117.

13. Ibid.

14. François and Max Armanet, *Ciné Kung Fu* (Turin, Italy: Éditions Ramsay, 1988), 19.

15. Metropolitan Film Distribution is one of France's biggest importers and exhibitors of films and video.

16. Christophe Gans is also the director of *Crying Freeman* (1995) and *The Brotherhood of the Wolf* (2001).

17. Individuals of Asian descent are only part of *HK*'s translation team.

18. "Edito," *HK Orient Extreme Cinema* 0 (October 1996): 3. This and all subsequent English translations of the journal's original French text are my own. The original French was deleted in this version at the request of the publisher because of word limitations.

19. *HK Video*'s superior quality controls positioned its operations as distinct from the many other fanzine and commercial videocassette operators who conduct business under less fastidious standards. For example, Video Search of Miami, the video distribution arm of *Asian Cult Cinema* (formerly known as *Asian Trash Cinema*) in the United States, offers videocassette versions of Hong Kong and Japanese films that are not of the highest-quality standards. Even Taiseng Video, operating out of California and serving as the primary videocassette distributor of Hong Kong films in the United States, has regularly compromised the film's original aspect ratios; this has resulted in many of the English subtitles being truncated. In the United Kingdom, strict censorship policies against the depiction of certain types of screen action means that many Asian action films were released with key scenes missing, such as Bruce Lee's signature fights scenes with the *nunchaku*.

20. Given a choice, French customers clearly preferred *la version française* over *la version originale,* since the latter accounted for only three thousand (15 percent) of the total. Philippe Christin, interview with author, Paris, France. 18 July, 2000.

21. In 1999 Polygram launched a new series of five Hong Kong *polar noir* films on videocassette under the label "Hong Kong Connection" to challenge *HK*'s position on the market. See Benjamin Rozovas, "Hong Kong Connection," *Impact* 79 (April 1999): 36–37.

22. Philippe Christin, interview.

23. "Edito," (October 1996): 3.

24. "Edito," *HK Orient Extreme Cinema* 5 (December 1997): 3.

25. *Fengshui* is explained as "a Chinese belief that foretells good and bad fortunes based on the orientation of objects." See STL, "Le Tao du Vampire," *HK Orient Extreme Cinema* 10 (March 1999): 43.

26. Hervé Dante, "Opération Gros Dragon," *HK Orient Extreme Cinema* 10 (March 1999): 34.

27. Ibid. Matthieu is France's version of Barbara Streisand and her haircut is indeed *dépassé* and unglamorous, but according to Dante, Matthieu's is still nowhere as untamed as Hung's own.

28. "Edito," (October 1996): 3.

29. Ibid., 3.

30. This includes only the *départements* of the French hexagon, plus Corsica, but excludes the *Départements d'outre-mer et Territoires d'outre-mer* (Overseas Departments and Territories) (DOM-TOMs).

31. The British fanzine-turned-professional-journal (or "prozine"), *Eastern Heroes*, also had a regular film journal and videocassette sales component in its operation. It even boasted its own retail store, called Eastern Heroes: The Shop, in Camden Town, London. Its videocassette series featured only Hong Kong films, were released under the label "Hong Kong Cinema," and were divided into categories such as "Late Night Collection" and "Over the Edge."

*Eastern Heroes* began as the Jackie Chan U.K. Fan Club, releasing its first newsletter in 1988. It became a fanzine in 1989 and, starting with issue 4, went by the title *Jackie Chan Newsletter.* It officially took the label *Eastern Heroes* for the first time in issue 8, sometime between 1990 and 1991. After a total of fifteen issues since its 1988 start, it officially switched to being a prozine in 1992. *Eastern Heroes* marked this metamorphosis by designating the prozine issues as the start of volume 2. The prozine was available in the United Kingdom, United States, Germany, Australia, and New Zealand. Its videocassettes were available nationally in major retail outlets such as Virgin, H.M.V., Tower Records, John Menzies, Our Price, and Forbidden Planet. By 2000, *Eastern Heroes* had ceased business operations. See Lisa Tilston, ed., *The Essential Guide to the Best of* Eastern Heroes (London: Eastern Heroes Publications, 1995).

32. Philippe Christin, interview.

33. Ibid.

34. Ibid.

35. Ibid. A half-hour *Best of HK Video* videocassette was included with issue number one on January 1997, containing clips of *HK*'s video catalogue. A subsequent problem that arose was the high rate of mail theft of the videos. More-secure hard-plastic coverings were required so that both the complementary video and the journal would arrive safely to *HK*'s subscribers.

36. The first fifteen issues and eleven complementary videocassettes are:

0) Le Tournage de *Zu* (The Filming of *Zu: Warriors from the Magic Mountain*)
1) *Polar+Best of* HK Vidéo
2) Tsui Hark
3) *The Blade*
4) John Woo+*Tiger on the Beat*
5) Takeshi Kitano+*City Hunter*
6) *Once Upon a Time in China+L'Arnaqueur de Hong Kong*
7) Bruce Lee+*Wonder Seven*
8) Godzilla+*L'Exorciste Chinois*
9) *Chevalerie Chinoise+Beach of the War Gods*
10) *Kung Fu Comédie+Operation Scorpio*
11) John Woo *Inédit+In the Line of Duty 3*
12) Heroic-Fantasy+*Supercop 2*
13) Asian Monster Show+*In the Line of Duty 4*
14) Ringo Lam+*Once a Thief*

37. The retrospective featured *Hand of Death* (1976), *Princess Chang Ping* (1976), *Last Hurrah for Chivalry* (1979), *Heroes Shed No Tears* (1983), *A Better Tomorrow* (1986), *A Better Tomorrow 2* (1987), *The Killer* (1989), *Just Heroes* (1989), *A Bullet in the Head* (1990), *Once a Thief* (1991), *Hard Boiled* (1992) and *A Better Tomorrow 3: Love and Death in Saigon* (1990, directed by Tsui Hark). Of these films, only *A Better Tomorrow*, *A Better Tomorrow 2*, *The Killer*, *A Bullet in the Head*, and *Hard Boiled* were previously released in France.

38. A second run was held in the Latin Quarter the following year.

39. "Edito," *HK Orient Extreme Cinema* 1 (January 1997): 3.

40. "Allen Fong," *HK Orient Extreme Cinema* 3 (July 1997): 52.

41. The *HK* venture was affected by the arrival of the internet and DVD. *HK Orient Extreme Cinema* ceased publication in Spring 2000 after issue fourteen. New videocassette releases also ended. Both components of the *HK* venture embraced the new DVD format. The film journal shifted focus to provide a detailed print insert that accompanies the DVD releases. The complete line of videocassette and DVD titles are available at www.hkvideo.fr.

According to an email interview with Philippe Christin on October 16, 2008, the unique collection of people, passion, and power behind the *HK* venture underwent a number of structural challenges in 2000. First, their high production standards required an enlarged customer base. The inclusion of the complementary videocassette starting with issue four was designed with this in mind. Unfortunately, it did not reach the level of expansion that was hoped for. Second, the expenses involved in creating two language versions for the videocassettes (*version originale* and *version française*) and the ending of the government subvention starting with issue twelve took their eventual toll. The final stress point occurred when Christophe Gans began directing *The Brotherhood of the Wolf* (2001). As the mastermind behind the *HK* venture, everything happened with Gans' participation and approval. As Gans became more involved with the completion of the film, he had less time and energy to devote to the *HK* venture. Consequently, this led to delays in production with many of the writers for the film journal becoming involved with new projects such as www.dvdvision.fr.

# 4

# Wong Fei-Hung in Da House

## *Hong Kong Martial-Arts Films and Hip-Hop Culture*

Frances Gateward

As many cultural critics have noted or, perhaps more accurately, lamented, mainstream American popular culture is synonymous with international popular culture. American mass media dominates the globe, from the unfortunate and unprecedented popularity of the television series *Baywatch* to the phenomenon of Michael Jordan (or Qiaodan, as he is known in China), who remains one of the most recognizable figures in the world, more widely known even than Mickey Mouse. But the road that pop culture travels is not a one-way street. In the last few decades, there has been within the United States the growth of "World" music, the popularization of Kente cloth, a fascination with Asian-influenced youth fashion, and the success of *anime*—from *Speed Racer* in the 1970's to the more recent examples of *Pokemon* and *Yu-Gi-Oh*. Although Hollywood has set the narrative and stylistic conventions for cinema and remains dominant on global screens, it too has not escaped foreign influence. Film scholars have traced the effects of Soviet cinema and German Expressionism in the 1920s, the French New Wave in the 1960s, the political and stylistic radicalism of Latin American cinema, and now Hong Kong cinema's influence on action choreography and editing. In fact, one could argue that Hong Kong cinema has been the cinema most influential to Hollywood in the last twenty years.

The "blockbuster syndrome" that began in the 1970s has become the standard mode of operation for the major Hollywood corporations, with action-adventure films now functioning as the barometer of yearly profits.

The importance of this often critically dismissed and denigrated genre is such that it, perhaps more than any other, affects every aspect of the industry—from the advances in cinema technology often invented and innovated within the genre, changing the aesthetics of the medium, to the increasing reliance on the summer season of action spectacles for box-office revenue, both locally and internationally. The Hollywood film industry became increasingly dependant on overseas audiences to guarantee and maximize profits, and by the mid-1980s it needed to reinvigorate what had become a stale and stagnant genre. It did so by looking to one of the most successful cinemas in the world, the industry that, until recently, dominated Asia—Hong Kong cinema.

The cross-cultural flow in the last few decades has now gone beyond the distribution of film and video to include a "migration" of Hong Kong talent to the West: actors Jackie Chan, Jet Li, Michelle Yeoh, Shu Qi, and Chow Yun-Fat; action choreographers Donnie Yen, Yuen Woo-Ping, and Yuen Cheung-Yan; as well as directors Tsui Hark, John Woo, Kirk Wong, and Ronny Yu. Such has been the impact of these cultural and personnel flows, that we may safely claim that since the 1990s, virtually all Hollywood action scenes are Hong Kong derived, from the climactic light-saber battle in *Star Wars Episode I: The Phantom Menace* (dir. George Lucas, 1999) to the mayhem of *The Bourne Supremacy* (dir. Paul Greengrass, 2004). Quentin Tarantino is (in)famous for having jumpstarted his career by remaking Ringo Lam's *City on Fire* (1987) and then resurrecting his career by expropriating the entire history of Japanese and Chinese action films for *Kill Bill* (2003) and *Kill Bill 2* (2004). It would be quite an arduous task to try and find, for example, a gun battle that does *not* contain a slow-motion shot of a hero or heroine flying through the air, firing automatic weapons with both hands à la John Woo. As I argue in this chapter, the impact of Hong Kong cinema on American media culture goes beyond the screens of the multiplex. Hong Kong action films, in particular the *wu da pian*[1] (martial-arts film), have functioned as a significant component of African American youth culture for the last thirty years, its tropes appropriated into the various aspects that make up hip-hop subculture.

At first glance, it seems that Hong Kong film culture and hip-hop have little to do with each other given the disparate historical, political, and social contexts, and that they are indeed different cultures. Despite these dissimilarities, hip-hop creators and consumers have bridged the cultural chasm by embracing Hong Kong martial-arts films and other aspects of Chinese culture. As I will demonstrate, close examination reveals that the two cultures hold so many themes in common that the African-American-defined subculture's affinity for Hong Kong martial-arts films will no longer seem incongruous.

As Dick Hebdige so clearly demonstrated in his groundbreaking book, *Subculture: The Meaning of Style* (1988),[2] the expressive cultures of youth groups create identities that represent specific responses and forms of resistance to oppressive hegemony through their use of ritual and style. Certainly that can be said of the hip-hop youth culture developed by African American, Caribbean American, and Latino American young people in and around New York City in the 1970s. This post-Civil Rights era youth subculture, recognized for its transformation of dance, painting, film, fashion, and video, is perhaps most well known for the development of a new music form—rap. Borrowing its lyrical style from African diasporic oral traditions (the call-and-response form common in ritual; the griot-storytellers and oral historians; jazz-derived scat singing; performed monologues common in soul music; a long tradition of political poetry; the recordings of words set to music by the Last Poets and Gil Scot Heron; the verbal boxing of Muhammad Ali; "playing the dozens;" and Jamaican dancehall), rap music, with its numerous subgenres and signifying styles, originated as a political and artistic form of expression rooted in the experience of marginalized working-class, urban, Black, and Latino American youth. It also draws significantly from the culture of Hong Kong, specifically the tradition of kung fu films.

In 1999 a television advertising campaign for Sprite, produced in the spirit of a classic *wu da* film, stunned audiences with its elaborate *mise-en-scène* and kinetic dynamism. The commercials, placed in heavy rotation on the MTV and BET cable networks, were designed by the Chicago-based Burrell Communications Group, the largest African American advertising agency in the United States. The Five Deadly Women campaign, derived from the 1978 Hong Kong film classic *The Five Deadly Venoms*, featured five female rap artists: Eve as the Blonde Bee, Angie Martinez from the Terror Squad as the Fire Fly, Mia X as the Lady Bug, Amil as the Praying Mantis, and Roxanne Shante as the Black Widow. The commercials were directed by the young African American filmmaker Antoine Fuqua, director of the *Replacement Killers* (1997), the first American film starring Hong Kong sensation Chow Yun-Fat. The narrative of the soft-drink advertisements is serialized over five commercials. In the first installment, a courier delivers a scroll to Dr. Ultra (Kool Keith) issuing a call for the most skilled female lyricists to "put it down" for Sprite, using beats recorded on a prized digital audio tape (DAT). Declaring that the women don't have the rhyming skills, Dr. Ultra declares that "it will never work." As the series of commercials continue, the Five Deadly Women confront Dr. Ultra individually and in pairs or trios, each attacking with her distinct rhyming skills and unique arsenal of weapons. In each spot, they take possession of the DAT, but cannot thoroughly defeat their nemesis. They quickly realize they must combine their lethal styles and martial-arts techniques to triumph. This advertising campaign certainly was not the first to use rap artists, nor, in fact, was it the first appropriation of an Asian popular-culture form to hawk soda pop.

A year before, in July 1998, another five-part commercial serial designed by Burrell Communications made its debuted. It too was for Sprite, and like the Five Deadly Women advertisements, this series of commercials featured rap performers. Using both contemporary and old-school rap artists, the campaign was an allegory about forgoing differences (in this case, styles and regional animosities) for the purpose of collective action. It featured Common (from the Midwest), Fat Joe (from New York), Mac 10 (an artist based in Los Angeles), the Goodie Mob (from the South), and Afrika Baambata of Soul Sonic Force, one of the New Yorkers considered a founder of the music form. Using the Japanese animated series *Hyakujuu ou Go Lion*, known in the United States as *Voltron: Defender of the Universe*, the advertisements concerned a most dire situation: King Zarkon, the evil villain from Planet Doom, sends a Ro-Beast to Earth to destroy every facet of hip-hop culture, namely the rhyming, deejaying, breakdancing, and graffiti art. Each of the artists take on the Ro-Beast alone, using his own robot (mechanized lions), but are readily defeated. Afrika Baambata determines that the only hope of victory is through unification. They combine their individual robots into one Voltron, promptly defeating their antagonist.

I find both these commercial campaigns intriguing: they are of African American design, they feature African American celebrities, and are targeted toward African Americans, yet they appropriate film styles and cultures from Asia—a continent with which African Americans are not usually associated. Even more compelling is the fact that the Five Deadly Women series works as a virtual compendium of the history and range of Chinese martial-arts film, revealing an intimate knowledge of the Hong Kong martial-arts-film tradition. While the iconography and wirework of the opening commercial borrows from films like *Once Upon a Time in China* (dir. Tsui Hark, 1991) and *Fong Sai Yuk* (dir. Corey Yuen, 1993), subsequent ads draw inspiration and imagery directly from old-school masters like director King Hu (with a forest battle much like that of his masterful *A Touch of Zen*) and the legendary Bruce Lee (in a recreation of the hall-of-mirrors scene in the climax of *Enter the Dragon*).

This kind of recombined expertise may also be witnessed in another postmodern melding of television, hip-hop, and kung fu cinema: rap recording artists, along with celebrity athletes, provide the voices for Kung Faux, a video series produced by Dubtitled Entertainment and Tommy Boy Films, a subsidiary of the hip-hop recording label Tommy Boy Records. The series, which made its debut in 2003, uses feature-length Hong Kong martial-arts films, editing them down to a taught thirty minutes. The films are also provided with new sound track—re-scored with breakbeats and hip-hop music, new sound effects, and dialogue steeped with hip-hop jargon. The program, which made its debut in the United States on the cable network FUSE, can now be seen in more than a dozen countries, including Spain, Brazil, and the United Kingdom, and has even spawned a number of ancillary products, from tee shirts to action figures. If these lush, visually compelling commercials and hip reworkings of old-school movies seem like an aberration, further research reveals long-standing interconnections between the African American community and kung fu films.

## Everybody Was Kung Fu Fighting

As David Desser (2000) notes in his study of America's fascination with Hong Kong martial-arts films,[3] during the week of May 26, 1973 something occurred in the film industry that, interestingly enough, had never happened before and has never happened since—the domination of foreign films on American movie screens. *Fists of Fury* (dir. Lo Wei, 1971), *Deep Thrust: The Hand of Death* (dir. Feng Huang, 1972), and *Five Fingers of Death* (dir. Jeong Chang-Hwa, also known as Cheng Chang Ho, 1973) were ranked first, second, and third, respectively, on *Variety*'s list of the top box office hits. Even more remarkably, these films and the kung fu movies that followed drew audiences at the same time that another short-lived genre experienced great commercial success: Blaxploitation. At no other time in North American film history have so many films featuring non-White characters been so well received by American moviegoers. It was not uncommon to see the films together, billed as double features, or to see their advertisements paired on the pages of important Black newspapers like the *Chicago Defender* (Figure 4.1). As *Variety* and box-office earnings show, Hong Kong films were widely popular. What they do not show is the fact that the Hong Kong kung fu films were particularly enjoyed by African American audiences. Indeed, African American audiences had their own "kung fu craze," prefiguring the mania that would sweep the mainstream.

It is generally accepted that the film that began the national fascination in the United States is *Five Fingers of Death*. Released in mid-March 1973, it was the first Hong Kong action film to get theatrical distribution in the United States. Yet an advertisement for *Deadly Duo* (dir. Chang Cheh, 1971) and *The Water Margin* (dir. Chang Cheh, 1972), also known as *Seven Blows of the Dragon*, appeared on March 3 (Figure 4.2) in the *New Amsterdam*, the most widely circulated Black newspaper in the five boroughs of New York City. Chinese theater owners clearly recognized the market for the *wu da* films, as the theater in this advertisement—the Music Palace—is located not in the Bronx, Harlem, or Bedford-Stuyvesant, but in the lower part of Manhattan in Chinatown.

In Washington DC, one of the most segregated cities in the United States, kung fu films played at such theaters as the K-B Langley, Queens Chapel Drive-In, Riverdale Plaza, the Tivoli, the Republic, and the

Figure 4.1 Black action and martial arts advertised side by side in the November 3, 1973 edition of the *Chicago Defender*.

Hampton Mall, located in neighborhoods with a predominantly African American population or in Prince Georges County, the Maryland suburb noted for its population of middle- and upper-middle-class African Americans. The success of what was called "chopsocky films" would quickly inform Black action film and vice versa.

In *Superfly* (dir. Gordon Parks, Jr., 1972), for example, we see the main character Priest spending time in a martial-arts studio, and in all of Pam Grier's films she engages in hand-to-hand combat, a first for women in American action films, though certainly not in Chinese films. Eventually, producers would see the advantage of going beyond the double-feature model by linking characters in a single film. "A Black cat from Watts" (Timothy Brown) and a "Kung Fu cat from Hong Kong" (Alan Tang) were paired on U.S. soil in *The Dynamite Brothers* (dir. Al Adamson, 1974). The new Black action heroine was teamed up with the Chinese woman warrior when Tamara Dobson, in *Cleopatra Jones and the Casino of Gold* (dir. Charles Bail, 1975), travels to Asia and, along with a female Chinese partner, Mi Ling (Tanny), defeats international drug runners. That same

Figure 4.2 From the pages of the *New Amsterdam*.

year, Jean Bell, as T.N.T. Jackson in the film of the same name, travels to Hong Kong and the Philippines to find her brother and battle heroin traffickers (Figure 4.3).

Other transpacific-traveling African Americans include Cal Jefferson in the Filipino-produced and Hong Kong based *Bamboo Gods and Iron Men* (dir. Cesar Gallardo, 1974) (Figure 4.4) and Ron Van Clief in *Black Dragon* (dir. Lu Chin-ku). Van Cleif, a former Hollywood stuntman and a five-time world champion trained in the arts of jiu-jitsu, shotokan karate, and wing chun, became the first "round-eye" to get star billing in Hong Kong. Carl Scott, while still a teenager, fought the likes of Lo Meng and Yuen Biao on Hong Kong screens. And of course, one cannot fail to mention "Black Belt Jones," international middle-weight karate champion Jim Kelly, who debuted in the Bruce Lee film *Enter the Dragon* (dir. Robert Clouse, 1973) before enjoying a brief but high-profile career in American action films. In 1978 he too went to Hong Kong, battling Bolo Yeung in the film *The Tattoo Connection*, directed by Lee Tso-Nan.

One aspect of note is the practice of movie-watching itself. According to researchers such as Cindy Hing-Yuk Wong (1999),[4] the only viewers

Figure 4.3 T.N.T. immediately explodes upon her arrival in Hong Kong. *Cleopatra Jones and the Casino of Gold.* Dir. Charles Bail. Harbor Productions, 1975.

Figure 4.4 Poster art for *Bamboo Gods and Iron Men.*

of Hong Kong films in the United States, in the theater or in video form (videotape, digital video disc [DVD], and the ubiquitous video compact disc [VCD]), are emigres from Asia who purchase the videos in Chinatown shops or view them in Chinatown theaters. They also argue that the only other place to find kung fu films is in art theaters. But as late as 1986, more than a decade past the end of the kung fu cinema's popularity, a theater in the heart of a Black neighborhood in southwest Washington DC, The American, was still screening such feature films. And

Figure 4.5 Video storefront in Harlem.

currently it is difficult to find Hong Kong videos in DC's Chinatown. Where are they? Downtown—in a specialty shop near Metro Center that caters to a primarily African American clientele. In New York it is common to see African American vendors offering bootlegs on the streets of Chinatown and "across one hundred and tenth street," in Harlem. This store, located between 124th and 125th Streets on Harlem's main thoroughfare, Lexington Avenue, offers African American and Chinese videos to local residents (Figure 4.5). Of course, all of this is not lost on the media moguls.

In the late 1990s, Xenon, the video company that distributes low-budget B movies whose rights have been obtained with minimal expense, released classic Shaw Brothers and Golden Harvest action features on VHS and later DVD. These re-releases are divided into four series: The Shaolin Dolemite Collection (linked to Rudy Ray Moore, a comedian and star of Blaxploitation films, whose claim to fame is the character Dolemite), Brooklyn Zoo, 36 Chambers, and the Wu Tang Collection. The films released include *Ol' Dirty Kung Fu* (previously known as *Dirty Kung Fu*) and *Hellz Windstaff* (previously released as *Hell's Windstaff*)—with changes in the titles as an attempt to appeal to hip-hop consumers. *Ol' Dirty Kung Fu* is a reflection of the popularity of hip-hop recording artist Ol'Dirty Bastard. The conversion in spelling of "Hells" to "Hellz" reflects hip-hop's common appropriation and transformation of the English language. The 36 Chambers collection takes its title from the name of the recording studio owned and operated by the hip-hop artists Wu Tang Clan, who adapted it from Liu Chia-Liang's immensely popular 1978 film, *The 36 Chambers of Shaolin*.

In addition to the link forged by these re-releases, there are many contemporary films that feature team-ups between well-known martial-arts stars, both Chinese and White, and African American celebrities, indicating the continued importance of the African American audience. They include *Drive* (dir. Steve Wang, 1996), starring Marc Dacascos and Kadeem Hardison; *The Glimmer Man* (dir. John Gray, 1996), with Steven Seagal and Damon Wayans; *Double Team* (dir. Tsui Hark, 1997), featuring Jean Claude Van Damme and Dennis Rodman; *Rush Hour* (dir. Brett Ratner, 1998), with Jackie Chan and Chris Tucker; *Rush Hour*'s sequels, *Rush Hour 2* (dir. Brett Ratner, 2001), set in Hong Kong, and *Rush Hour 3* (dir. Brett Ratner, 2005); *Romeo Must Die* (dir. Andrzej Bartkowiak, 2000), where an interracial love affair is alluded to between Jet Li and hip-hop recording artist Aaliyah; *Exit Wounds* (dir. Andrzej Bartkowiak, 2001), with Steven Seagal and rapper-turned-actor DMX; and *Cradle 2 the Grave* (dir. Andrzej Bartkowiak, 2003), with Jet Li and DMX.

There are also *Above the Law* (dir. Andrew Davis, 1988), which featured Blaxploitation star Pam Grier as partner to the policeman played by Steven Seagal, and the television series *Walker Texas Ranger*, with Clarence Dillard Jr. as a law enforcement officer who works with Chuck Norris. In an effort to increase the ratings for the action-drama *Martial Law* (1998–2000) in its second season, CBS Television Network removed white actor Louis Mandylor from the cast and added African American Arsenio Hall to the show, which featured Sammo Hung and Kelly Hu (Figure 4.6).

Something of a benchmark was achieved with the production of Berry Gordy's *The Last Dragon* (dir. Michael Schultz), a martial-arts film featuring an African American cast. Released in 1985, the film was a homage to the beloved Golden Harvest and Shaw Brothers martial-arts films that by the mid-1980s were rarely being produced. In *The Last Dragon,* a common theme in the period Chinese films—the struggle against injustice and the survival of the family or clan—was adapted for a modern, urban locale. Even the iconography and symbolism of Japanese aggression in films like *Five Fingers of Death* and *Fists of Fury* were utilized. The Shogun of Harlem, Sho'nuff, who sports Hakama pants, a Japanese-inspired vest with flared shoulders, and the rising sun prominently displayed on the bridge of his sunglasses, threatens the peaceful community and the family of Leroy Green, a young man who dresses in the style of a Chinese commoner and seeks only to perfect his mastery of kung fu. The threat of Sho'nuff to the Chinese-defined African American community is made known early on, when he and his gang intrude on a screening of *Enter the Dragon*. Their disruptive presence denies the moviegoers cinematic recompense, as the interrupted scene is of Lee's (Bruce Lee) triumph over O'Hara (Robert Wall),

Figure 4.6 The cast of *Martial Law*: Sammo Hung, Arsenio Hall, and Kelly Hu.

the White man who participated in the assault and attempted rape of Lee's sister Su Lin (Angela Mao). Following the formula of the *wu da* film, the reluctant Leroy is driven to use his martial-arts prowess after violence is wrought upon his family and love interest.

## Outside the Frame

Beyond the world of film, in the area of music, there is recording artist Foxy Brown, who took her name from the film of the same name starring Pam Grier and who sports on her arm prominent tattoos of Chinese characters that translate as her name. Rapper Jeru, who refers to himself as the "Taoist professor," released a song called "The Sun Also Rises in the East," and the Mob Squad released the album *Game of Death*, the title of Bruce Lee's last film. The most renowned hip-hop recording artist associated with kung fu is the aforementioned Wu Tang Clan, a group of artists that emerged from New York's underground scene in 1993, transforming the music genre. The members include RZA, the primary producer for all their work, Ol' Dirty Bastard, Raekwon, Method Man, Ghost Face Killer, and Cappadonna. It is their popularity, along with the availability of Hong Kong films in rental stores, that is most likely responsible for the Xenon re-releases: Their first album is titled *Enter the 36 Chambers* (Loud/RCA Records, 1993), *36 Chambers* also being the name of one of the Xenon video's series. Ol' Dirty Bastard's first solo single is "The Brooklyn Zoo," and there is, of course, the Wu-Tang Collection itself.

Like that of many rap artists such as Erik B. and Rakeem, Poor Righteous Teachers, and Lakim Shabazz, the lyrics of the Wu Tang Clan are informed by the philosophy and beliefs of the "5 percenters," an offshoot of the Nation of Islam that considers themselves part of the Asiatic Black Nation. The original meaning of the "5 percent" itself is taken from the *Lost Found Moslem Lesson No. 2*, written in 1934 by Nation of Islam founder W. D. Fard. Essentially the breakdown is as follows:

- The 85 percent are those who do not know the living God or their origin in the world; they are easily led in the wrong direction, and are hard to lead in the right direction.
- The 10 percent are the rich, the slave-makers of the poor, who teach the poor lies.
- The 5 percent are the poor righteous teachers who do not believe in the teaching of the 10 percent. They are wise, and know the living God, and teach that the living God is the Supreme Being, realized in the Black man of Asia. Their philosophy also involves teaching freedom, justice, and equality to all the human families of the earth.

An example of the ethos is Lakim Shabazz's title cut from the album *The Lost Tribe of Shabazz* (Tuff City Records,1990):

*My people were took from the motherland by the other man*
*Brought to the wilderness, like a ventriloquist*
*Played my people like puppets by playing fear in their heart*
*Nowadays most of us don't even know where to start*
*10 percent of us can help but don't feel the need*
*They love greed, and this really bothers me*
*85 percent of us are totally ignorant*
*Walking around with a nigga mentality*
*5 percent of us are ready to die for the cause, so pause, the source is Elijah.*

But the Wu Tang clan's association with Asian culture goes beyond their faith as 5 percenters, as evidenced by their chosen name, the references in their work and work methods, in their videos (one shot in Hong Kong), and even their likenesses in the video game *Wu Tang Style*, which features each member using martial-arts techniques with distinctive skills and weaponry. In these two excerpts from their lyrics, kung fu is used to create metaphors for their rapping skills:

(From "Da Mystery of Chess Boxin" from the album *36 Chambers)*
*The game of chess is like a swordfight*
*You must think first, before you move*
*Wu style is immensely strong and immune to nearly any weapon*
*When it is properly used, it's almost invincible.*

*(From "Bring da Ruckus")*
*Shaolin shadowboxing and the Wu Tang sword style*
*If what you say is true, the Shaolin and the Wu Tang could be dangerous*
*Do you think your Wu Tang sword can defeat me?*
*En garde, I'll let you try my Wu Tang style*

This competitive and confrontational aspect is common in rap—also common in kung fu films, where characters often boast of their physical skill. Many film plots, for example, are constructed around a martial-arts competition. Early rap shows were structured in the same manner, with deejays and emcees competing to prove their musical prowess. Arguably, this connection between rap and Chinese film culture began during the height of the kung fu craze and at the moment of rap's development, in the 1970s. Those who proved themselves worthy of distinction would take on the monikers of Master and Grand Master, following in the martial-arts tradition. Similarly, break-dancing was often performed in competition. Opposing crews would "battle" in parks, showcasing their moves, many of which, like the windmill, were adapted from kung fu fighting forms.

The Wu Tang Clan's appropriation of aspects of *wu da* also includes sampling from the dialog of dubbed kung fu films, using the sound track to demonstrate their roles as poor righteous teachers. For example, from the album *Wu Tang Forever* (Loud/RCA, 1997), the interlude before the track "Reunited:"

*I have given it much thought. It seems disaster must come, at best only postponed.*
*If Shaolin kung fu is to survive, it must now be taught to more young men. We must expand, get more pupils so the knowledge will be spread.*

Their commitment to community uplift is also one of Confucianism's three imperishables, to leave worthwhile teaching. The other two are to be virtuous and to perform meritorious deeds—all three common goals of the heroes and heroines of *wu da* films. Another common event in kung fu films, often seen as clichè, is also derived from Confucianism, what one may describe as "clan centrism." The family is central to the philosophy.

Quite often in kung fu films the event that sets the narrative in motion is the murder, and sometimes rape, of a family member or the murder of one's *sifu* (master teacher). If the latter is the case, then the family is represented by the martial-arts school. The Wu Tang Clan has thoroughly embraced this tenet of Confucianism. Although every member of the group has the power to negotiate solo deals with any record company, all productions released as solo artists are released under the name Wu Tang Productions. Each member contributes 20 percent of their earnings as solo artists back to Wu Tang Productions, and all share equally in the profits.

## Black Power Meets Yellow Power

But the aspect that most closely links hip-hop to Hong Kong martial-arts films, to facilitate its appropriation, is ideology. Hip-hop has always been a rich space for the development and exploration that grows out of cultural exchange, having emerged out of an amalgamation of African diasporic cultures: Cuban, Jamaican, Dominican, Puerto Rican, and African American. As George Lipsitz reminds us, "[A]s people in different places around the world face similar and interconnected kinds of austerity, inequality, and social disintegration, a transnational culture speaking to shared social realities starts to merge."[5] Hip-hop attempts to negotiate the experiences of marginalization, brutally truncated opportunity, and oppression within the cultural imperatives of African American and Caribbean history, identity, and community, while in kung fu films, the Chinese attempt to negotiate the same in relation to Japanese, European, and sometimes—as in the case of Bruce Lee and *Enter the Dragon*—White American powers. A new Chinese nationalism emerged in Hong Kong during the 1960's, one that addressed the local as well as the diasporic. It grew at the same time that frustration with the failure of particular aspects of the Civil Rights movement in the United States fueled the growth of Black nationalism, which, like Chinese nationalism, addressed both the local and the global. One function of Black nationalism has always been to elide the national categories to turn national minorities into global majorities by affirming solidarity with peoples of color around the globe, as demonstrated by coalitions formed on both the east and west coasts of the United States among Asians, Asian Americans, and African Americans. Together, organized groups and dedicated individuals struggled against cultural imperialism, colonialism, political subordination, and the repression of human and civil rights. The Black Panther Party distributed and made use of Mao Tse-Tung's *Little Red Book*. Harlem resident Yuri Kochiyama was an activist in both the Civil Rights Movement and the Black Liberation Movement, a friend of Malcolm X and a member of the Organization for African American Unity. She is still active in numerous causes today, from the Mumia Abu-Jamal case to the protection of affirmative action. Lee Lew Lee served as a liaison between the Harlem branch of the Black Panthers and the I Wor Kuen (IWK), a Maoist organization operating in Chinatown. Richard Aoki was a charter member and Field Marshall of the Black Panthers while at the same time a member of the Asian American Political Alliance.

As the Cultural Studies critics of the Birmingham School informed us, popular culture is a rich, viable, and imperative area of study. Forms of play frequently enable members of an aggrieved community to express indirectly aspects of their identity that might be dangerous to present by more direct means. Within this cultural context, Hong Kong kung fu films of the 1960s and 1970s provided African American youth pleasure through the triumph of non-White heroes and secularized, self-reliant protagonists like Wong Fei-Hung, a Chinese nationalist who lived from 1847 to 1924. Immortalized in more than eighty films, Wong, a scholar and master of several martial-arts forms, was devoted to the cause of justice and battled against political corruption, abusive law enforcement, and foreign political and cultural domination. It is this aspect of the kung fu film that strikes a cord with African Americans, who, as many would argue, live a sociopolitical existence as an internal colony within the United States.

The martial-arts films' emphasis on the body holds particular currency within the African American community. The body as a site of resistance is significant, for as Michel Foucault has demonstrated, the body, and its control, is an important site for oppressive practices. For the colonized, the working class, and those subjected to oppressive regimes, the body is the primary resource as well as the means for self-articulation. As Yvonne Tasker reminded us in her groundbreaking book *Spectacular Bodies*, Frantz Fanon discussed the importance of fantasy, how the powerlessness of a colonized people can serve to highlight the relationship between physical fantasy relations of power:

> The first thing which the native learns is to stay in his place, and not to go beyond certain limits. This is why the dreams of the native are always of muscular prowess; his dreams are of action and of aggression. I dream I am jumping, swimming, running, climbing; I dream that I burst out laughing, that I span a river in one stride, or that I am followed by a flood of motor cars which never catch up with me. During the period of colonization, the native never stops achieving.his freedom, from nine in the evening until six in the morning.[6]

This concentration on the body, which we saw adapted into American action films, is highlighted throughout the kung fu genre, particularly in scenes of training, which, as Simon During points out, emphasize an ascension to power and control—a process not of being, but becoming.[7] The use of the body as revolutionary tool and identity as a source of pride is perhaps best demonstrated in the films of Bruce Lee, as noted by such scholars as Stephen Teo in his 1997 book *Hong Kong Cinema: The Extra Dimension* and David Desser in his 2000) essay "The Kung Fu Craze."[8]

In an increasingly global culture, media messages that easily cross national boundaries may provide images of possibilities and alternatives to perhaps staid or retrograde images. This cross-cultural mixing and crossover, a culturally hybrid approach to identity, can be considered a transgressive act, for it subverts categorical oppositions and hence may aid in the creation of cultural reflexivity and change. African Americans have a tradition of appropriating popular culture and modifying it to reflect African American culture—taking Betty Boop and transforming her into Betty Boops, or rendering Mickey Mouse, Batman, and Bart Simpson Black. As Peter Parisi argues in his essay about the Black Bart Simpson, these appropriations serve a sociopsychological function akin to the soul strategy of the blues tradition, increasing feelings of solidarity, boosting morale, and strengthening consensus.[9] Rather than portraying Chinese traditions as exotic in the form of Orientalism, or erasing the culture's origin in the process of appropriation, this adaptation is more like an embrace. After all, the motto of Jeet Kune Do, the martial-arts style developed by Bruce Lee, is "Absorb what is useful."[10]

## Notes

*Acknowledgments:* An earlier version of this chapter was presented in 2000 at the "History, Technology, and the Future of Transnational Chinese Film and Television" symposium, School of Communication, Hong Kong Baptist University. I would like to acknowledge Jenny Lau, David Desser, Gina Marchetti, Chuck Kleinhans, and Peter Feng for their support and insight throughout the process of getting this chapter to print.

1. In Hong Kong cinema, *wu da pian* is the generic term for kung fu or unarmed combat films. Sometimes known as *dong zhuo pian*, or action films, this genre has come to encompass gunplay films. "Martial-arts films" is a general term for *wu da pian*, including *wu xia pian*—swordplay or knight-errant films.

2. Dick Hebdige, *Subculture: The Meaning of Style* (New York: Routledge, 1988).

3. David Desser, "The Kung Fu Craze: Hong Kong Cinema's First American Reception," in Poshek Fu and David Desser, eds., *The Cinema of Hong Kong: History, Arts, Identity* (New York: Cambridge, 2000), 19–43.

4. Cindy Hing-Yuk Wong, "Cities, Cultures, and Cassettes: Hong Kong Cinema and Transnational Audiences," *Postscript* 19.1 (1999): 87–106.

5. George Lipsitz, *Dangerous Crossroads: Popular Music, Postmodernism, and the Poetics of Place* (New York: Verso, 1994), 7.

6. Franz Fanon. *Wretched of the Earth* (New York: Grove Press, 1963), 52: cited in Yvonne Tasker. *Spectacular Bodies: Gender, Genre, and the Action Cinema* (New York: Routledge, 1993).

7. Simon During, "The Global Popular," *Critical Inquiry* 23 (1997): 808–834.

8. Stephen Teo, *Hong Kong Cinema: The Extra Dimensions* (London: British Film Institute, 1997) and David Desser, "The Kung Fu Craze," 19–43.

9. Peter Parisi, "Black Bart Simpson: Appropriation and Revitalization in Commodity Culture," *Journal of Popular Culture* 27.1 (1993): 125–142.

10. Bruce Lee, *Tao of Jeet Kune Do* (Burbank: Ohara Publications, 1975).

# 5

# Same Difference

## *Racial Masculinity in Hong Kong and Cop-Buddy "Hybrids"*

GAYLE WALD

*They come from different cultures. But on a case this big, they speak the same language.*

—TAGLINE FOR *RUSH HOUR* (BRETT RATNER, 1998)

*Media images of Asian-American men are changing from meek and mild to macho.*

—"WHY ASIAN GUYS ARE ON A ROLL," *NEWSWEEK* (FEBRUARY 21, 2000)

In an early scene from *Lethal Weapon 4* (dir. Richard Donner, 1998), Los Angeles police lieutenants Martin Riggs (Mel Gibson) and Roger Murtaugh (Danny Glover) are out for an evening pleasure cruise and fishing expedition when they inadvertently intercept a ship whose main "cargo" turns out to consist of illegally smuggled Chinese men, women, and children. Realizing that they have stumbled onto a crime scene, the two board the ship and quickly dispatch with its creepy crew. Once the gunplay has ended, however, there is still the troubling matter of the human shipment. As the ship's blanket-clad passengers are brought ashore, they discuss the situation with a jaded Immigration and Naturalization Service (INS) official, who coolly informs them that the Chinese, having survived a grueling six-week sea journey, now face imminent deportation.

Their conversation, filmed in medium close-up with a lingering emphasis on the reactions of Danny Glover's character, Murtaugh, goes as follows:

INS AGENT [GESTURING TOWARD THE SHIP]: Coast guard interdicts about one of these a month.

MURTAUGH: Pretty raggedy looking.

AGENT: Six weeks locked in a hole with one toilet. Rice, a little fish to eat. Lousy deal for thirty-five grand a head.

RIGGS: Thirty-five grand? Where did they come up with that kind of money?

AGENT: Didn't. Got to work it off. [Camera on Murtaugh] And the snake heads, the smugglers? They sell them as cheap labor.

MURTAUGH: *Sell* them??

AGENT: Like slaves. [Jazz saxophone riff]

RIGGS [GESTURING TOWARD THOSE GETTING OFF THE SHIP]: Guess these must be the lucky ones, huh?

AGENT: Eh, they'll claim asylum, say they were persecuted like everybody else. And we'll send 'em packing. Cost you and me a goddamn fortune.

MURTAUGH: What happened to "Bring me your tired, your poor, your wretched masses yearning to be free"?

AGENT: Now it reads No Vacancies.

MURTAUGH: [Smirking] I guess your parents were Native Americans.

This conversation between the INS agent and our two heroes sets the plot of *Lethal Weapon 4* in motion. On one side is the agent, a white male government official who invokes the interest of U.S. "taxpayers" as a means of solidifying national identity with the two officers, one black, one white. For the agent, what unites "us" against "them" is that "we" are citizens, while they are not. Although the Chinese have suffered during their journey, it is Americans who will pay the price.

On the other hand is Murtaugh, the African American officer whose concern here is unusually roused by the spectacle of the ship's bewildered, voyage-weary, and frightened passengers, in whom he sees the image of his own enslaved African ancestors. The film underscores Murtaugh's empathetic identification by focusing on the image of his face when the INS agent refers to the future of the Chinese refugees as unwaged laborers, and by inserting a brief—and, in this context, fully overdetermined—saxophone cool-jazz riff that punctuates the sound track when he utters the word "slaves."

What are the conditions that set this ship—and with it Murtaugh's journey of self-discovery—in motion? *Lethal Weapon 4* never responds to the first of these questions with any precision, and to be fair, sociopolitical analysis is neither its forté nor its primary intention. But through Murtaugh it does hint at an answer. If, in the "old" global economy, sixteenth-century colonial powers found in the transatlantic slave trade a means of expanding wealth and empire, then in the "new" global economy, the interests of power create miseries that require the displacement of entire populations of the poor and dispossessed. The film is vague in defining what "the interests of power" are, beyond imagining them in the sinister figures of Chinese Triad leader Wah Sing Kun (played by Jet Li) and Chinatown mob boss Uncle Benny (Kim Chan). One thing is clear, however: Although its passengers may have volunteered for the journey, the Chinese cargo vessel is a slave ship of the new millennium.

The most explicit exploration of this metaphor comes in a subsequent scene in *Lethal Weapon 4* that becomes a defining moment in the development of Glover's character. Explaining to Riggs why he has chosen to risk his position as a newly promoted police captain to harbor a whole family of the smuggled Chinese immigrants in his home, Murtaugh says, "The way I see it, these are slave ships out there. And I'm freeing slaves, I'm freeing slaves. Like no one did for my ancestors." The elisions of such an analogy are legion, and it would take another chapter to explicate them fully. More to the point, in any case, is the film's equation of contemporary Chinese refugee-immigrants with earlier African subjugation, and with it Murtaugh's personal identification with the Chinese refugee-laborers. For it is precisely in and through his self-identification as a raced subject—that is, a subject formed through a consciousness of racial oppression—that Murtaugh "recognizes" himself in the Chinese passengers of the ship. In effect, it is not until he confronts the brutal indifference of the INS agent to the Chinese that Murtaugh himself "becomes" raced in the film (previous to that he was, like Riggs, just doing his job in the manner of a "raceless" member of the Los Angeles Police Department [LAPD]). Moreover, by identifying himself implicitly as a descendent of African slaves (here the jazz riff is an aural reminder of Africa), Murtaugh is able to reject the INS agent's appeal to "taxpayer" dollars as a strategy of separating "us" (taxpayers) from "them" (the Chinese). In the end, then, where the agent seeks to use national identity to draw an imaginary circle of "citizenship" around the three men, securing their "us"-ness through the notion of shared national identity that transcends race, Murtaugh finds in a consciousness of himself as a racialized citizen a means of questioning the violence of such moves and resisting the impulse to deploy national identity as an exclusionary discourse, a discourse of forgetting. (What about the Statue of Liberty?, he asks). All of us are American male officers of the state, we imagine the reasoning going, but some (one) of us are (is) also black.

Such racial self-consciousness on the part of the African American buddy character is rarely articulated in cop-buddy films of the late 1990s, in which, as Cynthia J. Fuchs explains, racial difference is presented as spectacle even while it is alternately denied through the assertion of white heroes and mythologies or effaced through retreat into "the less traumatic and more familiar crisis of masculine identity."[1] In such films, that is to say, the very spectacle of racial difference that allows the black-white buddy team to function as a hetero "couple" must be carefully managed—not only for race to dissolve as a source of tension but for the bond between men to remain safely within the realm of nonsexual friendship. In *Lethal Weapon 2*, to cite only the most bizarrely outrageous example, the tension dissipates as Murtaugh comes to understand racial apartheid in South Africa through Riggs. And even in *Lethal Weapon 4*, a film that develops Murtaugh's racial self-consciousness more than any of the other films in the series, his primary identification remains that of a late-twentieth-century national subject committed to the notion of America as a color-blind society.

The fluidity of Murtaugh's identifications is alluded to from the outset, as his self-recognition as someone whose ancestors were slaves comes into conflict with an official discourse—as symbolized in the motto on the Statue of Liberty—of America as a nation welcoming those in need. He is, in fact, both a man who recognizes slavery as part of his heritage and a man who recognizes himself within American national narratives of citizenship and national solidarity. In the end, it is Murtaugh's charitable gesture of "adopting" a Chinese family that conveys the film's liberal politics of a citizenship that remains "blind" to race or ethnicity. He begins the film positioned as the descendent of slaves who will uphold the ideals of America, welcoming immigrants even if the nation will not. Yet the film's ultimately insipid resolution to the "problem" of the Chinese immigrants through friendship never ultimately addresses the question of Murtaugh's location within the nation or of the terms on which the Chinese family might be accepted into the national family. In other words, what happens to the film's critique of the racialization of certain citizens in its ultimate celebration of the national multicultural family (quite literally, since a significant subplot of the film involves the pregnancies of Rigg's girlfriend and Murtaugh's daughter)?

Some of these contradictions in *Lethal Weapon 4* are predictable. Nevertheless the film marks an important transition in the U.S. imagination of race, masculinity, and citizenship, which are rendered in narrative terms through the cop-buddy film. In particular, it portends a shift from the 1980s and 1990s buddy-film paradigm of coupling black and white male characters to a model that specifically pairs Asian and African American men—imagining them not primarily as antagonists (that is, noncitizens versus citizens, immigrants versus natives, job-stealers versus job-seekers) but as "multicultural" cop protagonists whose partnership conspicuously complicates an earlier logic of representing race in U.S. buddy films in terms of a black-white binary.[2] The shift is alluded to in the relationship Murtaugh develops in *Lethal Weapon 4* with Hong (Eddie Ko), the patriarch of the Chinese refugee family, although it acquires subtle shading as well through the presence in his office of an Asian American officer, Detective Ng (played by Calvin Jung). The line between Asian immigrant and Asian American citizen is still clearly demarcated in *Lethal Weapon 4*. Yet it will be through the of the introduction of the "Asian" buddy in male cop-buddy films of the late 1990s that Hollywood films ultimately begin to negotiate, in cinematic terms, questions of the relationship between African

Americans and Asian Americans within the "multicultural" American nation.

The new twist on the old cop-buddy formula is significant for at least two reasons. First, it replaces the strategy of using the Japanese enemy "other" to solidify the bond between black and white men, a strategy evident in Hollywood films as recent as *Rising Sun* (dir. Philip Kaufman, 1993). It was this strategy of homosocial male bonding that was so crucial to an earlier cinematic imagination of racially transcendent but emphatically gendered national unity. (Women are indeed dispensable here, fetishized either as objects of desire or as idealized figures in need of male protection.) One only has to watch the trailer of *Rising Sun* to recognize in its positioning of the Asian bad guy a reprise of World War II-era films that construct the solidarity of U.S. male soldier-citizens through their confrontation with a common "yellow menace" enemy. Second, and more important for my argument, the changes intimated in *Lethal Weapon 4* reveal important shifts in the dominant U.S. discourse of race and nation since the 1980s. The multiculturalism these changes advocate is consistent—rather than in tension—with nationalism, and in fact it is under the banner of a United States welcoming to all that the nation take strides in exercising power over "others" deemed foreign, a shifting and slippery categorization. Thus, even when, at the exegetical level, *Rush Hour*, the film I discuss next, focuses on a black and Asian (not Asian American) pairing, its subtext is the "multicultural" (that is, black, white, Asian, and Latino) U.S. nation, and the limits of citizenship within what I call a "millennial multiculturalism," or the "multicultural imaginary" of the new millennium.

As a transitional text, *Lethal Weapon 4* deploys both "old" and "new" paradigms, its representation of "Asian-ness" split between its portrayal of the Chinese villains behind the smuggling operation (the Asian as "other") and its sentimental depiction of a Chinese immigrant nuclear family (the Asian as "us," which is to say, the Asian as docile and nonthreatening, the Asian as obedient within the terms of the nation). Where the latter is concerned, the bonding between Murtaugh and Mr. Hong over shared family values is necessary to the film's liberal message on immigration. The Chinese are seen as fit for American citizenship inasmuch as they are already American (or Chinese in a manner that the nation deems acceptable): They embrace the same values; they are quiet and take up little room; they are resourceful but not devious; they are family members, not workers who will steal "our" jobs. (They are also cute, as embodied by the little boy Ping [played by Steven Lam], who saves the day and steals the show). Insofar as it is rooted in heterosexual family narratives, moreover, the film's message about immigration is further mediated through gender, carefully delimiting the erotic frontiers of male-on-male intimacy.

*Lethal Weapon 4* gestures toward a "multicultural"—not merely an "interracial" (which suggests a racial binary)—bonding of men across lines of race and ethnicity. The film that completes this shift is *Rush Hour*, a movie that represents an Asian and an African American cop who, while initially antagonistic toward one another, end the film giddy and relaxed, bound for a Hong Kong vacation, much as you might imagine any two newlyweds on a honeymoon. Like the short-lived late-1990s television show *Martial Law*, a police comedy that sought to imitate the film's success, *Rush Hour* is a generic hybrid in the sense that it appropriates conventions of Hong Kong martial-arts cinema as a means of updating the buddy genre in the context of changing U.S. racial discourse.[3] In terms of both its racial representation and its marketing, *Rush Hour*'s hallmark is its pairing of a relative newcomer, fast-talking African American comedian-actor Chris Tucker, with Jackie Chan, an established Hong Kong film star. This particular pairing is anticipated in *Lethal Weapon 4*, where comedian Chris Rock plays Murtaugh's son-in-law and the villain is played by martial-arts icon Jet Li (whom Roger Ebert rather embarrassingly referred to as a "newcomer" with "a lot of neat moves" ).[4] It was later taken up in *Martial Law*, which by its ninth episode began pairing fading African American comedian Arsenio Hall with its star, Hong Kong veteran actor Sammo Hong.

Such casting decisions speak to the various commercial exigencies that contribute to what I have been heretofore discussing largely as a shift in cultural representation. But as the transition from *Lethal Weapon 4* to *Rush Hour* makes clear, the fact that Hollywood begins to make room in cop-buddy films for Hong Kong film stars beginning in the late 1990s is hardly just a case of film culture mirroring changes in the zeitgeist, as though suddenly the old paradigm of black and white male bonding had given way to black and Asian male bonding. The trend also reflects the intensifying reliance of major U.S. film studios on non-U.S. audiences for "acceptable" profit margins (hence the use of actors who are recognized stars throughout Asia), as well as important shifts brought about by changes in the Hong Kong film industry as a result of the July 1, 1997 "return" of Hong Kong to the People's Republic of China after more than one hundred fifty years of British rule. The Hong Kong handover, in particular, meant the decline of a once-thriving film industry and, with it, the need for local stars to look elsewhere—especially to Hollywood—for employment.

To say that economic factors have been a driving force behind the heightened visibility of actors like Sammo Hong, Jet Li, Jackie Chan, and others in U.S. action comedies since 1997 is not, however, to imply that the presence of "Asian" faces on U.S. screens is explainable solely in economic terms. Indeed, the welcome presence of such "foreign" faces corresponds to changing needs within U.S. national discourse to represent the nation as "multicultural." Made at a time of heightened awareness about the approach of the millennium, and with that new attention to what *Time* magazine (in a starkly essentialist fashion) once called "The Changing Face of the Nation," the multicultural cop-buddy film affirms the solidarity of different "minority" subjects within the embrace of the nation.[5] Gone are some of the usual tensions of films like *Lethal Weapon 1*, replaced by new ones that emerge in the context of a dominant discourse that both celebrates this multiculturalism and worries over its consequences as the "minorities," together, begin to overtake the "majority," at least in sheer numbers.

My central claim about *Rush Hour* is that, like *Lethal Weapon 4*, it simultaneously represents and contains the threat posed by the bonding between differently racialized male subjects. Just as *Lethal Weapon 4*'s critique of the racism of contemporary anti-immigrant discourse does not cancel out its nationalist subtext, so *Rush Hour* reinscribes dominant racial and national discourses even as it successfully imagines an alliance that might challenge these discourses through the spectacle of "minority" togetherness. In particular, the film evidences such contradictions through its representation of gender and its insistence that the Asian male buddy *not* be American.

In *Rush Hour*, Tucker plays Carter, a bumbling Los Angeles police detective who is paired with Inspector Li (Jackie Chan), an ultracompetent Hong Kong officer called to the United States at the urging of the Chinese consul, whose daughter has been kidnapped and is being held for ransom by a group of Chinese criminals led, it turns out, by a white British Hong Kong ex-official who passes under the Chinese moniker Jingtao. (He is an ex-official, of course, because the handover has just been completed; thus *Rush Hour* incorporates, at the level of plot, some of the very economic and social forces that motivate its production.) Carter and Li come together when Carter, as punishment, is given the lowly assignment of "babysitting" Li so that the latter does not interfere with the FBI's investigation of the kidnapping; and their initial encounter is, predictably, fraught with Carter's resentment. The two, in fact, could not be more different: Dressed in a black suit and red tie, Inspector Li, looking more like a corporate power broker than a police officer (or perhaps he has been taking sartorial counsel from the guys from *Miami Vice*?) deplanes from a Gulfstream private jet at Los Angeles Airport. He is met there by Carter, wearing a flashy ensemble and exiting an old Corvette. Adopting a comedic "speak-loud-to-foreigners" approach, Carter nearly shouts at Li, "I'm Detective Carter. Do you speak-a any English? Do you understand the words that are coming outta my mouth?" When he gets no answer to this query, only a look of confusion and a polite smile from Li (who is busy anyway thanking the Chinese flight crew), Carter turns his back on his new partner and mutters to himself (and to us, the viewers), "I cannot *believe* this shit! First I get a bullshit assignment, now Mr. Rice-a-Roni don't even speak American."

In this humorous scene (at least when I saw it at a theater in Washington, DC it elicited big laughs from a racially diverse audience), *Rush Hour* makes a point of representing Carter's antipathy to Li as racist as well as xenophobic. Carter invokes every predictable stereotype in the anti-Asian arsenal, from imitating "Chinese" accents ("speak-a" for "speak") to making fun of "Chinese" food (the reference to Li as "Mr. Rice-a-Roni," a term that also impugns his masculinity). What ultimately earns the big laugh in the scene, however, is Carter's own ignorant confusion of language and national identity, especially when this mix-up is paired with the actor's delivery of his lines in a voice that deviates from the standard English vernacular (for example, he pronounces "mouth" as something that sounds more like "mouf").

The scene is admittedly complex, allowing the audience to enjoy stereotypes and at the same time to maintain a critical distance from Tucker's character. On the other hand, it is doubtful whether the humor would seem so innocent or pleasurable here if the voice of racism and xenophobia belonged to, say, Riggs from *Lethal Weapon 4* rather than to a young black comedian playing the role of the parochial Angeleno who has barely ever left the city limits. Where, in other words, does our laughter at Carter's ignorance intersect with laughter at the black character who embodies such ignorance? How much does the film's positioning of Carter as a black police detective (he is represented as being out of his league among the white FBI agents who are the primary investigators in the case of the consul's missing daughter) enable him to be the "innocent" (that is to say, forgivable) agent of racism and xenophobia? Are white viewers accountable for the racial and ethnic dynamic of this scene if they are not somehow a direct part of it?[6]

Subtle extradiagetic allusions make these already urgent questions even more pressing. One allusion, of course, is to Jackie Chan's arrival in Los Angeles for the launch of his Hollywood film career as a comic action-film actor. The airport scene at the beginning of *Rush Hour* (titled "Meet Inspector Li" in the digital video disc [DVD] "chapter stops") winkingly stages the "real-life" arrival of Chan in Los Angeles (private jet and all) and his incorporation into a cinematic world in which he will have to work primarily or entirely in English to get leading roles. Carter's ambivalent welcome of Li (Chan) is thus something of a stand-in for Hollywood's embrace of a Hong Kong legend whose limited English relegated him, at least initially, to roles with little dialogue.

The other extradiagetic allusion—to U.S. media representations since the 1990s that have fetishized the interethnic scuffles of urban "minorities," particularly blacks and Asians in urban centers such as Los Angeles—is both subtle and more powerful. That is, through its *mise-en-scène* in southern California, the film encourages viewers to read the airport scene as though Chan's character were an immigrant, not a visitor or a tourist or a special guest of a diplomatic consul. Such representations support a racialized dynamic of spectatorship in which the (white) viewer looks on from a position of superiority and distance: Once again it is not "we" who have to learn how to get along in (in Rodney King's famous phrase), but "they."

The triangulation of "race" (through the figure of the implicitly white, nonracialized spectator) is especially crucial in managing the tricky issue of Carter's racism. In particular, it facilitates a reading in which he does not have the "right" to deride Li's accent or difference from an imagined norm because he himself speaks black vernacular. This perhaps also explains the puzzled look on Li's face, which Carter interprets as noncomprehension and perhaps "funny" Asian mannerisms but which can also be read as Li's own bafflement at Carter: Is this black detective a "real" American? Is he an educated American, up to Li's standards, or will he be a hindrance to the investigation (Li quickly arrives at the latter conclusion)? Can he speak "black" English and still look down on Li as "Mr. Rice-a-Roni"?[7] Can a black man represent the LAPD?

The film returns twice to the joke of whether Li understands—in the first instance when we discover (a few scenes later) that he does speak English, just cannot be bothered to correct his partner. "I'm not responsible for your assumptions," Li informs him, matter-of-factly. It is a giveaway line that nevertheless invites us to imagine whether Carter might not understand what it means to be the object of others' (racialized) assumptions. Does Carter at this moment see and hear himself in Li's rebuke? Is he amused or shamed by Carter's suggestion that he is the racist who relies on "assumptions"? Is this a moment of buddy "coming together" or of painful division, in which the two men become aware of a gap that divides them? Does the fact that Carter (or Murtaugh in *Lethal Weapon 4*) has been the object of false "assumptions" render him any less likely to make them? If so, what kind of moment of instruction or enlightenment is this?

The second time we return to the joke is in the final scene, in which Carter and Li settle comfortably into the first-class cabin for their trip to Hong Kong. As the two discuss the logistics of the trip, a Chinese female airline attendant approaches and offers them peanuts. Carter refuses, greeting the attendant and thanking her in polite Cantonese for her kindness. Li looks taken aback. "You never told me you spoke Chinese," he offers. "I never told you I didn't," Carter corrects him. "You *assumed* I didn't." Meanwhile, we discover that Li has picked up a few new words of his own. Appearing here for the first time in the film looking relaxed, wearing a loose-fitting jacket with no tie, he promises Carter excitedly, "We can hang in my crib. I will show you my hood." "No," Carter quickly follows up, "you can show me a couple of them Chinese girls 'cause when I get over there I want a massage 'cause I wanna get butt wild."

Carter's fantasy-image of "Chinese girls" with whom he can "get butt wild" predictably reintroduces heterosexual desire into this scene of buddy-togetherness. It does so, notably, in a way that also reintroduces racial and national difference, not merely through gendered stereotypes of lascivious black men and pliant Asian women, but through Carter's characterization of Hong Kong as a site of sex tourism. Hence, while in circling back to the joke about language from the scene of the two detectives' initial encounter, *Rush Hour* would seem to have resolved the narrative through the achievement of "cross-cultural understanding," this final scene also considerably muddies any easy recuperation of "multicultural" understanding. In particular, by announcing his intention to use Hong Kong as a place to "get butt wild," Carter re-secures his identity as a national (U.S.) subject for whom Asian (Chinese) women are purchasable commodities. Whereas the film's subplot has revolved around the stealing of Chinese art objects—all of which, including huge but fragile vases, are spectacularly saved in hair-breadth fashion in the film's penultimate showdown with the Jingtao bad guys—in the end Hong Kong and China no longer signify "priceless ancient culture" but "sex tourism." Here, then, is where notions of tradition figuratively abut late-twentieth-century global capitalism.

Li responds to Carter's babbling about Chinese massage girls after the fashion of kids from Los Angeles: He puts on his headphones to shut out the noise. The music that comes out of them (transitioning into the title and credits) is Edwin Starr's "War," a soul-funk classic from 1970. This, too, is a flashback to an earlier scene—one set on the streets of Los Angeles's Chinatown, where the two detectives are staked out awaiting their chance to raid a Chinese restaurant that fronts for the headquarters of the kidnapping ring. As Li and Carter exit Carter's Corvette, "War" is playing on the radio. Jackie Chan's character hums along with the song's famous chorus: "War (huh). What is it good for? Absolutely nothing. Say it again!" Carter is incredulous. How can a "nerdy" Chinese guy from Hong Kong possibly know the English words to this antiwar soul anthem? (One answer, of course, has to do with the global circulation of African American music, but that is for another chapter.) To Carter's accusatory "You don't know nothing about [the song] 'War,'" Li responds matter-of-factly, "Everybody knows 'War,'" and continues singing. After another joke at the expense of Chan's pronunciation of "y'all" (as "you all"), the music increases in volume and the sound track takes over. To thumping sounds punctuated by James Brown-style "Uhs" and "Good Gods" (reminiscent both of the Church and the bedroom), the two perform a sort of cop-buddy voguing, striking poses. Carter shows off his funky-corny dance moves, while Li displays the "kung fu" moves he learned at the police academy back in Hong Kong. The substitution of music for dialogue suggests that what is being created here (the love between Li and Carter that will also have to be "heterosexualized") is ineffable, or at least beyond the capacity of expression in either man's native tongue.

In this scene that seals the bond of intimacy between the protagonists—so that they may redirect erotic energy in mutual antipathy for the villain—we literally watch as Li and Carter go from being strangers to being intimates who come to know each other, if not through sexual encounter, then nevertheless in and through the semiotics of their raced and gendered bodies. In contrast to the scene on the airplane, here the song "War" symbolizes the resolution of conflict through a "multicultural" sharing of distinct national and cultural knowledge. An important part of what is at play here, that is, is the mediation of male intimacy through racialized images and narratives circulated via global entertainment industries. The notion is of bonding through the "universal language" of international entertainment commodities, as Carter lets slip when he observes that Chan's character looks like some guy out of a "karate" movie.

What's further interesting is that these particular cultural commodities—soul-funk music and dance and martial-arts films—have also served to establish political solidarity among symbolically "third-world" subjects in their resistance to U.S. imperialism and struggles for radical social reform. "War," for example, the 1970 song Li already knows the words to, is a Vietnam protest song that simultaneously references African American resistance to U.S. nationalism, imperialism, and racism, both domestic and "foreign." Similarly, in Carter's attempt in the scene to pantomime moves he has seen in martial-arts films, *Rush Hour* tacitly references the ongoing history of African American cultural appropriations of such films as rich and productive sites for the cultural imagination of alternatives to white supremacy and U.S. hegemony.

In promoting *Rush Hour*, the actor Tzi Ma, who plays consul Han, was quoted as saying, "To the best of my knowledge, this is the first Hollywood film with two heroes of color. That's exciting to me. This movie is really a melting pot." Elizabeth Peña, the actress who portrays Johnson, Carter's partner in the LAPD and an explosives expert whose skill helps save the consul's daughter, similarly was quoted as saying that she liked "the idea of two men of totally different ethnic backgrounds who come together." These comments neatly summarize what Raymond Williams might call a "dominant" reading, an interpretation of the film as it wants audiences to see it—that is, as a parable of cross-racial, cross-national "coming together."[8]

Yet the "War" scene's insistence on the primacy of the *body* as the conduit of such interpersonal, intercultural instruction and male bonding complicates this reading. In celebrating the raced male body as the site of a certain culturally specific "style" and gender performance, the scene threatens to symbolically feminize African American and Asian men by representing them in terms of embodied spectacle, which is of course how women (particularly women of color) are coded in U.S. discourses of gender and sexuality. What is interesting in this context is that, because both men are feminized, the film is not as concerned as is the *Lethal Weapon* franchise with parrying anxiety about homosexuality with homophobic "humor." Unlike *Lethal Weapon 4*, *Rush Hour* contains no nervous litany of gay jokes, and Peña, as the tough sidekick to Carter, plays the (possibly lesbian) butch to his macho femme.

Taglines for *Rush Hour* advertised the film as one in which "the fastest hands in the East" meet "the biggest mouth in the West," neatly contracting bodily metonymy (hands and mouth) with national synecdoche (East and West). Here, as in the scene between Murtaugh and the INS agent in *Lethal Weapon 4* and in the scene in which Carter and Li first meet, *Rush Hour* can successfully delegate to Chris Tucker (as Carter) the role of representing the West, but only insofar as it may successfully ascribe Easternness to Chan (as Li). Indeed, no amount of buddy-bonding can transcend national difference, or change the "fact" that Li is an outsider, even in the pointedly "multicultural" city of Los Angeles where the film is set. No matter how culturally or linguistically fluent in "American" the latter's character becomes through his bonding with Carter, that is, Li must always produce the signs of his foreignness for their pairing to "stick." Likewise, the portrayal of an African American man as a national subject depends, in *Rush Hour*, on this "other" who, no matter his citizenship status, cannot so easily be folded into a national narrative.

Would such a narrative of bonding be possible if the plot were altered so that Li's character could be played by a Chinese American—especially one who does not speak "accented" English as does Chan? To put it another way: To what degree is the film's portrayal of Li as a "buddy" protagonist who facilitates the film's image of a "multicultural" America paradoxically predicated on his Chinese, not American, citizenship?

To hazard a preliminary answer to these questions is to confront the issue of the political value of the representation of the "multicultural," cross-national buddy alliance. As *Lethal Weapon 4* illustrates, the representation of affinity among differently raced subjects across lines of national difference does not necessarily pose a threat to U.S. nationalist narratives; indeed, Hollywood films have increasingly demonstrated an ability to deploy images of multiculturalism in the service of nationalism, where U.S. exceptionalism is redefined as our ability to incorporate "others" into the symbolic fold of the nation. Such self-conscious deployment of images of multiculturalism does not, moreover, address questions of citizenship or the persistent embodied particularity of certain U.S. citizens. Here the noncitizenship of Inspector Li in *Rush Hour*, or of Mr. Han in *Lethal Weapon 4*, as symbolized in their accented English, is crucial to the ability of the films to smoothly incorporate them as the buddies of African American men. Indeed, the evidence of *Lethal Weapon 4* suggests that it is through the coding of Asian masculinity as "foreign" that the films negotiate the thorny and ultimately inadmissible issue of the history of the noncitizenship of African Americans, those national subjects who have most had to represent "race" within U.S. racial discourse.

What is the value of the spectacle of the bonding of raced masculine subjects that the films banish from their field of vision? Such a spectacle would almost certainly disrupt the prevailing narrative of domestic relations between Asian Americans and African Americans as one of "minority" scuffles along the lines of those the media so relentlessly displayed in the aftermath of the Rodney King verdict and, more subtly, in debates over affirmative action and college admissions. Moreover, it might give lie to the racialized structuring of the rhetoric of Asian Americans as a model minority, revealing the degree to which this "elevation" of Asian Americans as national subjects who are able to transcend seemingly narrow racial interests is predicated on the degradation of African Americans as a racially despised minority.

The questions these films pose lead me, in conclusion, back to issues of gender and sexuality. In February 2000, less than two years after *Rush Hour* was released, *Newsweek* magazine ran an article titled "Why Asian Guys Are on a Roll."[9] Written by an Asian American woman, Esther Pan, the article assures readers that Asian American men have "made it"—both as national subjects and as men—because white women now want to date them. (On the other hand, the white women interviewed for the article precisely attribute their attraction to Asian American men to their perception that they are not as "masculine"—that is, as patriarchal—as white men, and yet can be counted on to earn a good living.) The article celebrates such an "achievement," yet like the cop-buddy films discussed here, its optimistic tone is premised on various racial contradictions. For one, it cites the heightened visibility of Chinese actors Jet Li and Chow Yun Fat to support the claim that Asian American men are now sexualized subjects who do not have to compromise masculinity. Second, and more tellingly, the elevation of the coupling of Asian American men and white women—as a sign of the declining significance of race and the nation's successful incorporation of "others" into the national fold or family—can be understood only in the context of the historical threat posed by black male sexuality—to white women and hence to the American nation.

Lurking behind the "positive" representation are the model minority discourse (Asian American men are good catches for white women because they are stable and nonthreatening) and animosity between Asians and blacks (because of their particular positioning as nonthreatening, Asian American men are not a threat to the purity of the nation the way that African American men are). Like the films, the article envisions a multicultural nation that is itself "on a roll." (To illustrate the pun, the article pictures an Asian American guy on all-American roller blades—not, say, on the basketball court.) And yet, as in both *Rush Hour* and *Lethal Weapon 4*, this multiculturalism is ultimately self-aggrandizing, a multiculturalism that best serves not those "minorities" who must perpetually produce and perform it, but a myth of the raceless American nation.

## Notes

1. Cynthia J. Fuchs, "The Buddy Politic," Steven Cohen and Ina Rae Hark, eds., *Screening the Male: Exploring Masculinities in Hollywood Cinema* (New York: Routledge, 1993), 202, 206. Fuchs's reading of the buddy film builds off of Michael P. Rogin's "Make My Day!: Spectacle as America in Imperial Politics," *Representations* 29 (1990): 99–123. Beyond the *Lethal Weapon* franchise, begun in 1987, other early examples of cop-buddy films include *Black Rain* (dir. Ridley Scott, 1989), *New Jack City* (dir. Mario Van Peebles, 1991), and *The Rookie* (dir. Clint Eastwood, 1991).

2. This chapter examines the representational politics of such transracial, transnational pairing by focusing on *Rush Hour* as a paradigmatic text. A discussion of subsequent films that fall into the same general category as *Rush Hour—Rush Hour 2*, *Shanghai Noon*, *Shanghai Nights*, *The Tuxedo*, *The Medallion*, and *Cradle to the Grave*—would both complicate and enrich this discussion. So, too, would a consideration of films such as *Romeo Must Die* (dir. Andrzej Bartkowiak, 2000), which imagines the curiously asexual erotic pairing of an African American woman (the late rhythm-and-blues singer Aaliyah) and an Asian man (kung fu star Jet Li) as contemporary "star-crossed lovers." These, however, lie outside the scope of the present discussion.

3. In terms of visual spectacle, this means that some of the adrenaline-producing pyrotechnics of the former are replaced by the awe-inspiring fight scenes of the latter.

4. For Ebert's review, see http://rogerebert.suntimes.com/apps/pbcs.dll/article?AID=/19980710/REVIEWS/807100303/1023 Accessed July 22, 2008.

5. See "Special issue: The New Face of America: How Immigrants Are Shaping the World's First Multicultural Society," *Time* 142.41 (Fall 1993).

6. There are numerous outtakes at the end of *Rush Hour*, much like the outtakes that are a stock-in-trade of Hong Kong action films. Yet in *Rush Hour* the humor is not only in action scenes gone wrong (as when Jackie Chan messes up a difficult stunt), but in scenes where both actors mispronounce their lines.

7. Korean American scholar Elaine Kim explores some of these questions by reading the various media representations of the aftermath of the Rodney King verdict and the riots in Los Angeles, also known (for Korean Americans and others) as Sa-I-Gu. See her "Home is Where the Han Is," in Robert Gooding-Williams, ed., *Reading Rodney King/Reading Urban Uprising* (New York: Routledge, 1993), 215–235.

8. It is hard to overlook Peña's perhaps unintentional pun on male homoeroticism. The pun is complicated by the fact that it is her (possibly lesbian) character's burden to continually rebuff Carter in his constant references to her sexuality (for example, "What color panties are you wearing?"). Although it lies outside the scope of this chapter, it would be interesting to explore further the possibility of the character Johnson's position as the "strong, assertive" lesbian who mediates male heterosexuality in a film in which women are largely ignored and in which neither man is given a female romantic interest. Of course, the film also revolves around the missing little girl, who proves herself equally tough as a protégé of Inspector Li.

9. Esther Pan, "Why Asian Guys Are on a Roll," *Newsweek* (February 21, 2000): 50. The article is accessible online at http://rogerebert.suntimes.com/apps/pbcs.dll/article?AID=/19980710/REVIEWS/807100303/1023. Accessed July 22, 2008.

# 6

# American Popular Music and Neocolonialism in the Films of Edward Yang

Emilie Yueh-yu Yeh

> *Xiao Maowang (Little Elvis): I sent my demo tape to Elvis and he wrote me back! Your sister translated the letter for me. Elvis said: "I am surprised to know that my songs are so popular on a remote, unknown, tiny island." He said that he was very happy, and he even gave me a memento. Guess what it is?*
>
> —Edward Yang, *A Brighter Summer Day*

Music in Edward Yang's film oeuvre is characterized by a wide variety of styles. Disparity and disjunction seem to be key to Edward Yang's work. The disparity between the English and Chinese titles in several of his films[1] points to Yang's embodiment of a hybrid identity: American, Chinese mainland, and Taiwanese. Born in Shanghai of Hakka origin, raised in Taiwan as a second-generation mainland émigré, and trained and employed as an engineer in the United States, Yang shuttles between his Chinese upbringing and a cosmopolitan sensibility. Compared to the films of another Taiwan director, Hou Hsiao-hsien, who prefers rural motifs, Yang's works are marked by urban themes and, more importantly, "glocalization," hybrid, cultural sentiments, and wry humor.

Yang's disparity registers in the facts that he has never made films outside Taipei and he is never interested in issues unrelated to the Taipei metropolitan culture. Yang has marked the capital of Taiwan as a global locale through *In Our Time: Expectations* (*Zhiwang*, 1982), *That Day, on the Beach* (*Haitan de yitian*, 1983), *Taipei Story* (*Qingmei zhuma*, 1984), *The Terrorizers* (*Kongbu fenzi*, 1986), *A Brighter Summer Day* (*Kulingjie shaonian sharen zhijian*, 1991), *A Confucian Confusion* (*Duli shidai*, 1994), *Mahjong* (*Majang*, 1996), and *Yi Yi: A One and a Two* (*Yiyi*, 2001). *Taipei Story* takes place in Taipei, but refers to Tokyo, Los Angeles, and Williamsburg, Pennsylvania. The Chinese title of *The Terrorizers* (*Kongbu fenzi*; also translatable as "terrorists") recontextualizes a post-cold-war global paranoia in a newly developed but increasingly confusing urban space. *A Brighter Summer Day* links Shanghai, Guangzhou, and Taipei into a geography of the postwar Chinese diaspora. In *A Confucian Confusion*, complex business and interpersonal relationships are developed in the transregional connections of Taipei, Hong Kong, Guangzhou, Xian, Shanghai, and Beijing through the traffic of capital, raw materials, sex, and commodities. This spiral relationship linking various East Asian capitals is further compounded in *Mahjong* and *Yi Yi*. For example, the sound-track album for *Mahjong*, "Qu Xianggang kankan," is titled in English *What Ever Happen to Hong Kong* [*sic*]. The title apparently addresses the then-impending 1997 deadline for the handing over of Hong Kong to the People's Republic of China (PRC), although the music on the album is for the most part not to be found in the film. In addition, a local hairdresser, a character named Hong Kong, embodies Hong Kong's stock images: flashy, predatory, and tricky, blended into a tale of cosmopolitan treachery.[2] The film's title, *Mahjong*, referring to the most popular Chinese gambling game, is also a witty conceit, echoing Taiwan's beguiling democratic development in the 1990s. To complicate the already entangled regional network, Yang adds a Londoner and a Parisian to lay out an increasingly globalized East Asian urban imaginary. In *Yi Yi*, the Taipei-Chicago-Tokyo triangle is rendered through business travel, the information-technology economy, male bonding, and old romance. In Edward Yang's films, social relations become ever more reified and identities are constantly destabilized and negotiated in an increasingly complex network of transnational capitalism. So, how may we sort out the perplexities of Yang's style?

In *A Brighter Summer Day*, Yang clearly pays homage to the era when Taiwanese teenagers were dazzled by American popular music. At the end of the film, it is through a letter written by Elvis Presley, in response to a recording of "Are You Lonesome Tonight" that Little Elvis sends him, that the island's fans are identified and recognized and "come alive." The peculiar adherence to postwar American popular music, as shown in *A Brighter Summer Day* and other moments in Yang's work, reveals a preoccupation with American culture, which paradoxically constitutes the core of a Taiwanese collective memory. Perhaps a baby boomer like Yang can go back to the good old days only in film and sound-track albums, but in Taipei cityscapes, golden oldies do not necessarily signify a bygone age. "Smoke Gets Into Your Eyes," for example, continues to play in the Hard Rock Café, at TGI Fridays, and at Ruth's Chris steak house; the song is no longer a personal memory but part of a "national," fully commercialized, assimilated Taiwan culture.

Edward Yang is concerned with the interface between local and foreign cultures more than with the integrity of a Chinese identity. He wants to explore the impact of Western culture and its ideological implications. This vision opens a window to further investigate issues of neocolonialism. Here, music illuminates these issues. The arguments to be developed are the following. First, the bifocal importance of American music: American music in Edward Yang's films signifies neocolonial history and simultaneously functions as an agent for youths' self-assertion and deviance. Second, the music in Yang's films, particularly in *A Brighter Summer Day*, illustrates a performative appropriation of neocolonial cultures. The music of this film goes beyond the function of enhancing images. In addition, it elicits a conscious self-mockery, a "metanarrative" of Taiwan's neocolonial appropriation of American music.

## A Brighter Summer Day: Youth Rebellion in the Cold War Era

> *The environment of the 1960s might have strengthened or dampened your will. Either way, it influences the 1990s. That era provides a lot of clues for us to look plainly at the present.*
> —Edward Yang[3]

The appeal of *A Brighter Summer Day* lies primarily in its music. American music, particularly the industrial type for mass consumption, constitutes a powerful aural narrative of neocolonialism. The use in this narrative of hit songs of the 1950s evokes Taiwan's continuing dependence on the United States after the end of the Korean War in 1952.

*A Brighter Summer Day*[4] is based on an actual murder case that made newspaper headlines in 1961. Yang stated in an interview that he wanted to make the film as a tribute to his childhood memories of postwar Taipei—in other words, a film "tracing the past" (*sujiu*).[5] For a postwar baby boomer like Yang (b. 1947), life in the 1960s was never safe and comfortable, but it was very different from the comfortable bourgeois lifestyle portrayed in his 2001 film *Yi Yi*. Yang chooses to remember his youth as a time of dangerous living, a closed world of corruption, high libido, betrayal, and epiphany. It is also a memory of a collective youth oppressed by several apparatuses—the educational system, political suppression known as White Terror (*baise kongbu*), and organized crime. The film's emphasis on youth counterculture is clearly stated in its prologue, with the following text:

> Millions of Chinese migrated with the Nationalist government to Taiwan around 1949. Most of these people wanted only a secure job and a stable environment for their children. However, as the young generation was growing up, their hard-working parents were living in fear and uncertainty. Under such an insecure atmosphere, these young people often organized gangs to expand their primal and powerful surviving will.

Diaspora—in this case motivated by political change—forced older mainland émigrés to focus on matters of survival, stability, and security. The younger generation was left to face a new life on its own. It is in this context that Edward Yang depicts his childhood memories. The film's Chinese title, *Gulingjie shaonian sharen shijian*—literally "Youth Murder Incident on Guling Street"—refers to a real case: a fifteen-year-old teenager, Mao Wu, stabbed his girlfriend to death out of anger at her unfaithfulness.

The intention to insert a historical truth into fiction is evident in the first shot of the opening sequence, where the subtitle gives the date "48th Year of the Republic" (or 1959). In the scene, Mr. Zhang, father of the protagonist Xiao Si (Little Four), asks a schoolteacher to double-check his son's test score so that he can be reconsidered for entrance into a better high school. The accents of these characters mark their regional background and their social condition, namely, Nationalist émigrés from China settling in Taiwan after the Communist takeover in 1949.

Aside from Xiao Si's success in certain scholastic rites of passage, his school life proves to be a disaster. He hates the repressive atmosphere in the school and gets involved with gangs; this later leads to his suspension. On top of this personal trouble, his father is arrested for being an acquaintance of communist infiltrators. Finally, his girlfriend, Xiao Ming (Little Brightness), dumps him for his rich best friend. Unable to deal with this series of traumas, he kills her and spends his prime years in a detention center.

Youth violence provides the thrust of the story. Three youth gangs are featured in the film: Tiny Park (Xiao Gongyuan), 217, and South Sea (Nanhai). The latter two consist of hoodlums who are into gambling and extortion, and Tiny Park is mostly involved in organizing concerts and showing off its flashy lifestyle. Edward Yang is less interested in reworking the gangster genre than in rewriting the role of gangsterism and rackets in the context of Chinese diasporas in postwar Taiwan.

217 is a group of thugs who cheat and exploit. They dress in white undershirts, baggy pants, and, interestingly, Japanese wooden clogs; this garb points to a collective experience of colonialism under Japanese occupation, an experience these mainland orphans did not have. The structure of the gang resembles an extended family: the thugs, most of whom lost their families during the civil war on the mainland, live in a pub run by their leader, Shandong (named after his home province of Shandong in northeast China). The gang's quasi-familial structure illustrates its diasporic condition, which in turn refers to the exile of the three million mainland Chinese in Taiwan. The gang's indifference to the Nationalist ideology marks its rejection of education and military training, and its refusal to seek local alliances predestines its bleak future. In a night raid mobilized by Tiny Park, 217 is exterminated inside its compound.

The portrayal of 217 as a group of underdogs contrasts with the lively depiction of Tiny Park. The latter, unlike the ingrown 217, seems to promise a future for the young generation of mainlanders. There are two keys to this future: traditional masculinity and Western culture. Tiny Park adheres to the rules of Chinese outlaw culture, the honor code of the "rivers and lakes" (*jianghu*) knights-errant who are committed to justice, loyalty, and reciprocal respect. Honey, the leader of Tiny Park, immerses himself in martial-arts stories. His belief in the old-fashioned world of swordsmen wins him the support of a local Hokkienese-speaking rival gang called Wanhua after the oldest area in Taipei, which was once known for its old colonial docks. Eventually, this gang teams up with Tiny Park to overtake 217. However, what makes Tiny Park unique is its infatuation with rock 'n' roll. Aside from being involved in gang fights, Tiny Park runs a rock band that holds regular concerts, covering ten-year-old American pop songs.

As in Edward Yang's previous films, rock's explosive energy is repeated here as an essential component of youth images. The insertion of rock 'n' roll in the narrative is always diegetic, played either by the characters on records or in live performances. The first appearance of rock music in the film takes place when Tiny Park holds a small dance party in a neighborhood cafe. The scene begins with the lead vocalist, Tiaozi (Copster), singing Frankie Avalon's 1959 hit "Why." As Tiaozi sings, a group of people led by his rival Huatou (Slippery Head) steps into the café, passing the dancing couples and heading straight for the kitchen. When Tiaozi's partner, Xiao Maowang (Little Elvis), picks up the female vocal part ("I think you're awfully sweet / Why? Because I love you. / You say I'm your special treat / Why? Because you love me"), Tiaozi rushes to the kitchen, where he confronts Huatou, accusing him of selling out their own gang by collaborating with 217 and other rival gangs for the upcoming rock concert.

The next diegetic use of rock in the sound track also accompanies an intense gang scuffle. The scene begins when Xiao Si greets his girlfriend, Xiao Ming, in the same café. When Xiao Ming arrives, she immediately fills the empty café with music by playing a record. As the record begins to play, the song "Mr. Blue" slips into the aural space: "Our guardian star lost all his glow the day that I lost you / He lost all his glitter the day you said no / And his silver turned to blue." Listening to the song, the young couple look at each other quietly, trying to remain in the magical musical world. The romantic aura accompanied by the blues harmony is soon short-circuited by a sudden intrusion—the café's proprietor stops the record for no apparent reason. Within seconds, a group of Tiny Park members rushes into the café, breaking up the couple's enchanted aura.

The third instance that features rock within the diegesis is a grand concert held in Taipei's Sun Yat-sen Hall. It is juxtaposed with the film's most intense event, namely, the murder of Honey. Inside the concert hall, Tiaozi sings "Poor Little Baby" and happily receives cheers and applause from his fans. Outside the hall, Tiaozi's brother, Honey, has a talk with Shandong, the leader of 217. Unaware that his own murder has been premeditated,

Honey challenges Shandong to a fight. Pretending to be stunned, Shandong pushes Honey toward the middle of the road in front of an approaching bus. As the bus runs over Honey's body, the concert reaches its climax—the famous band Telstar (Dianxing) performs "Don't Be Cruel" as if in accompaniment to the murder.

These three examples indicate the metanarrative function of the musical sound track. Songs do more than correlate to actions of confrontation, interruption, and betrayal. They are not simply ironic counterpoints. Instead, they evoke an otherworldly space that is both aloof and beckoning to the claustrophobic territoriality of the young gangsters. American songs offer a kind of escape hatch, not only to the protagonists but also to contemporary spectators who, like Yang himself, are invited to relive an era of brighter prospects.

## Neocolonial Rock: Restaging Mimicry Through Nostalgia

The appearance of the band Telstar in *A Brighter Summer Day* clearly shows Yang paying tribute to the cover bands of the 1960s. Telstar, retired by the time the film was made, was *the* band of the 1960s. They covered American pop songs, and covered them extremely well. Yang invited them to perform in the film to refresh spectators' memories as well to authenticate the historical representation. Interestingly, they appear in the film as they look *now* rather than how they looked *then*. Yang does not mind showing an aging band as long as its members still throb with the music. Here, nostalgia is activated primarily by aural means and accented by visual representation. It is a striking musical anachronism that works, in musical terminology, like a descant, soaring above and along the main narrative events.

Like Telstar, the Tiny Park band is interested only in covering popular American songs, not in creating its own music. This may seem like secondhand, cheap imitation by the standard of orthodox rock practice, but it accurately reflects Taiwan's cultural practice at that particular neocolonial period—superficial, limited in quality, and lacking originality. After the Korean War, Taiwan became the anti-Communist bulwark for America in exchange for military and financial aid to assist the Nationalist government in maintaining its hegemony and developing Taiwan. Military and diplomatic dependence parallels cultural dependence, and not even youth subculture is immune to it.

After the Korean War, two major forces dominated Taiwan's politics and culture: the Nationalist government, which had taken Taiwan as a temporary base from which to prepare for the future invasion and recovery of communist China, and the United States, which used Taiwan as a convenient military satellite for continuing its surveillance of China. This situation was not identical to the classical colonial model, but is what can be called a neocolonial, codependent state of semiautonomy and semidependence.

The most striking critique of this neocolonialism has come from the nativist literature of the 1970s. New Cinema directors and scriptwriters followed the lead of the nativist writers and used the victimization of women to form an allegory of Taiwan's dependence on the first world. Cinema and fiction appear to share a critique of the country's "shameful" past. In the case of *A Brighter Summer Day*, however, neocolonialism appears as a rather sweet memory.

The release of the sound-track album bears evidence to the film's nostalgia, at least for the producers. Titled *Guling Street Youth Band* (*Gulingjie shaonian hechangtuan*), the album was released simultaneously with the film, in July of 1991. It is dedicated entirely to American pop of the 1950s and the early 1960s, although all the songs are covered by the ad hoc Guling Street Youth Band, which also plays the Tiny Park band in the film. Aside from an apparent marketing strategy, the album itself extols a heavy-handed nostalgia. The first three songs, "This Magic Moment," "Only the Lonely," and "Peggy Sue," do not appear in the film and are listed in a separate category as "pop hits of the 1950s." Clearly the album is an anthology of the music of historical periods. In addition, the catalogue illustrates the album's other intent: period accuracy. According to the liner notes, Edward Yang personally supervised the production of the album to ensure the acting band's covers were as close as possible to the original recordings. The band's style also shows an emphasis on period authenticity: hairstyle, dress, and performance simulate some of the classical rock bands of the 1950s, namely, Buddy Holly and the Crickets.

This is the first sound-track album ever released from one of Edward Yang's films. Yang's active role in the album's production shows his personal interest in seeing the resurrection of these dated American songs on the local pop charts. Other songs on the album include "Why," "Poor Little Fool," "Angel Baby," "Never Be Anyone Else But You," and Elvis Presley's "Are You Lonesome Tonight." These songs were selected because they were supposed to represent the period as well as rock's significance for Taiwan's youth culture—that is, the discovery of sexuality and romance.

Originally sung by Frankie Avalon in 1959, "Why" is a teenybop song characterized by mild sexual expression. "Angel Baby" is a 1960 ballad by Rosie and the Originals; like other "girl groups," Rosie and the Originals sang of teenage girls' craving for love. Two rockabilly songs, "Poor Little Fool" and "Never Be Anyone Else But You," by Ricky Nelson represent the prototypical California suburban rock that featured youthful cheer and energy. A tribute to the 1960s would be incomplete without Elvis. "Are You Lonesome Tonight" (1961), one of Elvis's best recordings in his post-army period, blends a soft blues flavor with a slow, balladlike chanting. In

Elvis's interpretation, the song evokes an unrestrained longing for romance.

Covering American songs is one thing; singing precisely like the originals is another. Xiao Maowang, or Little Elvis, a young gang member, has committed himself to singing like the King. He imitates Elvis even though he knows no English. This type of mimicking seems to fit well with what Homi Bhabha (1983) has called "grotesque mimicry."[6] Mimicry means an act of imitation; it resembles the original object without being identical to it. However, mimicry does more than just copy; it also entails a parasitical double. An association that derives from biology provides a better explanation of mimicry in the colonial context. One dictionary definition of "mimicry" is "a superficial resemblance that some organisms exhibit to another or to the natural objects among which they live and thereby secure concealment, protection, or some other advantage." And for "mimic," the dictionary indicates "a usually edible and harmless animal that escapes predation by being mistaken by potential predators for a distasteful or venomous animal."[7] The biological definition explains the necessary conditions for mimicry to take place in nature. Mimicry, in the biological realm, does not simply indicate a superfluous or pointless imitation; the superficiality of the resemblance is precisely the point. Mimicry is a matter of survival for certain insects and reptiles, which survive by imitating other stronger animals. The Arsenura moth of Panama, for instance, imitates dead leaves to avoid the attention of its predators; the king snake often scares away most animals because its red-and-black stripes resemble those of a poisonous coral snake. By mimicking the coral snake, the harmless king snake enjoys a carefree life.[8]

This biological view helps us understand Bhabha's concept of "grotesque mimicry." According to Bhabha, the term indicates the colonial subject's "desire for an originality" and the wish to replicate and even consume the original. A colonial subject depends on imitating the colonizer in order to survive. Mimicking, no matter how closely it resembles the original, is doomed to be superficial. Nevertheless, that superficiality can be profoundly disturbing, even menacing. This instability, according to Bhabha, is built into the structures of colonial discourse itself, in spite of the markers of race, gender, and culture that differentiate the colonizer from the colonized and regardless of whether colonial subjects activate that instability for their own purposes (Bhabha, 1983: 27). Mimicry is, therefore, a sign, a recognition of the irreducible difference between the copy and the original that renders the mimicking grotesque. The grotesque is not only inauthentic, but also monstrous, intimidating, and powerful—an inescapable problem for the colonial mission to civilize.

Because of his height, Little Elvis has to stand on a stool to reach the microphone when he performs on stage. In his rendition, "Are You Lonesome Tonight" becomes something quite different from Elvis's deep, lazy, masculine singing. Little Elvis's voice is prepubescent, and he sings the song in a high, girlish, piercing voice. Neither Little Elvis nor his band seems to distinguish the "grotesque mimicry" from their earnest emulation of Elvis. They are happy with their covers, so long as the music is generically American and the singing is quasi-Elvis. Does this awkward but fascinating audiovisual covering disclose the deep colonization in Taiwan's youth culture of the 1960s? Or is it a surrogate for something else?

## Redirecting Neocolonial Criticism

One may argue that the music in *A Brighter Summer Day* typifies America's cultural colonization of Taiwan in the postwar era. This kind of symptomatic reading, which fails to consider internal politics, tends to give a simplistic diagnosis of Taiwan's neocoloniality. It is true that neocolonialism has to do with the unequal distribution of resources between the first and the third worlds, but we need to caution against a cultural reading based on external economic and political determinations. Taiwan's internal struggles during the cold war also have much to do with the formation of cultural dependence on the West. Taiwan's cultural field of the 1950s appeared stagnant because of martial law and anti-Communist dogmatism. Guided by the monumental slogan "Oppose Communism, Resist the Soviet Union" (*fangong kangE*), the nation devoted most of its resources to future action against the socialist bloc. Every aspect of social, political, and cultural life was consequently subsumed by this political and military mission.

To the young rebels in the film, the adults' culture appears pathetic and dead. It is this feeling of death and obsolescence that makes room for Western culture. The members of the younger generation cannot and will not identify with their parents, let alone their parents' music. They refuse to cocoon themselves in the memory of old times marked by war and migration. It is the 1960s and it is the age of youth, the age of rock 'n' roll. Western culture arrived in Taiwan in a neat, enticing package, full of pleasure, wonder, and knowledge. Restless youth caught between the old generation's nostalgia and unfamiliar local customs embraced rock without hesitation.

The allegiance to Western culture is not simply a reflection of cultural colonization, but rather part of the international, intracultural youth rebellion. Rock is not just a way in which young people show their admiration of American culture; it empowers them and provides them a means for asserting a distinct identity, albeit a problematic one. The way the music appears in the film and the way characters perform the music both embody empowerment and conscious performativity. All the American songs are diegetic; they appear either through the band's live performance or as part of the diegetic sound track.

Live performance is the heart of Hollywood musicals, what Rick Altman calls the "synchronic constituent."[9] In *The Hollywood Musical*, Jane Feuer suggests that the importance of live performance lies in its first-person quality and that it tends to address the audience directly.[10] In the early rock 'n' roll musicals such as *Jailhouse Rock* (1957; dir. Richard Thorpe), *Rock Around the Clock* (1956; dir. Fred F. Sears), and *The Girl Can't Help It* (1956; dir. Frank Tashlin), rock performance occupied a large portion of the narrative. In these films, live rock 'n' roll, like any number in conventional musicals, constitutes a *spectacle* that provides the pleasures of identifying for both rock fans and the film spectator.

Music and stars dominate the way performance is structured in rock films.[11] Yet what is at issue is how to represent rock 'n' roll and its performers in a truthful or "original" fashion. In *A Hard Day's Night* (1964; dir. Richard Lester), a film about the Beatles and Beatlemania, an on-the-spot approach is adopted in constructing the Beatles' star personae. Frequent close-ups of the Beatles' lips, eyes, and other facial features convey to the spectators an "authentic" aura of, as well as an intimate relationship with, the Beatles.

Authentic spectacles such as *A Hard Day's Night* emphasize live rather than canned productions such as lip-synching or studio recording. Rock performances in *A Brighter Summer Day* follow this model closely. But in terms of showing the audience's reaction, a necessary syntagma to legitimize the performance, Yang's film goes the other way. Yang deviates from standard practice in Hollywood musicals, especially musical biopics intent on documenting celebrity: we expect reaction shots of the audience inside the hall when they watch the performance of the Tiny Park band. But this is deliberately withheld in Yang's film. According to Jane Feuer, "the use of theatrical audiences in the films provides a point of identification for the audience of the film" (Feuer, 1982: 338). By such use, an "immediate and fluid" relationship between the performance and its audience can easily be transformed into one between performer and the film audience. In *A Brighter Summer Day*, however, Yang is not interested in this relationship. Only one instance in the concert sequence shows the enthusiastic reaction of the audience toward the Tiny Park band. The lack of sufficient-shot and reverse-shot alternation suggests that the film's priority is to treat the performance as self-empowerment of the gang members, not as entertainment. Its concern is less with these young people's popularity and appeal than with their performing power, independence, and individuality.

For the teenagers in *Summer Day*, singing American songs is not just one of their many ways of "looking for fun" (*zhao lezi*); it is also a way of expressing themselves and inventing a shelter in the midst of boredom, gang violence, and alienation. Even though Edward Yang never hesitates to reveal the contradictory nature of rock, the performance of the youth gang is presented as a pure, transcendental, and timeless practice. When Little

Elvis sings, he is no longer the little guy always bullied by the vicious and incompetent schoolteacher; nor is he just a grotesque mimicry of American pop. He is someone who injects all his energy into singing Elvis, conjuring the King out of nothing. Similarly, Tiaozi turns from an anonymous gang member into a charismatic rock performer when he sings "Never Be Anyone Else But You" on stage.

Rock gives youth gangs an escape from the drudgery of everyday life. More important, it provides a new identity, free from historical and political burdens. Andrew Jones, in his analysis of the PRC rock musician Cui Jian, provides a similar reading. Jones argues that the meaning of Chinese rock 'n' roll is located in the context of authoritarian politics, especially the official suppression of individual expression.[12] The meaning of Cui Jian lies not just in his individual defiance against a repressive Chinese society; he also represents the rise of a new, collective, youth-dentity that plays off of a conflicting official tune. Similarly, the subcultural practice in Edward Yang's film must be recognized as a reaction against Taiwan's internal politics and a repugnant national identity.

As Lawrence Grossberg argues, rock identity is defined not just by what fans listen to but "what they do not listen to."[13] This dialectic explains the noninclusiveness of youth culture. It suggests that youth culture is defined by its (counter)relations to the social, cultural, economic, and sexual practices outside itself. The "negative" identity of Yang's teenagers shows that they cannot listen to those archaic, patriotic art songs that are twenty years older than they are. They cannot identify with Hokkien pop, a derivative of Japanese *enka*, which is also irrelevant to their lives.

At the end of *A Brighter Summer Day*, Little Elvis finally receives a letter from Elvis Presley thanking him for sending his recording of "Are You Lonesome Tonight." In the letter, Elvis expresses his appreciation and surprise at his popularity on this "tiny island" and encloses a ring for his devoted fan. Little Elvis delivers a copy of his recording and another letter to the penitentiary where Xiao Si is imprisoned, hoping Xiao Si will be able to share his joy. His package is received with courtesy by the penitentiary officer but is thrown into a trash can immediately after Little Elvis leaves the reception desk. Xiao Si apparently has no chance to share the joy of his good friend. It is through the offscreen voice-over of Little Elvis that we finally learn what the letter says. A postcolonial reading would quickly reveal the colonial residue in Yang's nostalgia toward the 1960s. But for mainland émigrés who were sandwiched between a dead "ancestral country" (*zuguo*) and a despised "provincial island" (*xiaodao*), America the superpower with its all-conquering pop is a safe and desirable host.

This brings us to a scene in which the film's English title is mentioned for the first and only time. Xiao Si's sister, a college student with an American dream, is helping Little Elvis transcribe the lyrics of "Are You Lonesome

Tonight." After several tries, she still cannot get down all the words correctly. She begins to doubt her hearing:

> Record: "Does your memory stray to a bright summer day . . ."
> Elder Sister: "This is so strange. He obviously sings "a *brighter* summer day."
> Elder Brother: "But 'a brighter summer day' is not grammatical! Brighter? Bright summer day?"

Perhaps "a brighter summer day" is not all that ungrammatical, considering the pleasure and freedom represented by American pop music for young men stuck on a closed, semitropical island. In a stifling-hot summer season, Elvis, Frankie Avalon, Ricky Nelson, and Rosie and the Originals do not bring just one bright day but a *brighter* day that dazes and confuses the restless young souls.

## Notes

This chapter is a revision based on an earlier essay "Elvis, Allow Me to Introduce Myself: American Music and Neocolonialism in Taiwan Cinema" published in Modern Chinese Literature and Culture 15.1 (Spring 2003): 1–28.

1. Edward Yang tends to discriminate between the Chinese and English titles of his films. *Taipei Story*, for example, has a quite different Chinese title, *Qingmei zhuma*, meaning "Childhood Romance." The Chinese title for *A Brighter Summer Day* is *Gulingjie shaonian sharen shijian* (literally, "The Youth Murder Incident on Guling Street"). The Chinese title of *A Confucian Confusion* is *Duli shidai* ("The Age of Independence").

2. For an insightful analysis of gangster culture in *Mahjong*, see Gina Marchetti's "Taiwanese Triads in the Transnational Imagination: *Mahjong* and *Good-bye South Goodbye*" in *From Tian'anmen to Times Square: Transnational China on Global Screens* (Philadelphia: Temple University Press, 2006).

3. Huang Jianye, "A Confucian Confusion: Edward Yang Discusses His Career from Age Forty to the Making of *A Confucian Confusion*"/Ruzhe de kunhuo: Yang Dechang tan cong erli zhi nian dao *Duli shidai*," *Dianying xinshang* 12.5 (1994): 23.

4. *A Brighter Summer Day* has two versions—the theatrical-release version and the director's cut. The one used for this chapter is the longer version, almost twice the length of the theatrical release.

5. Huang Jianye, *Studies on Edward Yang's Films/Yang Dechang dianying yanjiu* (Taipei: Yuanliu, 1995), 154.

6. Homi Bhabha, "The Other Question: Stereotype, Discrimination and Discourse of Colonialism," *Screen* 24.6 (Nov.–Dec. 1983): 18–36.

7. For both definitions, see Webster's Third New International Dictionary (New York: Merriam, 1981), 1436.

8. There are many more examples of mimicry in the wild. See Wolfgang Wickler, *Mimicry in Plants and Animals*, trans. R. D. Martin (New York: McGraw-Hill, 1968).

9. See Rick Altman, *The American Film Musical.* (Bloomington: Indiana University Press, 1987).

10. Jane Feuer, *The Hollywood Musical* (London: Macmillan, 1982), 23.

11. The famous examples are Elvis Presley in *Jailhouse Rock*, the Beatles in *A Hard Day's Night*, the Who in *Tommy* (1975; dir. Ken Russell), Jimmy Cliff in *The Harder They Come* (1973; dir. Perry Henzell), and Diana Ross in *Lady Sings the Blues* (1972; dir. Sidney J. Furie). But the most "authentic" representation of rock stars comes from rockumentary—for example, Bob Dylan in *Don't Look Back* (1967; dir. D. A. Pennebaker) and Madonna in *Madonna: Truth or Dare* (1991; dir. Alex Keshishian).

12. Andrew Jones, *Like a Knife: Ideology and Genre in Contemporary Chinese Popular Music* (Ithaca, NY: East Asia Program, Cornell University, 1992), 115–128.

13. Lawrence Grossberg, "Is There Rock after Punk?" in Simon Frith and Andrew Goodwin., eds., *On Record: Rock, Pop and the Written Word* (London: Routledge, 1990), 115.

# 7

# Hollywood and Taiwan

## *Connections, Countercurrents, and Ang Lee's* Hulk

Gina Marchetti

Many filmmakers from Taiwan have staked out a claim on world screens; however, no other director from Taiwan has enjoyed Ang Lee's commercial success. As Shu-mei Shih has noted:

> Ang Lee's success has been perceived as Taiwan's national pride, even though Ang Lee refrains from expressing any Taiwan nativist sentiments about Taiwan's independence from China. His fame is considered a reflection of Taiwan's ascendancy in the global cultural arena.[1]

Like many other ethnic-Chinese directors working transnationally (including Wayne Wang, Evans Chan, and many others), Lee negotiates a career that spans Hollywood, Taiwan, Hong Kong, the People's Republic of China (PRC), American independent films, and Asian American film cultures. As a result, situating his oeuvre—not only geographically, but ideologically, culturally, and aesthetically—can be challenging.

With *Hulk* (2003), Lee lets one of his "bottled-up" (as Bruce Banner's mother describes her toddler-Hulk son) protagonists step out of the closet. Lee has always been a master of repression (*Sense and Sensibility*, 1995), of

---

From *Film Appreciation Journal* No. 120 (Summer 2004), 80–90 (translated into Chinese). Reprinted in English in *Film International* No. 12 (2004), 42–51. Reprinted in this volume with permission.

the decay of the patriarchal family (*The Ice Storm*, 1997), and of enduring paternal power (the "father knows best" trilogy of *Pushing Hands*, 1992, *The Wedding Banquet* 1993, and *Eat Drink Man Woman*, 1994) in the face of inevitable social change. Lee knows what it is like to be on the losing side (*Ride with the Devil*, 1999), within a corrupt empire (*Crouching Tiger, Hidden Dragon*, 2000). With *Hulk,* Lee collaborates again with writer and production partner James Schamus and with cinematographer Fredrick Elmes to revisit these themes.[2]

*Hulk* brings to a boil what has been churning in his oeuvre for a decade. In the commercial American film industry, it takes guts, after 9/11 and the wars in Afghanistan and Iraq, to let a man of color (albeit green) take on the United States military in the desert and survive. Given Hollywood's bottom line of profitability, the fact that Lee would let an out-of-control nonwhite "alien" rip army helicopters out of the sky and escape into the camouflage of a third world jungle needs to be given credit. The A-bomb be damned—the Hulk condenses the Viet Cong, Osama Bin Laden, and Saddam Hussein into one gargantuan challenge to the U.S. military-industrial complex. Could Ang Lee, like accused spy Wen Ho Lee, also from Taiwan, be feeling the pinch of not being white in America? Does the Hulk's anger go beyond adolescent hormones out of control to tap into a different rage coming from a third world location? Do the Hulk's associations with Latin America and Vietnam through his jungle hideaway resonate with the wars in the deserts of the Middle East? Like his creator Lee, the Hulk also seems to hail from Taiwan, from the Chinese diaspora, from Asian America, from the ranks of American minorities visible below the glass ceiling, targeted as "threats to national security" and under surveillance by the U.S. government. An Orientalist fantasy gone awry, *Hulk* shows that within the white, Western, establishment male (and, by extension, the American body politic) lurks the repressed man of color, perpetually angry, on the margins and on the loose, waiting to emerge as the apocalyptic destroyer of Western civilization or, perhaps, its ultimate salvation.

## Rooting Out the *Hulk*

In Lee's film, Lou Ferrigno, the television Hulk (1978–1982 series run), and Stan Lee, one of the creators (with Jack Kirby) of the Marvel-comic-book Hulk (original run 1962–1967), walk out of protagonist Bruce Banner's (Eric Bana's) lab building dressed as security guards complaining about lax security. The joke may be there to satisfy either television or comic-book fans in the know—even though those fans may be a generation removed from the adolescent and young adult males whose movie-theater attendance drives the production of Hollywood action films like *Hulk*. However, it also signals that Lee's film walks away from the Hulk's earlier incarnations. This is not the Ralph Bakshi cold-war-animated Hulk who fights the "yellow peril" Leader, also known as Khanga Khan, in the mid-1960s. This is also not the post-Watergate Hulk of the Jimmy Carter years. The late Bill Bixby played Dr. David Bruce Banner to Ferrigno's Hulk, hunted relentlessly not by a cold-war evil empire or megalomaniacal villain but by a Woodward-Bernstein wannabe, down-and-out tabloid journalist Jack McGee (Jack Colvin).

The Hulk still seems to represent science out of control, though, with his roots in *Frankenstein* and *The Strange Case of Dr. Jekyll and Mr. Hyde*, as well as the "id monster" from *Forbidden Planet* (1956). Because of his nuclear connection, he has a certain affinity to Godzilla, Gamera, Mothra, and other radiation victims or creations from Japan. He resembles mutant superheroes who find themselves both debilitated and enhanced by lab experiments gone wrong or nuclear explosions of various sorts in the post-Hiroshima era.

Gangly, out of control, misunderstood, unable to communicate effectively in the adult world, the Hulk becomes the adolescent past of the adult Banner—not a bad kid, just "green" and in need of a little self-control. In the 1970s television show, the middle-aged Banner just cannot see himself as the Hulk. He suffers through an internalized generation gap, a crisis in the representation of self in the mass media (hence, the journalist as villain), as well as a crisis of authority in the post-Watergate era when a fugitive accused of murder has more to fear from being hounded by the tabloids than from facing the criminal-justice system. (If it were not for journalists, Nixon would have gotten away with "murder.") The fact that the Hulk represents an America at war with itself because of color (black, not green) and corruption (usually rooted in the quest for the greenback) also marks this incarnation of the Hulk.

Fracturing the Hulk further, Ang Lee splits Dr. David Bruce Banner from the live-action television series into David and Bruce, making David's impulse to rid the world of Bruce, or the preschool Hulk, much less benign. Rather than using the accidental deaths of Banner's wife and a female lab associate that are at the root of the television series' narrative, Lee's film substitutes David Banner's murder of his wife as a botched attempt to kill the Hulk in the making—that is, his son Bruce. Lee plays on the idea of the divided self, questioning more than in other incarnations of the character the white mask of Bruce Banner in relation to the "authentic" nonwhite self outside of white authority. In *The Death of the Incredible Hulk* (1990), Bixby's Banner makes much of the fact that he has never seen the Hulk, but in Lee's film, the image of the Hulk looms in the mirror and Banner certainly sees himself as others see him.

Lee returns twice to Bruce Banner shaving in a steamy mirror—first with a dissolve to green presaging his eventual transformation and, later, during a hallucinatory moment when the Hulk bursts through the steamy mirror and tries to strangle Banner while shaving. It seems foolish that Bruce can rid himself of all the hairy associations with out-of-control primitive beasts like King Kong by shaving or that he may assure himself of his own maturity and keep the childlike Hulk at bay by engaging in an act that marks his adulthood. Lee provides the first version of the Hulk in which the character is conscious of seeing himself as others see him and aware of the impact his physical body has on the world around him. Like Fanon's image of white masks that hide black skin or W.E.B. DuBois' characterization of the "two-ness" that defines African Americans, the Hulk looks through the mirror to see how the white world views him. DuBois' words resonate with Lee's depiction of the Hulk:

> It is a peculiar sensation, this double-consciousness, this sense of always looking at one's self through the eyes of others, of measuring one's soul by the tape of a world that looks on in amused contempt and pity. One ever feels his two-ness—an American, a Negro; two souls, two thoughts, two unreconciled strivings; two warring ideals in one dark body, whose dogged strength alone keeps it from being torn asunder.[3]

However, Lee's Hulk is torn asunder. This Hulk exists in layers—adolescent and childhood fantasies vie with elements that seem to highlight questions of race and ethnic difference. However, although this Hulk may be similar to his earlier Marvel and Universal Television manifestations, Dr. Banner, elder and younger, has changed. Dr. Banner has stopped fighting the villains, stopped seeing his Hulk condition as "temporary" and subject to a "cure," and he has stopped trying to vindicate himself. This Dr. Banner (the elder played by Paul Kersey and Nick Nolte) is not just accused of killing a woman; he did, indeed, kill his wife, attempt to kill his son, and set mutant dogs on his son's girlfriend. This Dr. Banner (the younger) admits that he likes being the Hulk. While Betty, his former girlfriend, appears to be obsessed with a "cure," Bruce does not seem quite so eager to go back to "normal," to being a "puny human." This Hulk appears to be at home away from the white establishment, happy to be in the jungle, and none too eager to "cure" himself of his so-called "primitive" impulses.

As a creature of the 1960s, the Hulk owes a debt to Pop Art as well as Marvel Comics. Both part of American cold-war paranoia and its critique, Pop Art and popular comics arose out of the postnuclear age, the McCarthy hearings, the Cuban Missile Crisis, the assassination of John F. Kennedy, and the escalation of the Vietnam War. The comic-book aesthetic, exemplified by the work of Roy Lichtenstein (whose son, coincidentally, played Simon in Lee's *The Wedding Banquet*), could cordon off the moment, intensify the emotion, magnify the detail, and revel in the surface of comic-book mass culture that dealt with all the personal and global traumas of the postwar era abstracted and contained by oil on the artist's canvas. Ang Lee seems to be doing much the same with his filming of the Hulk comics. Lee aesthetically comments on the world of comic books, uses the split screen to reference popular culture but keep it at a remove, and explores the new- world-order (rather than cold-war) implications of the Hulk.

A Pop Art figure, the Hulk does well out of his original context, and he easily adapts, much like his creator Ang Lee, to new political, cultural, and aesthetic circumstances. Difficult to situate ideologically, *Hulk* can be read as an allegory of the American body politic finally accepting itself as multiracial, with the Hulk as hero, or *Hulk* may represent the reinvigoration of the myth of the threateningly primitive nonwhite pointing to the failure of the white American mainstream to maintain control. Perhaps, though, the Hulk should not be viewed as an emblem of American concerns at all, but as an icon of the Chinese diaspora, on the move around the world, burdened by history, race, and ethnicity as much as by the onus of modern science and human hubris. The Hulk is slippery and not that easy to pin down—existing as he does, and as Ang Lee does—somewhere between Hollywood and Taiwan.

## An Oedipal or a Confucian Tale?

If earlier incarnations of Banner/Hulk presented a divided character, Lee depicts Banner father/Banner son/Hulk as an indeterminate entity. In previous versions, the Hulk was simply the misunderstood, alienated child of the nuclear age, with Banner acting as the creature's creator and father—the child as the father of the man in reverse. Banner was at odds with General Ross in order to win from him his daughter Betty. In the film, the oedipal dimension of the comic-book-formula structure (set aside in the live-action television series) remains as the General and Bruce duke it out in the desert after Ross has warned Bruce to stay away from his daughter in no uncertain terms. Lee's film adds another layer by including another Dr. Banner as the *pater familias*, the Western patriarch who can dispose of the members of his extended family as he sees fit in order to maintain his control.[4] David Banner condenses a range of myths associated with Judeo-Christian and Greco-Roman civilization as he oscillates between the patriarch who must destroy his son to save the nation, like King David, or sacrifice his daughter for victory in battle, like Agamemnon. *Hulk* can be read as the story of Abraham and Isaac with a different ending.

Of course, the oedipal aspect of the film takes on another dimension as the narrative offers a fantasy of the son growing up to challenge the corrupt authority of the father, who had "punished" ("castrated" as Freud would say) the mother behind closed doors. *Hulk* returns repeatedly to this "primal scene" of the parents having a fight (as the child imagines, or sex, as Freud says) behind the closed bedroom door. When the door swings open, the son witnesses the penetration of the mother—sex turned into violence in the child's imagination, as Freud would have it. The mother dropping as the A-bomb destroys the lab in the distance conjures up the orgasmic images of sex and mass destruction that have become a clichéd part of the cinematic lexicon at least since Bruce Conner's *A Movie* (1958) and Stanley Kubrick's *Dr. Strangelove* (1964).

Edith Banner (Cara Buono) does resemble the dark-haired, dark-eyed Betty Ross (Jennifer Connelly), and this resemblance keeps the oedipal element in play. Bruce battles his biological father to possess the memory of his murdered mother as well as to claim Betty, who has been mesmerized by the old man (his father). Bruce also takes on the father-figure writ large, General Ross, in order to wrest Betty out from under the old man's (the general's) control. Before the film begins, Betty has already dumped Bruce, and, again, looking at the narrative from an oedipal perspective, the film becomes a quest for the remasculinization of the castrated Bruce as he struggles to assert his virile domination over an environment that includes his reluctant love object as well as very potent father figures.

Oedipal complexities aside, *Hulk* remains a global work that must travel outside the West. In fact, Lee's Hulk owes at least as much to Confucius as to Homer's epics and the Bible. In fact, the Hulk is not the first transnational green screen creature to be linked to Chinese culture and Confucian morality. Golden Harvest's *Teenage Mutant Ninja Turtles* (1987), for example, owes a heavy cultural debt to Chinese civilization with the Confucian bent of its mutant rat leader, and *Star Wars*' Yoda also condenses green skin and Chinese philosophy into a single futuristic body. The generational conflicts presented in *Hulk* really have as much, if not more, to do with Confucian notions of order and a Chinese conception of the patriarchy as they do with Oedipus and Freud. In fact, filial piety becomes a key issue in the development of not only the relationship between Bruce and David Banner, but also in the relationship between Betty and General Ross.

Lee often talks in interviews about his rocky relationship with his own father. Lee's father was disappointed that his son did not do well on the college entrance exams in Taiwan and that he was a "late bloomer" pursuing a career in the arts. Although Lee's father said nothing about the "father knows best" trilogy, which featured ethnic-Chinese families,[5] he did go to see *Hulk*. Reportedly, he had a favorable impression of his son's version of the comic book.

In *Hulk*, both David Banner and General Ross represent patriarchs in a Confucian universe where family relationships mirror the welfare of the nation-state. Visually, no boundary exists between the desert military installation in which they work and the suburban tract homes in which they raise their families. The younger generation, out of control, threatens not only the hierarchy that is based on age and gender within the nuclear family; it threatens the very foundations of the nation as Bruce Banner becomes a potential weapon of mass destruction and Betty his possible accomplice.

The conflict becomes classically Confucian. The welfare of the individual family is at odds with the greater good of the nation. David Banner cannot refuse his wife's request for a child, and the need to perpetuate his lineage (even if it is mutant and monstrous) becomes a greater imperative than the well-being of the state. The individual patriarchal unit that is out of sync with the state can bode only ill for all involved, and David Banner struggles throughout the narrative to regain control of his offspring.

No doubt David sees Bruce as belonging to him, and he demands the respect and filial devotion that he perceives as his due. David treats Bruce's body as his rightful property—taking the blood of the toddler and demanding the flesh of the adult. When David describes lunging at the toddler with a knife, he calls it "doing a father's work." Just as filial Chinese children dutifully give their flesh and blood to concoct medicines to cure ailing parents, David demands Bruce's flesh in order to "stabilize" his own mutant condition. However, the film shows the tender, as well as cruel, nature of patriarchal privilege. The recurring image of Bruce and David playing out a fight by using a stuffed toy dinosaur and a monkey indicates the way in which warmth and violence cannot be separated in their relationship. Bruce's first and last memories of his father involve tenderness, and an image of Bruce's father as a young man wishing him "sweet dreams" precedes the Hulk's descent into oblivion at the hands of the massive force David Banner has become at the film's climax.

The scene in which David insists on seeing Bruce in exchange for his surrender to the authorities, for example, unleashes all the nightmares that sons face when confronted by paternal power. It is a very theatrical scene. David makes his entrance in a large, dark, cavernous room, with two spotlights crisscrossing the stage on which Bruce sits opposite a second empty chair waiting for his shaggy, unkempt father to sit. Taking his seat, David has the advantage in not being strapped down like Bruce. He can freely move around, gesticulating wildly, during the conversation that turns into a harangue. He looms close to Bruce as he expresses extreme disappointment in his son, whom he calls a "superficial shell." He has come to see his "real" son—that is, his virile son, the son capable of serving him and perpetuating his ambitions. Bruce has broken down in tears. Angrily, David tells him to stop "bawling" as if his son were still four years old and not living up to the patriarch's expectations that the boy "act like a man."

While the broken Bruce has issues with the man he loves, who also killed his mother, David has another axe to grind—not with his son, his family, but with the nation-state. Even David's mad scientist veneer cannot really take the sting out of his tirade against the U.S. military: "Think of all the men out there in their uniforms, inflicting pain around the globe, think of all the harm they've done to humanity." While David may have megalomaniacal dreams about the Hulk as a new hero who can "save" the world from civilization, he does have a point about the mess his own complicity with the American military-industrial complex has created. At this point, David Banner comes close to J. Robert Oppenheimer with second thoughts about the purposes to which his scientific discoveries may be put. His experiments were originally designed to strengthen the "men out there in their uniforms," not destroy himself and wreak havoc on his own family line.

The crisis in Confucian orthodoxy comes when the older generation of fathers cannot clean up the mess they have made of their families and the state. Bruce is pulled apart by the rivalry between the General and his father. Mad-scientist David Banner wants to continue his experiments with "his real son," the Hulk, while the General wants to keep the Hulk (Bruce) imprisoned indefinitely. Bruce has fond memories of the man who tucked him in at night and rage against the man who killed his mother. He knows he is out of control, but likes it, since the virile Hulk, ironically, brings him closer to Betty.

Betty, the figure who should be the "new woman," liberated and beyond patriarchal control, ends up as the postfeminist figure of compliancy and complicity in *Hulk*. Following a neo-Confucian model, the General does not take much interest in his daughter. Betty intimates that he is "emotionally distant," and Bruce assumes she is estranged from him. Quite the contrary, when Betty has problems first with Talbot and later with Bruce, she immediately turns to the General with implicit trust.

Even when the General drops the A-bomb on the poor Hulk, Betty comforts her father by putting a hand on his shoulder—paralleling the hand that he put on her shoulder when they watched the desert lab go up in atomic smoke thirty years previously. Although by their final phone conversation Betty seems to have finally gotten the message that her father is not a "nice guy," she also must admit it is far too late to make amends. If Bruce is still around, he must, by now, know that contact with Betty spells trouble. Even if she does not turn him in at this stage, the General's wiretaps will do the job for her.

Although he may feel nostalgia for paternal authority and continue to hope for the "sweet dreams" of his boyhood, the rebellious son, rather than the pseudo-liberated daughter, remains the bulwark against Confucian orthodoxy in *Hulk*'s universe. He carries within him anger against the power of male authority, outrage at the injustice of the dominant system, and the constant threat that he may come out of hiding, return, and end the repression on which the social order is founded.

## From Bruce to Wen Ho Lee

The tearful confrontation between Bruce and David before David bites into an electric power cord and sends the entire army bunker into pandemonium reminds me of the scene between Hsiao Kang and his father in the gay bathhouse in Tsai Ming-Liang's *The River* (1997). The father fucks with, fucks up, and fucks over his son. In the case of Hsiao Kang, the son just takes the slap in the face afterwards, while, in the case of Bruce, in the final apocalyptic moment, the son associates it all with "sweet dreams."

Two diasporic Chinese directors—one from Malaysia who has settled in Taipei and one from Taiwan, the child of displaced Kuomintang (KMT) mainlanders, who has settled in the United States—meet around this image of a father and son. Before Nixon went to Beijing in 1972, the buildup of all that military power in the American desert was there to fight a Cold War in which Taiwan, the Republic of China, was a major player. *Hulk* begins in 1966 as the war in Vietnam was escalating, as Taiwan's importance as a staging ground for U.S. military operations in the Pacific was becoming even more vital. Certainly, David Banner's as well as General Ross's misguided allegiance to the U.S. military parallels the KMT's faith in American support against the PRC. Ross and Banner, like their KMT counterparts, represent a generation of old men out of touch with reality, creating weapons for a war that will never be fought, and ruining the lives of their children in the process. The Hulk's innate talent for *qing gong* gives the character an even clearer Chinese identity, linking him to a tradition of lighter-than-air Chinese martial heroes favored by the Hong Kong and Taiwan martial-arts tradition in the cinema, and it seems appropriate that Ang Lee goes back to "Bruce" (as in Bruce Lee) for the Hulk's given name.

The Hulk's circumstances also seem to resonate with the misfortunes of another diasporic Chinese from Taiwan. As Ang Lee and his collaborators were creating their cinematic Hulk in 2002, Wen Ho Lee's battle with the U.S. government was still quite topical. Dan Stober and Ian Hoffman's *A Convenient Spy: Wen Ho Lee and the Politics of Nuclear Espionage* was published in 2002 by Simon and Schuster, and Wen Ho Lee's own account, written with noted Civil Rights advocate Helen Zia (who had established her reputation with another case involving a miscarriage of justice revolving around an Asian American, Vincent Chin), *My Country Versus Me: The First-Hand Account by the Los Alamos Scientist Who Was Falsely Accused*, came out around the same time from Hyperion Press.

After being incarcerated for nine months, much of that time in solitary confinement, without bail or the benefit of a trial because he supposedly posed a "threat to national security," Wen Ho Lee finally pleaded guilty to charges considerably reduced from treason and espionage and was sentenced to time served. However, the case exposed a raw nerve involving racial profiling and the xenophobic targeting of Asian Americans, specifically ethnic-Chinese immigrants. Janet Reno's characterization of Dr. Lee could easily apply to either Dr. David or Dr. Bruce Banner:

> Dr Lee is no hero. He is not an absentminded professor. He is a felon. He committed a very serious, calculated crime, and he pled guilty to it. He abused the trust of the American people by putting at risk some of our core national security secrets. He had one of the highest security clearance levels possible, granting him access to the most sensitive of nuclear weapons information. . . . He had access to the Los Alamos computer system that was designed precisely to be secure against unauthorized intrusions.[6]

Born in Taiwan and himself married to an ethnic-Chinese scientist (a microbiologist, thus closer to the Banners' field than to Wen Ho Lee's), Ang Lee may have felt some particular affinity to the plight of both Drs. Banner because of the Wen Ho Lee case. Given that the film's *mise-en-scène* is peppered with nuclear explosions, desert laboratories, and dense concentrations of computer screens, the world of Wen Ho Lee's Los Alamos does not seem to be far removed from the desert military installation that gave birth to the Hulk. Like Wen Ho Lee, both David and Bruce Banner are incarcerated in the narrative. Bruce's incarceration is vividly depicted on screen, and many of the specifics directly mirror Wen Ho Lee's imprisonment—bound hand and foot, placed in solitary confinement, and kept in isolation. Bruce's unconscious face in his coffinlike box transported under heavy guard by military helicopter provides a particularly eerie evocation of Wen Ho Lee's confinement. The nine months that Wen Ho Lee spent in custody may well have started as the "indefinite" sentence given to Bruce by General Ross because of the Hulk's "threat to national security." [7]

Like many KMT members and their children who ended up in Taiwan after 1949, Wen Ho Lee would seem to anyone with an ounce of historical or political sense a highly unlikely candidate to sell anything to Communist China. However, Ang Lee provides another angle on the situation of Asian American scientists frustrated by the glass ceiling and the lack of control over their intellectual labor by introducing Talbot, not as a minion of General Ross, but as a former member of the military establishment who has gone over to the much more vicious and unscrupulous industrial establishment. The steps from military secret to basic science to bankable intellectual commodity for corporate exploitation are not that hard to imagine.

In fact, Talbot emerges as a much more sinister villain than either of the battling patriarchs. As a representative of Atheon—that is, the industrial rather than the military establishment—Talbot terrorizes Bruce for profit rather than for any semblance of "national security." In a nightmare of privatization, Talbot at one point wrests authority from General Ross and takes over the experiments involving the Hulk. The machinations that turn the tables on Ross and allow Talbot, a civilian, to take command remain opaque. However, the film intimates that, at some level, the profit motive plus tacit government support for the corporate sector outweigh any consideration of the national good. Transnational profits trump national security. Just as Talbot and Ross dance around control of the Hulk, the U.S. government waltzes around the profound contradictions between official foreign policy and corporate interests. Money drives America's push-and-pull policies, for example, in relation to Taiwan, in which it is heavily invested both financially and militarily, just as Ross and Talbot struggle over the fate of the Hulk with little regard for Bruce's, the Hulk's, or the general welfare of either the nation or the planet.

## Rooting for the Hulk

The massive, "primitive," angry Hulk, however, shows as little concern for making a profit as he does in furthering U.S. military interests. The Hulk is nonaligned. The Hulk takes command of the desert, leaping through Monument Valley (and all it represents from its appearances in John Ford's westerns) to the strains of Middle-Eastern-inspired techno-world music. While the American western and Bruce's mother dream of a garden in the desert ("desert flowers" from Ford's *The Man Who Shot Liberty Valance* [1962] turn up as Mrs. Banner's favorite perfume), the Hulk sticks to the barren landscape, preferring its majesty to the "puny" attempts of white civilization to destroy its beauty. Even after the U.S. military has turned his territory into a "parking lot," as so many bombing missions in Hanoi and Baghdad were supposed to do in those places, the Hulk emerges unscathed.

With the Hulk inside him, Bruce hides out in the jungles of Latin America, another third world realm under assault from white "civilization." He knows he is a creature of the third world, and like the rest of the third world he is a creation and victim of European-American military expansionism and neocolonial corporate greed. The contra-like bandito who harasses Bruce at *Hulk*'s conclusion keeps the first world's penetration into the third world in the foreground. As Trinh T. Minh-ha has pointed out, within every third world there is a first world and vice versa, so that the Hulk's "primitiveness" comes directly from the most advanced Western science and his rage cannot be disengaged from that fact. The Hulk lurks in the shadows of the first world, always ready to reemerge from the margins if provoked.

The U.S. military has nuked him, corporate America has tried literally to bleed him dry, and liberal humanism has thrown up its hands after its intimate links to the military-industrial establishment have been exposed. Saying "sorry," as General Ross does near the end, may simply not be enough. However, the Hulk remains ambivalent. After threatening the Golden Gate Bridge, one of the monuments often listed as imperiled by foreign terrorist groups, the Hulk latches onto a military jet that is flying out of control in an effort to save this American symbol. The image is reminiscent of King Kong being harassed by planes atop the Empire State Building, except that in *Hulk* the symbol of American technological mastery is saved by the creature, not by the American planes; this also redeems another image of airplanes penetrating another American icon, the World Trade Center in New York, on September 11, 2001 (instead of villains from the third world destroying an American icon, a representative of the non-white (green) third world saves the Golden Gate). Again, the Hulk's allegiance vacillates and his sympathies remain unclear.

Ideologically overdetermined as a disgruntled worker, an angry minority professional outraged by the glass ceiling, a displaced child of the KMT, an Asian American targeted by racial profiling, and a rebellious son unable to cope with the patriarchy, the Hulk can never represent a clear political position. (The Wen Ho Lee incident happens during Bill Clinton's presidency, for example, whereas General Ross reports to a young African American woman who resembles Condoleezza Rice, and she, in turn, reports to a president off on a fishing trip who resembles George W. Bush). Just as the specific political administrations remain difficult to pin down in *Hulk*, the Hulk himself remains a figure of general frustration, as much in tune with the dilemma of teenage nerds who cannot get a date on Saturday night as with Wen Ho Lee, Osama Bin Laden, Saddam Hussein, or any other real or imagined threat to the U.S. government and the American nation.

The Hulk is also something "more," as David Banner enjoys reminding his son, since the Hulk, additionally, concretizes the cutting edge of computer-generated imaging (CGI). In many respects, he is less a character and more an "image," subject to the abilities and limitations of digital technology at Industrial Light and Magic.[8] As a product, *Hulk* circulates as much as psychological drama, comic nostalgia, action-adventure, and digital virtuosity as it does as any sort of ideological critique or political intervention.

## Against the Hollywood Grain

Perhaps asking the Hulk to carry the burden of the complex interconnections between Taiwan and America within global film culture demands too much of the big green guy. In fact, other filmmakers operating somewhere between Taiwan and the United States have looked at this relationship more critically. Shu Lea Cheang's feature film *Fresh Kill* (1994) provides just one example of a film that resonates with *Hulk* in certain key respects.

In *Fresh Kill*,[9] Cheang creates a science-fiction vision that links the cavalier treatment of nuclear waste and industrial pollution to global politics stretching from Taiwan's Orchid Island to New York's Staten Island. As in *Hulk*, Taiwan is imaginatively linked to the U.S. military, corporate greed, and out-of-control Western technology. Through editing, *Fresh Kill* connects the urban spaces of Staten Island with the remote rural fishing villages of Orchid Island. However, more than just a cleverly matched montage connects these spaces. The squatters' village in New York really does not seem that different from the fishing village on Orchid Island. Ang Lee has made a similar point in an interview: "Although their bodies are not in the United States, they are immigrants psychologically. . . . What is the difference between living in Flushing, New York and Taipei? Except that one knows America better and sees more Americans, there is not much difference."[10] Televisions, tee shirts, and tourists penetrate both spaces. Both environments allow for military and corporate dumping, and both suffer the contamination of these excesses of American capitalism.

As Seth Silberman has pointed out in his analysis of *Fresh Kill*,[11] Cheang's film fits into the category that Fredric Jameson has termed the "conspiratorial text." An argument can be made that *Hulk* fits within this category as well. For Jameson, the conspiratorial text has less to do with the veracity of what is brought to light than with modeling a process of cognitive resistance: "Nothing is gained by having been persuaded of the definitive verisimilitude of this or that conspiratorial hypothesis: but in the intent to hypothesize, in the desire called cognitive mapping—therein lies the beginning of wisdom."[12]

Both *Fresh Kill* and *Hulk* blend fictional issues with actual events that seem more incredible than fiction and are subject to elaborate cover-ups. However, *Fresh Kill* refuses to envision a world beyond the need for political action, demonstrating the continuing currency of political critique outside the confines of *Hulk*'s cartoon frames and the generic conventions of the Hollywood action-fantasy.

## Notes

1. Shu-Mei Shih, "Globalisation and Minoritisation: Ang Lee and the Politics of Flexibility," *New Formations* 40 (2000): 94.

2. For more on the production process, see David E. Williams, "Temper, Temper," *American Cinematographer* 84.7 (July 2003): 34–45.

3. W.E.B. DuBois, *The Souls of Black Folk*, 1903 (NY: Dover, 1994), 2.

4. For more on the oedipal nature of *Hulk*, see Rob White, "The Rage of Innocence," *Sight and Sound* (August 2003): 34ff; http://www.bfi.org.uk/sightandsound/2003_08/hulk.php.

5. Interview with Ang Lee, "The Long and the Shirt of It," *Guardian Unlimited* (July 6, 2003): http://film.guardian.co.uk/interview/interviewpages/0,6737,992144,00.html.

6. PBS, On-Line News Hour (September 26, 2000): http://www.pbs.org/newshour/bb/law/july-dec00/wenholee-congress_9–26.html. Accessed December 2003.

7. It is interesting to note that Ang Lee makes the lab personnel lily-white, with the exception of an African American security guard. To show that the film is not "about race" and not "about" Wen Ho Lee, *Hulk* does provide one unnamed Asian

aide-de-camp as General Ross's personal assistant, houseboy, and secretary, who answers the phone for him and brings him documents. His service to the white general tacitly shows that the American military is not racist, but open to all races and ethnicities. Thus, the Asian assistant imaginatively covers up any implicit anti-Asian bias alluded to in the film that might alienate viewers.

8. For more on the digital creation of *Hulk*, see Ron Magid, "Growing Pains," *American Cinematographer* 84.7 (July 2003): 46–57.

9. For more on *Fresh Kill*, see my "Cinema Frames, Videoscapes, and Cyberspace: Exploring Shu Lea Cheang's *Fresh Kill*," *positions: east asia cultures critique* 9.2 (Fall 2001): 401–422.

10. Quoted in Shu-Mei Shih, "Globalisation and Minoritisation," 95. From *China Times Weekly* 65 (March April 1993), 75.

11. Seth Clark Silberman, "Fish Lips and Television Sets: *Fresh Kill*'s Critical (Queer) Consciousness," *Fifteenth Anniversary Asian American International Film Festival* (catalogue). (Washington, DC: Asian American Arts and Media, 1996), 28.

12. Fredric Jameson, *The Geopolitical Aesthetic: Cinema and Space in the World System* (Bloomington: Indiana University Press, 1995), 3.

# 8

# Becoming Hollywood?

## *Hong Kong Cinema in the New Century*

CHUCK KLEINHANS

Hong Kong news-item headline, April 2000: "Tung sees into SAR's [Special Administrative Region's] future after Disneyland visit." Photo with caption: "Taking the Mickey. Tung Chee-hwa pats Minnie Mouse as Mickey looks on in a visit to California's Disneyland. He met Disney's chief executives Michael Eisner and president Robert Iger." The write-up:

> Tung Chee-hwa came face-to-face with the future of Hong Kong tourism yesterday—eagerly re-acquainting himself with Mickey Mouse, patting Minnie Mouse on the cheek and bumping into popular Chinese heroine Mulan. . . . "It's been a wonderful visit for me personally," he said after a tour in vast contrast to his two days of congressional lobbying and White House and State Department meetings in Washington. . . . [He adds,] "It has made me even more confident that the building of Disneyland in Hong Kong will strengthen Hong Kong's economy and bring our tourism to world-class standards. Disney's innovation and technology is unbelievable and I am sure will upgrade our own entertainment industry". . . . He returned to a San Francisco residence he owns and will be on leave until he comes home at the weekend.[1]

I am not an expert on Hong Kong or Hong Kong cinema, nor on Chinese cinema, but I do feel confident in making some observations about

Hollywood cinema. So when I was asked to participate in a Hong Kong conference that asked, "Do we need to follow Hollywood to become more competitive," I felt that I had something to say. Initially I proposed to answer this question by examining some films made within Hollywood by Hong Kong directors and actors and considering what is gained and lost in the transnational crossing.[2] However, on further thought, I realized that this was not a sufficient base for analysis because actual conditions are much more complicated than any bipolar model of Hollywood and Hong Kong has assumed.

Consider *Romeo Must Die* (2000), starring Jet Li and Aaliyah, directed by a Polish-born cinematographer who worked in Hollywood throughout the 1980s and 1990s, Andrzej Bartkowiak. Shot in Vancouver, although set in San Francisco and Oakland and including a side trip to Hong Kong, the film presents the familiar Romeo-and-Juliet story with the lovers' families presented as warring gang families: one Chinese American, the other African American. Simply laying out this sketchy outline reveals the film as a transnational and multicultural text. Is it then also a Hong Kong film, a Hollywood film, a hybrid, or something else? I want to address that question in the process of developing my discussion, but I also acknowledge that this set of concerns is apparently of little interest in the United States—where it is just assumed to be an American film—but of considerable interest in Hong Kong.

A quick survey of a Web site for Hong Kong film critics[3] shows that both films directed by Hong Kong directors working in Hollywood and U.S. films starring Hong Kong actors have garnered compelling critical interest and are basically treated as part of Hong Kong cinema.[4] Thus the site presents key reviews of *Maximum Risk* (dir. Ringo Lam, 1996), *Double Team* (dir. Tsui Hark, 1997), *Mr. Magoo* (dir. Stanley Tong, 1997), *Face/Off* (dir. John Woo, 1997), *The Replacement Killers* (dir. Antoine Fuqua, 1998), and others. These can be added to the substantial body of work of Jackie Chan overseas, as well as one-shots such as the Jean-Claude Van Damme vehicle *Knock Off* (dir. Tsui Hark, 1998, Hong Kong/United States). At the Hong Kong conference, Kin Yan Elyssa Szeto discussed *Anna and the King* (dir. Andy Tennant, 1999) as a Hong Kong-Hollywood hybrid, and has continued by examining transnational Asian American martial-arts films.[5] Even the nominally Taiwan-U.S. production of *Crouching Tiger, Hidden Dragon* (dir. Ang Lee, 2000) used a Hong Kong crew as well as Hong Kong stars. In subsequent years, the pace of cross-fertilization has increased, and we could add to the list easily.

We know the familiar story of the reception of Hong Kong action cinema in the United States: the initial interest in Bruce Lee and Kung Fu films in the 1970s spawned development of a U.S. product containing domestic martial-arts stars such as Chuck Norris and later Steven Seagal, as well as foreign arrivals such as Van Damme. Initially, the imported Hong Kong cult film was domesticated as a U.S. low-budget genre. But at the same time, Hollywood itself was undergoing a large change, both economically and in terms of genres and style: the emergence of the "high-concept" film, and specifically the blockbuster masculine action film most recognizable in the 1980s in the series of Sylvester Stallone vehicles and flourishing through successful series such as *Lethal Weapon* and *Die Hard*.[6]

It is also now familiar legend that portrays figures such as Quentin Tarantino, video-store clerk and enthusiast for Hong Kong action films during the 1980s (especially the work of John Woo), who imitated those films in their own work. Two points are worth remarking on here. First, if we are concerned with a primarily linear history of development populated by auteur directors and stars, this legend has considerable explanatory purchase. Second, the legend replays the simple logics of imperial absorption and countercultural resistance. Thus the West can be charged with Orientalizing and expropriating on the large scale and also with resisting and appreciating on the small scale. Fan culture—in the small sense of kung fu film cultists, but also in the larger sense that includes knowledgeable practitioners of martial arts, members of the Chinese diaspora, and (some) academic specialists in Asian cinema—provides for the production of another knowledge.

But before drawing any quick conclusion, we would also have to account for what seems like a postmodern appropriation of stylistic flourishes: in Tarantino's *Reservoir Dogs* (1992), the heist shootout and later gun-to-gun confrontations; in *True Romance* (dir. Tony Scott, 1993), the final slow-motion shootout among multiple opposed groups and individuals; and the bullet or knife point-of-view (POV) shots in *Natural Born Killers* (dir. Olive Stone, 1994). These are rather obvious borrowings that are not particularly profound in terms of influence. Rather, they are best seen as part of the endless absorption of stylistic elements that has made the Hollywood cinema so powerful in its classic period and beyond.[7]

In the largest sense, the Hollywood model of narrative cinema has been the overarching and dominant style for world cinema, especially during and after the 1920s. Thus we would recognize that greater Chinese cinema in general and Hong Kong cinema in particular share a broad set of concepts that govern dramatic organization, storytelling, and the way film technology is used. In that framework, it is easy to see how a figure such as John Woo can be influenced by Hollywood films, which were, of course, readily available to him growing up in Hong Kong. He has said as much in interviews, often remarking on how dance sequences in Hollywood musicals shaped his understanding of how to organize the gunplay sequences for which he is so well known and regarded. Woo was always already within the shadow of Hollywood as he began filmmaking. But of course he would not be so notable or influential if he had not also developed within the traditions, practices, and themes distinctive to Hong Kong cinema.

Most important, Woo worked with particular stars whose talents and images contributed to his recognizable authorship in the cinema.

So, when we speak of Hollywood and Hong Kong cinemas, what are we most concerned with, and what lies below the surface of the discussion? What is the aim of the comparison, and what are its anxieties? Are we addressing a matter of national cinema, even if we now recognize Hollywood as transnational in finance, production, and distribution, and Hong Kong was never a nation, going straight from colony to SAR without the phase of postcoloniality? Is the discussion about the status of auteur directors and stars when they cross over? By looking at significant changes from the Hong Kong films to the Hollywood films of these directors and stars, we can ask if author and star-image identities are being changed, erased, or redeployed in the cross-cultural transition. Is crossover viable, and if so, at what price?

Let me take what may seem like an odd detour here to gain some distance on the question. A historical analogy may be useful. Part of the genius of the Hollywood system, as we all know, has been to use imported talent: stars, directors, and technicians. From Charles Chaplin and Rudolph Valentino to Slavko Vorkapitch and Marlene Dietrich through Alfred Hitchcock, Carmen Miranda, and Douglas Sirk to Paul Verhoven, Salma Hayek, and Jean Reno and even Godzilla. So now it's John Woo, Chow Yun Fat, Michelle Yeoh, and Jet Li.[8] Consider Austria, which never had a strong film industry, but which sent a remarkable group of directors to Hollywood: Erich von Stroheim, Josef von Sternberg, Fritz Lang, Billy Wilder, Edgar Ulmer, Otto Preminger, and Fred Zinneman. We could even try to constitute an Austrian cinema in exile (although I don't think this is the most productive way to think of these figures) by marking the recurrence of certain themes in their work such as depictions of central Europe, memory, the exile's experience, an interior exile out of time and out of place, a particular sense of loss after World War II, and especially in Wilder and Ulmer, a dark cynicism and bitterness about the United States.

Should we be trying to read the U.S. work of Hong Kong directors in the same way—as reflecting an essential "Hong Kongness" that travels with them? Is Stanley Tong's version of *Mr. Magoo* a continuation of certain aspects of Hong Kong culture and identity? Should the film be bracketed along with *Happy Together* (dir. Wong Kar Wai, 1997) as Hong Kong cinema set in another place? Or is Tong simply an opportunistic sellout seizing the main chance? I provide this ridiculous example only to underline that for Hong Kong critics (or at least the ones I have access to) there is always a deeply ambivalent approach to Hong Kong identity and its existence in attenuated forms when actors and directors work abroad.[9] As an outsider I cannot add to that discussion, but only be aware of it and find it remarkably refreshing to observe the openness to consider all questions, to criticize and comment on all matters of change, displacement, and incessant transition. At the same time, however, I have to notice a downside of an obsessive anxiety among Hong Kong intellectuals about Hong Kong identity.

The question of an essential Hong Kong identity can be examined beyond the perhaps subtle auteur expressions of directors and considered more openly with actors. While Jackie Chan developed his career within the framework of being a Hong Kong superstar, how he is read changes with his own global transition.[10] (A movement highlighted most explicitly in *Who Am I?* [dir. Benny Chan and Jackie Chan, 1998], itself often read as an allegory of the 1997 handover of Hong Kong to the People's Republic of China.) As various critics have noted, Jackie becomes "cute" in his Hollywood biracial buddy incarnations with Chris Tucker and Owen Wilson.[11] While the most successful international star on a worldwide scale, his work has faltered in some recent films.[12] Yet he also exists as a star property in internationally syndicated television animation ("Jackie Chan Adventures") and continues to "go global" with vehicles such as *Around the World in 80 Days* (dir. Frank Coraci, 2004). Does this transnationalization imply a loss of Hong Kong identity? In Hong Kong or in the East Asia region, or among fans who can appreciate the culturally specific skills in films such as *Drunken Master* (dir. Yuen Woo-ping, 1978), Chan's earlier films maintain a tension between modernity and social tradition. But clearly something is lost in the process of marketing a star image on an international platform. While Jackie Chan has been imported to the United States as "lovable" (but not notably sexual), as he ages that quality is harder to retain—one reason the animation version of Jackie may have a longer career in the future than the cinematographic version.

Similarly, the importing of other Hong Kong male stars such as Chow Yun Fat and Jet Li presents problems of ideological translation, particularly around Western expectations of normative masculinity and the Hollywood norm of a double plot of drama and love. The classic Hollywood film narrative uses two lines of action, one of which is a heterosexual romance.[13] In the United States, the romance line involves conspicuous markers of masculinity that are emphatically enacted in scenes involving the couple. In other cultures, the proper markers of masculinity may more obviously involve the male role within the extended family and social standing in the community. Furthermore, in much of the world, intimate displays are not appropriate for public consumption. Thus the cross-cultural problem here involves the structural nature of the dominant Hollywood convention and the culturally different markers of appropriate masculinity. The cultural difference in expectations has repercussions for Asian male stars. Thus, in discussing *Romeo Must Die*, Richard Corliss praises Jet Li's martial skills but notes "a romance so tepid it is consummated with a hug."[14] Similarly, in his Hollywood incarnations, Chow Yun Fat has been handicapped by cultural limits on playing the romantic hero. While his Hong

Kong roles display a range of characters (for example, police officer, hit man, and god of gamblers) and show a talent for comic, dramatic, and action acting, in general his masculinity is granted a priori by social role and bearing, and thus it is simply presented, not performed in romantic behavior.

But further analysis requires a baseline reorientation. Cultural analysis must be linked to political economy before it flies off into wishful thinking. In recent years Hollywood has attained new heights in revenue.[15] In 1998, domestic (North American) theater admissions hit $1.4 billion. Box-office revenue reached $6.88 billion. Worldwide home video revenue was $8.1 billion. The blockbuster hit *Titanic* returned $3.2 billion in 1998 on a $200 million investment. At the same time costs are rising. The worldwide revenues for blockbuster films easily override cases of domestic box-office failure (as happened with *Godzilla* in 1998), thus spurring increasing commitments to simultaneous global openings. Hollywood relies on overseas revenue as never before. The economic logic of blockbusters continues relentlessly for the studios. The mammoth hits are necessary to carry the overhead of the operation and the inevitable losers. And today the hits are potentiated through multiple revenue streams represented in different media (theatrical, television, video rental, digital video disc [DVD] sales, soundtrack recordings, and so forth) and in licensed merchandise encompassing music, print publishing, theme parks, retail stores, resorts, video games, and television spin-offs.

At the same time, through the primary vehicle of the Motion Picture Association of America (MPAA), Hollywood and its parent conglomerates have been extremely aggressive, and for the most part very effective, in attacking trade barriers to film and other media entertainment throughout the world. Attaining World Trade Organization status produces abolition of media trade barriers. The results for local and regional markets has been extreme, undercutting local film production in many countries and sharply reducing regional overseas revenue for Hong Kong and other centers of film production that previously depended on export revenues. At home the MPAA and media conglomerates have successfully extended copyright, so that, for example, Mickey Mouse, who was about to enter the public domain in 2003, is now protected for another twenty years. And Hollywood has been especially concerned with issues of software piracy, particularly in Asia. It has also been moving rapidly to accomplish a new technological change in distribution—digital projection via satellite—that holds the promise of simultaneous worldwide premieres and a reduction in piracy through signal encoding, while also making existing projection systems economically obsolete and thus reducing competition by weeding out those who cannot afford to work at the same technical level. At the same time, Hollywood is strategizing on how to respond to the growth of commercial and pay television abroad, as well as the changing nature of foreign markets, which show declines in theatrical exhibition as populations acquire greater home access to more channels and other television options.

In the United States, the pressures for putting more and more money into blockbusters has produced a situation in which big films keep getting bigger and more expensive. Stars are now taking "back-end" deals, participating in first-dollar grosses, while studios seek to spread their risk by co-financing and splitting rights with other studios. The number of medium-budget films have been drastically reduced while there has been an expansion of low-budget niche-market product—for example, the independent or "Sundance" film, which itself becomes more and more uniform as it is brought into the mainstream. The odd result is globalization on the high end and fragmentation and niche marketing on the low end.

With this context in mind, I want to turn to an aesthetic analysis, David Bordwell's notable "Aesthetics in Action: Kung Fu, Gunplay, and Cinematic Expressivity."[16] In a comparative analysis, using the original *Lethal Weapon* (dir. Richard Donner, 1987) and *Hearty Response* (Law Man, 1986) as his examples, Bordwell points out that Hollywood action film uses a predominant style that maximizes movement: action in every image, usually showing no movement completed; a short shot length; and camera movement along with actors in motion. The result, he argues, is that performance is minimized while other techniques compensate for this change. The overall effect is to produce a feeling of "general excitement." In contrast, Hong Kong films show more kinetic impact and are more "readable," using a "pause-burst-pause" pattern in actor movement and cinematic technique. Thus actor performance is more pronounced and prominent in the Hong Kong films. Bordwell's analysis is clear and convincing and demonstrates how a much more modest and thrifty production process can produce important aesthetic features in a dramatic narrative.

In his comparative analysis of late 1980s action cinema, Bordwell validates the Hong Kong film by validating its superior economy of activity, but his essay does not exhaust the subject. Hollywood action films tend to combine elements from a variety of actions: most obviously the chase, the shootout, and hand-to-hand combat. Each of these can be further subdivided and elaborated. Thus the vehicular chase in the James Bond films always includes special features and weapons built into the car, and the auto chase reaches a notable high point in *The French Connection* (dir. William Friedkin, 1971), after which directors tend to outdo each other in clever additions to the number of vehicles and crashes, and to extend the types of transportation (motorcycles, cars, trucks, busses, trains, subways, boats, planes, and so forth) and places involved. Hong Kong does not provide the same range of places for pursuit as southern California, say. (Increasingly, Hong Kong films are being made elsewhere: for example, Thailand, Malaysia, and Vancouver, as are Hollywood films seeking economic breaks.) But it is also obvious that modestly budgeted work literally cannot afford to tie up vast amounts of public space and transportation to stage a large-scale chase or develop and incorporate elaborate computer-generated imagery (CGI) work to substitute for location shooting. Hollywood's immense capital resources can create grander spectacles, more-elaborate special effects, and so forth. Thus aesthetics are tightly bound with production pragmatics.

But more significantly, fight choreography in the action film itself typically proceeds through combinations, sometimes developed through specific martial-arts styles,[17] and in Hollywood productions often through a combination of chase, gunplay, and hand-to-hand combat combined with spectacular sets and special effects. Regarding Bordwell's contrast of *Lethal Weapon* and *Hearty Response*, subsequent Hollywood films seem to have taken up the difference with yet another stylistic absorption. *The Matrix* (dir. Andy Wachowski and Larry Wachowski, 1999) uses Yuen Woo-ping and *Romeo Must Die* employs Corey Yuen as martial-arts choreographers (a position the latter also held in *Lethal Weapon 4*—as if Hollywood deal makers were carefully following Bordwell's aesthetic analysis). It seems that Hollywood has partially, but significantly, adapted the "pause-burst-pause" technique by importing the very people who developed it as specialist technicians. For the same results or less? My initial conclusion is "somewhat less," but this fits with what we have come to expect of Hollywood aesthetic hegemony: a gradual absorption, not a decisive transformation.[18] At the same time, Bordwell's argument validates certain continuing strengths of Hong Kong cinema. For example, Johnnie To's *The Mission* (1999) includes superbly dramatic scenes, such as a shopping-center shootout with an extreme emphasis on stasis, employing an existing location that can be rented for filmmaking during off hours.

The history of Hong Kong's Golden Harvest studio, from upstart in the early 1970s to major presence in a short time, demonstrates what can be accomplished by creating alternative action heroes, such as Bruce Lee and Jackie Chan, who negotiate modernizing cultures and traditional Chinese family values with extraordinary skill, and in Chan's case who add irreverent local comedy to the martial-arts mix. Golden Harvest's films are different from Hollywood's in that they are grounded in a distinctive local performance tradition and appeal to diasporic Chinese communities as well as East Asian regional audiences. Golden Harvest became so successful that they expanded into distribution and theater ownership (three hundred in the region) and were exporting 150 films a year in the early 1990s. The studio even tried to break into the U.S. major market but managed only one certifiable hit, 1990's *Teenage Mutant Ninja Turtles* (dir. Steve Barron), which had a $13.5 million budget and returned $135 million in U.S. theatrical gross and $67.6 million in U.S. video rentals. But when the East Asian economy tanked in the early 1990s, uncertainty reigned in commercial film. Hollywood responded with aggressive (and largely successful) attempts to remove trade barriers and capture more of the East and South Asian theatrical market at the expense of regional production and distribution.

Jackie Chan's evolving career as a deliberately transnational star shows some of the problems in crossing over. For the past ten years, Chan has alternated between productions based in Hong Kong and Hollywood while aiming for films marketed around the world. For example, *The Tuxedo* (2002) was produced by U.S.-based companies lead by Dreamworks SKG, directed by Kevin Donovan from a U.S.-generated script. Immigrant New York City taxi driver Jimmy Tong (Chan) is hired as chauffer for a James Bond type of secret agent. When the boss is injured, Chan takes over pursuit of the villain, aided by a neophyte government agent (Jennifer Love Hewitt) while wearing a high-tech tuxedo that grants him superhuman skills. Fitting Chan into the Hollywood framework alters his trademark martial-arts actions in several ways. First, because of Hollywood finance protocols and production insurance rules, he cannot perform all his stunts but must employ a double.[19] Second, increased special effects, plus wire-work and editing between the double and the star, remove the "realism" of the viewer's knowing that Chan is doing his own stunts. Third, much of the action is attributed to the clothing, not Chan's performing body, and the first big action sequence features fancy stunt driving, not Chan's body in motion. Budgeted at $60 million, the film returned a disappointing $50 million theatrical return in North America, boosted by $48.6 million in non-U.S. showings. Critical response was largely negative, with Chan fans disappointed by the changes. The implausibility of the pairing with Hewitt was aggravated by her character's inconsistency: part science nerd, part sexy agent. Inexplicably, she repeatedly expresses girlish fear in fight sequences while exhibiting aggressive and effective physical attack skills.

Chan returned to U.S. screens the following year in *Shanghai Knights*, a re-pairing with Owen Wilson based on the highly successful *Shanghai Noon*. But later in 2003, the Hong Kong produced *The Medallion* (dir. Gordon Chan) bombed. Budgeted at $41 million, the film had a U.S. theatrical gross of $22.1 million and a non-U.S. theatrical gross of $4.4 million. Continuing the previous problems, many actions are done with stunt doubles and wirework. The 1980s Hong Kong characteristic Bordwell noted of fully articulated body and performance oriented action is now changed to a stuttering form which denies Chan many of his old style action and comic opportunities.[21] Part of the problem is relative and contextual. Employing its characteristic absorption of commercially effective new styles, Hollywood adopted the comic action formula quickly. With many new digital effects available, Hollywood churned out effective glossy stunt action work such as *Charlie's Angels* (dir. McG, 2000) and *Charlie's Angels: Full Throttle* (dir. McG, 2003), using female actors without martial arts and stunt training, a complete contrast to the marketing of 1995's *Rumble in the*

*Bronx* as "Jackie Chan: No Fear. No Stuntmen. No Equal." Adaptation to the Hollywood market remains awkward. *The Medallion* puts forward a totally unconvincing romance interest when Chan as a Hong Kong police officer is paired with an Interpol officer (Claire Forlani). On their first encounter, she slaps him for not having stayed in touch after they had worked together 3 months earlier. (Comic outtakes of this shot are repeated in the end credits.) Clearly the gesture narratively signals that they had been sexually intimate during the previous assignment, yet the acting throughout belies any personal allure between the couple. While Chan is marked from the start as a bold police officer, fulfilling a firm masculinity established by position, rank, and action, the addition of the romance line seems grafted on: fulfilling Hollywood conventions and painfully implausible. Taken literally, the Chan character would have to be regarded as a "love 'em and leave 'em" hero—hardly an admirable masculinity in Asia or Western society, and contradictory to narrative and character throughout the film, as well as Chan's star image.[22]

So to return to the question—"does Hong Kong need to follow Hollywood to be more competitive?" We can answer in this way: On the high end of the global blockbuster with big stars, elaborate special effects, and world wide marketing, no other national cinema or even partnership (for example, the European Economic Community) can compete with or successfully challenge Hollywood on its own turf. At least not at this stage. As Thomas Schatz has concluded:

> As the major studios partner up on megabudget global blockbusters designed for that "much larger group who care to be entertained," they are reinventing the oligopoly structure of old, cooperating (if not actively colluding) to control the movie marketplace, insuring their profits and securing their status as an exclusive cartel. By partnering on high-end pictures, on the films that dominate the global market and generate the lion's share of the revenues, the studios virtually guarantee that the budgets for both production and marketing will be so high that no one can possibly compete, thus creating "barriers to entry" at the most lucrative level of the business.[23]

To put it simply, if John Woo is going to make big-budget action films like *Mission Impossible 2*, there is only one place to go: Hollywood (a global economic entity, not a geographic location, since almost all of *Mission Impossible 2* was shot in Australia, which gave a better budget break).

At the other end, the small independent end, there may seem to be more freedom, but there is actually a fairly limited diversity. What works best is highly formulaic, a fact much bemoaned by observers of the U.S. independent film scene, if by "best" we mean economically successful. Moments of transition always allow some openings for new expressions, but not always effective challenges to the dominant system. The independent sector remains wavering between a "cockroach- capitalist" response to the dominant system and the creation of a waiting area for those who hope to be called into the main arena.

Does Hong Kong have to follow Hollywood to compete? I have argued that technological and marketing dominance by Hollywood create conditions that make it virtually impossible to compete with it directly, head-on, and that its overall system absorbs foreign elements, changing only in style rather than allowing significant "working from within." A competent response has to find an alternative strategy, but this involves asking what is "success" in this competition: economic? ideological? or artistic?

## Notes

An earlier version of this article was presented at the conference "Year 2000 and Beyond: History, Technology and the Future of Transnational Chinese Media," held at Hong Kong Baptist University and organized by Jenny Kwok Wah Lau, Hong Kong, April 2000. Subsequently it appeared in *Film Appreciation* (Taiwan, Chinese-language translation by Yeh Yueh-yu), November 2000. For comments and encouragement, I want to thank Jenny Lau, Gina Marchetti, Kin Yan Szeto, Ting Wang, L. S. Kim, Frances Gateward, David Desser, Ben Kim, Evans Chan, David Leiwei Li, and Julia Lesage.

1. Gregg Torode (in Washington), *South China Morning Post* (April 17, 2000), 3. The biggest local story in Hong Kong at the same time involved a high official of the SAR announcing that all discussion of Taiwan in the press, radio, and television should cease because "Taiwan has nothing to do with Hong Kong matters." The local press, intellectuals, and independent legislators immediately protested.

2. For purposes of my analysis here, I am bracketing questions of aesthetic quality. I want to generate a discussion of economic, institutional, structural, and historic factors. This does not mean that I think aesthetic matters are negligible, rather that they can be addressed adequately only when contextual frames are clear.

3. Hong Kong Film Critics Society, http://filmcritics.org.hk.

4. Thus in a paper given at the 1998 East-West conference in Hong Kong, "Postcolonial Hong Kong Culture in the Age of Global Capitalism," Chu Yiu Wai discussed *Tomorrow Never Dies* and *The Replacement Killers* along with work produced and directed in Hong Kong.

5. Kin Yan Elyssa Szeto, "The Cosmopolitical Martial Arts Cinema of Asia/America: Gender, Ethnicity and Transnationalism," diss. (Northwestern University, 2004).

6. Justin Wyatt, *High Concept: Movies and Marketing in Hollywood* (Austin: University of Texas Press, 1996).

7. The definitive source for such analysis is David Bordwell, Janet Staiger, and Kristin Thompson, *The Classical Hollywood Cinema: Film Style and Mode of Production to 1960* (New York: Columbia University Press, 1985), especially 365–384.

8. Yeoh is a former Miss Malaysia, yet also a Hong Kong star, reminding us—as Maggie Cheung does also—of the perils of a purely national analysis.

9. For a very self-aware discussion of Tong (and others) working in Hollywood, see Cheung Suk-yee, "Hong Kong Filmmakers in Hollywood," Law Kar, ed., *Border*

*Crossings in Hong Kong Cinema* (Hong Kong: Twenty-fourth Hong Kong International Film Festival, 2000), 124–137.

10. Steve Fore provides a thorough discussion of Chan's work, centering on his first big U.S. theatrical hit, *Rumble in the Bronx* (dir. Stanley Tong, 1995), in "Jackie Chan and the Cultural Dynamics of Global Entertainment," *Transnational Chinese Cinemas: Identity, Nationhood, Gender,* Sheldon Hsiao-peng Lu, ed. (Honolulu: University of Hawaii Press, 1997), 239–262. He updates and elaborates the discussion in "Life Imitates Entertainment: Home and Dislocation in the Films of Jackie Chan," Esther C. M. Yau, ed., *At Full Speed: Hong Kong Cinema in a Borderless World* (Minneapolis: University of Minnesota Press, 2001), 115–141. Gina Marchetti considers Chan in relation to African American culture in "Jackie Chan and the Black Connection," Matthew Tinkcom and Amy Villarejo, eds., *Keyframes: Popular Culture and Cultural Studies* (London: Routledge, 2001), 137–158.

11. *Rush Hour* (dir. Brett Ratner, 1998), *Shanghai Noon* (dir. Tom Dey, 2000), *Rush Hour 2* (dir. Brett Ratner, 2001), *Shanghai Knights* (dir. David Dobkin, 2003), *Rush Hour 3* (dir. Brett Ratner, 2007).

12. Among those given major release in the U.S. market: *The Tuxedo* (2002, budget $60 million; U.S. theatrical gross $50 million); *The Medallion* (2003, budget $41 million; U.S. theatrical gross, $22 million, non-U.S. theatrical gross $4.4 million); *Around the World in 80 days* (2004, budget $110 million; U.S. theatrical gross $21.4 million), www.imdb.com.

13. David Bordwell, Janet Staiger, and Kristin Thompson, *The Classical Hollywood Cinema: Film Style and Mode of Production to 1960* (New York: Columbia University Press), 1985.

14. Richard Corliss, "No Cooling this Jet," *Time* (April 3, 2000): 80.

15. My debt is considerable here to Thomas Schatz, "Show Me the Money: In Search of Hits, the Industry May Go Broke," *The Nation* (April 5/12, 1999): 26–31 and to Carl Bromley, "The House that Jack Built: How Valenti Brought Hollywood to the World," *The Nation* (April 3, 2000), 39–41. Toby Miller, et al., *Global Hollywood* (London, British Film Institute, 2001), is authoritative. Also, I surveyed the independent-film sector in: "Independent Features: Hopes and Dreams," Jon Lewis, ed., *New American Cinema* (Durham: Duke University Press, 1998), 307–327.

16. "Aesthetics in Action: Kung Fu, Gunplay, and Cinematic Expressivity," *Fifty Years of Electric Shadows* (Hong Kong: Urban Council of Hong Kong, 1997) 81–89. Bordwell has elaborated his discussion of "pause-burst-pause" patterns in his *Planet Hong Kong: Popular Cinema and the Art of Entertainment* (Cambridge, MA: Harvard University Press, 2000).

17. Aaron Anderson, "Violent Dances in Martial Arts Films," *Jump Cut* 42 (2001) http://www.ejumpcut.org/archive/jc44.2001/aarona/aaron1.html.

18. Peter X Feng's chapter in this volume, titled "False Consciousness and Double Consciousness: Race, Virtual Reality, and the Assimilation of Hong Kong Action Cinema in *The Matrix*," elaborates another aspect of Hollywood's blurred multiculturalism in which not only are plots cross-generic (the mix of New Jack gangster and Hong Kong martial arts in *Romeo Must Die*, for example), but even action stars themselves exhibit a peculiar multicultural blurring, as in *The Matrix*'s Keanu Reeves (Chinese Hawaiian father, English mother, raised in Canada). Reeves's earlier teen roles marked him as white American. Today there is a critical mass of actors who represent the entertainment-business version of de facto multiculturalism, such as Cameron Diaz, Mariah Carey, and Vin Diesel. For a critical take on some subsequent implications, see Evans Chan, "War & Images," *Film International* 5 (2003): 10–23.

19. Capital outlay is so large that all aspects of production are covered by insurance. On-set insurance dictates that stunt-doubles are substitutable elements, whereas stars cannot be replaced if injured. Thus, none of Chan's famous dangerous Hong Kong actions can be performed in the big-budget framework. Bordwell's "pause-burst-pause" style is not only aesthetic, it is also grounded in economies of production.

20. Bordwell describes the new dominant Hollywood style in a masterful essay: "Intensified Continuity: Visual Style in Contemporary American Film," *Film Quarterly* 55.3 (2002): 16–28.

21. Chan's Hong Kong produced work since 1995's *Rumble in the Bronx* often contains problems that stem from the film's being significantly reedited for Western distribution. Fan publications often note changes between the East Asian version and the North American edit. In his 1997 essay ("Life Imitates Entertainment), Fore describes various changes—aesthetic and cultural—between the two versions of *Rumble* ranging from the music track to reducing characters and narrative. He calls the process of change "disembedding," a process that reduces cultural specificity and depth to gain a global market.

23. Thomas Schatz, "Show Me the Money," p. 30.

# PART II

# Questions of Genders

# 9

# "From Behind the Wall"

## *The Representation of Gender and Sexuality in Modern Chinese Film*

ZHOU XUELIN

> *The entire garden is bursting with spring colours,*
> *A spray of red apricot blossom peeps out from behind the wall.*
>
> —YE SHAOWENG, A POET OF SOUTHERN SONG DYNASTY (CA. 1195–CA. 1264)

The morning after their first night together, the young woman (a sign painter) brings a Western-style breakfast to Long Xiang (a rock kid), who is still sleeping in bed. She leaves her apartment key beside the pillow and says to the young rocker who has just become her lover: "I leave the key here. If you like, you can take it with you." After these words, she goes out to work. Sitting in bed against the wall covered with pinups (of Western star beauties) and staring at the key in his hand, Long looks puzzled. The shot freezes; and so ends the film *Rock Kids* (*Yaogun qingnian*, dir. Tian Zhuangzhuang, 1988). This scene is significant in modern Chinese cinema. First, it deals with the issue of sexuality in a beautiful and explicit way. The girl's nightdress and Long's blanket-covered nudity maintain some restraint, but the suggestion of what has happened is clear.

Second, theirs is a premarital sexual relationship. The young couple met only recently at a subway station. They then had a few brief encounters on the street and at the dance place. They hardly knew each other's name. Such a relationship was considered illegal in the past and had to be condemned with no hesitation by the mass media (including film). But in the 1988 film their relationship was far from negatively represented. Third, it is not even slightly implied that the couple is going to get married. Long's final stare and gesture are ambiguous, suggesting that his feelings remain ambivalent.

In many respects, the ambiguity and ambivalence of Long Xiang were echoed by an art exhibition held in Beijing toward the end of the same year.

The Exhibition of Oil Paintings of the Human Body (*Youhua renti yishu dazhan*), held at the China Art Museum from 22 December 1988 to 8 January 1989, struck a raw nerve in the nation. During the eighteen days of the exhibition, the museum was visited by approximately 220,000 people from all parts of the country coming to "appreciate" more than 130 paintings of the human body, in most cases the female body. To many Chinese at that time, the exhibition was a shocking breakthrough, as explicit images of the body, especially the female nude, held direct associations of sexuality, and sexuality in turn tended to be associated with "moral decadence" and "vulgar appetites." It was abnormal to talk about sex-related issues either privately or as an academic topic. A retrospective look at the mile-long queue outside the Museum would trigger the question: how many of those standing and waiting in the icy cold were truly art lovers? Some random comments from the public overheard during the exhibition seemed to supply some explanation for the excitement stirred up by the event. For example, a middle-aged man elbowed his way out of the museum with a blushing face and the comment, "Damn it! I seem to have been to a women's bathroom." Within the exhibition hall, a middle-aged woman pointed to two young men and said to her colleagues with anger, "Look at those two guys. They are just itching to get their hands on the person in the painting."[1]

On a broad scale, the sensation caused by the exhibition revealed a dilemma in which Chinese people had been trapped over the issue of sexuality. While the event indicated some kind of political and ideological relaxation, it also drew attention to the constraints that remained. Although the body, especially the female body, might not be a taboo idea or a forbidden topic, it was still far from fully exposed to the light of day. From this perspective, a traditional Chinese saying helps express the situation—the beauty of a woman's body still "remained semi-hidden by the *pipa* (lute) in her own hands (*you bao pipa ban zhe mian*)."

Before examining the issue of gender and sexuality treated in modern Chinese film, a brief historical look seems necessary.

The sensation caused by the Art Exhibition was not the first time such issues had arisen in China. A similar event occurred much earlier in 1926, when a young painter named Liu Haisu (1896–1994) proposed offering classes on the human body at his privately run Shanghai Art School. Liu made this proposal to a startled Shanghai, by far the most westernized and industrialized city in China at the time. The reverberation soon reached many other parts of China. Conservatives denounced the painter's plan as "shameless" and "decadent," and cursed him as "a traitor to art." The "incident" was vividly recorded in Huang Shuqin's *Hua hun* /*The Soul of the Painter* (1994), a film about a Chinese female painter's road from brothel to art museum. A scene in the film shows a group of people from all walks of society breaking into an Art School class, driving students and the nude model away, and smashing their drawings on the floor. In real life, the attacks against the idea lasted for ten years and the whole school was later closed down. But Liu did not give up; his perseverance worked in the end.

The conservative veterans' eventual withdrawal from this issue was certainly not just an outcome of Liu Haisu's individual efforts. Liu's success should be put into a social context. From the very start, Liu won support from the leaders of the New Culture Movement, a movement that took place in 1916 and was spearheaded by leading intellectuals such as Cai Yuanpei (1868–1940), Hu Shi (1891–1962), Chen Duxiu (1879–1942), and Lu Xun (1881–1936). The Movement criticized Confucian-based traditional culture and heralded the coming of "Mr. Science" and "Mr. Democracy" from the West. In its aftermath, the May Fourth Movement further removed other shackles of historical residues, in particular some patriarchal attitudes and practices associated with Confucianism. In the autumn of 1919, Peking University, a privileged educational institution and a revered place for Chinese intellectuals, opened its doors to female students for the first time. This "open-door policy" was soon followed by other universities across the country and had a subsequent domino effect on society at large. Urban intellectuals talked openly about issues related to sex and regarded the talk as a sign of liberation from traditional fetters. According to Frank Dikötter, "Literary writers exposed their personal sexual experiences to the public, young intellectuals clamoured for sexual equality, educationalists campaigned for the enlightenment of youth through sexual instruction, and social improvers undertook to reform the sexual habits of the nation."[2] For a while, talking about "women's emancipation" became a fashion in Republican China (1919–1949).[3] People claimed that "liberated" women now had free choice in love, marriage, and even divorce, with their marriage no longer needing to be arranged by parents or brokers. Consensual unions became more common among youngsters. Young women also began to join Ibsen's Nora and walk out of "the doll's house" into most fields of society. Meanwhile, books and journal articles on sex-related issues were published, as it was believed that "to strengthen the country, one should first strengthen the race; to strengthen the race, one should improve sex education."[4]

At first sight, this trend of "women's emancipation" and "sexual permissiveness" seemed to flow through to the early 1950s. One of the first regulations issued by the new Communist regime was the *Marriage Law of the People's Republic of China* (1950), which "outlawed arranged and venal marriages and ratified monogamy based on the free choice of partner as the only legal form of marriage."[5] Women were allegedly announced to have equal status as men in society and were defined as the upholders of half the sky.[6] Liberating as it was, this version of monogamy has been regarded recently as little more than an expression of a "patriarchal-socialist system,"[7] because this gender equality was based on the "politicization of the individual body."[8] Woman's emancipation became absorbed as a component of proletarian liberation. Women were now conceived as little more than an organic part of the machinery of the Party organization. With this gender policy, the government could boast itself as being distinct from previous administrations, representing a progressive force in the building of socialist modernity. It was certainly true that in terms of gender ideology this policy brought a form of equality, which, however, involved a loss of difference. It was a kind of masculinization of feminine appearance and behavior, the purpose of which was to bring women out of their private space and into the public sphere. For many Chinese women, even marriage became "a 'cell' of the entire cause of revolution, something important to the interests of society as a whole."[9] Their criteria for choosing partners were based more on collective interests. Those with insufficient revolutionary ethos were less likely to be selected. For example, in a 1957 film titled *Hushi riji /A Nurse's Diary* (dir. Tao Jin), the female protagonist deserts her fiancé after finding out that "he cared for nothing else except himself, his wife, his children, and his family." In a more recent Chinese film *Molihua kai /Jasmine Women* (dir. Hou Yong, 2004), a melodrama about the lives and fates of three generations of Chinese women in one family respectively in the 1930s, the 1950s, and the 1980s in Shanghai, the petit-bourgeois Mother of the early 1950s marries herself off to a former classmate from a working-class family against the grandmother's will because the young man was the only Party member at the school.

Partly to echo the gender policy promoted by the Party, many films made in the 1950s had women, especially young women, as lead characters. But what was ironic about these films was that, despite the government's attempt to uplift women's position, the official status of these young women remained awkward and was subtly revealed, wittingly or unwittingly, by the title of a film of the period—*Dang de nüer/Daughter of the Party* (dir. Lin Nong, 1958). In the two classic revolutionary films of the 1950s—*Qingchun zhige/Song of Youth* (dir. Cui Wei and Chen Huaikai, 1959) and *Hongse niangzijun/Red Detachment of Women* (dir. Xie Jin, 1959)—the female leads were represented to be initially living in misery and poverty, suffering from the old society in general and brutal male figures in particular (e.g., landlords and Nationalist Government officials as representatives of society). The misery of the women's lives would sooner or later end in the course of the film, but not until the appearance of a male Communist Party's representative (*dang daibiao*). Usually it was only through various kinds of trials "in blood and fire" and the Communist male's ultimate phoenixlike death that the young women were finally saved and formally named as true revolutionaries (by being accepted into the Party as members). Even in films set in the contemporary 1950s, such as *Nülan Wuhao/Girl Basketball Player No. 5* (dir. Xie Jin, 1957) and *Wu Duo Jinhua / Five Golden Flowers* (dir. Wang Jiayi, 1959), the existence of the "patriarchal-socialist system" was visible in that the male protagonist remained in the focus of the female attention, with the latter being either viewed and pursued as "objects of desire" (*Five Golden Flowers*) or coached and disciplined by a male figure (*Girl Basketball Player No. 5*).

In general, the 1950s witnessed Chinese women in a paradoxical position, being squeezed between the Communist Party's constant efforts to uplift women's position in society and its simultaneous persistence in regarding women as its docile and dutiful daughters to be saved and enlightened. The consequence was that women were further deprived of sensual or sexual opportunities. Therefore, it was rare to see women spend time on their external appearance in Chinese films of the 1950s; neither was there any trace of erotic beauty and fashionable clothes associated with them. (If any such trace appears on the big screen, it would unambiguously refer to an enemy character.) This said, the female body had not yet entirely disappeared in Chinese films of the 1950s. The (female) identity was still recognizable through their sportswear (*Girl Basketball Player No. 5*); cheongsam (*qipao*, in *Song of Youth*); short skirts (*Red Detachment of Women*); and colorful ethnic clothes (*Five Golden Flowers*). These remaining traces of femininity, however, were soon to be completely eradicated, with the image of the female body becoming utterly invisible in the decade of the Cultural Revolution. In its place, a new gender culture was formed and presented "as a simple signifier of bodily constraint and containment, and of puritan morality."[10] Throughout the revolutionary year, women dressed like men and wore the same colors and styles, unless they were willing to risk being labeled "self-seeking temptresses."[11] Any suggestion of sexual interest, no matter how slight, was considered ideologically incorrect; any artistic work with the vaguest suggestion of love or marriage, to say nothing of sexuality, was repudiated as a "bourgeois poisonous weed." Any film with romantic scenes, no matter how understated, was considered obscene and decadent and had to be withdrawn from circulation. In the eight "revolutionary model performances" (*geming yangbanxi*) that dominated China's cinema screens during much of the Cultural Revolution, female protagonists were portrayed as simply lacking any elegant and attractive trace of femininity or bodily beauty.[12] As women, they had ceased to listen to the claims of their individual bodies and were devoting themselves instead to the grandiose project of socialism, being reduced to anonymous and faceless members of a large collective group identity—sisters of the proletarian class. They were seldom, if ever, shown to have husbands or children, and the filming never presented their bodies in a sexual way. What received prominent emphasis was the concept of class solidarity and class struggle as embodied through them.

Such genderless and asexual imagery flooded cinema screens in China in the new cultural context and contributed a unique colony of pictures in the gallery of world cinema. In *Zhiqu Weihushan/Taking Tiger Mountain by Strategy* (dir. Xie Tieli, 1970), a story set in the Civil War (1945–1949), the romantic feeling between the head of a Communist squad and an army nurse in the original novel was eliminated and replaced by puritanical camaraderie. *Baimao Nü/The White-haired Girl* (dir. Sang Hu, 1972) and *Hongse Niangzijun/The Red Detachment of Women* (dir. Pan Wenzhan and Fu Jie, 1971) were based on 1950 and 1959 films with the same titles. In the 1950 version of *The White-haired Girl*, Xi'er and Dachun (a young peasant of the village) are in love with each other. She is later kidnapped by the village landlord and raped by the landlord's son. She then flees to the wild mountains and gives birth to a baby before her anger turns her hair white. In the 1959 version of *Red Detachment of Women*, Wu Qionghua, a slave girl on the tropical island of Hainan, is saved by the head of the women's detachment, a Party's representative. In the process of Qionghua's awakening to issues of self-identity and class conflicts, a romantic emotion, though somewhat thin and veiled, begins to emerge deep in her heart. When these two films were "transplanted" into model operas between 1971 and 1972, all the romantic and sexual elements were removed.

These stereotypes were followed by even more extreme examples. Jiang Shuiying, the female protagonist in *Longjiang Song/Song Of The Dragon River* (dir. Xie Tieli, 1972), shows no signs of femininity and simply busies herself making serious and imposing gestures while instructing the masses about the necessity and importance of class and class struggle. Only a tiny label, which reads "honorable soldier's family" on the door of her house, ambiguously suggests that she has a partner somewhere. There is not even such a label for Fang Haizhen, the heroine of *Haigang/On the Docks* (dir. Xie Tieli and Xie Jin, 1972–1973). That she is a leader of the Shanghai dockworkers deters viewers from asking questions about her private life. The scene where she guides a younger colleague through an enormous "class education" art gallery has been described as one of the "most interminable sequences in Chinese film."[13]

The representation of gender and sexuality in Chinese film between the1950s and the1970s throws light on at least two things. First, "gender equality" surfaced. Gender oppression gave way to class struggle, and in the process gender differences were repressed. Second, "gender neutrality" dominated. Tremendous care was given to minimize the presence of female beauty and the female body. A contradiction, however, emerged here. In one sense, many films produced during the period could be described as extraordinary attempts to neutralize the "male gaze" that film theorists had identified in Western cinema. In another sense there was something very male about the canceling out of a whole range of traditional female experiences and pleasures. Women ceased to be an "object" for male desire but the price for this was the negation of their own body.

By 1976 when the Cultural Revolution ended, half a century had passed since Liu Haisu initiated the proposal to use nude models in a fine arts class. No substantial changes had occurred in China in terms of its attitude to and treatment of issues associated with gender and sexuality. It was not until the late 1970s when there started to be an awakening consciousness of the body in Chinese society. The economy-oriented open-door policy also brought in Western concepts and conduct. As early as 1979, a poem asking for "sexual openness" appeared on the Democracy Wall in Beijing.[14] The following years saw in urban China a sexual reawakening, which was no longer deemed as posing a threat to public morality but as "a sign of progress."[15] Young urbanities had adopted a more liberal and tolerant attitude toward love and marriage, gender and sexuality. Their aspirations were becoming increasingly different from those of their elders. The concept of desexualization was ridiculed as just another example of the Cultural Revolution's intentions to distort human nature.

In these circumstances, issues of gender and sexuality became subjects of unprecedented attention in Chinese cinema. The human body, especially the female body, was configured as the classic focus of sexuality, sparking the fascination of the public. A small stream soon turned into a big river. As if to make up for the loss of the previous desexualized decades, numerous films were screened to reshape the image of women. On the pretext of challenging Confucian morality and body repression, filmmakers of the 1980s presented a parade of feminine beauties and female rebels against the patriarchal order, often identified with an old and brutal or childish and innocent man.[16] In the course of their struggle, these female characters exposed their own sexual desires in "a total liberation and desperate triumph of the body."[17]

But these films were either set "in wild mountains" or in an ambiguously identified past. While many of these films engage in portraying sex-related issues, the treatment is suggested only coyly. The implicit treatment of sex was as much the release of the repressed human desires as cultural allegory, serving as polysemous texts for audiences and critics, at home and abroad, to think and digest. More explicit exploration of sexuality came with some youth-oriented films set in contemporary urban areas. Young urbanites in these films, by standing ahead of the historical tide, moved faster than people of other age groups in accessing and accepting new concepts, including those of sexuality. Side by side with *Rock Kids*, other films focusing on the private behaviors and social pursuits of young adults include *Lunhui/Samsara* (dir. Huang Jianxin, 1988), *Wanzhu/Masters of Mischief* (dir. Mi Jiashan, 1988), *Dachuanqi/Out of Breath* (dir. Ye Daying, 1988), *Yiban Shi Huoyan, Yiban Shi Haishui/Half Flame, Half Brine* (dir. Xia Gang, 1988), and *Fengkuang De Daijia,/Obsession* (also known as *The Price of Frenzy*; dir. Zhou Xiaowen, 1988). Partially through their awareness of the increased tolerance of the nonmarital cohabitation in the West, young protagonists of these films determined to challenge the strictures of Confucian patriarchy and Communist puritanism.

While these youth films are significant for the various themes they examined, they share one thing in common: a comparatively candid and true-to-life representation of gender and sexuality, which is mainly expressed through some cohabiting scenes. Although premarital sexual relationships were officially disapproved, cohabitation became a common practice among young urbanities in the 1980s. An investigation conducted then showed that more than 40 percent of urban youth approved of premarital sexual relationships.[18] The issue of cohabitation was explored at length in these youth-oriented films and with a matter-of-fact acceptance. For example, Zhang Ming and Wu Di in *Half Flame, Half Brine* meet each other in a park and talk about sex before they know each other's name. Zhang tells Wu that he has slept with more than one hundred women, and the latter comes to believe him after an exchange of a few remarks. After bumping into each other again on the high street, they go off to have sex. The eroticism and sensuality of the scene are achieved with elegance and subtlety by relying on a careful manipulation of sound effects and lighting. Unlike that in *Half Flame, Half Brine*, the cohabiting scene in *Samsara* is approached differently and in more detail. Throughout, the body of the young female protagonist, Yu Jing, is greatly emphasised. The scene starts with Yu Jing, in loose nightdress, walking softly in the dim-lit corridor against stylish and slow-rhythmed soundtrack. A point-of-view shot shows that she stands beside the opened door, goddess-like, with her face cast in high-key lighting. The subsequent four shot-reverse-shots suggest the lovers' mutual apprehension and appreciation, as well as their shared excitement and expectation. She then walks towards Shi Ba in slow motion. The whole scene is distinguished by a sense of beauty and purity.[19]

However, by the late 1980s China was not yet ready to see a full-fledged "sexual revolution." Perhaps not purely out of coincidence, the young men and women in the cohabitating scenes of both *Half Flame, Half Brine* and *Samsara* are in each case closely observed by a pretty yet firm-looking young woman from a big poster picture on the wall. Given the fates that await the woman protagonists, this female look from the poster is prophetic and sarcastic at the same time. Despite the established value system undergoing sweeping changes in the more tolerant 1980s, patriarchal influence was not completely indiscernible. While Chinese society might no longer weigh down woman adulterers with stones and drown them in water, some attitudes of the past did survive the extremism of the Cultural Revolution. When examining some problems in researching and representing women in Chinese cinema, Chris Berry observed that "even after over forty years of women's liberation, it is still commonly felt that a respectable woman should not be alone with any man other than a member of her family, a party representative, or a responsible government official."[20] Even in the youth-oriented films, the idea that fidelity to patrilineage was a central virtue demanded of a woman; and chastity, the crucial expression of female fidelity, continues to linger in the minds of many "liberated" and "rebellious" young women. There was still resonance in such old sayings as "to die of hunger is a trifling matter; to abandon chastity is a grave matter." Not infrequently in these films, once a young woman has "lost her body" to a man to whom she is not married, her life becomes problematic even though she may not be sneered at by those around her. She is more likely to lose her self-confidence and dignity. Such contradictions between tradition and modernity, reflecting the ambivalence and confusion of society in matters of gender and sexuality, are revealed in both Yu Jing and Wu Di. Yu Jing, an award-winning student at a dance academy, scales back her promising career after marriage and develops a hobby of collecting recipes. She is gradually reduced in status to a chorus-line dancer, making these sacrifices only to support her crippled (mentally as well as physically) husband. Wu Di, a foreign-language university student, meets Zhang Ming and moves in with him. She becomes increasingly dependent and loses interest in study. When she is deserted by Zhang, her revenge is to abuse her own body by having causal sex with multiple partners. After Zhang is arrested for blackmailing foreigners, she commits suicide.

The following conversation between Yu Guang and Ding Xiaolu in *Masters of Mischief* occurs early in the morning after they have spent a night together. (Ding was portrayed as a conventionally mainstream youth with a sense of commitment and responsibility.)

> DING: Did you sleep well last night?
> YU: Yes, I did. Why did you get up so early?
> DING: I have to go to work today. I can't always stay away from work. Do you want to eat something? There is milk in the fridge outside.
> YU: No, I don't feel like eating. I usually don't have breakfast.
> DING: Your life lacks pattern. It's not good for your health.
> YU: I don't want to live to a hundred years anyway. I don't care if my health is good or not.
> DING: Yu Guang, if there's anything. . . . Well, forget it. I know you won't even need my help. I just want to say, come whenever you want to.

Xiaolu's words are reminiscent of Pan Yuliang's action in *The Soul of the Painter.* After receiving some fair treatment from a local governor in Huang Shugin's movie, Yuliang (the would-be prostitute) is so moved that she goes over to the bed and begins undressing herself without saying a word. She offers her body to the governor, as she thinks that her maiden body is the most precious gift she can present in return for his "greatest kindness." Xiaolu is certainly not Yuliang, but their behavior rings a similar tone. If some "good" reasons can be suggested to defend Yuliang, Xiaolu's offer of her body in the new social and cultural context sounds more confusing and contradictory. As "young women rebels" influenced by traditional legacies, Wu Di, Hu Yi, and Xiao Lu are at the same time playing the role of a nurturing woman in the contemporary context.

Zhou Xiaowen's 1988 hit *Obsession* provides another example. A film about the rape of a teenager girl (Lanlan) and the revenge taken by her elder sister (Qingqing) against the rapist, it is not so much telling a revenge story as contemplating some traditional interpretations of chastity for girls in modern China.[21] As a consequence of the sexual assault, Lanlan is in the spotlight of neighbors' stares at home and finds it impossible to return to her normal life. At school, she is separated from other children at the physical education class (a well-intentioned move). Meanwhile, her sister's obsession with revenge hardly brings Lanlan any consolation. Far from that, the obsessive Qingqing is becoming less and less sensitive to Lanlan's feelings, and more and more haunted by the desire to catch the man who has taken her sister's chastity. While Qingqing can accomplish her task only with the help of an old, retired (male) policeman, she does this at a high price—not only losing "her previous roles as loving sister, capable daughter, doctor, and friend,"[22] but also making herself a transgressor into the patriarchal terrain. (That she kicks the rapist off the tower to his death is itself an offense against the law.)

In one way or another, the obsessive ideas that torture Qingqing are not distinctive from Wu Di and Yu Jing's contradictions in *Half Flame, Half Brine,* and *Samsara,* or from Ding Xiaolu's paradox in *Masters of Mischief.* Together they reveal that the female body in 1980s China was still the site of both a literal and an ideological struggle for possession. Commenting on a classic scene when Grandpa and Grandma "made it" in the wild sorghum fields in Zhang Yimou's 1987 *Hong Gaoliang/Red Sorghum*, Mo Yan, the writer of the original story, said that he had wished to have Grandma fully undressed so that her pure and pretty body could be exposed fully to the light of the day.[23] But the time was not ripe yet. Writing about the position of women in new Chinese cinema, British film critic Tony Rayns notes, "There can be no such thing as a radical-feminist Chinese cinema until social and political changes pave the way for it."[24] Surely, relaxing controls on conceptual or ideological levels are not sufficient for a candid and honest treatment of issues of gender and sexuality in literary and artistic works (including films). Other factors can also function as restrictions. First, there is the national economy, the development of which plays a crucial role in the process. Given that China is currently a developing country still in an initial stage of socialism, Chinese women still have a long way to go before they can declare independence in a true sense. Second, there is the surviving influence of cultural traditions, which have been inhibiting a fully candid representation. Any attempt at crossing the line may mean trouble for the filmmaker and the film as well. Third, concern about the issues of gender and sexuality "has not become generalized across Chinese society and institutions in the same way as has occurred in most English-speaking countries," according to Berry.[25] These seem to be good reasons to suppose that Chinese filmmakers will continue to stand in the same awkward position in the foreseeable future. While they cannot present a complete picture, they will not give it up. In other words, they will continue to dance with shackled feet.

Zhou Xiaowen opens and ends his *Obsession* with a "lyrical title sequence, set soft-focused in a women's shower-room,"[26] where a group of nude women are washing themselves and each other in steaming water. These two scenes have been described as "utopian," suggesting that "there is no room for women in society apart from this dreamlike, enclosed space. The world outside the bathhouse is violent and unsafe, and women are powerless to change this."[27] While the remark reveals some truth it may also sound an exaggeration. Maybe one should not be too pessimistic. It is just a matter of time before the steaming curtain between the camera and the shower-room in *Obsession* is removed in a figurative sense to reveal the "spring colours" "from behind the wall."

## Notes

This chapter was originally published in *Asian Journal of Communication* 11.2 (2001), 1–17. Reprinted with permission.

1. Zheng Sili, *Zhongguo Xingwenhua: Yige Qiannian Bujie Zhijie/Sexual Culture in China: A Knot Tied by a Millennium* (Beijing: Zhongguo Duiwai Fanyi Chuban Gongsi, 1994), 2.

2. Frank Dikötter, *Sex, Culture and Modernity in China: Medical Science and the Construction of Sexual Identities in the Early Republican Period* (Honolulu: University of Hawaii Press, 1995), 1.

3. *Women in Republican China*, edited by H. R. Lan and V. L. Fong (Armonk, NY: M. E. Sharpe, 1999), provides an excellent sourcebook with regard to the relationship between the May Fourth Movement and the emancipation of Chinese women.

4. Dikötter, *Sex, Culture and Modernity in China*, 2.

5. Harriet Evans, *Women and Sexuality in China: Dominant Discourses of Female Sexuality and Gender since 1949* (Cambridge and Oxford: Polity Press, 1997), 2.

6. Mao Zedong, "Letter to the CCP Committee of Hunan Province: Fully Bringing Out Women's Initiative in the Revolution and Construction," in *Hongqi/Red Flag* (October, 1971): 63.

7. For an enlightening explanation of the principles and contradictions of patriarchal socialism, see Judith Stacey, *Patriarchy and Socialist Revolution in China* (Berkeley: University of California Press 1983), 203–247; and Harriet Evans, "Fashioning Identities, Consuming Passions: Public Images of Women in China," *Culture/China: A Journal of Culture/Theory/Politics* 40 (Spring 2000): 118–120.

8. Mingyan Lai, "Female but not Women: Genders in the Chinese Socialist Texts," Carol Siegel and Ann Kibbey, eds., *Forming and Unforming Identity* (New York: New York University Press 1995), 293.

9. Elizabeth Croll, *The Politics of Marriage in Contemporary China* (Cambridge: Cambridge University Press 1981), 6.

10. Harriet Evans, "Fashioning Identities," 117.

11. Feng Yu, "Jintian de funü fuzhuang wenti (The Question of Women's Dress Today)," *Zhongguo funü* (*China Women*), No. 3 (1955); quoted in Evans, "Fashioning Identities," 118.

12. Despite the generalization, there were two possible exceptions, both involving ballet films. The tight-fitting silk pajamas of Qionghua (the female lead in *The Red Detachment of Women*) and Xi'er (the female lead in *The White-Haired Girl*) were featured in popular pinups in many Chinese homes and dormitory rooms during the period. I am obliged to Paul Clark for suggesting this to me.

13. Paul Clark, *Chinese Cinema: Culture and Politics since 1949* (Cambridge: Cambridge University Press 1987), 134.

14. The Democracy Wall Movement occurred in the winter of 1978–1979, a time of unprecedented relaxation in contemporary Chinese history. The first two stanzas of the poem (*Xing Kaifang/Open Sex*) ran like this:

> *Friend, are you an April Fifth youth?*
> *Let us stand together to advocate open sex.*
> *Oh, you are studying English,*
> *Good, please remember this new phrase:*
> *(Open sex.)*
>
> *1979, it will be Open Sex Year,*
> *If we take a figure of speech:*
> *This year is a girl,*
> *"Open sex" is the little wool hat on her head,*
> *If you do not put it on,*
> *You are not modern at all.*

The translation is from Fang Fu Ruan, *Sex in China: Studies in Sexology in Chinese Culture* (New York: Plenum Press, 1991),160.

15. Sandra Burton, "The Sexual Revolution Hits China," *Time* (12 September 1988): 65.

16. This is true, for instance, in *Yellow Earth* (*Huang tudi*, dir. Chen Kaige, 1984), *A Girl from Hunan* (*Xiangnü Xiaoxiao*, dir. Xie Fei, 1985), *Good Woman* (*Liangjia Funü*, dir. Huang Jianzhong, 1985), and *In the Wild Mountain* (*Yeshan*, dir. Yan Xueshu, 1985). More well-known examples to Western audiences include Zhang Yimou's "women's trilogy": *Red Sorghum*, *Judou* (1990) and *Raise the Red Lantern* (*Dahong Denglong Gaogao Gua*, 1991).

17. Zhang Yingjin, "Ideology of the Body in *Red Sorghum*: National Allegory, National Roots, and Third Cinema," *East-West Film Journal* 4.2 (1990): 40.

18. For details, see Wu Luping, "Hun Lian Xing Guannian De Biandong Guiji/ Changing Concepts of Marriage and Sex," *Zhongguo Qingnian Yanjiu/China Youth Study* 5 (1999): 25.

19. In an interview, the film's director Huang Jianxin claimed that cinematography, *mise-en-scène*, and sound effects were used to make the particular scene "beautiful and pure," so that the young people's conduct could be accepted by a wider range

of audiences. See Zhang Ziliang and Zhu Zi, eds., *Huang Jianxin Zuopin Ji/Selected Works of Huang Jianxin* (Xi'an: Huayue Wenyi Chubanshe, 1989), especially 223–224.

20. Chris Berry, "Representing Chinese Women: Researching Women in the Chinese Cinema," A. Finnane and A. McLaren, eds., *Dress, Sex and Text in Chinese Culture* (Clayton: Monash Asia Institute, 1999), 210.

21. For a critical study of gender inequality as represented in this film, refer to Elissa Rashkin, "Rape as Castration as Spectacle: *The Price of Frenzy's* Politics of Confusion," Tonglin Lu, ed., *Gender and Sexuality in Twentieth-Century Chinese Literature and Society* (Albany: State University of New York Press 1993), 107–119; and Tonglin Lu, "How Do You Tell a Girl from a Boy?: Uncertain Sexual Boundaries in *The Price of Frenzy*," William Burgwinkle, Glenn Man, Valerie Wayne, eds., *Significant Others: Gender and Culture in Film and Literature East and West* (Honolulu: College of Languages, Linguistics and Literature, University of Hawaii and the East-West Center 1993), 63–74.

22. Elissa Rashkin, "Rape as Castration as Spectacle,"113.

23. Mo Yan, "Ye Jiao 'Honggaoliang Jiazu' Beiwanglu/Another Memorandum on *Red Sorghum Saga*, *Daxibei dianying/Film in the Northwest* (April, 1988): 4.

24. Tony Rayns, "The Position of Women in New Chinese Cinema," *East-West Film Journal* 1.2 (June 1987): 43.

25. Chris Berry, "Representing Chinese Women," 206.

26. Paul Clark, "Chinese Cinema in 1989," *Ninth Hawaii International Film Festival* (Honolulu: East-West Center, 1989), 40.

27. Elissa Rashkin, "Rape as Castration as Spectacle," 114.

# 10

# Beyond the Western Gaze

## *Orientalism, Feminism, and the Suffering Woman in Nontransnational Chinese Cinema*

Andrew Grossman

Since the 1919 May Fourth Movement, Chinese feminism has been caught between a struggle for Chinese national identity and the imperialist legacy of Western ideas. Despite indigenous attempts at non-Western feminism before May Fourth, such as the gender egalitarianism espoused by the Taiping Rebellion, it was the modernity that Chinese intellectuals adopted after the 1911 Republican revolution that quickly established Western prejudices. Mainland feminist Wang Zheng has characterized May Fourth feminism as a battle between two kinds of liberal humanism: a progressive philosophy positing women as separate from but equal to men, and a masculinist ideology in which the "human" in "humanism" referred to the modern, first-world male that Chinese revolutionaries should emulate.[1] To achieve equal rights, women following this latter humanism's male slant should impersonate and effectively become neutered men, something like Lin Ching-hsia's butch, cross-dressing Republican revolutionary in Tsui Hark's *Peking Opera Blues* (1986).

Wang calls this masculinized scenario the "Mulan subject position," after the legendary heroine Hua Mulan, who dutifully impersonated a male soldier when her ailing father was unable to fight. It was ironic, though, that revolutionary Chinese women looked toward Mulan: her tale regurgitates filial piety and other outmoded Confucianisms, and she, as impersonated

From *Bright Lights Film Journal* 35 (January 2002). http://www.brightlightsfilm.com/35/chinesefeminism1.html

by Ivy Ling Po in *Lady General Hua Mulan* (1964), continually alternates between masculine power and female (hetero)sexuality without being able to synthesize the two. Later, Maoists would exploit this alternation, for the Mulan archetype afforded communist women a unisexual image of politico-economic power while denying them individualistic sexuality. But the Mulan subject position was only the tip of the iceberg, for revolutionary women's political problems were actually argued by male revolutionaries, who saw in women's liberation a universal allegory for their own liberation from Confucianism and dynasticism. Analogously, as few female-directed Chinese films are exported to the West, the cinematic window through which we transnationally view Chinese "women's issues" has been forever fogged by the (male) likes of Zhang Yimou.

Indeed, in Chinese film the ideological tensions between Eastern and Western feminism have been trumped by the splendiferous depictions of melodramatic female suffering advanced by the Fifth Generation filmmakers. While representations of feudal suffering were common tools both Republican revolutionaries and anti-Confucian Maoists used to critique the *ancien régime*, the persistence of this aesthetic in film has submerged *any* kind of gendered politics beneath a commodifiable aesthetic of cinematographic prettiness, in which the systems critiqued are paradoxically presented romantically, nostalgically, and, in a word, sexily. True, East Asian tragedy has traditionally emphasized suffering, from Mizoguchi's lowly whores, to the fatalistic courtesans of *huang mei* opera-films, to Tong Shu Shuen's classic *The Arch* (1970), about a Ming Dynasty woman valorized for her self-depriving chastity. But Zhang Yimou's expensive, transnationalized images of female pain placed a new, exclusive, international commodity value on the antiquated aesthetics of suffering. If feminism should critique the tyranny of the physical appearances that preserve male and female as biologically—and economically—exclusive and unequal terms, it is ironic for Zhang's *Raise the Red Lantern* (1991) to purportedly critique patriarchy while burying its themes beneath the economically exclusive physical appearances of high-class cinematography.

The twinned evils of orientalism and transnational consumerism now constitute a hackneyed film-studies argument: E. Ann Kaplan,[2] Rey Chow,[3] Dai Jinhua,[4] and Chris Berry[5] have already critiqued the Fifth Generation's exportation of the resplendent aesthetics of rural female suffering.[6] Mainlander Dai Jinhua has argued that Zhang's self-orientalization renders him passively feminine: just as mad Gong Li flails within the patriarchal house of *Red Lantern*, so is Zhang imprisoned within the Western patriarchy and economics of international film distribution. Yet if we narrowly identify artists according to passive-aggressive, female-male binaries, Zhang's actively prestigious, profitable films could be also coded "male" or "aggressive." Indeed, in the recent wake of Hollywood's appropriation of Jackie Chan and Jet Li, the commercialized chinoiserie of *Hero* (2002) and *House of Flying Daggers* (2004), and Zhang's 2007 staging of Tan Dun's East-West "fusion" opera *The First Emperor*, it has become fashionable to deride Chinese artists' opportunistic complicity in manufacturing orientalism.

Rey Chow has defended Zhang by arguing that Zhang's emphases on comely surfaces are not tricky diversions from textual emptiness, but signify a sort of "genuine" superficiality, an "oriental's orientalism" whose parody of the Western gaze juggles self-identity and international identity in a postimperialist, postcolonial struggle to transcend the two. It is questionable, however, whether Zhang would have orientalized himself as early as *Red Sorghum* (1987), before the economic viability of the Fifth Generation aesthetic became fully established. Yet it is more troubling that academics must continually marshal parody, that favorite first and last resort of postmodernism, to fob off a director's cowardly lack of political willfulness. Parody, hardly a salvation in itself, is rather the obligatory curse of transnational consumerism, dumbly pointing out the circuitry of the cross-cultural gaze without disrupting it. Joan Chen's *Xiu Xiu: The Sent-Down Girl* (1998) apotheosizes this nondisruptive (though economically viable) aesthetic of "parodic" orientalism. Although Westernized Chen propagates prodemocracy ideas that Zhang Yimou would not, her Anglicized feminism falls flat under the weight of its oriental prettiness, and her deterministic Maoist critique demands obligatory suffering and martyrdom of its Young Communist heroine *cum* rape victim.

Rather than further explore orientalism and Zhang Yimou-ism, however, we will examine female-centered Chinese films whose images of female suffering are *not* primarily aimed at Westerners, and whose rural exoticisms are intended for modern, post-Mao Chinese audiences who might be reconsidering the premodern values the Cultural Revolution overanxiously erased. First, we will consider a concurrence of barely exported Chinese films about "combed women," an indigenous tradition of deviant, late Qing marriage resistance particular to the Pearl River Delta, whose nonexploitive lesbian undertones further rebuff a heteronormative gaze. Although preoccupied with individuating women's bodily rights and erotic desires from both male and female authoritarian social groups, the three "rural" films I discuss[7]—the mainland's *Women Flowers*, Taiwan's *The Twin Bracelets*, and Hong Kong's *Intimates*—present feminism seemingly motivated by premodern, collectivized identities rather than Westernized individualism. While these films' directors might not intend their films to be labeled "feminist," the "comb sisters' " economic independence and marriage resistance are inherently a kind of anti-Confucian feminism predating May Fourth. However, even these films, despite their deviant subject matter, persist under the influence of orientalist romanticism (*Women Flowers*), obligatory female martyrdom (*Twin Bracelets*), and imperialistic Western feminism (*Intimates*), demonstrating that Chinese films not exported to the West can be equally guilty of the political clichés perpetrated by the ones that are. Furthermore, because their rural romanticisms are primarily intended for domestic audiences, these films produce an oriental's orientalism which cannot be the sly parody Chow suggests, but a sincere—if naïve and self-defeating—desire to renegotiate a disappearing nationalist aesthetic.

Margaret Topley[8] has chronicled the *fin de siecle* phenomenon of combed women, or comb sisters, who formed ritualized sisterhood communities, refused the Confucian oppressions of marriage, earned economic independence through local sericulture industries, and wore their hair defiantly bundled in a comb (a traditional marker of the unwed). While Topley, a second-wave feminist, tends to read regionally constructed political resistance in terms of personal freedom, Stockard[9] has since specified divergent marriage-resistance practices whose varying local customs within the Canton Delta inhibit a monolithically "feminist" interpretation. However, as *Women Flowers* and *Intimates* deemphasize the sisters' economic independence and bring to the foreground their erotic longings, they rewrite a collectivized reaction against patriarchy in terms of modern, individualistic desires. While any individualistic, Western feminism in China may raise the specter of imperialism, these Chinese directors are framing their nativist feminism in the inherently modern, transnational terms of the cinema anyway, just as they may semiconsciously orientalize themselves by indulging in romantically rural subject matter. Dai Jinhua attempts to rationalize this semiconscious orientalism by claiming that "Chinese intellectuals put themselves in a difficult position, since they themselves are deeply attached and rooted in the cultural tradition they came to objectify and reject" (192), but apologies of "deeply rooted" nationalism cannot excuse the sentimental unwillingness of artists—or politicians—to refute their own destructive histories.

Mainlander Wang Jin's *Women Flowers* (1994) begins with two comb sisters performing a sisterhood ceremony. Their exchanges of vows before the altar mimic heterosexual wedlock. However, the comb sisters' bitter matriarch, the vaguely lesbian Miss Sheng, also hypocritically pimps her girls into arranged marriages. While *Flowers* contains no explicit lesbianism, rosily lit scenes where Miss Sheng maternally strokes her favorite girl's face are clearly coded as such. But while the comb sisters' butchness may suggest rudimentary performativity, gender role-playing here is a one-way street, with females continually sliding toward and from the pole of anchored masculine power. The lesbian ambiguities of these combed sisterhoods are further abetted by the conspicuously cautious language of scholars. Topley coyly notes that "several sources refer to lesbian practices in connection with sisterhoods" (76) and that "several [of her] informants expressed a distaste for heterosexual relations" (79), and Hinsch[10] offers "heterosexual chastity" and "economic and social independence" (177–178) as reasons for rural Chinese homosociality, even while admitting "the related hairdressing ritual of the Guangzhou region seems to have been primarily nonsexual" (202n).

One of Sheng's girls, Ah Di, is kidnapped by the husband her deceased parents had arranged for her. Coming to her rescue, Sheng leads a phalanx of comb sisters to confront the husband's family. As they threaten collective suicide by raising scissors to their throats, female suicide becomes equated with the scissors' implication of castration, for in either instance the husband would be robbed of the chance of producing children and continuing his kinship. Intimidated by the sisters' bravado and Sheng's economic power, the groom's father suggests a scenario Stockard historically identifies as a "compensation marriage," wherein the economically independent comb sister appeases her husband by buying him a second wife so that she need not cohabitate with him. However, Ah Di is surprised to discover the fondness she harbors for her unexpectedly decent groom. This shifting emphasis on the comb sister's individual eros—as opposed to the economic independence afforded by her collectivized comb-sister identity—is crystallized when the camera acquires a conspicuous female gaze. When Ah Di's eyeline match ogles the bare-chested groom at a local dragon-boat festival, she suddenly resents being a sex-starved, cryptolesbian comb sister. While a traditional feminist reading might applaud the camera's privileging female desire, these heteronormative eyeline matches not only refute the sisterhoods' homosocial bonds, but stereotypically feminize Ah Di, ensuring she retreats into a passivity from which the groom ultimately can rescue her.

Planning to violate the nonsexual terms of her compensation marriage, Ah Di faces the threat of drowning by Miss Sheng, just as the rebellious women of Wang Jin's earlier *Village of Widows* (1989) face capital punishment for engaging in premarital sex. Deceiving the comb sisters, the groom impersonates Ah Di's executioner, and they flee the village before their romantic transgression can be punished. But then the plot tellingly fixes on Miss Sheng, who now confronts her former flame when he returns to insolently demand a concubine. As Sheng's repressed heterosexuality is climactically revealed, we understand that the tension between Ah Di's individual desires and her collective identity is merely a symptom of the gender binaries that stipulate that Sheng must either be powerlessly feminine or a masculinized exploiter of women. Enraged by her former lover's insolence and realizing she has remained a reactionary pawn with delusions of female power, Sheng climactically immolates the comb sisters' altar and roams the countryside as a madwoman.

While Wang Jin's confused melodrama is more multilayered than Zhang's "parodic" *Red Lantern*, it is ultimately as impotent as its heroine to advance beyond the either-or fallacy of the neurotic Mulan woman, whose agency exists in inverse proportion to her heteronormative passivity. In a sense, Ah Di and Miss Sheng represent complementary halves of the

Mulan subject position: Sheng is the neurotically masculinized half, denying her "inner" heterosexuality for so long that when its repressed specter (the former flame) finally returns she instantly plunges into lunacy, whereas Ah Di stands for the inner "real" woman—whose "reality" is equated with passivity—struggling to assert an individuality coded as and subsumed by heteronormativity. However, this unofficial incarnation of Mulan-ism is not the burgeoning modernity of May Fourth's urban intellectual elite, but a premodern dead-end, as the deviant socioeconomic powers of Miss Sheng's "economic lesbianism," having no rightful place within rural Confucianism, become identified with outright madness.

While transnational *Xiu Xiu* and *Red Lantern* peddle postcards of China to the West, the subdued lyricism and moderately pretty cinematography of the middle-budget *Women Flowers* romanticize a premodern past for a domestic Chinese audience still recovering from the Cultural Revolution and hopefully climbing towards transnational capitalism. Because the film tackles the issue of the Mulan woman in a premodern context, before Maoism made her into an asexual (or unisexual) communist, its deconstruction of Mulan-ism can undo the "damage" done to women during the Cultural Revolution, returning to them the essential (hetero)sexuality they exchanged for modernity, while taking back the economic power that was not theirs to begin with. Simultaneously, the film romanticizes the innocent, premodern context to which these gender contentions have been relocated. Therefore, the film's feminism is intractably caught between transnationalist progress and nationalist nostalgia, as rural premodernity becomes the site of both feminist critique and anti-Mao romance, and as nativism becomes a reflexive tool with which nativism itself must fruitlessly be attacked.

While Huang Yu-shan's *The Twin Bracelets* (1992) does not pathologize lesbianism like *Women Flowers*, its thesis schematically romanticizes the bankrupt aesthetic of female suffering. Although *Bracelets*, a modern-day Taiwanese narrative, exists apart from the "official" comb-sister narratives of *Women Flowers* and *Intimates*, its story of female marriage resistance and rural homosociality warrants grouping the three films together. The film's teenage heroines, Hsiu and Hui-hua, live in a modern-day fishing village whose sexist, anachronistic customs permit brides, who must marry in their teens, to visit their arranged (and promiscuous) husbands only three times a year, to procreate. Should these visitation rules be violated, the man must publicly thrash his wife, while he endures only social humiliation. Suffering *Women Flowers*' patriarchal worldview but lacking its economically independent women's societies, Hsui and Hui-hua swear a pact as blood sisters to avoid the abusive marriages looming in their futures: "We vow as sisters to be man and wife."

Four years later, Hsui must wed an arranged husband, but as the two girls share a bath, a threatened Hui-hua reiterates their earlier vow: "Which is the closer relationship? That between man and wife or that between sisters?" Unlike the conflation of heterosexual marriage and sisterhood implied by their original vow, now "man and wife" and "sisters" emerge as two practically separate categories. As their close proximity in the steamy tub discloses their feminism's lesbian undertones, they exchange the titular bracelets that will bond their hearts. In a rebuff of the man-hating scenario we expect, Hsui's arranged husband is a handsome saint—exactly as in *Women Flowers*—and the two fall in love; Hui-hua's parents, meanwhile, pawn her off to a local bully in exchange for his sizeable dowry. The film ends with a pregnant and thus futuric Hsui boarding a modern bus—a shockingly incongruous sight in a film that otherwise seems ages removed from our "modern" times—and returning to Hui-hua her bracelet for eternal keeping. Understanding that a better life awaits Hsui, Hui-hua knowingly accepts the bracelet, spurns her rapist husband, and stoically descends into the sea's suicidal depths. Although suicide was a well-documented type of rural marriage resistance, a pretext of unimaginative historical realism does not excuse the film—a voluntary fiction—from perpetuating nonconfrontational aesthetics of suffering.[11] Moreover, while not homophobic like *Women Flowers*, *Bracelet*'s brand of feminist lesbianism, like that of Deepa Mehta's *Fire* (1996), presents same-sex bonding not as an active choice but as a reactive mechanism whose immediate struggle is not for a better lesbianism, but a better heterosexuality.

The Hong Kong film *Intimates* (1997), directed by Jacob Cheung and written by Anita Tong, offers a liberalized version of these marriage-rebellion scenarios. Flashing back and forth between modern-day Hong Kong (where the values of Western feminism are still underappreciated) and rural, post-Revolutionary 1930s China (where combed marriage resistance becomes a catalyst to lesbian romance), the film introduces explicitly Western elements that the pre-Revolutionary scenario of *Women Flowers* cannot. The film also fits within a pattern of 1997-era Hong Kong films—such as Shu Kei's *Hu-du-men* (1996) and *A Queer Story* (1997)—whose championing of democratically queer identities seemingly challenged mainland homophobia. The film begins in the present day: Americanized Wai is stern with male employees but is taken advantage of by her unfaithful boyfriend (once again, economic competence is binarily opposed to [hetero]sexual competence). She cannot grasp the easy feminist confidence of her father's elderly maid, whom she is obliged to escort to her Cantonese hometown. When the maid, Foon, nostalgically caresses a comb, we flash back to the 1930s, where she, a comb sister, waits to be pawned off to an arranged husband. But generous Wan, the eighth wife of Foon's silk-merchant boss, reimburses the husband his dowry and frees Foon, lest she become like fatalistic Hui-hua in *Bracelets*. Soon, Westernized Wan, herself a former prostitute, develops a lesbian attachment to Foon, assuming that she, a homosocial comb sister, would be logically open to such advances. While

Foon cuts Wan's hair—an ironic version of combing—Wan ceremonially offers earrings to Foon, similar to the exchanging of fetishistic jewelry in *Bracelets*.

At a dragon-boat festival, combed yet apparently heterosexual Foon catches a handsome fisherman's eye and—precisely as in the dragon-boat scene in *Women Flowers*—the camera adopts a female gaze as an eyeline match is used to show Foon glimpsing his bare-chested athleticism. Yet in a thematically subtle (or ambiguous) scene, Foon accompanies Wan to a wealthy warlord's mansion, where impoverished Foon enviously watches Wan and her husband waltz in occidental dress. After the men depart, Wan playfully encourages Foon to dance, Wan adopting the male role in the dance and Foon the female. Yet each adopts these roles only after the other partner has defined them: intuitively finishing each other's sentences, Wan says, "I'll be the . . ." and Foon finishes her sentence with "man," while Wan finishes Foon's complementary sentence with the word "woman." Only in this Western dance scene is gender role-playing complicit, loving, and voluntary, unlike the seemingly tender—but in fact asexual—nativist masculinism of Foon's comb sisters.

Later, a flashback wherein Foon massages wounds Wan suffered during abusive heterosexual intercourse is intercut with a contemporary scene of an older Foon rubbing the back of an inebriated, sexually unsatisfied Wai. So although wealthy Wan attempted to coax a lesbian romance from poor Foon by extrapolating a Western-framed lesbianism from her comb-sister homosociality, a now-empowered Foon transfers this extrapolation into the present day (through film cuts) to a poor Wai as unemancipated from her callous boyfriend as Foon was from the sexual futility of the comb sisters. More simply, because the flashback structure codes the past as Chinese and the present as Western, and because what Westernized, heterosexual Wai needs is a good dose of *non*lesbian feminism, temporal *cum* social progress is orchestrated in Western terms that effectively dismiss the combed sisterhoods whose homosociality inspires the film's modern feminism.

In another flashback, an anxious Wan finally, passionately kisses Foon in a rare burst of honest emotion. But Foon responds, "We're women . . . it's impossible," a statement explaining to Wan the difference between combed homosociality and outright homosexuality. After Wan rescues Foon from a gruesome abortion necessitated by a taboo night of passion with the fisherman, Foon's defenses break down and the two finally make love. In a mawkish finale, Wan's husband forgives Wan for her lesbian transgression and implores her to accompany him by steamship to escape the Nanking Massacre. But Wan climactically leaps from the boat, opting to take her lesbian chances with Foon instead. We then make our final return to the present, where an elderly Foon nervously awaits her reunion with long-lost Wan. But in a genuinely surprising, bizarre twist, young Wai learns that the woman she—and we—thought was Foon is actually Wan! "I started asking for Foon so often, people started to call me 'Foon'," Wan says, thus totally reversing the identifications we had made all along, complicating to an impossible degree our attempt to extricate the film's premodern homosociality from its "bi-curious" modern feminism.

In the reunion scene, however, we are forbidden to see (the real) Foon's elderly face: as the camera is about to reveal her, we instead magically, nostalgically see Foon as the young woman we know from the flashbacks, and Wan is transformed likewise. While previously the film merely framed combed feminism within its modern flashback format, it now reinscribes those premodern identities into that modernity, as if the women's youthful lesbian identity were now being declared openly in democratic, "out" Hong Kong. In effect, director Cheung performs a kind of ideological cosmetic surgery on his heroines: we see the present-tense framing of premodern China in terms of modern democracy. On another level, because young Wai has shown no lesbian tendencies, the film conservatively offers solidarity in gender, and not in sexuality, as Foon and Wan's Chinese lesbian odyssey simply becomes transnational shorthand for overarching modern feminism.

We have examined *Women Flowers*, *Twin Bracelets*, and *Intimates* to see if they offer alternatives to Zhang Yimou-ism, for these are examples of moderately prestigious yet barely exported films that perpetuate rural romanticism while offering a Chinese feminism removed from both heteronormative and transnational gazes. But even though presenting a non-Westernized concern for female bodily autonomy and individual desire—and thus at first glance seeming to offer such alternatives—these films demonstrate that the failure of many generically rural films to adequately address women's issues is *not* reducible to the transnational or orientalist gazes Zhang Yimou-ism fosters. Therefore, we should examine a brief set of urban Chinese feminist films, by both male and female filmmakers, whose feminism turns on the *universal* criterion of *class* and not the particular criterion of nationality or nativism.

While some Westernized Chinese filmmakers have, of course, directly engaged American feminism, films such as Ann Hui's *Starry Is the Night* (1988), Clara Law's anti-Mao *Reincarnation of Golden Lotus* (1989), Sylvia Chang's *Mary from Beijing* (1992), and the omnibus *Conjugal Affairs* (1994) all engage middle-class feminism, not the class- and race-conscious "womanism" Western academies fostered as a panacea for feminism's bourgeois bias. Therefore, one must consider *The Mistress* (1999), whose director, Crystal Kwok, began not as an empowered auteur but (like many Hong Kong actresses) as a beauty pageant winner, one whose struggles against sexism mirror those of her film's heroines. Notably, *The Mistress* boasts a "category III rating," a censorship marker generally indicating either sex-and-violence exploitation or, more rarely, a film of sociopolitically sensitive subject matter (c.f., *If I Were for Real* [1981], *Cageman* [1992], and so forth). Kwok has expressed surprise at the censorship certificate: "It was classified category III. However, there is no nudity. . . . It explores female sexuality from a psychological point of view. It is a subject that is taboo in HK."[12] The film begins as University of California, Berkeley graduate Alex tutors tycoon Henry's mistress Michelle in English, the international language of capital, while Michelle, a mainlander versed in the hardships of poverty, tutors naive Alex in the universal language of concubinage. Michelle draws Alex into her world, first at a garish S–M party, and later when they humiliate a masochistic fat client by kicking him under a mahjong table while they gamble. "The more money they have, the more perverse they get," says Michelle, as the mahjong table comes to symbolize a Hong Kong economy seemingly managed by common citizens (they play the game) but which is really controlled by giggling, well-fed men behind (or in this case under) the scene.

When Alex becomes Henry's second mistress, and temporarily stands content in his boardroom, surveying at eye level the phallic skyscrapers surrounding her beyond the corporate windows, she has broken through the glass ceiling using the only "weapon" she has: bodily materialism. While in premodern *Women Flowers* and *Intimates* ascendant female desire was cued through eye-line matches directed at male sex objects, here the ascendancy of female material power becomes pessimistically equated with the negation of Alex's desires, for the objects of her skyline gaze are not flesh and blood but sterile phalluses of modernist steel. While *The Mistress* purports to examine desire from a female perspective, Alex's fantasies are masochistic, posit a male spectator, or both, and seemingly represent a female internalization of male desire. Initially, prompted by bizarre stories of sexual deviance she overhears, a sexually frustrated Alex has exuberant fantasies: businessmen dine on sashimi served upon naked women; she herself becomes a living sex doll; she joins Henry and Michelle in their "French maid" sex games; and Henry strikes pricey golden golf balls into her vagina. Each scenario posits a male spectator and female objectification (quite literally in the sex doll fantasy!), mentalities she adopts and internalizes upon her entrée into a masculine capitalism where the mistress becomes another replaceable commodity whose built-in obsolescence is hardly different from that of a car or microwave.

At a dinner party with Henry's business colleagues—all in attendance with their mistresses—Michelle does an expert impersonation of Henry, imitating his business rhetoric, chomping a cigar, and finally making a toast. "To Hong Kong! To the economy! To our country!" she says, with "country" optimistically referring to post-1997 China, not Hong Kong. Later in the film, the tycoon dinner-party scene is replayed, but now Alex attempts to duplicate Michelle's parody of Henry's machismo. Yet Anglicized Alex is unable to confidently smoke the Freudian cigar Michelle puffed so professionally—Alex will become an incompetent mistress because she, unlike former prostitute Michelle, does not know how to be successfully submissive. Driven to madness after Henry grows weary of her individualism, Alex destroys her mistress-gotten apartment and languishes in the gutters before an ironic coda image places her and Michelle on a fantastic stage, clad as chorus girls, singing a sarcastically cheerful anthem to female passivity. In the end, the lessons of their odyssey will have little influence on the sociological condition of women at large, and their travails, grounded in the old courtesan aesthetic of compulsory female martyrdom, at best produce a sense of irony as politically impotent as one of Zhang Yimou's oriental self-parodies.

In truth, people judge films the way they judge each other: by physical appearances. All the films we have discussed are, if not "A-level" productions, at least "B+" productions aimed at audiences with preconceived notions of bourgeois cinematic respectability; even *The Mistress*, winner of the People's Choice Award at France's Deauville Film Festival, encodes its capitalist critique in the fanciest visual terms possible, thus succumbing to a kind of capitalism in form if not content. So if we are still concerned with the orientalist agenda underlying the transnational commerce that decides which films receive Western distribution, we should ultimately turn our attentions to feminist films of such low budgets that they, although perhaps informed by Western feminism, have neither an interest in nor a possibility of reaching a sizeable Western audience.

While few category III films are as politicized as *The Mistress*, and fewer still are as artistically respectable, the category III rating's censorial conflation of sex and politics[13] has birthed sensationalistic subgenres preoccupied with women's bodily autonomy, usually understood in terms of horrific rape-revenge.[14] Just as Carol Clover has argued that exploitive rape-revenge thrillers, such as *I Spit on Your Grave* (1978), are actually more feministic than their mainstream counterparts, low-budget category III films, because they don't demand critical respect, can provide disempowered audiences and directors alike with a safe space to nakedly enact body politics that in mainstream cinema would be sanitized, coded with allegory, or disallowed entirely. Of course, low budgets alone do not guarantee "authentic" politics. While the furies of films such as Ho Meng-hua's prototypical rape-revenge potboiler *Kiss of Death* (1973) may gratify, their caricatured castration fixations—in addition to being symptomatic of neurotic male filmmakers—merely neuter patriarchy symbolically, rather than progressively remaking it.

Chor Yuan's *Intimate Confessions of a Chinese Courtesan* (1972), generally regarded as Hong Kong's first lesbian film, forms a bridge between the passive suffering of the courtesan film and the sexually emancipated violence of vengeful category III rape heroines. Director Clarence Fok has even acknowledged that his *Naked Killer* (1992), the *ne plus ultra* of category III, is a thinly veiled variation on *Intimate Confessions*. Chor Yuan's film begins when young Ai Nu is kidnapped into the hands of predatory brothel-keeper Lady Chun. Although Chun's "entrepreneurial" lesbianism is uncloseted and superficially feminine, unlike that of butch Miss Sheng in *Women Flowers*, her sword-wielding power is predicated on the social norms of martial violence that regularly construct masculine advantage and dominion. When Ai Nu refuses Chun's erotic advances, she is sold to four despicable men, and thereafter makes an unsuccessful suicide attempt. But unlike the suffering Hui-hua in *Twin Bracelets*, Ai Nu will not euthanize herself; deciding to seek revenge, she finally accepts Chun's love, feigning affection so that she, as Chun's favorite, can accrue power and secretly plot vengeance against her four rapists and captor. Whereas the lesbian heroines of *Naked Killer* are cutthroat yet sincere, we see through Ai Nu's pretensions and hardly believe her when she confides to Chun: "I think I'm becoming like you—hating men . . . this could mean that I'll love you more. . . ." Because Ai Nu's lesbianism is insincere, it cannot temper the gory, generically determined martial-arts violence she engages in to avenge her despoliation. Despite (or perhaps because of) its admitted visual artistry, *Intimate Confessions* has laid the either-or groundwork of rape-revenge, which mandates that women, pretending to libertarian autonomy, must reproduce masculinist norms of violence to cease their passive suffering.

Let us conclude, then, with a rare category III film that not only rejects the elitist economics of visually attractive art, but espouses a nonaggressive, anticapitalist agenda in lieu of the bloodletting that usually poses as "feminism" in the genre film. Although Ivan Lai's *A Fake Pretty Woman* (1995) is more of a sexploitation melodrama than the rape thriller the category III rating usually signifies, its themes of bodily violation and autonomy intersect with those of the rape film, an ideologically overarching category encompassing everything from sleazy horror to *Xiu Xiu*. *Fake*'s flat-chested heroine "May," conditioned by a breast-obsessed Hong Kong to believe she is unworthy, undergoes plastic surgery at the hands of female Dr. Wong to become precisely the type of fluffy fashion model most category III films promote as safe sexual icons. Her surgeries enable her to become a successful actress and the fiancé of a billionaire's son, yet a feministic deus ex machina mandates that a wayward truck demolish her wedding procession, leaving her hideously scarred by poetic justice. On learning from surgeons and scandal sheets that May is a "fake pretty woman," the wealthy groom-to-be abandons her, hypocritically disgusted by her bodily capitalism. Unlike the myopic postfeminism of Garry Marshall's *Pretty Woman* (1990), in *A Fake Pretty Woman* a woman cannot successfully mobilize her sexual bodily power, for in a world of limited options whoring (or self-commodification) is not an active choice but a built-in precondition.

Most notable, though, is the character of Dr. Wong, a female plastic surgeon who admits to profiteering from women's self-debasement. As with *Women Flowers*' pimping Miss Sheng, capitalist women operate as exploitatively as men, as passive-aggressive economics feed into and define gender binarism. Yet Wong's own feminist consciousness is piqued when she catches her adulterous husband entertaining a twenty-something bimbo. Although May is ostensibly the heroine, it is the middle-aged Wong, curiously, who narrates the film in voice-over ("I feel terrible when I think of the word 'old' "), and who considers plastic surgery herself after realizing that her performatively "masculine" profession doesn't spare her the indignities reserved for biological women. Only when treating a male friend of May's who was severely burned, and subsequently witnessing his girlfriend's devotion in spite of his hideous disfigurement, does she realize both her marriage and profession are shams. In the end, we see a divorced Dr. Wong with the happy couples she has treated, but she walks into the sunset alone—this is not the transcendental descent into the shadowy pleasure quarters that closes Mizoguchi's protofeminist *A Geisha* (1953), nor the noble false front of female perseverance climactically worn by Takamini Hideko in Naruse's *When a Woman Ascends the Stairs* (1960), but a defiant march to the upbeat tune of the closing credits. Admittedly, the inclusion of happy couples (monogamy) and the single defiant woman (asexuality) only redistributes to two parties the either-or binaries that underwrite normative-conservative sexuality, rather than having them occur alternately within the same woman as a feministic identity crisis. Nevertheless, *Fake*'s feminism unpretentiously demonstrates the coercive interrelationship between economics and sexuality while avoiding the predictable aesthetic of martyrdom indulged by *Xiu Xiu* and even *The Mistress*, but will be deemed beneath consideration by respectable critics and bourgeois audiences because its themes operate within a subgenre that is "low" and content-based (category III sexploitation) and not "high" and form-based (narrative arc of tragic suffering).

Meanwhile, *Xiu Xiu*, winner of numerous Golden Horse Awards, is essentially mainstream in Taiwan, but its tame, politically correct, liberal-humanist content is rendered through the Western politics of film distribution into something falsely, undeservedly oppositional, simply because *any* imported film seems oppositional when weighed against Hollywood xenophobia. In fact, the oppressions of surgical beauty that *Fake* decries are analogous to the oppressions of cinematographic beauty that *Xiu Xiu* advances: both oppressions are products of first-world technology designed to exploit the viewer's sensibilities for profit. Simply, both plastic surgery and expensive cinematography are in the business of selling an economic definition of beauty to reinforce classist sensibilities of appearance-based value—it is merely a puritanical hypocrisy that disparages the capitalism of plastic surgery as deceptive and praises the capitalism of prettified cinematography as aesthetically genuine.

## Notes

For an alternate version of this essay, see www.brightlightsfilm.com/35/chinesefeminism1.html.

1. Wang Zheng, *Women in the Chinese Enlightenment* (Berkeley: University of California Press, 1999), 17–18.

2. E. Ann Kaplan, "Problematising Cross-Cultural Analysis: The Case of Women in Recent Chinese Cinema," Chris Berry, ed., *Perspectives on Chinese Cinema* (London: British Film Institute, 1991), 141–154.

3. Rey Chow, *Primitive Passions: Visuality, Sexuality, Ethnography, and Contemporary Chinese Cinema* (New York: Columbia University Press, 1995), 12-14, 150-162

4. Dai Jinhua, "Rewriting Chinese Women: Gender Production and Cultural Space in the Eighties and Nineties," Mayfair Mei-hui Yang, ed., *Spaces of Their Own: Women's Public Sphere in Transnational China* (Minneapolis: University of Minnesota Press, 1999), 191–206.

5. Chris Berry, "Representing Chinese Women: Researching Women in the Chinese Cinema," Antonia Finnane and Anne McLaren, ed., *Dress, Sex, and Text in Chinese Culture* (Clayton, Australia: Monash Asia Institute, 1999).

6. I agree with Chow's critique of Kaplan, who overemphasizes the "dangers" of cross-cultural analysis. Nevertheless, both Kaplan and Berry caution against reducing all Western appreciation of Chinese cinema to a convenient common denominator of orientalism.

7. Other rural marriage-resistance films include Wang Jin's *Village of Widows* (1989) and *The Girls to Be Married* (1990), and Taiwanese Yeh Hung-wei's *Five Girls and a Rope* (1991).

8. Margaret Topley, "Marriage Resistance in Rural Kwantung," Margery Wolf and Roxane Witke, eds.,*Women in Chinese Society* (Palo Alto: Stanford University Press, 1975), 67–88.

9. Janice Stockard, *Daughters of the Canton Delta* (Palo Alto: Stanford University Press, 1989), 79.

10. Bret Hinsch, *Passions of the Cut Sleeve* (Berkeley: University of California Press, 1990), 177-78, 202n.

11. See director Huang's *Spring Cactus* (1999) for an urban twist on *Twin Bracelets*' themes of female martyrdom.

12. From an untitled interview with Kwok at http://www.ifrance.com/hkcinemagic/siteanglais/atsuihark/acrystal.htm (March 31, 2001).

13. Julian Stringer discusses category III body politics in "Sex and Violence in Postmodern Hong Kong," Christopher Sharrett, ed., *Mythologies of Violence in Postmodern Media* (Detroit: Wayne State University Press, 1999).

14. Cf., for example, *Raped by Angel* (1993), *Love to Kill* (1993), *The Wrath of Silence* (1994), and *Red to Kill* (1994).

# 11

# Disappearing Faces:

## *Bisexuality and Transvestism in Two Hong Kong Comedies*

Helen Hok-Sze Leung

### Bisexuality and the Conundrum of Gender

*I cannot recall, when I first dreamt of you*
*If you were wearing a neck tie or a dress*
*I cannot recall if that scent was your fragrance*
*Or your eyebrow steeped in smiles*

*I cannot recall, when I dreamt of you again*
*If you were wearing ear-rings or a moustache*
*I cannot recall if that bronze ring was your jewelry*
*Or your feigned nonchalance*

*You said you cried after reading a poem*
*I said I don't like writing gray words anymore*
*Is there even a relation, or are dreams speaking?*
*You said you love a severe winter*
*I said I no longer detest the hot sun*
*Is there even a connection, or are dreams conversing?*[1]
— Anson Mak, *Bisexual Desire*

This poem, which appears in the first Chinese-language publication on bisexuality to appear in Hong Kong, articulates bisexual desire by eroticizing the ambivalence of gender difference. The speaker in the poem invokes clichéd markers of gender (necktie, dress, earrings, moustache), but the neat lineup of binary oppositions is displaced by the speaker's pleasurable refusal to "recall" the difference between each pair of opposed terms. This deconstructive tactic is reminiscent of Hélène Cixous's famous pairings of masculinity and femininity in "Sorties," where Cixous offered one of the earliest feminist attempts to deconstruct gender in Derridean fashion.[2] Yet, the bisexual lover's imperative is not exactly the same as the feminist one's: it is erotic rather than critical. It does not aim so much to undo the hierarchical power structure of gendered signs as to eroticize their interchangeability. In the poem, it remains unclear (and it does not matter) whether the necktie or the dress is worn (or desired) by a female or male body. The erotic resides in the dreamlike atmosphere where it is impossible to tell the difference, and where the possibility of multiple and simultaneous configurations of sexed bodies, gender identification, and desire exists. In effect, Anson Mak's poem issues an erotic challenge to what Judith Butler has theorized as the "heterosexual matrix": that the logic that requires identification and desire be mutually exclusive, and that it presume "if one identifies *as* a given gender, one must desire a different gender."[3] Bisexual eroticism undoes this equation and opens room for a radically different understanding of gender and sexuality.

This notion of bisexuality—not as a political identity, sexual orientation, or descriptive category, but as a deconstructive principle—informs the primary argument in Marjorie Garber's *Vice Versa: Bisexuality and the Eroticism of the Everyday Life*, which documents in approximately five hundred pages the ubiquitous presence of bisexual desire in Western culture. For Garber, the apparently infinitely inexhaustible accounts of bisexuality's presence do not so much define bisexuality as reveal its radical openness:

> If bisexuality is . . . not just another sexual orientation but rather a sexuality that undoes sexual orientation as a category, a sexuality that threatens and challenges the easy binaries of straight and gay, queer and "het," and even, through its biological and physiological meanings, the gender categories of male and female, then the search for the meaning of the word "bisexual" offers a different kind of lesson. . . . The question of whether someone was "really" straight or "really" gay misrecognizes the nature of sexuality, which is fluid, not fixed, a narrative that changes over time rather than a fixed identity, however complex. The erotic discovery of bisexuality is the fact that it reveals sexuality to be a process of growth, transformation, and surprise, not a stable and knowable state of being.[4]

In Garber's study, bisexuality often serves as an interpretive strategy, a way of rereading texts previously understood simply as "gay" texts, or more often *failed* "gay" texts that recuperate heterosexual closures. As such, the consideration of bisexual desire and eroticism serves as an effective intervention into what Ellis Hanson, in the context of queer cinema, has criticized as the "politics of representation" model of reading. Hanson argued that ideology critiques that are preoccupied with prescribing positive or liberating images presuppose the possibility and desirability of an "authentic" representation while discounting complex mediating factors such as cinematic pleasure, spectatorial positions, and processes of (mis)identification.[5] Thus, films like *Personal Best*, *Henry and June*, or *The Wedding Banquet*, which explore the permeability rather than the absolute incommensurability of gay and straight desires, are often perceived to be not authentically representative of gay experience. Efforts like Garber's to reread them as bisexual rather than as failed gay texts call attention to the fluidity and unpredictability of sexual desire, which are not accounted for in the discourse of fixed "sexual orientation."

In the context of Hong Kong cinema, where the conscious and serious exploration of queer desire in cinema is only a very recent phenomenon—best exemplified by all of Stanley Kwan's films since *Yin +/– yang* (*Nansheng Nuxiang*, 1996) and the works of independent film and video makers such as Raymond Yeung and Yau Ching—the consideration of bisexuality provides a refreshing and useful perspective to interpret the strong undercurrent of homoeroticism in ostensibly "straight" genres such as action films and comedies. In comedies in particular, where irreverent and subversive subject matters are usually couched in humor and inevitably tamed by ideologically conservative endings, the representations of homoeroticism and gay desire often appear to provide nothing more than comic relief before disappearing to make way for heterosexual closures. One of the most popular tropes used to produce this kind of comedy is the transvestite disguise. The momentary misrecognition of a character's gender identity induces what appears to be homosexual desire but which becomes unmasked as "really" heterosexual when the transvestite disguise is removed at the end. While an ideological critique of such films yields many insights into the recuperative power of heterocentrism, it also tends to elide the intimate relation between transvestism and bisexual desire. It is no coincidence that *Vested Interests*, Garber's book on transvestism, is strikingly similar in structure and style to *Vice Versa*. In *Vested Interests*, transvestism—like bisexuality in the later book—was invoked as a deconstructive principle, what Garber called the logic of "the third":

> The "third" is that which questions binary thinking and introduces crisis . . . the "third term" is *not* a *term*. Much less is it a *sex*, certainly not an instantiated "blurred" sex as signified by a term like "androgyne" or "hermaphrodite. . . ." The "third" is a mode of articulation, a way of describing a space of possibility. Three puts

into question the idea of one: of identity, self-sufficiency, self-knowledge.[6]

While bisexuality challenges the logic of "sexual orientation" that fixes, once and for all, the relation between gender identification and sexual desire, transvestism calls into questions the putatively stable relation between sexed bodies and gender identity. The seemingly innocuous use of transvestite disguise in comedies often instigates bisexual pleasures that cannot be easily recontained by heterosexual closures. What I would like to show in the rest of this chapter is the various and complex ways in which transvestism generates bisexual spectatorial pleasure despite seemingly heterosexual resolutions.

## The Pleasures of the Fence

Peter Chan's two box-office smash hits, *He's a Woman, She's a Man* (*Jinzhi Yuye*, 1996) and the sequel *Who's the Woman, Who's the Man* (*Jinzhi Yuye II*, 1996), provide a useful point of departure for the discussion of bisexuality and transvestism in Hong Kong cinema. The sexual politics of the first film have been criticized for stereotypical representation of minor gay characters (such as the record producer played by Eric Tsang and the Cantonese opera singer played by Law Kar-Ying) and the film's restoration of heterosexual romance at the end.[7] Perhaps aware of or anticipating such criticism, the director Peter Chan even felt the need to make a disclaimer in the form of a short documentary that appears in the video release of the film. In his disclaimer, Chan states that *He's a Woman* "looks at a changing world purely through the lens of heterosexuality." In this "changing world," Chan and some of the lead actors went on to suggest, there is an increasing awareness in people of the possibility of latent gay desire. ("Everyone, at one time or another of their life, has probably considered the possibility that they may be gay.") Indeed, one of the film's plot lines follows the twists and turns of a man's exploration of this latent possibility. On the surface, then, the film seems to be about gay desire that appears and recedes in people who ultimately heave a sigh of relief at the reassurance that they are, after all, "really" heterosexual. Yet, despite the complete silence on bisexuality in popular discourses around the film, it is precisely bisexuality that structures the fundamental dynamics of desire in both this film and its sequel. Moreover, bisexual desire is instigated by and articulated through the practice of transvestism.

*He's a Woman* tells the story of Wing (Anita Yuen), a young woman of meager means who idolizes a glamorous show-business couple: the producer and songwriter Sam Koo (Leslie Cheung) and the superdiva Rose (Carina Lau), who rises to stardom under Koo's tutelage. Unknown to adoring fans like Wing, the romance between Koo and Rose is cooling down. In an attempt to curb his own tendency to fall for the newest female singer under his tutelage, Koo decides to sign an "ordinary young man" instead for his next recording project. Obsessed with meeting her idols, Wing disguises herself as a young man and shows up at the audition. Through chance, Wing actually wins the audition in spite of her mediocre singing talent. She moves in with Koo while being groomed as an upcoming recording star. Sexual attraction between Wing and Koo develops, despite resistance from both: Koo because of his homophobia and Wing because of her reluctance to break up Rose and Koo. Koo struggles with his homoerotic impulses before Wing's disguise is finally unmasked and heterosexual romance wins the day.

The film employs many of the generic conventions that Chris Straayer attributes to "the temporary transvestite film." Films in this genre, Straayer suggests, offer viewers "a momentary vicarious trespassing of society's accepted boundaries for gender and sexual behavior," while allowing viewers to "relax confidently in the orderly demarcations reconstituted by the films' ending."[8] Straayer's discussion of Hollywood films shows that their deployment of transvestite disguise sutures viewers into alternately or simultaneously heterosexual and homosexual subject-positions. This "fence-sitting" pleasure is generated through an unstable oscillation between different levels and elements of the film text. In Hollywood films, such an oscillation is usually stabilized at the end by the powerful reassertion of heterosexual closure. In *He's a Woman* and *Who's the Woman*, this spectatorial fence is constructed in more complex ways, by a multivalent bisexual epistemology that is not so readily recuperable by heterosexual closure.

Although never explicitly acknowledged, it is in fact bisexual desire that motivates Wing's transvestite disguise. In Hollywood films of the same genre, the transvestite disguise is usually purely functional. For example, Dustin Hoffman's character in *Tootsie* is driven by economic necessity to look for work disguised as a woman, while Robin Williams' character in *Mrs. Doubtfire* dresses up as a woman to be close to his children after he has lost a custody battle to his ex-wife. By contrast, Wing's disguise is *erotically* motivated by her idolatry of Rose and Koo as a couple. In a very comical opening scene, Wing weeps with joy in front of the television set as Rose declares her love for Koo on a live broadcast during an awards ceremony. In this scene, Wing is a spectator *par excellence*. The complex dynamics of her relation to the spectacle illustrate what Maria Pramaggiore characterizes as "bisexual spectatorship"— that is, "the spectatorial difficulty of clearly distinguishing between wanting to 'be' a character . . . and wanting to 'have' a character."[9] When Rose pronounces her love for Koo on the television screen, Wing repeats after her, "I love you too." It is ambiguous whether "you" refers to Rose (in which case Wing is desiring Rose through the gaze) or Koo (in which case Wing is identifying with

Rose through the gaze). This conflation between desire and identification is more dramatically realized in a later scene. Rose, certain that Wing is a man but uncertain whether "he" is straight or gay, decides to test Wing's attraction to her. After a romantic dinner together, Rose takes Wing back to her apartment and starts to undress in Wing's presence. Wing looks longingly at Rose's breasts and asks for permission to fondle them, mumbling, "I have never known what it feels like to have such big breasts." Wing is ostensibly experiencing a moment of envy, desiring to be like Rose. However, her narcissistic identification is channeled into a desire for (hence a wish to fondle) Rose's breasts. Besides Wing's conflation of desire and identification vis-à-vis (the spectacle of) Rose, she is also implicated in another common figure for bisexuality: the triangle. As the opening scene clearly suggests, Wing is initially attracted to Rose and Koo as a couple, with herself as an undefined third term rather than a replacement of Rose. In an early scene, Wing declares her wish for Rose and Koo to love each other forever, and for herself to become their "invisible angel." When Wing discovers that she has caused Koo and Rose to break up, her reaction is explicitly depicted as a moment of pain, rather than as pleasure or triumph. The erasure of Rose and the domestication of Wing into part of a heterosexual couple at the end of the film results from the characters' failure to acknowledge and explore the erotic possibilities of bisexuality, even though these possibilities have driven much of their previous action. More important, such an ending marks the film's failure to fully accommodate the complex demands of bisexual spectatorship.

However, the scene that actually ends the film is curiously not completely devoid of queer resonance, showing once again a fence-sitting impulse. Bisexuality resurfaces in Koo, who decides that he loves Wing *before* he clearly understands that Wing is "actually" a woman. Wing, wearing a dress in front of Koo for the first time, tells Koo that she is "really a woman." However, much as Dil (Jaye Davidson) in *The Crying Game* looks even less like a man when Ferghus (Stephen Rea) "restores" him/her to masculine attire, Anita Yuen with her cropped hair, waif-like figure, and minimal make-up also looks curiously at odds with her feminine clothing in this scene. Koo, understandably suspicious and unconvinced by Wing's claim, declares his love for Wing *bisexually*: "I love you, whether you're a man or a woman." Although this ending is very much a reinscription of heterosexuality on the narrative level, Koo's bisexual declaration, combined with Wing's androgynous appearance, swings the film at least momentarily back to the queer side of the fence.

The sequel adopts a more radical plot line that explicitly develops the latent bisexual content of the first film. In *Who's the Woman*, Koo and Wing have moved in together as a couple. Koo's portrayal becomes increasingly unsympathetic as he grows weary of Wing's constant demand for his company. As a selfish ploy to distract her, he encourages Wing to revive her short but promising career masquerading as a male recording star. Wing's androgynous image propels her to stardom. She is soon winning awards and being offered film roles, while her disguised male identity remains intact. Meanwhile, Fong (Anita Mui), a famous actress known for her transvestite roles, has moved into the apartment downstairs. Since early retirement, Fong has been traveling around the world with her assistant, a flamboyant young lesbian called O (Theresa Lee). Fong initially has an anonymous fling with Koo but later becomes very attracted to Wing, who continues to maintain her masculine disguise. Wing, in turn, becomes deeply attached to Fong, who is far more attentive to her than the selfish and arrogant Koo. In a subplot, Wing's best friend Fish Man (Jordan Chan) tries to pursue O, who rejects him repeatedly on the ground that she only desires women. The sexual tension between Fong and Wing culminates when they star together as lovers in a transvestite comedy, in which Fong plays a man and the supposedly male Wing plays a woman. Jealous of the developing attraction between the two women, Koo reveals to Fong that Wing is in fact a woman, assuming that his news will discourage Fong from falling for Wing. To his dismay, the knowledge does not affect Fong's attraction to Wing. An on-screen kiss between the women during a film shoot leads to off-screen sex in the apartment Wing shares with Koo. On the same afternoon, Fish Man dresses up as a woman and successfully seduces O, who is sleeping by the swimming pool and comically mistakes Fish Man to be the sexy actress Christy Chung. The film ends in Fong and O's departure from Hong Kong and the restoration of Wing and Koo's romance.

In this film, the bisexual triangle is more fully realized on the narrative level as Wing, Koo, and Fong have all been lovers with each other, developing the erotic configuration that could have happened between Koo, Wing, and Rose in the first film. More interestingly, some of the conventions of the temporary transvestite film are innovatively explored in scenes rich with self-referential allusions to the film's own queer undertone. For instance, the kiss between Fong and Wing in the film-within-the-film is a complex variation on what Straayer called "the paradoxical bivalent kiss":

> In this generic system the conflict between a character's actual sex and the sex implied by the character's disguise and performance functions to create simultaneously heterosexual and homosexual interactions. Narrative point of view and nonnarrative spectacle collaborate through contradiction to create a double entendre of simultaneous homosexual and heterosexual readings, identifications, and experiences in film viewers—viewers caught within the narrative and nonnarrative interpretations and by identification with a bi-sexed figure.[10]

The "bivalent kiss" plays on viewers' consciousness of the disguised character's real as well as fictive gender, thus instigating both homosexual and heterosexual pleasures. The kiss between Wing and Fong in *Who's the Woman* is an ironic play on this generic convention. The scene operates on three different levels: the narrative of the film depicts it as a lesbian kiss between Fong and Wing; the narrative of the film-within-the-film, which is parodically entitled *Now a Woman, now a Man* (*Hu Nan Hu Nü*), depicts it as a queer kiss between two transvestites; and the nonnarrative spectacle depicts it as a heterosexual kiss between a man and a woman. The film-within-the-film uses transvestite disguise while ensuring heterosexual closure by employing a female and a (supposedly) male actor, each disguised as the opposite sex, to play heterosexual lovers. Unknown to the audience-within-the-film, "actual" lesbian desire is present behind the kiss. Drawing attention to the fact that the cinematic medium is another site of disguise, this sly parody suggests that a film may contain ever-multiplying layers of disguise, provoking multivalent desire and identification in viewers, often without their full consciousness of the underlying dynamics. It also suggests that a seemingly heterosexual filmic resolution (including the film's own) may be ripe with all kinds of unacknowledged queer resonances.

In the sex scene that culminates from the kiss, the camera eschews any direct representation of the 'actual' lesbian sex between Wing and Fong, and focuses instead on the disguised 'lesbian' sex between Fish Man and O, a scene that turns Fish Man into a bi-sexed figure and O into a bisexual figure. This maneuver may be the film's attempt to straddle what Pramaggiore calls the "industrial fence"[11]: on the one hand to fully develop the bisexual plot, and on the other hand to placate homophobic viewers by visually showing sex between a man and a woman rather than between two women. However, the wildly funny sex scene between Fish Man and O, which may be called "bivalent sex" as it works in the same way as the bivalent kiss, is by no means a "straight" representation of heterosex. Fish Man's transvestite disguise is blatantly inadequate, but O, who is either too asleep or too drunk to notice—or perhaps slyly enjoying Fish Man's queer act of seduction—responds passionately to Fish Man *as though* he were a woman. She fondles his fake breasts, savors the smoothness of his shaved thighs and legs and squeezes his buttocks, all the while mumbling "Christy! Christy!" in ecstasy. This bivalent sex serves as a comedic foil to the sex between Fong and Wing in the background, resulting in a layered scene that oscillates wildly between multiple configurations of erotic desire.

The ending of *Who's the Woman*, like that of *He's a Woman*, is obviously a strained attempt at asserting heterosexual closure. It is less obviously also symptomatic of the way bisexuality disappears from the screen. The concluding scene takes place in an aircraft bound for "Africa." (The ridiculously vague reference reveals the film's problematic evocation—one that is disturbingly reminiscent of primitivist discourse—of an undifferentiated

"Africa" as a land of instincts, spontaneity, and inspiration.) Fong has just left Hong Kong again, and Wing, in complete confusion over her life, is going away on her own to where Koo has always claimed to be the place of his dreams. Koo finally catches up with Wing and tries to comfort her while she sobs. As Wing is dressed like a man, a stewardess (played by director Ann Hui in a cameo appearance) stares at the two uncomfortably:

> Koo: What are you looking at? I'm just comforting my wife.
> Stewardess: But, sir, he's a man.
> Koo: (annoyed) So what? Is that forbidden?
> Stewardess: (apologetic) No, no, of course not.

After this exchange, Koo promptly asks Wing to marry him, and the film ends as though heterosexual marriage resolves all of the characters' previous bisexual involvements with each other. The exchange between Koo and the stewardess is the film's feeble attempt to assert, against the heterocentric thrust of the narrative, that there is nothing wrong with gay desire. Yet, this aside brings up the prickly question of why Fong has to leave, at a point in the film when all the emotional and sexual tension has been built to culminate in *her* union with Wing. But then, how can three people make a romantic "couple"? Can bisexuality provide closure, and if so, how? Finding creative answers for these questions will surely chart a new erotic landscape in Hong Kong cinema.

## Bisexuality and Disappearance

The abrupt disappearance of Fong from *Who's the Woman* (like the less glaring erasure of Rose in the earlier *He's a Woman*) marks the disappearance of bisexuality. Most of the main characters, including Wing, Fong, O, Koo, Fish Man, and Rose, have displayed a capacity for bisexual eroticism, yet each character is forced to renounce either one of what are constructed as two mutually exclusive *kinds* of desire. Interestingly, as already presented here, the film's own production of spectatorial pleasure depends entirely on its viewers' enjoyment of bisexual eroticism. In other words, the film's use of triangles and transvestite disguise creates *both* homosexual and heterosexual subject-positions or, more properly speaking, bisexual subject-positions that do not exclude an object-choice on the basis of gender, do not distinguish clearly between identification and desire, and do not respond to multiple object-choices in multiple kinds of gendered configurations. The erasure of bisexuality at the end is thus, at the same time, an inability to acknowledge the dynamics of the film's own production of pleasure.

The problem of intelligibility is, of course, endemic to any discussion of bisexuality. Garber suggests at the beginning of *Vice Versa* that bisexuality is paradoxically constructed by "common wisdom" as being either everywhere ("Everyone is bisexual") or nowhere ("There is no such thing as bisexuality").[12] Such cavalier declarations of seeming truisms efface bisexuality as a distinct erotic capacity. Similarly, while most of the characters in the two films have the capacity for and, to varying degrees, the experience of bisexual eroticism, they all seem to interpret such capacity and experience as results of misunderstanding, confusion, or deception, hence fundamentally irrelevant to their "real" erotic capacity, which is presumably either gay or straight. Bisexuality here has become an unutterable sign—that which brings existent understanding of sexuality in crisis but remains unarticulated as such. In his review of *Who's the Woman*, the film critic Sek Kei relates this sense of confusion and inarticulation to the general state of Hong Kong during the postcolonial transition:

> Are the three principal characters gay or not gay? It is really not very clear. Perhaps one can only say that this film is about "identity crisis" and "gender complex." Perhaps this desire for everything, accompanied by an uncertainty of what exactly is being desired, is representative of a certain Hong Kong style confusion.[13]

Indeed, the predicament of bisexuality in these comedies—where bisexuality disappears from the screen not because it ceases to exist but because there is no acknowledgement of it as an erotic capacity as such—is closely akin to what Ackbar Abbas theorizes as the predicament of Hong Kong culture itself:

> As for Hong Kong, it was, in a favorite phrase, "a cultural desert." Not that there was nothing going on in cinema, architecture, and writing, it was just not recognized to be culture as such. This refusal to see is an example of reverse hallucination. . . . If hallucination means seeing ghosts and apparitions, that is, something that is not there, reverse hallucination means *not* seeing what *is* there.[14]

This predicament is intensified during the period of postcolonial transition, when not only Hong Kong's culture but also its language, lifestyle, political structure, economic function—in short, everything that has come to define Hong Kong—seem poised on the brink of disappearance, not because they will cease to exist, but because it becomes doubtful if they will continue to be *intelligible* as belonging specifically to Hong Kong. In relation to the new cinema that is emerging precisely during this volatile period of change, Abbas argues that Hong Kong as a subject matter cannot be represented without precipitating a crisis in representation itself: Hong Kong permutates so quickly that it appears to have always already disappeared by the time it is made into an image or narrated as a story. Abbas argues that the new cinema does not try to develop new content or invent new forms. Instead, it renders the act of viewing itself problematic:

> These . . . films of the new Hong Kong cinema . . . define for us the spatial conditions of viewing and of filmmaking, where the act of looking itself has become problematic: the more you try to make the world hold still in a reflective gaze, the more it moves under you. These films do not so much thematize Hong Kong culture as they give us a critical experience of Hong Kong's cultural space by problematizing the viewing process.[15]

This curious tactic of reproducing the problematic conditions of intelligibility, rather than trying to make something more intelligible, is also at work in these two comedies of bisexual desire. This argument does not mean to suggest that the films intend to use queer sexuality as a metaphor for Hong Kong's postcolonial predicament. On the contrary, sexuality is most likely meant to provide a playful escape from such serious concerns. Yet, the films' attempt to articulate what Peter Chan called a "changing world," where sexual desire no longer conforms to the dominant binary and monosexual discourse of sexual orientation, unwittingly reproduces the conditions of disappearance that structure—and are structured by—the "changing world" of Hong Kong's postcoloniality. The seeming restoration of "order" at the end of both comedies cannot entirely curb the excess of the queer humor, just as the enforced "order" of postcolonial transition has not stopped the debates over Hong Kong's cultural location and political identity.

The lesson of bisexuality's constitutive role and disappearance in these popular comedies may thus have important significance for Hong Kong culture in general. Many of the most insightful and nuanced accounts of Hong Kong culture, by critics such as P. K. Leung (1995), S.L. Li (1997), and Rey Chow (1998),[16] have focused on the *difficulty* of representing Hong Kong, as well as the hybrid, mediated, and layered expressions that writers, songwriters, and filmmakers must deploy to represent a rapidly changing culture, the specificity of which is in danger of being elided in the face of a homogenizing discourse about Chinese nationalism. This struggle for emergence is precisely the struggle of bisexual politics. Mak wove these two predicaments together in this way:

> Speaking of 'bi' or 'bai,'[17] one doesn't even know if one's speaking in English or Chinese. Hong Kong people often use words which can be spoken aloud but have no corresponding written characters.[18] Even if these are Chinese words, they only exist in Cantonese. I don't even know whether to be happy about such hyper localism or anxious about its exclusivity. Speaking of "bi" or "bai"

> is difficult not only because there is a lack of discussion on sexuality and desire in Hong Kong culture and hence a lack of adequate vocabulary, but also because there is no acknowledgement that bisexual desire even exists. . . . [19]

The lack of adequate expressions for bisexuality in Hong Kong, except through a kind of linguistic transvestism (where English words are "dressed" in Cantonese to the effect that one can no longer clearly determine if the word is English or Cantonese Chinese), fosters a cultural and political expression that cannot afford to rely on the certainty of categories and the fixity of identity. In the "changing worlds" of desire and politics, it is perhaps the only kind of expression that will survive and emerge as a new and vibrant form of discourse.

## Notes

1. All translations of Chinese texts are mine unless otherwise noted.
2. Helene Cixous, "Sorties," Elaine Marks and Isabelle de Courtivron, eds., *New French Feminisms* (New York: Schocken, 1980), 90.
3. Judith Butler, *Bodies that Matter: On the Discursive Limits of "Sex"* (New York: Routledge, 1993), 239.
4. Marjorie Garber, *Vice Versa: Bisexuality and the Eroticism of Everyday Life* (New York: Simon and Schuster, 1995), 65–66.
5. Ellis Hanson, "Introduction: Out Takes," Ellis Hanson, ed., *Out Takes: Essays on Queer Theory and Film* (Durham: Duke University Press, 1999), 6–10.
6. Marjorie Garber, *Vested Interests: Cross-dressing and Cultural Anxiety* (New York: HarperCollins, 1992), 11.
7. See Lee Cheuk-To, *Linli Theatre/Linli Yingxiang Guan* (Hong Kong: Subculture, 1996), 121–125 and Chou Wah-Shan, *On Tongzhi/Tongzhi Lun* (Hong Kong: Tongzhi yanjiu she, 1994), 290. Tongzhi, literally meaning "comrade" in Chinese, was coined by Hong Kong playwright Edward Lam when he launched a film festival in Taiwan in 1991, introducing the New Queer Cinema. The term caught on quickly and has since become the most commonly used term in Hong Kong to describe sexual minorities. However, other local and linguistically hybrid terms are also continually being coined and put to use (for example, see note 17).
8. Chris Straayer, *Deviant Eyes, Deviant Bodies: Sexual Re-orientations in Film and Video* (New York: Columbia University Press, 1996), 42–44.
9. Maria Pramaggiore, "Straddling the Screen: Bisexual Spectatorship and Contemporary Narrative Film," Donald Hall and Maria Pramaggiore, eds., *RePresenting Bisexualities: Subjects and Cultures of Fluid Desire* (New York: New York University Press, 1996), 282.
10. Chris Straayer, *Deviant Eyes, Deviant Bodies,* 54.
11. Maria Pramaggiore, "Straddling the Screen," 275.
12. Marjorie Garber, *Vice Versa,* 16.
13. Sek Kei, *Collected Reviews of Sek Kei/Shi Qi Yinghua Ji*, Vol.4 (Hong Kong: Subculture, 1999), 362.
14. Ackbar Abbas, *Hong Kong: Culture and the Politics of Disappearance* (Minneapolis: University of Minnesota Press, 1997), 6.

15. Ibid., 26.

16. See Rey Chow, *Ethics After Idealism: Theory—Culture—Ethnicity—Readin g* (Bloomington: Indiana University Press, 1998); P. K Leung, *Hong Kong Culture/ Xianggang Wenhua* (Hong Kong: Hong Kong Arts Centre, 1995); and S.L. Li, "The Colonial Historical Imaginary," Wong Wang-chi, ed., *Hong Kong: Unimagined: History, Culture, the Future/Fuoxiang Xianggang: Lishi, Wenhua, Weilai* (Taipei: Rye Field, 1997), 133–264.

17. *Bai* is literally the Chinese term for "defeat." Its Cantonese pronunciation is synonymous with the English term "bi." Transliterating English words in this way is a very common practice in Hong Kong. *Gei* (literally meaning 'foundation' in Cantonese), for instance, is very commonly used as the word for "gay."

18. The modern Chinese script is based on the dialect spoken by the educated class in the Beijing region. There are thus many words used in spoken dialects that cannot be written because they do not exist in the Beijing dialect. The brand of Cantonese spoken in Hong Kong is especially rich in these exclusively oral expressions.

19. Anson Mak, *Bisexual Desire/Shuangxing Qingyu* (Hong Kong: Hong Kong Christian Women's Association, 2000), 6.

# 12

# Staging Gay Life in China

## *Zhang Yuan and* East Palace, West Palace

CHRIS BERRY

*East Palace, West Palace* (*Donggong, Xigong*, 1996) is the first feature film from mainland China to deal with gay life there today. The title is taken from Beijing gay slang and refers to the two public toilets on either side of the Forbidden Palace on the north edge of Tiananmen Square. Much of the film takes place during the night at a similar location in a typical gay cruising zone of an inner-city park in Beijing and in the park police station. But the film is not slice-of-life realist. Developed originally as a stage play by director Zhang Yuan, it is highly dramatized, reminiscent to a western viewer of Jean Genet's work, perhaps. The main focus is an exchange between one of the men who frequent the park, A Lan (played by Si Han), and Shi Xiaohua (played by Hu Jun), one of the cops whose job it is to harass them. A Lan forms a masochistic infatuation with the cop and goes all out to get taken in for questioning. Alone with the cop in the police station, A Lan then spends the night revealing his fantasies and his past to him, simultaneously trying to provoke and seduce him. This is Zhang Yuan's fifth feature and his most critically acclaimed so far. Given the uneven quality of Zhang Yimou's recent work and Chen Kaige's lapse into the production of *chinoiserie* that out-Bertoluccis Bertolucci, *East Palace, West Palace* stakes a serious claim for Zhang Yuan to be the mainland director

From *Jump Cut: A Review of Contemporary Media* 42 (1998), 84–89. Reprinted with permission.

who has produced the most consistently interesting body of work so far in the 1990s.

Zhang Yuan has many gay friends and is also working on a documentary about China's first transsexual, the modern dancer Jin Xing, who went overnight from being referred to as "he" in the Chinese press to "she" without any explanation at all offered to readers. It is provisionally titled *Miss Jin Xing* (*Jin Xing Xiaojie*). However, Zhang himself is not gay, and indeed he wrote the script of *East Palace, West Palace* together with his wife Ning Dai. So, when I interviewed him in 1996 soon after completion of the film, one of my first questions was about his interest in the topic. "Many of my films are concerned with minorities living on the margins of society," he noted. "*Mama* (1990) looked at the disabled, *Beijing Bastards* (*Beijing Zazhong*, 1992) examined the rock music subculture, and *Sons* (*Erzi*, 1995) focused on alcoholism and unemployment."

In the discussion that followed, Zhang made it clear that as a filmmaker whose work is invisible but not actually illegal in China, he has a certain amount in common with gay men and other marginalized groups. The opening scenes of *East Palace, West Palace* indicate that although there is no law specifically forbidding homosexuality in China, gay people are not free from police harassment.[1] As the character we later discover is A Lan comes out of the stalls in the park men's room, a policeman washing his hands asks him a series of questions, starting with where he lives and ending with a request to see his identification and even his bike permit. In the next scene, the police round up the men in the park at night, punishing them by forcing them to squat down, beating them, telling them to slap themselves, and threatening to inform their employers.

In Zhang's case, the authorities dislike what he is doing so much that in 1994 they issued a notice forbidding anyone to cooperate further with him and a number of other filmmakers. When I asked him why they had not actually stopped him completely, he joked, "That's quite natural. I love my country and I love the Party, just like A Lan in my film loves that policeman." What kind of love does A Lan have for Shi Xiaohua? A Lan compares himself to a female thief in a Beijing Opera story. As the policeman naps on the sofa, he stands over him, saying, "The convict loves her executioner. The thief loves her jail keeper. We love you, we have no other choice."[2] Toward the end of the film, he repeats the same lines to the now conscious Shi Xiaohua, adding, "I love you. Why don't you love me?"

Indeed, although Zhang Yuan has worked outside the system throughout the 1990s without being stopped, *East Palace, West Palace* has provoked the most concrete government action against him as a filmmaker yet. No doubt this is at least in part because, of all his five features, this one has received the greatest international attention. The film was invited to take part in the *Un Certain Regard* section at the 1997 Cannes International Film Festival. Zhang should have been there in person for this career highlight, but the

Chinese authorities seized his passport to prevent him from leaving China. When the Cannes organizers refused to pull Zhang Yuan's film, Chinese authorities also pressured the producers of Zhang Yimou's new film, *Keep Cool* (*You Hua Hao Hao Shuo*), to withdraw from the festival.

Had he been able to attend the opening ceremony, I suspect Zhang Yuan would have enjoyed the little performance Cannes put on to address the Chinese government's actions. By placing an empty chair on the stage to symbolize his absence, they simultaneously made both him and his absence present to the audience.[3] Zhang is equally adept at dealing with the Chinese authorities. And he has also developed a strong interest in this sort of playing with performance and reality in a tension between high drama and high realism that runs through his work.

When I spoke to Zhang a couple of years ago after seeing his observational documentary about Tiananmen Square, *The Square* (*Guangchang*, codirected with Duan Jinchuan, 1994), he suggested that, to him, the square itself was like a large stage on which all sorts of people performed.[4] I reminded him of this after *East Palace, West Palace*, and he elaborated by saying, "If you want to say I strive for the authentic in my films, that authenticity has two aspects to it. One side is realism, and the other side is subjective truth. In *The Square* and *Beijing Bastards* I leaned more toward realism, but I think that in *Mama* and *Sons* I leaned more toward my own subjective truth. Actually, all of my films have a tension between the subjective and the objective, and in *East Palace, West Palace*, my subjectivity has been particularly strong."

In this chapter, I would like to look at *East Palace, West Palace* and China's emergent gay and lesbian culture by examining the connection between Zhang's interest in social marginality (including his own as an independent filmmaker) and his interest in highlighting and blurring the line between drama and reality. For, paradoxically, although the space of performance on stage or within a feature film is marked off from what we know as "the real world" in a mutually constitutive manner, acting is not so much outside the world as it is a special sort of doing *in* the world.

This insight has been both central and essential to the focus in Cultural Studies and Queer Studies on theories of performance and performativity in recent years. In the introduction to a collection of articles on the topic, Eve Kosofsky Sedgwick summarizes Jacques Derrida's deconstruction in "Signature Event Context" of J. L. Austin's *How to Do Things with Words*: "Where Austin, then, seemed intent on separating the actor's citational practices from ordinary speech-act performances, Derrida regarded both as structured by a generalized iterability, a pervasive theatricality common to stage and world alike."[5]

Breaking down the distinction between the space of the stage and the space of the real world on the basis of generalized citationality has various effects. First, as discussed most notably in the work of Judith Butler as well as that of Sedgwick, it suggests that "being" is based on the kind of "doing" that acting is. Furthermore, if identities in the real world are also performed rather than given, then they can be cited and read "wrongly" but productively in order to construct different identities and undermine seemingly natural givens.[6] As a result, much recent work in English-language academia has focused on the way in which existing social identities are performed or constructed as well as particular instances of their perversion, so to speak, in these productive misreadings and miscitations.

In what follows, I first want to identify some of the features of Zhang Yuan's work that also draws attention to the way being is connecting to the special kind of doing that acting is. I then want to draw attention, however, to some of the important differences between the kind of emphasis on performance found in Zhang's work and the emphasis on perversion (in the sense cited above) found in the work of Butler and others. I will argue that in Zhang's work, the emphasis is more on access to public discourse and the ability to find a place to stage a public performance at all. I will argue that this problematic is not only one that Zhang shares with gay men and the other Chinese social minorities he represents in his work, but that it is generalized across Chinese society today and results from the contradictions that characterize and constitute the contemporary Chinese postsocialist condition. On one hand, the relaxation of central control in the economic realm has produced a plural society composed of a wide range of different social groupings. But on the other hand, increasing central control in the ideological realm struggles to maintain strict limits on the ability of those social groupings to establish their identities and win public recognition for them. Perhaps the case of gays and lesbians in China is the most extreme example of this contradiction that Zhang Yuan has dealt with so far. But it is also a contradiction that extends to cover him and his fellow independent filmmakers who have worked outside the state sector to date.

Zhang's first film, *Mama*, a drama about a separated woman's struggle to look after her mentally disabled son, places a strong emphasis on the use of real locations as opposed to studio sets and includes some documentary elements. As the film demonstrates, not only do the needs of the disabled receive little attention from the underresourced state in China, most ordinary citizens even prefer to ignore them altogether. However, in most other ways, *Mama* is a comparatively conventional drama made within the studio system for Xi'an Film Studio. It is with Zhang's next film (his first independent one) that his interest in the permeability of the screen world and real life starts to make itself apparent. In *Beijing Bastards*, Zhang focuses on Beijing rock' n' roll youth subculture. No doubt he was partly inspired by the music videos (known as "MTVs" in China) that he had been shooting to make a living. But more important, the locations used are real and many of the actors are nonprofessionals drawn from the subculture the film represents. In this way, Zhang opens up the screen to another social group that has received little recognition or understanding in China to date.

In *The Square*, Zhang moves from features to documentaries and from including real-life people as performers of roles similar to themselves to showing the performance that is inherent in real life. He made this film directly after the issuance of a government "document" (*wenjian*) forbidding him to make more films and other people to cooperate with him.[7] Clearly, the decision to go and shoot in Tiananmen Square, the political heart of China, was politically pointed as well as a demonstration of his sheer ability to persevere.[8] However, as already noted, Zhang and codirector Duan Jinchuan not only document daily life in the square but show the square as a kind of stage that people come to from Beijing and around the country to perform on.

*The Square* is an observational film in the manner of Fred Wiseman, without voice-over commentary or extradiegetic music, and so it is open to many interpretations. However, what I see in *The Square* is a tension between ordinary people, who come there to exercise, fly kites, throw Frisbees and walk around, and the police, politicians, and other official groups who use it to stage their events. When visiting dignitaries arrive, the ordinary citizens are cordoned off. When the military police go for their jog, the old men exercising have to stand aside. Once the police have moved through, one of the old men comments, "They're gone now, let's get on." Furthermore, given Tiananmen's history as a site for larger public contestations of this sort, not only in 1989 but also on many other occasions during China's recent history, it is difficult not to think of this larger significance as one watches the film. Here, then, power and social identity are represented as a sort of performance in which the contest for access to public space is key.

Finally, in *Sons*, Zhang Yuan takes the whole intermixing of documentary and feature film making to a new level. He made this film when one of the amateur actors from *Beijing Bastards*, who lived in the same building as Zhang Yuan did at the time, approached him and suggested he make a film about his family's life. The parents in the family are members of a dance troupe. The father is an alcoholic, and both sons are unemployed and heavily into alcohol themselves. Zhang and Ning Dai interviewed the family at length, then had them reenact key scenes from their family history. In this way, a stage family in real life stages its own history on film, again placing into public discourse a variety of social problems and issues that are normally ignored.

Set against this developing problematic of stage and real life in his work, *East Palace, West Palace* may seem like a step away at first. Although the actor who plays A Lan is not a professional, he was not recruited from the Beijing gay scene but from Zhang's film crew. The rest of the actors in the film are not from the gay scene, either. And although studio sets are not used, the locations are not real-life Beijing cruising zones, possibly to avoid provoking crackdowns on those places. Furthermore, the film is highly dramatized. There are fantasies and flashbacks, as well as a tense dialogue between A Lan and the policeman that is certainly too highly crafted to seem real in any everyday slice-of-life sense. And the camerawork is highly crafted, too, drawing attention to itself as it communicates, through circling movements, the power-play and surveillance that constitute the film's general ambiance. For example, when A Lan's story of his humiliation and beating by one of his partners is enacted on the screen, the camera circles 360 degrees around A Lan again and again as his partner and his friend attack him. Similarly, after the policeman arrests A Lan and makes him squat in the little park police station, the policeman goes out and circles the building, looking in at A Lan through the windows. But toward the end of the film, when A Lan is turning the tables on the cop and the cop tells him to leave, it is A Lan who circles the building looking in through the windows.

However, I would argue that in light of Zhang's previous productions, what this highly dramatized quality draws attention to is the immense difficulty of putting China's real gay subculture into public discourse at the moment. Unlike with the disabled, the unemployed, alcoholics, or rock 'n' roll kids, the risk of reprisals is simply too great. At one point in my interview with him, I pointed out to Zhang Yuan that in its focus on nighttime cruising, toilet sex, masochism, cross-gender identification, and run-ins with the police, *East Palace, West Palace* was a long way from the cozy coupledom of a film like Ang Lee's *The Wedding Banquet* and might be seen as presenting a negative image of homosexuality to some. "I believe this dramatic situation and these characters are a true expression of the current circumstances gays in China live under," Zhang responded. "I interviewed many, many people, including my own friends and also sociologists who have carried out investigations of gay life in China and AIDS researchers. All the stories I heard, including those from the gay community itself, were bound by circumstances of oppression, discrimination, and control. In China today, there is no visible gay culture and no one understands gay people. It is very hard to find any gay friends who are living a happy, well-adjusted life under these circumstances, and in fact I cannot think of anyone I know like that."

What I would suggest is that what this circumstance—and Zhang's way of dealing with it in *East Palace, West Palace*—highlights is that his films are not so much about the way in which identities can be performed differently, which is a major emphasis in the work of Judith Butler and others on performativity, but rather on the whole question of how they can be performed at all. The generalized citationality that Butler and other contemporary theorists of performance and performativity emphasize requires that we also rethink the distinction between the space of the stage and the space of "real life." If the citation and iterability that have traditionally been used to distinguish the stage from "real life" are in fact everywhere, I would suggest that the stage and stage-like spaces are still differentiated from the other spaces on the basis of their public visibility. I do not wish to construct a binary distinction between the public and the private here, for I am aware that there are many degrees of public visibility and privacy. Nor do I wish to enter into debates about the public sphere. Rather, I simply want to suggest that some spaces for performance are "public" by virtue of having a greater social visibility and hence a greater power to disseminate widely than others and that access to public performance may be limited or facilitated by social power structures. In other words, we need to ground Butler's insights into the potential of performativity both socially and historically if we are to understand how it does not simply smuggle the liberal free subject back into the picture but instead inscribes agency as regulated and deployed differentially.

In *East Palace, West Palace,* this focus on performativity in relation to access to public space and public discourse is dramatized in the all-night exchange between A Lan and the policeman that takes up most of the film. In fact, A Lan's capacity to restage conventional scenarios and behaviors so as to seize agency has been illustrated earlier in the film. When the police seize the men in the park at the beginning of the film, A Lan is among them and is taken back by Shi Xiaohua for questioning. But on the way, instead of behaving as a captured criminal, he seizes the circumstances of their walk together to the police station as an opportunity to treat Shi Xiaohua as one of his nighttime partners. When A Lan kisses him impulsively, Shi is so shocked that he lets him go, and A Lan runs off. Furthermore, when Shi takes him in for questioning the second time, it is clear that he knows A Lan is the man who has sent him the book inscribed "To my love, A Lan," because he asks, "You're A Lan, aren't you?" So, from the very beginning, Shi's motives in taking A Lan in for questioning are blurred, and A Lan knows this as well as the audience does.

However, Shi sets up the circumstances as a conventional police interrogation in which a confession is expected. He makes A Lan squat down and tells him to speak as he prepares to write it all down. However, the police confession is a public record. A Lan seizes this opportunity as eagerly as the earlier walk back through the park. He uses these rare circumstances in which Chinese gay men achieve a certain public visibility to perform his role differently, perversely. He insists on using the confession not as a space to denigrate or incriminate himself but as a mechanism to tell his story and state his case, insisting that his masochistic gay engagements are love and insisting that the policeman stop saying they are disgusting.

At first, he answers Shi's questions straightforwardly. But, very quickly, he uses them to move away from the confessional mode. A Lan is married, and when Shi asks to whom, A Lan uses the question as an opportunity to speak about his first sexual experience with a man. Although he imagines himself as "the girl" in the encounter and it is by no means a simply positive and affirmative one, A Lan ends the story with an emotional assertion that the next morning "I knew I was alive!" Not surprisingly, the policeman gets angry, telling him to cool down. Later, when the policeman attempts to characterize him as trash, A Lan answers back, provoking the policeman to say, "Have you forgotten where you are? You're getting out of line." Indeed he is. By now, confession is moving toward seduction. A Lan tells Shi that his mother used to tell him to be good or the policeman would come to get him, but "I loved to hear that sentence." As an adult, he continues, looking up at Shi, "I saw a policeman walking through the park and suddenly my dream came true. He arrested me." It would be inappropriate for me to give away the outcome of this contest between seduction and confession. However, what I want to emphasize here is not only the way in which A Lan's performative perversity attempts to reconstruct and resignify his own identity differently, but also how that attempt depends on the ability to seek out and obtain access to public space, public discourse, and public record, however unpromising the particular circumstances might seem.

Of course, this question of access to and regulation of public discourse is relevant in any society, and I think it is important for any discussion of performativity that wishes to avoid idealism. But it seems particularly charged in the People's Republic of China, where the actions of the government in relation to this year's (1997) Cannes film festival are only the latest in a long series that asserts control over Chinese film and other media, not only within their own borders but internationally. In these circumstances where access is difficult, it is not only a question of the ways identities are cited and miscited, but also whether they are allowed to be—or are able to find ways to make themselves—visible at all. As Zhang Yuan points out in relation to his motivation for making *East Palace, West Palace*, "Although there are many stories recorded about gays in Chinese culture, after the Liberation of 1949 and especially during the Cultural Revolution [1966–1976], the very word 'homosexual' disappeared from all newspapers, books, and even public discussion."

The problem of visibility is something that affects not only gays in China but also many other social groups. Indeed it is a broad issue that seems to lie behind Zhang Yuan's concern with contemporary Chinese life, and particularly the lives of younger city people like himself. It is a concern he shares with many other filmmakers of his generation. Zhang graduated from the Beijing Film Academy in 1989. Because the academy is China's only film school and does not take in students every year, Zhang's class was the first to graduate after the so-called Fifth Generation, which included such now internationally famous names as Chen Kaige, Zhang Yimou, and Tian Zhuangzhuang. Therefore, some people refer to the new generation of young filmmakers as the "sixth generation," but this is an appellation that Zhang and his peers dislike. While they admire their predecessors, they would prefer to be treated separately and individually.

Nonetheless, it is the case that the graduates of 1989 do seem to have used the turn to contemporary life as a way of setting themselves apart from the Fifth Generation. The vast majority of the famous Fifth Generation films, from *Yellow Earth* to *Red Sorghum*, *Ju Dou*, *Raise the Red Lantern*, *Horse Thief*, *Farewell My Concubine*, *Shanghai Triad*, and *Red Firecracker, Green Firecracker*, have been set in an almost mythical version of the prerevolutionary past. Although those films have frequently been interpreted as metaphorical commentaries on the present, Zhang Yuan and his peers clearly had no patience with indirect games, possibly seeing in the resort to these techniques a compromise and effective submission that they wished to eschew in favor of a more direct visibility. Hence, not only all of Zhang Yuan's films, but also Wang Xiaoshuai's *The Days* and *Vietnam Girl*, Wu Ming's *Frozen*, He Jianjun's *Red Beads* and *The Postman*, and Lu Xuechang's *This Is How Steel Is Made*, not to mention the works of China's independent documentary video makers, are nearly all set in contemporary urban Chinese milieus readily recognizable to the viewer.

In many cases, these films are also concerned with making visible that which is usually hidden from view or denied a space in public discourse in the People's Republic of China. *The Days*, *Frozen*, and *Red Beads* all focus on alienated young artists and members of the middle classes. Like all of Zhang Yuan's films except *Mama*, these three films were made independently without the benefit of state-run studio involvement, which means there is no mechanism for submitting them for classification and release in China. *Vietnam Girl* looks at migration from the countryside to the city, often illicit, and prostitution, and *This Is How Steel Is Made* looks at alienated youth, including consideration of drugs, alcohol, sex, and rock 'n' roll. Both these films were produced in 1996 by Tian Zhuangzhuang (best known as the director of *Horse Thief* and *Blue Kite*) for his company, which is attached to Beijing Film Studio. However, apparently the latter film has had to be radically changed before being passed for release, and *Vietnam Girl* has only been permitted a limited release within China and no export.

*The Postman* is also an independent film produced outside the state system, and particularly interesting in this context for its shared interest in surveillance, silencing, and social marginality. The film follows a young postman who takes over a delivery route when his predecessor is sentenced to labor reform by his employers for opening mail.[9] Soon, the new postman is doing the same thing, and in the process he discovers what goes on behind closed doors in Beijing today, including drug use, prostitution, homosexuality, and various other subplots. He himself has sex in the back room of the post office one night with a fellow employee, but neither or them ever speaks about it again. Furthermore, he not only opens letters but also begins to interfere in the lives of the people on this route, often with cruel and disastrous results. Just as A Lan's masochistic desires seem to be a perverse and not necessarily an affirmative form of resistance, so the unusual performance of his duties by the postman seem to be formed by his environment—it is an act of resistance but at the same time highly ambivalent and disturbing.

As well as in the filmmaking world, it must be pointed out that regular Chinese citizens are also showing a greater interest in speaking openly and without scripting about aspects of their lives that they might well not have wished to air publicly before. This is particularly evident on Chinese television. A decade ago, it was almost impossible to see on-the-street interviews. Most documentary and news interviews with ordinary people were carefully controlled, and most citizens, if approached to speak publicly, might well have shied away for fear of saying the wrong thing. This has changed, and many people attribute this to the introduction of a daily ten-minute show on China Central Television in 1992 called *Dongfang Shikong* (unfortunately, usually translated as *Oriental Moment*). Here, ordinary citizens spoke about their lives and feelings in a relatively spontaneous manner. The show was a hit, and a more spontaneous approach prevails across the whole of the television world today.

Similarly, when in 1996 a Chinese journalist decided to use a home video camera to make an independent documentary about gay life, he was able to find six individuals and couples who were willing to go on camera for in-depth interviews about their lives, including one elderly man willing to describe how things were at the height of Maoism. Presumably, a video intended for very limited and controlled circulation would be less threatening in this regard than a feature film like *East Palace, West Palace*. The video, called *Comrades* in English, was shown at the San Francisco Gay and Lesbian Film Festival that year.[10]As well as interviews, the video includes footage shot around some of the main sites and venues in Beijing. One particularly moving scene is shot in a public park that is a popular cruising area. Apart from noticing that journalist did shoot the faces of the people who agreed to speak to him in the park, one cannot help but notice that the hand-held camera is shaky. The filmmaker told me this was because he was so nervous about what he was doing that he could not stop trembling. And of course, this is not a video that is publicly or commercially available in China today.

How are we to understand the contradiction between the government's efforts to control access to public discourse tightly and the evident increased willingness and eagerness of citizens to *engage* in public discourse? These two phenomena need to be understood as being simultaneously the product of and constituting China's postsocialist condition. Since 1979, the government has decentralized and rolled back control to allow the development of a market economy alongside the state economy and to encourage enterprise and independent initiative. This basic shift certainly underlies the cultural move away from a psychology of waiting for instructions from above and has provided the material conditions for the production of a socially plural society composed of many different groups. But the government appears to be concerned with asserting control over this burgeoning culture and still driven by a command economy mentality. Restricting access to the relatively privileged platform of public discourse is clearly one way of doing this.

In conclusion, I would like to point out that this is an ongoing contest that is difficult for all concerned. In the film world, the days of independent filmmaking may be over. In July 1996, using the rhetoric of encouraging the rule of law, the Chinese government introduced a new Film Law. This law specifically made it illegal to produce any film outside the studio system, which meant that Zhang Yuan was forced to find a studio to work with for his next production. Interestingly, but not surprisingly, he has found a topic that is also concerned with supposedly generous legal amendments. The film he has been researching focuses on prisoners who are on death row. A recent Chinese law allows model prisoners to return to their families for Chinese New Year. Zhang intends to structure the film around such a home visit, although it is not clear that he will perform this reunion in the warm and loving manner presumably envisaged by the drafters of the law.[11]

The new restrictions instituted in the Film Law can be seen as a direct response to the increased visibility and access to public space and discourse of the independent filmmakers in the 1990s. As they gained greater recognition, so they inspired stronger government response. This highlights the perils of the very visibility that they have sought out. This danger no doubt also applies to other socially marginalized groups. *East Palace, West Palace* shows that the absence of direct legal proscription is clearly not a sign of social tolerance or support, but the greater visibility that Chinese gays and lesbians are gaining at the moment may well lead to new struggles in the future. It is no accident that both of China's most prominent gay activists, Gary Wu and Wan Yanhai, decided to relocated at least temporarily to the United States in 1996. However, they too are as determined to find a way to continue their work as Zhang Yuan is.

## Notes

I want to acknowledge my discussions with Wan Yanhai in Beijing, Gary Wu by e-mail, Seo Dongjin of the Seoul Queer Film and Video Festival, and Professor Kim SoYoung of the Korean National University of the Arts, as well as my students at the Korean National Uiniversity of Arts and La Trobe University in Melbourne, for helping to form my thoughts in this article. I am also very grateful to Wouter Barendrecht of Fortissimo Film Sales for providing me with a videotape of *East Palace, West*

*Palace*, and to Zhang Yuan for speaking to me so frankly and answering so many questions.

1. For further details on gay life in China, see Paul Richardson, "Subcultural Revolution," *Attitude* 1.10 (February, 1995): 68–74, and Wan Yanhai, "Becoming a Gay Activist in Contemporary China," in Peter Jackson and Gerard Sullivan, eds., *Gay and Lesbian Asia: Culture, Identity, Community* (Binghamton, NY: Haworth Press, 2001), 46–64.

2. All dialogues are transcriptions of subtitles rather than retranslations that might give a fuller version of the original Chinese but make it more difficult for non-Chinese speakers to identify the scenes discussed.

3. http://www.tmiweb.com/Bigfree/Tpacfree/1069/Cannes/cannes2.html

4. Chris Berry, "Zhang Yuan: Thriving in the Face of Adversity," *Cinemaya* 32 (Spring 1996): 40–43.

5. Eve Kosofsky Sedgwick, "Introduction: Performativity and Performance," Andrew Parker and Eve Kosofsky Sedgwick, eds., *Performativity and Performance* (New York: Routledge, 1995), 4.

6. Judith Butler, *Gender Trouble: Feminism and the Subversion of Identity* (New York: Routledge, 1990).

7. As readers who have seen Zhang Yimou's *The Story of Qiu Ju* (1992) will be aware, law and regulation are complex matters in China. A "document" is a government announcement or directive. It is not the same as a law, and indeed its legal status is a little ambiguous. Zhang Yuan maintains that although he heard about this "document" and its publication in the newspapers, it was never actually delivered to him, and so he did not feel himself bound by it.

8. For further discussion of the production circumstances of this film, see the interview with codirector Duan Jinchuan included in Chris Berry, " 'We Live in a Country of Earthquakes': China's Independent Documentary Film Makers," *Metro* 113/114 (1998), 86–89.

9. In China, punishments like this can be administered directly by employers without recourse to the court system.

10. I have refrained from naming the filmmaker because, although he has been named in one or two other places, I am not sure that he wishes to be publicly identified.

11. Editor's note: In 1999, Zhang Yuan released *Seventeen Years* (*Guo nian hui jia*). Co-written by his wife, Ning Dai, with Yu Hua and Zhu Wen, this film is about a female model prisoner who returns to her family home during the Chinese New Year after seventeen years. A winner of the Special Prize for Direction at the 1999 Venice Film Festival, it featured a nonprofessional cast and received transnational funding. Since then, Zhang has worked in the mainstream industry. For a review of *Seventeen Years*, see Olivia Khoo, "*Seventeen Years*": http://wwwsshe.murdoch.edu.au/intersections/issue4/seventeen.html.

# 13

# Whose Fatal Ways

## *Mapping the Boundary and Consuming the Other in Border Crossing Films*

Li-Mei Chang

## Unwelcome Immigrants from the Other Side of the Border

On 19 June 1997, after fourteen rounds of talks that had begun in 1988, Hong Kong and China signed an agreement redefining their border. The new boundary was to follow a new course along Guangdong province and the Shenzhen special economic zone. The agreement was expected to make policing the border easier for Hong Kong, thereby aiding efforts against illegal immigration and smuggling. However, this agreement has not brought any major relief for Hong Kongers' increasing anxiety about the invasion of illegal immigrants from the mainland. "If you want to make Hong Kong work, you have to control illegal immigration," said John Holmes, chief inspector of the British colony's border police. Again, only two days before China took over Hong Kong, an essay in the *Economist* warned Hong Kongers that "an army of illegal immigrants from the mainland," not Beijing, would be the only conceivable outside threat to Hong Kong. It went on to say:

> Almost all of Hong Kong's 6.5 million people fled communism on the Mainland. Yet, whatever they may think of British colonialism and reunification with China, no one here is keen to share their immense good fortune with any of their former compatriots.[1]

---

From *Asian Journal of Communication* 11.2 (2001), 39–57. Reprinted with permission.

Hong Kongers' hostility toward immigrants from China runs deeper than sharing the wealth. Instead, when situated within the larger scale of sociopolitical conditions, it can be understood as a cultural anxiety about finding a Hong Kong identity.

First of all, in the 1970s, for the first time, more than half of Hong Kong's population had been born locally. Unlike their parents, the new generation had no memory of or few ties to the mainland. Although their ethnic identification with the Chinese remained strong, the only native place they knew and might come to identify with was Hong Kong. The Hong Kong government's localization policy since the 1960s–that is, the distribution of more political power to the local elite and the recognition of Chinese as an official language—also helped conjure up a sense of belonging. And the indigenization of popular music and film in the 1970s has further reinforced an increasingly distinctive culture made in Hong Kong.[2] The growing consciousness of belonging to Hong Kong reduced sympathy for Chinese immigrants, in particular the illegal ones, and they came to be perceived more and more as outsiders.[3]

Second, decades of geopolitical separation between Hong Kong and China had established two distinguishable societies across the border. While Hong Kong had created a world-recognized economic miracle and was marching triumphantly forward as an international financial center, China had just started its four modernizations in the aftermath of the Cultural Revolution. Being a former British colony, Hong Kong was profoundly influenced by Western culture, while China had only recently reestablished its connection with the West. Significant cultural and lifestyle differences among those who lived on both sides of the border separated Hong Kongers further from their former compatriots. As a result, the newcomers, most from rural areas and poorly educated, had difficulties assimilating into Hong Kong society and became less accepted and even marginalized by the local population.

Third, Hong Kongers were politically awakened by former British Prime Minister Margaret Thatcher's visit to Beijing in September 1982 and became aware of the impending expiration of crown colony status for Hong Kong in the year 1997. The ensuing negotiations between Britain and the mainland also alarmed Hong Kongers, who were concerned by the threat of aggression from the Communist state in Beijing. At a time when the "1997 issue" posed a serious question about the city's destiny, there was a collective anxious desire to define what Hong Kong is. To acquire a Hong Kong identity, as Susan Naquin once put it, is to define "what it is not."[4] Since Hong Kongers could not control the Communist state in Beijing, they used immigrants from the mainland as a resource to act out their anxiety about the future of Hong Kong. Immigrants were generally characterized as lacking social grace and as disrespecting law and order. An imagined boundary was hence drawn between "we" Hong Kongers and "they," the new immigrants.[5]

## The Cinematic Representation of the Mainlanders

Border crossing films tend to dramatize female illegal immigrants' bitter and exploited experience to appeal to the local audience's gaze.[6] In *Hong Kong, Hong Kong/Nan Yü Nü* (1983), one of the very early films that employ the issue of border crossing, the heroine is initially exploited by her male fellow migrants as an occasional sexual toy. To escape from this miserable and hopeless situation, she agrees to marry an old widower, who is desperate to have a son, in exchange for a better material life. In one (controversial) scene, the camera boldly lingers on the glittering young body of the heroine while the rough aged hands of her husband are caressing it. If the fetishized female body stands for the economically deprived mainland China, then Hong Kong is the childless man who worries about the possible end of his bloodline (the end of local history) and who anxiously seeks a way to produce a son (a future).

The consumption and objectification of the female immigrant body is hard to miss in films like *Amnesty Decree/Renshe* (1988), *HeartyResponse/Yi Gai Yun Tian* (1988), and *Long Arm of the Law III/Shenggang Qibing III* (1989). Each heroine in these films suffers from rape and violence by the "snakehead" who smuggles her into Hong Kong. Even in a romantic comedy like *Mary from Beijing*, the heroine Mary (played by the internationally known Chinese star Gong Li) has to go through the trajectory of objectification. Stricken by her beauty, her potential boss, the son of a wealthy family, takes her as his mistress. Yet he does not dare introduce her to his family unless she becomes properly cultivated (fluent in English, for example). It is only through her romantic encounter with a more sympathetic Hong Kong businessman that she is able to leave her possessive lover behind and gain her independence by working as a tourist guide.

In his account of migration movements on the U.S.-Mexican border, Nevzat Soguk points out that through a variety of representational strategies, migrants often become multiple signifiers. At times they are represented as deficient figures in contrast to the adequacy and completeness of citizens. In other instances, they are conceived as an anarchy that exists outside the domestic sphere. In a word, they become a double signifier of their own void and the completeness of the citizen, of (external) disorderliness as compared to (internal) security. Such a strategy of creating boundaries, Soguk continues, is aimed not only at constructing "referable" national borders but also at constructing "representable" cultural, political, and economic identities that ostensibly overlap with the physical borders.[7]

The cinematic representation of the mainlanders articulates a collective desire to make mainland China into a female "other" whose body can be gazed at, consumed, and controlled. By doing so, Hong Kong cinema expresses an attempt to construct a national self by consuming the other according to the physical borderline. In their cinematic representations, the mainlanders become double signifiers in that their differences are patronized in order to give the local people a good look at the other. Yet at the same time, local Hong Kongers strive to derive an identity precisely from the otherness of the mainlanders.

In the following, I will use *Her Fatal Ways/Biaojie Ni Hao Ye* (1990) to illustrate how Hong Kong cinema utilizes the physical border and the mainlanders to construct a referable cultural identity of Hong Kong. *Her Fatal Ways* bore an important dialogical relationship to the time and to the genre itself; it foreshadowed the transition from screen violence to political satire, and the changing representation of mainlanders from immigrants to law enforcers in the 1990s.

## Her Fatal Ways

Unlike most previous border crossing films, which tended to focus on the mainlander's bitter and exploited experience in Hong Kong, *Her Fatal Ways/Biaojie Ni Hao Ye* (Alfred Cheung Kin-Ting, 1990) is a political satire whose cinematic treatment of the mainlander is mixed with humor as well as self-commentary on Hong Kong society. The heroine of the film is no longer a poor rural woman from the mainland who longs for the material goods of the capitalist city. Instead, she is a somewhat lovable and laughable *biaojie* (literally, older female cousin, one of the nicknames Hong Kongers have for mainlanders) whose cultural differences provide much humor for local viewers and at the same time differentiate the mainlander from the local.[8]

A Chinese policewoman (Carol "Do Do" Cheng) and her sidekick A-Sheng (Alfred Cheung Kin-Ting), both die-hard Communists, are on a mission to escort a criminal hiding in mainland China to Hong Kong. Wu Wei-kuo (Tony Leung Ka-Fai) is the Hong Kong police officer assigned to show them around town. Wu's father happens to be loyal to the Taiwanese government (ruled by the Nationalist Party). Many jokes that are based on the characters' cultural and ideological clashes ensue.

Because *Her Fatal Way* was a box-office hit, its three sequels—released in 1991, 1992, and 1994—continued to exploit the theme of cultural differences. Apparently inspired by the success of *Her Fatal Ways*, several films such as *His Fatal Ways/Biaoge Ni Hao Ye* (1991), *Bodyguard from Beijing/Zhongnanhai Baobiao* (1994), *Rock 'n' Roll Cop/Shenggang Yihao Tongqifan* (1994), and *My Father Is a Hero/Xiegei Babade Xin* (1995) all take up the theme of the police crossing borders for the sake of law and order.[9] This change in the cinematic practice speaks to the collective anxiety due to the rapidly vanishing national boundary between Hong Kong and China. By addressing the issue of the Chinese police crossing the border, popular response to the satiric treatment in *Her Fatal Ways* displaces the collective tension about the Communist state coming over. Further, it attempts to construct a local Hong Kong subjectivity through laughter. Laughter, as Jonathan Hall argues, is charged with subversive power no matter how "innocent" it may seem. Laughter, "like the collective organization of laughter in the Carnival traditions, is a small revolution and/or counter-revolution."[10] Kathleen Rowe, in her discussions of theorizing about the genres of laughter, also points out that almost all comedic forms—from jokes to most narrative structures—"attempt a liberation from authority."[11] By drawing on cultural and political differences, the mocking and laughter produced by *Her Fatal Ways* works like the carnival traditions in an attempt to liberate Hong Kongers from the authority of the big threatening "Father" across the border. The film attempts to negotiate and construct a local Hong Kong subjectivity through consuming the other, whose differences motivate the narrative and at the same time provide the local spectator viewing pleasure.

The politics of discursive looking in *Her Fatal Ways* must be examined through the framework of the dominant relation of mainland China to Hong Kong. In political reality, it is mainland China that has the authority to watch, monitor, interpret, and regulate the Hong Kong "body" through a Foucauldian sense of "discipline and punish."[12] In *Her Fatal Ways*, those who look and those who are looked at are charged with the binary oppositions and power dominance of Hong Kong/ First World/ male and mainland China/ Third World/ female. The biaojie's cultural differences are constantly seen through the cinematic eye and her Hong Kong male counterpart's gaze, both of which initially belittle and ridicule her, then assume authority over her when she more intensely desires Hong Kong. Not only is she deprived of the agency of the gaze, but her body, where binary oppositions of self (Hong Kong) and the other (mainland China) are played out, also comes to signify the mainlander's ignorance and backwardness. By making her body a spectacle and then "describing it, restructuring it and dominating it,"[13] the film works as a cultural displacement, in that the dominating "Father" becomes a laughable and controllable female who will be seduced and restructured by the capitalist city (which is male). Positioned as the discursive viewing subject, the local spectator can seemingly take control over the mainland (the female) and define it, having authority over it through the consumption of her otherness.[14]

The opening sequence is organized around binarism, with Hong Kong positioned as the male, the first world, modernity, and the desirable, while mainland China represents the female, the third world, backwardness, and the laughable. By cross-cutting between two locations to introduce two major characters, the sequence ends when the biaojie encounters her Hong Kong counterpart's gaze. The opening image enunciates a discursive moment when mainland China becomes manageable through the control of the gaze. Inside a running bus, the camera first shows a close-up of a cigarette in a woman's fingers, then cuts to another close-up to reveal a woman's face that apparently does not belong to one of the locals and immediately calls attention to her differences. Her short, straight haircut is only a slight change from what used to be standard female hairstyles on mainland China. The dark thick glasses on her face give her a look both like the stereotype of women from Communist countries and an unattractive spinster. The song she is humming roughly tells us that she is from the rural area, that is, a marginal region even within China itself. When the camera moves to reveal her torso, her difference is further accentuated by the peasant-like clothes she wears and the dark, outmoded handbag sitting on her legs.

In contrast to the fragmentation and the fetishization of the mainlander's body, the Hong Kong male is situated as an entity in a secure high-rise space. The scene following the brief introduction of the supposed heroine takes us inside modern and shining police quarters, where polished local inspector Wu Wei-kuo is asked by his supervisor to show the upcoming biaojie around. Wu is reluctant but has to follow the order. We learn that a biaojie and her assistant, A-sheng, will be escorting a criminal who has been hiding in mainland China back to Hong Kong. The juxtaposition of these two images yields what Roland Barthes would call a second-order semiological chain. Being associated with signs of "third-worldness" (for example, the outmoded handbag and the rural-style dress), the female body is then transformed into the signifier of the mainlander's backwardness and lack of modern taste. Her presence in the film immediately signifies otherness and automatically invites the local audience's gaze. In contrast, the local inspector is associated with professional dress, modern technology (the computer), and high-rise space, all of which connote the "first-worldness" of Hong Kong. In this way, the binarism of Hong Kong/ male/ First World and mainland China/ female/ Third World is well played out.

This binarism is reproduced through the "looking relation" between the first world (male), who looks and interprets, and the third world (female), who is to be looked at and defined. In a hilarious spitting scene on the bus, the mainlander's otherness is exploited and ridiculed as an entertaining spectacle: When an elderly passenger coughs and accidentally spits on A-sheng's shoes, the upset A-sheng tells the elderly man and literally shows him that he should spit on the floor, not on someone's shoes. To correct and educate A-sheng, the biaojie opens a window and spits outsides instead. An unfortunate motorcycle driver happens to be close to the bus and the spit lands on his head. The association of the elderly and spit with the mainlander mocks the patriarchal rulers in mainland China. In popular discourse there have been political jokes about the Chinese elderly leaders' grotesque spitting and their loss of control of urine during political meetings. By making the biaojie finalize the spitting scene in an inappropriate gesture, the film condenses its critique of patriarchal rule (for instance, the violation of human rights and democratic resistance) onto the female body.

As the bearer of the condensation of the "wrongs" and "grotesqueness" of the Chinese Communist state, the biaojie's body becomes a decipherable site of meaning and cultural conflict. Perceived as what Hong Kong is not, the biaojie's ignorance and her lack of respect for human rights are soon expressed in the narrative. In the next scene, shot from Wu's point of view, the biaojie gets off the bus and meets with her Hong Kong counterpart. After a brief introduction, the biaojie asks A-sheng to hand the criminal over to Wu. To Wu's surprise, the criminal is packed into a huge bag and put inside the bottom trunk of the bus. Wu gives the biaojie an accusing look, which reminds the spectator of the First World's frequent accusation of the Chinese Communist's violation of human rights. She shows a defensive gesture yet seems to be fully aware of her wrongdoing.

From the moment when the biaojie meets with Wu's gaze, her body is constantly inscribed with signifiers of mainland China's Third-World-ness either through his gaze or through his focalization. In this phallic enunciation, the "wrongs" and "grotesqueness" of the female body motivate the narrative interest but often ends up calling attention to her own inadequacy, i.e. mainland China's lack of Western modernization and capitalist consumption. This metaphorical lack is enunciated both through the biaojie's mimicry of femininity and her lack of proper femininity. After the biaojie and A-sheng are accommodated in a hotel room, she spends a moment in the bathroom while A-sheng, without her knowing it, is engrossed in pornography on TV. With a cautious move, she takes lipstick out of her handbag and applies it to her lips in front of the mirror. She stares at herself in the mirror delightedly like a child secretly trying on her mother's makeup. She then wraps the lipstick with cheap paper, as if wrapping a treasure, and puts it back in the handbag.

The lipstick, a symbol of femininity, sums up the mainlander's lack of and desire for capitalist consumption. By mimicking femininity, the female body becomes the bearer of both the lack and the desire, which are then portrayed as Hong Kong's parental gesture to the mainland through the male gaze. During a night bus ride at Wu's invitation, the biaojie expresses admiration for the bright streetlights in Hong Kong and says that her mother would be very happy if she could be here. When Wu then assumes that her home village must be very dark at night, she defends it by saying, "It is quiet, not dark." Then, unexpectedly, her lipstick falls out of her handbag onto the bus floor. Wu sees it, picks it up, and wonders whose lipstick it could be, since he and the biaojie are the only two passengers on the bus. Embarrassed and nervous, the biaojie hides her eyes from Wu in silence when he asks her if it belongs to her. Just when he is about to throw the lipstick out of the window, the biaojie takes the lipstick from him. Under Wu's sympathetic gaze, she then puts the lipstick back into her handbag.

The imitation of femininity by the biaojie underscores her lack of proper femininity. In other words, the "wrongs" and "grotesqueness" are inscribed through her body. When the criminal A-Niu manages to escape, the biaojie is forced to stay longer and helps Wu arrest the criminal. During their China–Hong Kong cooperation, which she emphasizes but Wu discounts, the biaojie expresses contempt for Wu's emphases on the law and evidence. Being impatient with the Hong Kong police's "inefficiency," she decides to act by herself. To intimidate the criminal, according to her explanation, the biaojie makes her body into a grotesque spectacle by painting her eyebrows in an exaggerated way. She then goes off to the office of Soo, A-Niu's big boss, and demands that he hand over A-Niu. Unsuccessful, the biaojie is thrown out by Soo's employees and pushed into a police car. Inside, an already informed Wu is waiting for her. He gives her an angry, reproachful look and is shocked by her painted eyebrows. "What happened to your eyebrows?" he asks.

Since the self-image of Hong Kong in the narrative is constructed through the representation of the other, is also aware of the differences among Chinese living in mainland China, Taiwan and Hong Kong. With the female body standing for mainland China's Third-World-ness, the narrative inserts Wu's father to represent the residual nationalist ideology in Hong Kong. In a descriptive shot, signs of the Nationalist Party (Kuomintang, or KMT), including portraits of three presidents of Taiwan, are hung all over the living room of an apartment where Wu resides with his father. We soon learn that Wu's father is a veteran of the KMT who strongly opposes the Chinese Communists. When Wu has to accommodate the biaojie and A-sheng in his apartment after an assassination attempt occurred in their hotel, an ideological clash between Wu's father and the biaojie becomes unavoidable. Mediating between these two and identifying with none of them, Wu strives to represent a sense of "Hong-Kong-ness" through his association with Westernization, i.e., the computer, and English. That night, as Wu's father and the biaojie are staging a symbolical war between the nationalist and the Communist through their singing, Wu is seen working on the computer. Next morning, on seeing both his father and the biaojie wearing uniforms at the breakfast table, Wu returns to his room and comes back with his Hong Kong inspector's uniform. His "Hong Kong-ness" is also represented through his ability to use chopsticks with both hands while Wu's father insists on the correctness of using the right hand and the biaojie contradicts him by using the left hand. As the breakfast leads to an argument between them again, Wu stops them from fighting and concludes in English, "We are all Chinese, OK?" Their failure to understand this foreign language—in a sense, Wu's hybrid identity—stops them from further arguments.

Wu's gaze not only objectifies the female body but also takes authority over her. During their cooperation, the biaojie is by no means passive. But her actions are always sanctioned by Wu's gazes which indicate approval, disapproval, or ridicule. As their investigation continues, they travel to a village called Little China, where many new immigrants from different provinces of China reside, to attempt to find the criminal A-Niu's associates. Apparently having no understanding of the community, Hong Kong policemen simply go from door to door to ask. Perceived as outsiders, they are not welcome by the villagers. The biaojie then steps in, under Wu's authorizing look, and chats with the villagers about their homes which they left behind in China. Many become moved and respond to her talk of homeland China until she shouts, "Let's go back to China." They become silent all of a sudden. Aware of the change in the atmosphere, the biaojie shifts attention by inviting them to have home-flavored noodle soup together in the village. When the biaojie, along with the villagers, walk away from the village square, the camera cuts to Wu giving a smiling, approving look.

This final look secures Wu's dominant position as the first-world subject and observer while the female body represents Little China's third-world identity as object. In contrast to the filmic image of Hong Kong as modern capitalist space earlier on, Little China is represented as a slum where undereducated immigrants live without tap water. A-Niu's Little China background hence indicates his immigrant status in Hong Kong. His crime—smuggling drugs—speaks of Hong Kong's revulsion toward those new immigrants, since in popular discourse they tend to be associated with smuggling and robbery. This marginal space is conceived as a threat to Hong Kong's first-world identity (prosperity) and, in a sense, fractures the Hong Kong subjectivity enunciated through Wu's image. By associating Little China strongly with the biaojie while Wu, the Hong Kong male, observes the entire scene, the film displaces Little China's third-world identity onto the female body. Wu's gaze indicates a superior distance between the first-world male subject and the third-world female object. Through the male's consuming and controlling of the female body, the local viewing subject is positioned as an observer of this third-world nation from a distance rather than from within. The threat that Little China carries is then removed from modern Hong Kong's discourse and displaced onto the other (the female body).

The binarism of Hong Kong (the first world and male) and mainland China (the third world and female) is also played out through space. Presented as a third-world body, the biaojie is allowed to prove her competence only when in Little China, a third-world space. When she is in a modern Hong Kong space, her body becomes a signifier of difference and a spectacle to be mocked and ridiculed. After she succeeds in collecting useful information about A-Niu's frequent associates, she and Wu go to a nightclub where A-Niu's lover used to work. There, karaoke singing is going on. Wu invites her to perform a song because she finds the songs others are performing unbearable. When she goes on the stage and starts singing in the name of "purifying Hong Kong society," it proves to be a disaster. The camera cuts back and forth between the biaojie singing on the stage and Wu's gaze, along with the gaze of other male clients, to assure the female body as spectacle. In a state of shock on hearing her song, Wu spills the glass of wine in his hand onto his face; one client's glass is broken into pieces.

The biaojie's inability to deal with modern Hong Kong's space is further revealed in a scene in an elevator where she and Wu are confined because of a sudden power shortage. Not knowing what is really happening, she loses all her control and becomes hysterical. She keeps screaming and asks for Wu's hands. After they get out of the elevator and go back to Wu's apartment, Wu leaves her in the living room after making sure that she is back to a normal state. Through the cinematic gaze, the spatial economics are transformed into the sexual economics of Hong Kong (male) and mainland China (female), with the female body seduced by the male. Alone in the living room, the biaojie is seen in a state of erotic excitement, which has apparently been caused by Wu after her "most intimate experience with a man" (we learn this from her letter to Wu upon her departure in the ending sequence).

Portrayed as an unattractive spinster, however, the biaojie is denied the potential to pursue any romantic relationship with Wu. This eroticism allegorizes the biaojie's seduction by the capitalist city and at the same time reinscribes her body as the bearer of mainland China's inferiority because her desire (either for Wu or for the capitalist enjoyment) is denied by the state. Shortly after this allegorical seduction, the biaojie tells Wu about her wish to own a toilet. Wu offers to buy her one but is refused because, she replies with a slight sense of frustration, being a state employee, she should not have material goods that the people do not have. Because it is contradictory to the desire of the state, her desire must be repressed and remain unfulfilled.

The biaojie's seduction by the capitalist city not only keenly illustrates the desire and inferiority she bears, but also points to the narrative desire to transform the mainland as the female (grotesque) body into a desirable body. When the Hong Kong police are informed that Soo invites his important associates from mainland China to a nightclub every night and takes different girls back home, they need a woman to play the bait. The biaojie is willing to risk herself since no one will do the job. Refusing her female counterparts' help, she prepares herself to look like a nightclub girl. Under Wu's gaze, the biaojie walks out with makeup like a Beijing opera singer while still wearing her peasant-like clothes and carrying the outmoded handbag with her. By making her body an excessive and grotesque spectacle, the biaojie shocks all of the Hong Kong police in the room. Wu clearly ridicules her and sees her lack of modern urban taste (in a sense, modernity), yet has to persuade her to change her makeup and dress. In his words, she has "to be modernized." He then asks one of his female colleagues to help her. When the biaojie is seen again, she has been redefined and is presented as a desirable body for the capitalist phallic gaze. With soft lyrical music in the background, the biaojie walks out, under Wu's gaze, with sophisticated makeup, a low-cut dress, high heels, and stylish hair. Her dark thick glasses are gone and the outmoded handbag is replaced with a chic purse. Everyone is enthralled by the charm of her new body; Wu, in particular, gazes at her with slight erotic desire, while the biaojie, under all those gazes, seems unconscious of herself for a while.

As a signifier for mainland China, the female body is discursively inscribed as the "wrong" body, which must be mocked, ridiculed, belittled, and made grotesque in the narrative until it is "righted" by the capitalist city and meets with its phallic gaze. Literally, in restructuring the third-world female body from the laughable to the desirable for the first-world's male erotic gaze, the film enunciates an "internal Orientalism" over the mainland (the other). Orientalism, according to Edward Said, can be conceived as a Western way of systematic dominance over the Oriental through "dealing with it by making statements about it, authorizing views of it, describing it, by teaching it, setting it." In short, Orientalism appears as "a Western style for dominating, restructuring, and having authority over the Orient."[15] Said particularly uses Orientalism to speak of ethnic and geographic differences between the Western and the Oriental. Since both the proximity of and the ethnic ties between Hong Kong and the mainland lack such differences, I will use "internal Orientalism" to describe this discursive dominance over mainland China through the representation practiced here. The term partly borrows from bell hook's use of "internal colonization" to describe the white population's dominance over African Americans within the nation-state.

In *Her Fatal Ways*, Hong Kong's dominance over mainland China is enunciated through a "looking" relation and through spatial and sexual economics. As a third-world female body located in capitalist Hong Kong, the biaojie acts, but ends up making mistakes, then relies on the male to rescue her. For example, she manages to find out the name of Soo's warehouse but ends up going to the wrong place and beating the wrong people because she fails to comprehend that there are many identically named warehouses in Hong Kong. Her inability to master modern Hong Kong's space deprives her of the agency of leading to closure through arresting the criminal in the film. It is Wu who locates Soo's warehouse and finds the evidence of his drug smuggling. And it is Wu who, with the help of Wu's father and other KMT veterans, finally arrests Soo along with his illegal cohorts. In this scene, the female body—as the bearer of all the "wrongs" and "grotesqueness" of the Chinese Communist state—also gets "righted" by accepting the concept of human rights. When A-sheng beats one of Soo's colleagues, the biaojie attempts to stop him by questioning him: "Don't you know what human rights mean?" This sequence ends with the biaojie and Wu shaking hands and cheerfully claiming "the success of

China-Hong Kong cooperation," while Wu's supervisor, arriving after they arrest Soo, is merely concerned about his future promotion.

However, even though the third-world body gets corrected, educated, and righted as a proper body by the capitalist city, it cannot become a first-world body. The allegorically united China-Hong Kong body (cooperation) is disavowed at the end. The narrative closure enunciates the desire to maintain the national boundary between Hong Kong and mainland China. Standing on the physical borderline between Hong Kong and China, Wu and his father say farewell to the biaojie and A-sheng and see them crossing the border. When they are gradually out of Wu's sight, the biaojie reveals in a voice-over what she has written in the letter that she gave Wu on her departure. She apologizes for not understanding the Hong Kong system and concludes with deep thoughts on differences between the two societies. The camera fixes on Wu's looks as the film's final image. His contemplation corresponds to the opening image of the biaojie's "to-be-looked-at-ness." Thus, through the politics of the looking relation throughout the film, the binarism of the Hong Kong (first-world) male)—who looks and defines—and the mainland China (third-world) female—who is to be looked at and inscribed—is made final.

## Notes

Support for this work by the Chiang Ching-Kuo Foundation under a dissertation fellowship is gratefully acknowledged.

1. *The Economist* (28 June 1997).

2. Yat-ming Siu, "Population and Immigration: With a Special Account on Chinese Immigrants," Mee-kau Nyaw and Si-ming Li, eds., *The Other Hong Kong Report 1996* (Hong Kong: The Chinese University Press, 1996), 184.

3. Helen F. Siu, "Remade in Hong Kong: Weaving into the Chinese Tapestry," Tao Tao Liu and David Faure, eds., *Unity and Diversity: Local Culture and Identities in China* (Hong Kong: Hong Kong University Press, 1996), 187.

4. Quoted in Helen F. Siu, "Remade in Hong Kong," 178.

5. Ibid.

6. For an overall analysis of the cinematic representation of immigrants from mainland China (or Vietnamese refugees) in the 1980s, see Cheng Yu, "Uninvited Guests," in Li

Cheuk-to, ed., *The China Factor in Hong Kong Cinema* (Hong Kong: Urban Council, 14th Hong Kong International Film Festival, 1990), 98–101.

7. Nevzat Soguk, "Transnational/Transborder Bodies: Resistance, Accommodation, and Exile in Refugee and Migration Movement on the U.S.-Mexican Border," Michael J. Shapiro and Hayward R. Alker, eds., *Challenging Boundaries* (Minneapolis: University of Minnesota Press, 1996), 287.

8. Hong Kongers use various nicknames for the mainland Chinese, including *biaojie, biaoge, biaoshu*, and d*alumei*. *Biaojie* (which literally means an older female cousin) tends to suggest a set of negative characteristics: backwardness, unfashionableness, lack of proper etiquette and culture, and an inclination to use bribery. She has a male counterpart, the *biaoge* (an older male cousin), who may be innocent in a

positive way, old-fashioned, or engaged in criminal behavior such as robbery. Both terms might originate from the term *biaoshu* (a less-than-second-degree uncle), used in the Cultural Revolution model play "Red Lantern" as a code name for underground Communists during the anti-Japanese war in China. *Biaoshu* served as a metaphor for the generational difference and distant blood relationship between China the "motherland" and its putative "child," Hong Kong. *Dalumei* (which literally means little sisters from mainland China), circulated in both Hong Kong and Taiwan, refers to a Chinese woman who in most cases serves as a prostitute.

For an elaboration on the feminization of the mainlander through the circulation of *biaojie* and *dalumei* in popular narrative, see Shu-mei Shih, "Gender and a New Geopolitics of Desire: The Seduction of Mainland Women in Taiwan and Hong Kong Media," *Signs* 23.21 (1998): 287–319.

9. Hong Kong scholar Cheuk Pak Tong identified those films that deal with the police crossing borders for the sake of law and order as "Chinese police films" (*Gongan Pian*). See Cheuk Pak Tong, "Jiuling Niandai Xianggang Dianyingzhong Gongan Xingxiang de Gaibian," *Xianggang Dianying Leixing Lun* (Hong Kong: Oxford University Press, 1997), 153–168.

10. Jonathan Hall, *Anxious Pleasures: Shakespearean Comedy and the Nation-State* (London and Toronto: Associated University Presses, 1995), 21.

11. Kathleen Rowe, "Comedy, Melodrama and Gender: Theorizing the Genres of Laughter," Kristine Brunovska Karnick and Henry Jenkins, eds., *Classical Hollywood Comedy* (New York and London: Routledge, 1995), 44.

12. In *The Fall of Hong Kong*, Mark Roberti details how mainland China interfered in Hong Kong affairs long before it was returned to China. See Mark Roberti, *The Fall of Hong Kong* (New York: John Wiley and Sons, 1994).

13. Edward W. Said, *Orientalism* (New York: Vintage Books, 1977), 3.

14. Ibid.

15. Ibid.

# 14

# Asian Martial-Arts Cinema, Dance, and the Cultural Languages of Gender

AARON D. ANDERSON

Asian martial-arts films hold many possibilities—and many Eurocentric traps—for Western film theory. The possibilities lie mostly in the ability to look outside the naturalizing influence of European American culture and thus be able to question otherwise invisible assumptions; but conversely, the traps lie mostly in failing to recognize that these same European American cultural assumptions are not necessarily universal. These traps are compounded by the fact that while film theory's purview is rapidly expanding, the tools used to analyze films are not always reformed as rapidly.

Historically, Western film theory investigated only *high art*, and action film's locus as a body-genre with simplistic narratives excluded it from consideration. More recently, film theory redefined its parameters by analyzing previously excluded *low* forms such as action films. However, the language used to analyze these films often remains tied to the static language of high art, with its historical emphasis on painting, sculpture, and literature. This incongruence has forced much scholarship on action films to focus on issues related to passive bodies-on-display. Hence, several scholars describe the action that defines action films as merely secondary to a passive display of muscular bodies. For example, Yvonne Tasker follows Richard Dyer in theorizing that "any display of the male body needs to be compensated for

From *Asian Journal of Communication* 11.2 (2001), 57–78. Reprinted with permission.

by the suggestion of action. Thus sports pin-ups and the portrayal of the feats of near-naked action heroes both offer the body a to-be-looked-at whilst refusing the 'femininity' implied by that very passive position."[1] Unfortunately, this theoretical framework leaves little room for action films to be seen as anything other than thinly veiled excuses for homoerotic displays of the male body, which, in turn, leaves little room for Asian action stars to be seen as anything other than a sexualized, and therefore largely fetishized, *other.*

In response, some scholars have conversely noted that the "perpetual motion" of many Asian action stars contradicts the masculine ideal of "male immobility" characteristic of most iconic Western action heroes.[2] Such work points out that similar connotations of masculine power in Asian martial-arts films are more often demonstrated through movement ability than through static posture or rigid strength and thus "[challenge] the notion that Western models of masculinity reflect a monolithic global ideal."[3] However, these arguments still use a bifurcated language of universal gender. According to this language, whenever Western *immobility* is coded as masculine, the opposite, Asian *avoidance*, becomes invariably coded as feminine. Thus the very language of the discussion reinforces postcolonial notions about the *feminine* nature of the Asian male body, while also ironically disallowing strong or authoritative female characters from being seen as anything other than *masculine.*

How then, given these two seemingly contradictory extremes—martial-arts action as compensation for a passive and therefore feminine body, and this same action as feminizing in and of itself—may one describe anything about Asian martial-arts films without eroticizing the Asian male body when it is immobile on the one hand, or defining it on the other hand as feminine when it is in motion? And where, within the confines of these same contradictions, is any possibility for strong or powerful female characters to be coded as anything other than masculine?

One way to avoid the contradictions of gender construction that so often leave Asian performers in a perpetual state of erotic *otherness* is to follow up on the methodological consequences of theorizing movement as a fundamental part of the film medium. In this sense, one way to analyze a martial-arts film is to analyze it in term of its movement, which in turn means using models and methods already developed to accomplish this task, in particular those developed to analyze dance.

One of the most basic definitions of dance suggests that there are at least four components that distinguish dance from nondance activities: 1) dances have a purpose; 2) dances have intentional rhythm; 3) dances contain culturally patterned sequences; and 4) dances have extraordinary nonverbal movement that has value in and of itself.[4] Since dance analysis is itself largely concerned with describing attributes of the body that performs the dance, even this basic definition can be used as a model to allow a systematic investigation into the ways in which filmed martial-arts movements may reflect or reify cultural ideas about the nature of the body in motion.

## Jackie Chan and the Art of the Film Fight

Jackie Chan, for example, often describes his fight scenes' choreography and performance not as representations of actual physical violence, but rather as danced spectacles. In a 1998 interview, Chan described his philosophy on the contrast between *dance* and *violence*: "It's like tap dance. Before I choreograph the fighting, I write down all the tempos—because our fighting is so long—then music. When the music comes up, you just keep punching, keep kicking. And then, 'ah, yeah'—it's not violent anymore."[5]

In accordance with our definition of dance, Chan's description here gives primacy to elements of *intentional rhythm* in his choreography. As dance, this choreography may have meaning on several other levels as well, including an "extraordinary" quality to the movement that "has value in and of itself."

In this sense, part of the pleasure of viewing is simply the sheer spectacle of watching Chan's body move through and interact with space. A large part of his films' appeal has to do not only with Chan's agility, but also with his ability to transform everyday objects into weapons, props, and obstacles around which to fight, defend, and perform. In the same interview, Chan described his use of the environment as a type of art:

> I want to show audiences I can grab everything; everything becomes a weapon. And when you choose a weapon, it's not like, "wham, wham." I want fighting to be like dancing. Everything is pretty. It's like dancing. Even fighting somebody, it's all pretty. At the end, you have a pose like a ballet. That's what I want. I want to show audiences fighting is an art. It's not like, "I want to kill you." It's an art.[6]

Many of the fight sequences in Chan's films follow this same philosophy. For instance, the set-piece fight sequence from *Rumble in the Bronx* (dir. Stanley Tong, 1996),[7] the film that successfully broke Chan into the American film market, includes the use of bottles, cue sticks, skis, chandeliers, chairs, television sets, sliding doors, shopping carts, ottomans, refrigerator doors, and even pinball machines as weapons.

Likewise, Chan's choreography often displays an almost uncanny ability to find and use the empty space around him. Most of Chan's adversaries move through space and attack as one would expect in an actual fight, with strong vertical stances and deliberately direct attacks. Chan, on the other hand, moves and fights along all the planes of movement. When attacked directly, he moves to the oblique. When knocked to the floor, he attacks from the horizontal. When attacked on the ground, he leaps in the air. When his base of support is pushed from beneath him, he rolls with the fall, finding new surfaces on which to move and fight. In this way Chan's use of space becomes almost a partnership with the environment, or, as novelist Donald E. Westlake puts it, "Jackie Chan is Fred Astaire, and the world is Ginger Rogers."[8]

Westlake's comment here hints at other connections between the movement sequences in martial-arts films and dance-centered musicals. Both genres incorporate similar sequences in which movement is used as spectacle. In this sense, a martial-arts training sequence in an action film may serve a similar function to a solo dance in a Hollywood musical, a one-to-one combat sequence creates a spectacle not unlike a duet, and multiple attackers echo the grand spectacle of an ensemble piece. Furthermore, innovative use of the environment is characteristic of many forms of dance spectacle, linking Chan's choreography not only to Hollywood musicals but also to other movement innovators such as Charlie Chaplin, Buster Keaton, and Harold Lloyd (all of whom Chan credits as role models).

In part because of Chan's links to these larger traditions of slapstick comedy and dance, few people challenge his assertion that his movement spectacles are forms of art. However, definitions of art are endlessly subjective and open to interpretation. In *The Modern Dance*, early dance critic John Martin defines movement art in the following way:

> When the word "art" is used it may be taken to mean the process whereby one individual conveys from his consciousness to that of another individual a concept which transcends his powers of rational statement. This concept need not be anything profound or esoteric, else we would have to exclude the decorative arts. It may be merely that contemplation of abstract perfection which never ceases to titillate the aesthetic sensitivity by exquisite design. The cover of a book, the design of a wall, the border on a dress, may all produce an aesthetic effect through form rather than through content. Form, then, is capable of operating of itself. It may, indeed, be defined as the result of unifying diverse elements whereby they achieve collectively an aesthetic vitality which except by this association they would not possess. The whole thus becomes greater than the sum of all its parts. This unifying process by which form is attained is known as composition.[9]

Chan's skilled use of mundane props as weapons clearly falls within the description of unifying diverse elements to achieve collectively an aesthetic vitality that, except by this association, they would not possess, and his choreography clearly includes a large degree of creative form and composition. It follows, then, that at least subjectively the whole of the movement in this example from *Rumble in the Bronx* may be considered greater than the sum of its parts. Ultimately, though, it is the very existence of subjectivity itself that allows for any definition of *art*. Movement art, in particular, depends on elements of subjectivity as pathways of communication.

Movement art implies kinesthesia, which in turn implies a phenomenological—or bodily—involvement in reception. In this way, viewed movement evokes different phenomenological perceptions (perceptions *felt* rather than *thought*) and bodily memories (sensations remembered *as* feelings rather than as consciously considered recollections) within each body engaged in interpretation. Movement in and of itself is the medium through which kinesthetic (felt, body-to-body) communication takes place, and so the transference of any movement's "meaning" always involves a range of nonlinear elements. For example, as already mentioned, choreographic rhythmic patterns within, or accompanying, movement can contribute significantly to the enjoyment and understanding of any movement performance. This may be, in part, because everyone *feels* the presence of his or her own internal rhythmic heartbeat and breathing patterns and most people also learn a more esoteric understanding of rhythmic cycles of time (waking into sleeping, day into night, changes in season, and so forth). Possibly because of these phenomenological roots, choreographed rhythmic patterns inherently refer to bodily rhythmic patterns, and therefore choreographed movement patterns assist in the recall of phenomenological memory or bodily feelings. Thus rhythmic patterns such as those found in dance and choreographed fights may increase or decrease aesthetic appreciation and understanding of movement, which in turn can affect one's subjective definition of the movement's artistic nature.[10]

In any event, whether or not Chan's movement spectacle qualifies as art to all viewers, it clearly may qualify as such to some. To these viewers, at least, Chan's movement may be both art and dance. Following our definition, then, this movement has a purpose, which according to Chan is to show audiences that fighting can be an aesthetic (and therefore no longer *violent*) art like dancing in which everything in the room may become part of the spectacle. Following this same logic, the intentional rhythm of Chan's film fights may also intensify viewers' physical reaction to the movement by acting directly on their phenomenological bodily memories; and further, these same fights have value (and because of their extraordinary nature, possibly art) in and of themselves. The last part of our definition of dance refers to the *culturally patterned* nature of the movement sequences. To consider at this point these cultural patterns of movement in terms of Chan's international appeal leads to some illuminating complications for theories of gender.

## Dancing Across Culture: Gendered Movement

In Western culture, hand-to-hand combat is usually considered in terms of a teleology of male aggression, or at the very least as the almost exclusive purview of masculine movement (as when Western boxing is referred to as the "manly" art of self defense). Dancing, in contrast, is often considered a feminine or feminizing activity. However, at odds with these supposedly natural or universal divisions, Chinese martial-arts movements are not so easily divided into masculine and feminine, fight and dance.

Jackie Chan's martial-arts movements originate from his early childhood training in the Beijing Opera. This training combined elements of dance and acrobatics with a variety of *ch'uan fa* (popularly known as *kung-fu*) styles. Many styles of Chinese kung fu are, in turn, also derived from or practiced as elements of dance, as in the modern educational and performance syllabus of *wushu*, often combining stylized dance-like sequences modeled on the movements of animals such as the tiger, crane, snake, monkey, or praying mantis, or mimicking human conditions, as in the case of *drunken* kung fu. In fact, throughout the long history of Chinese movement forms, the connections between kung fu and dance have been particularly strong.

Asian martial arts offer other challenges for Western understanding of movement as well. Many Asian martial-art forms incorporate into their practice what might be described as spiritual or philosophical elements, and these are difficult, if not impossible, to separate from other, functional elements in the practice of the forms themselves. In fact, the underlying philosophy of the practitioners is sometimes the primary factor distinguishing one form from another. Perhaps the most obvious example of this is the philosophical division that separates *external* or *hard* forms of kung fu from *internal* or *soft* forms. The weapons used in both of these types of forms are so similar as to be almost indistinguishable: similar swords, spears, knives, and other such *armed* weapons as well as similar use of *unarmed* weapons such as the feet, legs, arms, and hands. What distinguishes these categories from one another is often not so much what weapons are used, but rather that the divisions themselves derive from philosophical understandings about the methods of their use. For instance, the external or hard martial arts focus primarily on strengthening the muscles and bones involved in the proper execution of technique, whereas the internal or soft arts focus mainly on the cultivation of *Chi* (intrinsic power) and the ability to physically "listen" to an opponent's movement.

In kung fu, these ideas about matters of technique are fundamentally tied to other philosophical ideas about the nature of *Chi*, which are in turn tied to Buddhist, Confucian, and especially Taoist understandings about the nature of the universe. However, in practice, external styles often incorporate what would otherwise be considered internal techniques into the functional execution of certain movements (such as avoiding rather than blocking an incoming punch), and internal styles often incorporate what would otherwise be considered external techniques into the functional execution of their movements (such as blocking and counterpunching rather than avoiding an incoming punch). Thus, in practice, any given style is rarely only external or internal in the functional execution of movement. In such cases, what separates external movement from internal movement is often only a matter of the philosophical beliefs of the person executing the movement. For instance, any movements—such as blocking a punch, stepping into distance, and throwing the opponent—may be executed in both external and internal styles. Functionally, the movement patterns may appear exactly the same, yet the two (hypothetical) people executing the movement may identify the movement in different terms (for example, as either external or internal) depending on their understanding of the *style* of their performance or training. In this case, what distinguishes the movement style is not as much a matter of function as it is a matter of the self-identification of the person doing the movement. It is sometimes said that "there are not any entirely internal or external martial arts. . . . there are [only] internal or external martial artists."[11] Furthermore, because divisions between external and internal, hard and soft, are not entirely rigid or exclusive, practitioners are always free to move between external and internal, hard and soft techniques or self-identification, as desired or as necessity dictates.

One of the ways of understanding the seeming contradictions of this duality lies in the philosophical concept(s) of *yin* and *yang*. Yin and yang are familiar in the West mainly as a male-female dichotomy-combination usually represented by two "fish" encircling each other to form a circle, one "fish" black with a white "eye" and the other white with a black "eye." However, the concept of yin includes much more than a simple signifier for *female*, just as yang represents much more than simply *male*. In Chinese Taoist philosophy, and hence in most Chinese martial arts,

> Yin and Yang are two movements of the formed universe—one contracting, the other expanding; one cold or hot, male or female, day or night. Although nothing is solely Yin or Yang, everything has either a Yin or Yang expression. [In martial-arts combat] a forceful move such as a punch or push is Yang, while yielding is Yin. A foot that is weighted is Yang, while the unweighted is Yin. [If attacked] one yields to the opponent's Yang and fills in what is Yin. Yin and Yang are complimentary parts of the whole and harmonious in nature.[12]

The result of these philosophical considerations is that Chinese martial-arts movement cannot necessarily be considered or described in terms of a static dichotomy of masculine versus feminine. In contrast to Western conceptions of movement paradigms, in Chinese martial arts to fight is not always to be male, to yield is not always to be female, and attack and defense are not always opposites.

The complex nature of reading movement in terms of culture is particularly evident in Jackie Chan's 1992 film *Police Story III: Supercop*,[13] which won Chan the Golden Horse Best Actor Award in Taiwan. Chan's costar in this film is a former Miss Malaysia, Michelle Yeoh. Her character, Police Director Yang, is shown as a strong leader and proficient martial artist (both traits contradictory to Western stereotypes for former beauty queens). Chan's character likewise contradicts Western stereotypes for action heroes, as he is sometimes shown as timid and less proficient than his female counterpart. Similar contradictions are evident throughout much of the film.

For instance, the initial meeting between Chan and Yeoh in the film immediately sets up contradictions for Western paradigms of masculinity and femininity. For instance, Yeoh's character first appears wearing a "masculine" military uniform and is briskly efficient in her movements and posture. Her job title, "Chief of Security," likewise evokes traditional Western paradigms of masculine power and protection. Chan's character, in contrast, appears timid and inefficient in his bearing and posture, and during a photo session that refers to his Beijing Opera heritage, he even wears "feminine" makeup and lipstick. The narrative joke is that his manner belies his nickname, "Supercop Chan of the Royal Hong Kong Police," which itself refers to quintessentially "masculine" power. The film's contradictions in its characterization are not easily reconciled within Western paradigms of gendered movement. But from the perspective of dance—in which *culturally patterned* movement sequences play a fundamental role—these seeming contradictions can be understood by analyzing the movement not in terms of a static masculine-feminine dichotomy, but rather as a dynamic interchange between the philosophical, and thus cultural, elements of yin and yang.

In this manner, Yeoh's character's name, Comrade Yang, Chief of Security for the Chinese Police, makes direct reference to yang, the "masculine" essence of strength; thus the name plays against her actual gender and simultaneously comments on the official gender-blind philosophy of Communist China. Chan's character, on the other hand, draws on the other side of the equation, yin. Thus when Chan appears in "female" Beijing Opera makeup, the makeup both plays against the masculine nature of his "supercop" status and comments on his well-known early training in that performance form. In fact, throughout the entire film, Yeoh's strength and movement ability are highlighted in terms of yang energy while Chan is shown to have great indirect movement ability and agility in the manner of yin.

Yeoh's character is in almost constant control and power throughout the film. She, not he, uses a rifle (a quintessential Western phallus symbol) to shoot Chan's pursuers. Armed and perched like a sniper, she becomes Chan's protector during a staged prison break. In this scene, her "masculine" (yang) role as immobile, strong protector is directly contrasted with the "feminizing" (yin) aspect of Chan as the mobile, pursued character. In addition, throughout this scene, Chan's movement abilities are highlighted not in terms of yang aggression or strength, but in terms of yin avoidance and vulnerability, as when he desperately pants for air while running up a steep hill. Later, when the police again try to capture Chan, Yeoh comes to his rescue, and again she ends up holding the gun.

Throughout the film, Yeoh's physical ability to fight is shown to be as good as, if not better than, Chan's. For instance, when Chan is immobilized with a stun gun and she literally leaps to his defense, her movements are strong and fluid, her pose tall and graceful. And when Chan is again stunned, she again physically defends him, this time showing an extreme mastery of kung fu by using thrown chopsticks as weapons. Chan is juxtaposed as inept at using this particular weapon, so that the juxtaposition clearly shows how the yang in Yeoh's character matches that of any (even "super") man.

However, as with all things having to do with yin and yang, neither Yeoh nor Chan is shown as possessing only one or the other characteristic. Although Yeoh's character clearly is predominantly associated with yang energy, she is also shown in very yin-like, feminine pigtails disguised as Chan's little sister. And she occasionally performs traditional "feminine" roles, as when she helps Chan avoid detection by pretending to massage his back, or as the erotic object of a male gaze when Chan's character accidentally walks in on her undressing. Likewise, although Chan's character throughout the film is predominantly associated with yin energy, many of his martial movements are unmistakably yang in nature. In fact, almost all the stunts for which Chan is famous involve yang-like, expansive energy, as when he leaps from a rooftop onto a suspended rope ladder, or when he desperately clings to this same ladder as it hurtles high in the air beneath a flying helicopter.

Because the divisions are not rigid, separations of yin from yang are never entirely clean in actual cultural practice, and clearly there are other kinds of references to yin-yang in the film as well. For example, the macho Communist woman has become a standard comic role in recent Hong Kong films, so that the yang in Comrade Yang can also be seen as a joke referring to the caricature. Also, in the Beijing Opera tradition, a male (usually a young boy) historically would have played the role of heroic or strong woman. Thus we must also acknowledge a distinction between women's actual cultural status and that implied by analyzing the representations flowing from this performance tradition. In actual cultural practice, the divisions of yin and yang are often anything but equitable; instead they must vie with strict (some would say oppressive) Confucian notions of gender hierarchy. My point is simply this: movement in this film cannot be fully understood by simply referring to rigid Western categories of masculine and feminine movements. The division of movements seems, rather, aligned in terms of a unification of energy, with both Chan and Yeoh displaying an overall aesthetic of grace and power. In addition, these unified elements of grace and power—yin and yang—take on distinctly political overtones in one of the film's more spectacular fight scenes. Because the interactions between yin and yang in this fight are so fluid, it will be useful to look at this scene in detail.

Early in the film, after his photography session in Beijing Opera makeup, Chan's character is led by Yeoh's on a tour of a Communist Chinese martial-arts training facility. The trainees in this facility are all shown wearing various "masculine" uniforms. Chan himself is the only one not wearing a uniform, which visibly distinguishes the individualist nature of his origin in Hong Kong with the uniformity of Communist China. This contrast is then developed in terms of yin and yang in the movements that follow.

The Chinese police train in hard-style *Qikung*—breaking boards and bricks against their muscular bodies—and are thus depicted in terms of yang energy.[14] When Chan says that he has "avoided" such training because he is "too delicate," his comment plays against Chan's star persona and reputation for physical resilience while also referring to elements of yin in his character. Likewise, when Chan and Comrade Wang, the Chinese military police coach, engage in a hand-to-hand martial-arts demonstration, the entire exchange can be viewed in terms of muscular Chinese yang expansion against reluctant, yet not weak, Hong Kong yin agility.

This fight begins with Comrade Wang wearing a red "muscle" tee-shirt. He is aggressive, muscular, strong, and proficient in hard-style qikung (as evidenced by the many boards and bricks broken over his uniform-clad body). Chan, in contrast, dresses as an individual in jeans and a white (nonmuscle) tee-shirt and moves with casual ease. The Chinese Communist audience "takes seats" in position around the demonstration area with crisp, military precision and uniformity, whereas Chan engages in the demonstration only indirectly and reluctantly. The demonstration begins as Wang takes a classic hard-style pose with muscles flexed, rigid, and strong.

Chan, on the other hand, circles around the perimeter of the fighting area with his body loose and shoulders rounded in classic soft-style manner, relaxed and in constant indirect motion. Chan does not attack but instead gives his opponent an almost "feminine" wink and a smile, which in turn provoke Wang to attack with direct hard-style punches and kicks. Chan thus begins the fight as yin: on the defensive, avoiding and blocking the attacks, counterattacking only by filling in the spaces left by Wang's attacks. The fight's attacks and defenses present a unified whole of yang flowing into yin in a display of both combatants' movement agility.

However, when Chan is forcefully struck in the stomach, he returns the attack with a yang kick of his own. Although Chan's kick sends Comrade Wang sliding back across the room, Wang outwardly shows no signs of pain. Chan, on the other hand, visibly displays his pain by doubling over and grabbing his stomach. This is in keeping with many of Chan's movement performances, which visibly show the effort of moving while at the same time presenting an amazing degree of movement virtuosity. Although Chan's movements may at times appear to stretch the limits of human potential, his facial expressions and visible shows of effort almost always ascribe to his characters a human, everyday normality. In contrast, Wang is presented as almost machinelike in his single-minded relentlessness and lack of outward signs of pain.

As the fight continues, Chan moves back and forth between hard and soft styles of kung fu, first coming on guard in an angry hard-style stance and then deliberately softening, smiling, rounding his shoulders, and loosening his movements. With the opening of the second phrase in the fight, Chan first jabs twice in rapid succession to test Wang's defenses, and then jabs twice more, opening a path through the defenses, but ends up literally hurting his hand on Wang's head as Wang blocks the follow-up punch with the hard qikung of his own forehead. Wang then uses the yang strength in his head like a battering ram and pushes Chan backward across the floor. Chan attempts to push back but is overpowered by the stronger opponent. When Chan tries to grapple with Wang, he is again overpowered and put into a headlock. Chan escapes, not through strength but through superior agility, first flipping his opponent into a cartwheel and then using the momentum of this flip to flip himself over Wang's back. Wang turns and attempts a hard kick to Chan's leg, which Chan, yin-like, avoids. After blocking a second kick from Wang, Chan follows up this motion with two rapid hard-style kicks to Wang's chest and face, which themselves are immediately followed by a hard-style jumping knee strike to Wang's head and a spinning back-kick to Wang's chest. This last attack sends Wang flying backward into a concrete pillar, but once again Wang shows no outward pain. Chan returns to a hard-style guard but then, as before, deliberately softens his posture—rounding his shoulders and loosening his movements. In this phrase, Chan's character demonstrates superior martial ability, not through superior strength but through superior mobility coupled with the tactical ability to shift between both hard and soft fighting styles.

In the third phrase of the fight, Chan combats Wang directly, hard style against hard style, using direct blocks and absorbing blows with his body. Here as before, Chan's facial expressions clearly show the effort of the motions and the pain of the blows while Wang remains robotlike in his own movements. Chan ends the movement sequence by unexpectedly twisting Wang's nose with his thumb—figuratively tweaking the nose of Communist China. As Wang begins to advance again, Chan retreats, disarming the situation through the very yin-like movements of retreating and asking for a "time-out." Chan's movements in this sequence, as before, display a superior martial ability over that of his opponent. Although this sequence shows that Chan's character can move and fight in a yang-like hard style, it also demonstrates that he has greater success using yin-like indirect or unorthodox tactics. Chan's movements in this fight therefore cannot be described as either wholly "masculine" or wholly "feminine," but are probably better described in terms of a continual flow between yin and yang. The dual nature of this movement is further amplified through other elements in the scene that are codified as Chinese yang aggression against Hong Kong yin agility. Thus, these movements may also be read as transmitting aspects of an underlying anxiety about the then-impending 1997 return of Hong Kong to Communist China. These political overtones resurface again at the end of the film as Chan and Yeoh quarrel about which government—China's or Hong Kong's—should get the recovered money. Here Chan ends the quarrel by asking, "What difference does it make? After 1997 we'll be working together, eh?"

## Conclusion

As film theory expands its purview, so too must it expand its tools of analyses. Investigating new genres—such as action films—requires the development of new methods of examination. This is especially important when considering films that do not conform to Western stereotypes. Failing to see the necessity of this risks perpetuating the blindness of colonialism by relegating all non-Western films—and therefore all non-Western performers—to the nebulous realm of exotic "other." Here, I have suggested that an alternative way of analyzing Hong Kong martial-art films is to read them as dance. This approach emphasizes that movement plays a fundamental role in any understanding of bodies—and thus gender—in the genre. This approach also emphasizes that kinesthesia—and thus subjectivity—plays a central role in movement's reception: therefore different people may interpret the gender of any given movement in various ways.

Ultimately, there is no single method for understanding movement. I have argued for an interpretation of filmed martial-arts combat as dance in relation to culturally specific concepts of yin and yang. According to this model, political overtones in the dance-combat may reflect cultural aspects of the movement in terms of anxiety about Hong Kong's (then) impending return to Communist China—in effect, reifying the culture of Hong Kong in comparison to the impending merger with Communist China. By contrasting this reading with the otherwise strict dichotomy of Western concepts of masculine versus feminine movement, I hoped to illuminate some of the ways in which understanding martial-arts movement as dance might both create categories of understanding and leave elements of these categories negotiable within and between cultures. Yet this, of course, is far from the last word.

Alternative interpretations lie within other subjective bodies, the end result being simply that any given movement's "meaning" must be considered in terms of a dynamic exchange rather than as a static condition. Once we recognize the possibilities opened through this understanding, we might also then begin to avoid the trap of believing that European American divisions of movement, and of gender, are necessarily universal. In turn, perhaps we Western scholars will also eventually see the contradictions within our own cultural ideas of gender and stop having to define the bodies of *others* in terms of our own static, and often contradictory, dichotomies.

## Notes

1. Yvonne Tasker, *Spectacular Bodies: Gender, Genre and the Action Cinema* (New York: Routledge, 1993), 77. Cf. Richard Dyer, "Don't Look Now," *Screen* 23.3–23.4 (1982): 61–73.

2. Mark Gallagher, "Masculinity in Translation: Jackie Chan's Transcultural Star Text," *Velvet Light Trap* 39 (Spring 1997): 27–29.

3. Ibid., 25.

4. Constance A. Schrader, *A Sense of Dance: Exploring Your Movement Potential* (Champaign, IL: Human Kinetics, 1996), 10; based on Judith Lynne Hanna, *To Dance Is Human: A Theory of Nonverbal Communication* (Chicago: University of Chicago Press, 1987).

5. Jackie Chan (interview), *Jackie-Chan-a-Thon* (Chicago, IL: Turner Network Television [TNT]) (October 9–11, 1998).

6. Ibid.

7. Jackie Chan (actor) and Stanley Tong (director), *Rumble in the Bronx* (New Line Cinema, 1996); previously released as *Hong Faan Kui* (Hong Kong: Golden Harvest, 1995).

8. Cited in Richard Corliss, "Go West, Hong Kong (John Woo and Jackie Chan meet Hollywood)," *Time Magazine* (February 26, 1996): 67.

9. John Martin, *The Modern Dance* (New York: A.S. Barnes, 1933), 35.

10. For a more detailed description of the process of kinesthesia in film fight sequences, see Aaron Anderson, "Kinesthesia in Martial Arts Films: Action in Motion," *Jump Cut: A Review of Contemporary Media* 48 (2006), http://www.ejumpcut.org/archive/onlinessays/JC42folder/anderson2/index.html.

11. Ron Seih, *Martial Arts for Beginners* (New York: Writers and Readers Publishing, 1995), 66.

12. Ibid., 80.

13. Jackie Chan (actor) and Stanley Tong (director), *Supercop* (Dimension Films, 1997); Previously released as *Police Story III: Supercop* (Hong Kong: Golden Harvest, 1992).

14. *Qikung* is both a part of and separate from kung fu. *Qikung* deals specifically with directing *Qi* (or *Chi*) to various parts of the body to promote defense, offense, health, or all three.

# PART III

# At the Millennium and Beyond

# 15

# Singapore as a Society of Strangers

## *Eric Khoo's* Mee Pok Man, 12 Storeys, *and* Be With Me

Tan See-Kam

In Singapore it is no secret that Eric Khoo (b. 1965), one of the twelve children of the late hotelier-tycoon Khoo Teik Puat, was born with a silver spoon in his mouth. Despite his upper-class upbringing, Khoo has—as a filmmaker—demonstrated passion for making verité-like films about the downtrodden, the fragile, and the weak of contemporary Singapore society. His films excel at bringing to sharp focus the grit on the underbelly of the proudly capitalist, conspicuously affluent, and unapologetically consumerist global nation-state that Singapore has become. They frequently deal with subject matter that polite society would find unpalatable or disdainful, if not downright offensive: prostitution, suicide, child abuse, incest, alternative life-styles, euthanasia, even necrophilia. For the most part, the films portray Singapore as a society of strangers populated with dysfunctional individuals, families, and communities. All these underscore Khoo's awareness about the need to provide alternative ways of "seeing" the affluent nation-state.

Hooked on cinema from an early age, Khoo started to play with his mother's Super 8 Cannon camera at the age of eight, and by the time he was thirteen, had dreams of becoming a filmmaker.[1] He was schooled at the United World College of Southeast Asia (Singapore), which primarily caters to children of well-heeled locals or expatriates living and working in Singapore or the surrounding region. Later he went to City Art Institute in Sydney, Australia, where he studied cinematography. Around this time, Khoo started to make short films: *Barbie Digs Joe* (1990), *August* (1991),

*Carcass* (1992), *Symphony 92.4 FM* (1993), *Pain* (1994), and more recently, *Home VDO* (2000). In 1995 he directed his first feature film, *Mee Pok Man*, followed by *12 Storeys/Shi Er Lou* (1997). His third full-length film, *Be With Me* (2005), had the honor of opening the Festival de Cannes Director's Fortnight (2005). Khoo's films generally had a significant local following; they also traveled well on the international film-festival circuits, with some playing to critical acclaim and winning festival awards. He was conferred the National Arts Council's Young Artist Award for film in 1997 and the Singapore Youth Award in 1999, both in recognition of his contributions to the local arts community. In 1998 *Asiaweek Magazine* named him one of twenty-five exceptional Asians for his influence on film and television, and a year later listed him as one of the new millennium's leaders in the fields of society and culture. In 2007 he received the Cultural Medallion (film), Singapore's highest arts honor. Khoo has additionally worked on local television productions such as *Drive* (1997) and *Seventh Month* (2004), and has been supportive of budding local filmmakers such as James Toh, Abdul Nizam, and CheeK, who codirected the country's first digital video (DV) film, *Stories About Love* (2000), and also Royston Tan of the notorious *15—The Movie* (2004), a docudrama about real-life teenage delinquents and street gangs.

Eric Khoo's filmmaking efforts, chiefly via Zhao Wei Films—which Khoo cofounded with his sister, Jacqueline Khoo, and which produced the above films, sometimes with partial funding from the Singapore Film Commission (SFC)—contributed to the revitalization of Singapore's cinema in the 1990s. Eric Khoo is now Zhao Wei Films' principal producer, director, and scriptwriter, while his sister, a banker by training, primarily handles financing, distribution, and legal matters. In addition to making independent films, Zhao Wei Films has collaborated with Mediacorp Raintree Pictures, the filmmaking arm of the state-controlled Media Corporation of Singapore. Established in 1998, also the year when SFC was set up, Mediacorp Raintree Pictures is the country's most prolific studio and also the largest recipient of state funding for filmmaking. It actively fosters ties between the television industry and the filmmaking community in the country, aggressively seeks transnational collaborations, keenly churns out genre films, and ultimately aims to make "borderless" films that it hopes will have long-range success in the global film market.[2]

*Mee Pok Man*, *12 Storeys*, and *Be With Me*, sometimes referred to as Eric Khoo's trilogy on contemporary Singapore life, are so far this filmmaker's best-known works. These critically acclaimed and multiple-award-winning films, like Khoo's shorts, strive to be locally attached. They feature local talent in almost every aspect of the production process and contain content that carries an aura of cultural resonance and national distinction that would accord with Tom O'Regan's notion for national cinema in which "the local people-among-themselves framing their histories, their stories, their lifeways, their locations" is typical.[3] They generally cast amateur actors, with some literally playing themselves—most notably, Theresa Chan of *Be With Me*, which appends fictional stories about "love, hope and destiny" to Chan's autobiography. They occasionally draw on trained actors from the stage, film, and television scenes. The stories are primarily about Chinese Singaporeans; ethnic minorities (such as Malay, Indian, and Eurasian) mostly play bit-parts or walk-on roles. This mixing of different ethnicities helps configure and project a multiracial, multicultural, and multilingual country (in which ethnic Chinese constitute the vast majority). The films' sociolect smorgasbord works to reinforce the construction. It features standard English and Mandarin, and contains languages that Singapore officialdom has consistently dismissed and vilified as the tongues of the uneducated and the uncultured, deemed as detrimental to Singapore's development as a globally connected city-state and which it has accordingly sought to eradicate—namely, Singlish and Chinese dialects such as Hokkien, Cantonese, and Teochew. Last but not least, real-life persons and reel-life personae walk the filmscape of Khoo's "art house" films. This, together with the visual style of gritty realism that slips between verité compositions and fictional constructs, grants the films a docudrama quality.

## Going Against the Grain

Eric Khoo's "art-house" films generally portray a dark, dreary, desperate, even deviant side of the nation-state, displaying alternative urges, resistant impulses, and oppositional inclinations that show up the sterility of the state's triumphal tales about economic achievements, good governance, and obedient citizenry. These are tales which produce and are in turn produced by the ideological fabric that weaves what Kenneth Paul Tan has referred to as "One-dimensional Singapore"—a socio-political entity presided over by "an authoritarian and paternalistic government" which anxiously and vigilantly guards its dual roles as "the provider of material comfort and the definer of meanings and values through coercion, regulation and censorship".[4] The films reject "the authorized image [that Singapore is] wholesome, clean, upgraded and upwardly mobile"[5] by, for example, "[juxtaposing] the public, global 'face' of Singapore as an ultramodern, hygienic, orderly, rational, Confucian nation-state with the underbelly of Singapore's colonial past, transnational sex trade, urban blight, racism, political oppression, and economic inequities".[6]

The particular putting of the torch to the dark side of the Singapore moon raises questions less immediately about the political legitimacy of the People's Action Party (PAP) government that has ruled Singapore continuously, paternalistically, and authoritatively since 1965 than about the consequences of this government's nation-building agendas, social engineering policies, and economic-development programs, which, while successful at churning out economic miracles, have correspondingly created anomie, alienation, purposelessness (other than for material pursuits), and other forms of social malaise. Khoo's approach to issues as such is never politically direct or explicitly confrontational. As critique, Khoo's "slice[s] of life" (Khoo's term) work more at the level of the semiotic, the interpretive: they index social malaises, while simultaneously "exposing and concretizing the contradictions" at the heart of affluent Singapore.[7] They encourage self-reflexivity in regard to "what is going wrong with the ways people think, act, and learn to be Singaporean, and how one [might set] these right,"[8] and also with regard to the need to strike a balance between materialist pursuits and humanist goals that are characterized by strong interpersonal bonding based on care and compassion. If the ellipses in his films—those created by loose structuring that throw narrative linearity askew, unmotivated intercuts that render narrative causality ambivalent, and narrative jumps that fragment both time and space—actively work to invite viewers to fill in the gaps, then they also concurrently draw attention, in analogical ways, to an affluent society where human compassion appears lacking. Little wonder, then, that pimps, prostitutes, maids, hawkers, students, security guards, disabled people, and other socially marginal members of contemporary Singapore society, including emotionally stunted and psychologically scarred dwellers of Housing Development Board (HDB) homes,[9] have come to populate Khoo's films; the films flesh out tragic stories about dysfunctional individuals, families, and communities coping with a rigid and yet fast-paced society marked by harsh norms, rules, and regulations.

Khoo's films have indeed shown a strong, even clear, preference for lingering in the less affluent side of town. While exposing and showing concretely the contradictions at the heart of contemporary Singapore society, this particular preoccupation has attracted the charge that Khoo's "fascination with the poor [has stemmed] from a fascination with the Other rather than empathy for the Other": this kind of fascination makes his films "disturbingly voyeuristic," says Chua Beng Huat, who then attributes the matter to Khoo's upper-class background.[10] The charge is, however, a hasty one, as it relies on simple and static binary oppositions to secure its grounds. As Gina Marchetti has observed elsewhere, the contradictions fleshed out by Khoo's films are not reducible to class differential alone: gender, ethnic, and other social divides, including generational ones, also factor into the ways Khoo imagines and constructs social identities of Singapore as diverse, as "somewhat out of control and in crisis."[11] That charge also needs to be rethought in the light of the fact that the "other" in Khoo's work now includes rich Singaporeans living in luxury condominiums or semidetached houses: like dwellers of HDB housing, they too lead atomized or spiritually empty lives. Finally, Khoo's close association with HDB-dweller Royston Tan—in his capacity as mentor to this *enfant terrible* of Singapore cinema, and also as fundraiser to Tan's film projects—does point out the possibility of making connections across the class line (and other social divides) in contemporary Singapore.

## Atomization, Alienation, and Anomie

Khoo's trilogy is chiefly set in the HDB estates. Originally founded on democratic socialist principles for "creat[ing] social justice" and provid[ing] a" 'safety net' [for] . . . families who [do] not have enough to meet their minimum needs,"[12] the HDB offers subsidized public housing. Its success has since become a definitive statement for the PAP government's vision and achievements, granting political legitimacy to the regime. Now home to about 85 percent of Singaporeans, including foreigners who have permanent resident status, HDB estates give Singapore its distinctive uniform and monotonous skyline: they are as varied as Lego blocks. They are "literally concrete reminder[s] of the pervasive presence of the government."[13] To prevent "racial enclaves," the HDB sets strict occupancy quotas for ethnic minorities such as Malays (who are the indigenous population), Indians, Eurasians, and other non-Chinese races in each HDB block and neighborhood.[14] With 78 percent of the country's population being of Chinese descent, the HDB estates thus have a highly visible Chinese Singaporean presence.

Khoo's trilogy reflects this presence. The storylines invariably center on Chinese Singaporean households. Not all characters live in HDB housing, however: the more affluent ones live in luxury apartment blocks or semidetached houses. The tree-lined Orchard Road shopping mecca, and the glass–and-marble skyscrapers in the Central Business District, including the seedy parts of town where sordid back alleys, squalid old buildings, and sleazy prostitution haunts are found, also appear in the trilogy's filmscape. Locations as such give a fuller picture of Singapore's highly urbanized environment. In its midst are Singaporeans of other ethnicities, including foreigners.

Whether rich or poor, Khoo's characters all live atomized lives and for the most part endure seemingly voluntary isolation. In his trilogy, communities—whether within or across class and other social groupings—are portrayed as lacking cohesive communalism. In *Mee Pok Man*, its young, unnamed, speech-challenged male protagonist (played by Joe Ng) is a noodle hawker who lives alone and does not appear to have friends. (*Mee pok* is a Hokkien name for a kind of Chinese string noodle.) When not working at his stall in a shop located somewhere in the red-light district, Mee Pok Man spends his free time in his HDB apartment "talking" to his late father's picture; or else he wanders about aimlessly in back alleys and HDB foyers. He is attracted to a disillusioned prostitute, Bunny

(Michelle Goh), who eats at his stall from time to time. He occasionally stalks her.

The other stalker in Khoo's society of strangers is the shy and friendless Fatty Koh (Seet Keng Yew) of *Be With Me*. Fatty Koh desires Ann (Lynn Poh), a high-flying executive who works in the same office block where he is a security guard. At work, he keeps a constant lookout for her, going as far as using the closed-circuit security cameras in the sentry office to track her movements through the building's public areas. After work, he follows her into shopping malls or hangs around the perimeter of her home, watching and worshipping her from afar. Eventually he plucks up the courage to write her a love letter, but is killed before he can deliver it to her. Before his death, he lives with his father (Ng Sway Ah) and brother (Lim Poh Huat) in an HDB apartment. Like Mee Pok Man, he suffers from an inferiority complex. Like Mee Pok Man, he grew up in an abusive family environment.

Bunny resides in an HDB apartment with her mother (Wang See Eng) and younger brother (George Chua). She does not relate well to them: they hardly talk to each other, let alone interact. Bunny keeps a secret diary, but its intimate content is progressively revealed through voice-over when her brother inadvertently discovers it and reads it. Bunny has an English lover, Jonathan Reese (David Brazil). She wishes to break away from her pimp, Mike Kor (Lim Kay Tong), dreams of a better life in the West, and considers Reese her potential emigration ticket. However, unbeknown to her, Reese is a porno-photographer from a European skin syndicate who preys on unsuspecting prostitutes (Tan, Lee, and Aw 2003—see endnotes). She thus labors under the tragic illusion that she is in control of her life and that she will succeed in "using men to achieve her hopes."

One night, Bunny meets with a hit-and-run accident. As Mee Pok Man takes the wounded Bunny home rather than to a hospital, the narrative slips into the twilight zone. In his claustrophobic apartment, the young man nurses her injuries, feeds her, talks to her, and sleeps next to her on the floor. He eventually wins her trust. At one point, they attempt to have sex; during that attempt, she dies. He keeps her corpse in his apartment and tends to it lovingly, pouring his heart out to Bunny, whose body, in the meantime, has been decomposing. Necrophilia in the context of *Mee Pok Man* thus becomes a powerful, deadly metaphor for critiquing a society that cannot foster healthy human relations (Tan et al. 2003). (See Figures 15.1 to 15.3.)

Characterized by spatial and temporal discontinuities, the montage sequence containing *Mee Pok Man*'s final scenes heightens this social critique about spiritually empty lives and socially alienating spaces. The visual track intercuts between Mee Pok Man's apartment and various exterior locations around the island-state. In these shots the outside world is filmed in the style of documentary verité. Intercut are rapid glimpses of passengers in a moving Mass Rapid Transit (MRT) train and the "HDB-scape" from

Figure 15.1 Mee Pok Man sings to dead Bunny. *Mee Pok Man*. Dir. Eric Khoo. Zhao Wei Films, 1995. Courtesy of Zhao Wei Films.

Figure 15.2 Mee Pok Man bends over to kiss Bunny's decomposed hand. *Mee Pok Man*. Dir. Eric Khoo. Zhao Wei Films, 1995. Courtesy of Zhao Wei Films.

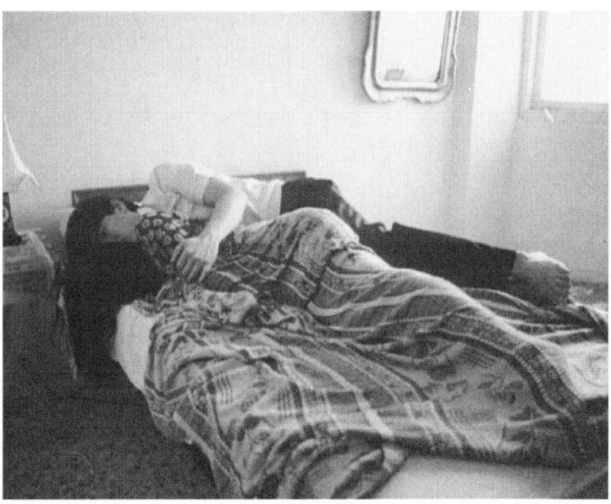

Figure 15.3 Mee Pok Man snuggles up with dead Bunny in his bed. *Mee Pok Man*. Dir. Eric Khoo. Zhao Wei Films, 1995. Courtesy of Zhao Wei Films.

Figure 15.4 Meng does his stretches while San San sits on a bench, each lost in his or her world of thought. The slide (foreground) serves as a visual grid for separating the two, highlighting alienation in an urban environment. *12 Storeys*. Dir. Eric Khoo. Zao Wei Films, 1997. Courtesy of Zhao Wei Films.

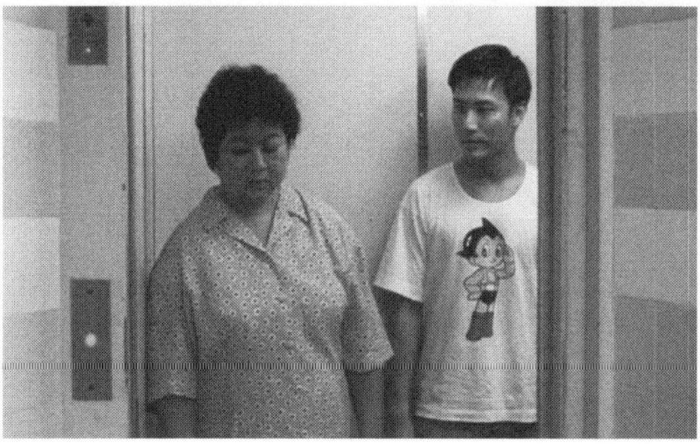

Figure 15.5 In a lift, San San turns away from her neighbor, avoiding contact. There is certainly no neighborly friendliness here. *12 Storeys*. Dir. Eric Khoo. Zao Wei Films, 1997. Courtesy of Zhao Wei Films.

the windows of that train. Outside, the distant HBD apartment blocks look clean, functional, and yielding. Elsewhere, glistening glass-and-concrete towers loom tall in the Central Business District where the crowd, including immaculately dressed white-collar workers, moves about as if on urgent yet futile missions. In yet another part of tropical downtown Singapore, an equally faceless, nameless crowd mills about Orchard Road. Here the thick air of Christmas festivities hangs heavily over the country's shopping mecca. The view presents a picturesque consumer-land, with fairy lights dotting the landscape's orderly pavements, trees, and malls and concurrently throwing a cheery glow on a gigantic jolly snowman, around which are reindeer figurines and other motifs from the "snow land" in the West. This collage is a compilation of still and moving shots. It gives a tourist's view of affluent Singapore that stands in surreal contrast to Mee Pok Man's apartment, including the seedy red-light district seen earlier in the film. After this excursion, the montage returns to Mee Pok Man's apartment. The hawker now makes an offering to his late father's photo on the wall. Then he proceeds to eat breakfast. Unbeknown to the son, the father, for the first time in the film, makes a ghostly appearance. Sitting next to the son silently, he watches him vacantly. After breakfast, Mee Pok Man goes back to bed and snuggles up to Bunny, seeking comfort from her dead body (Figure 15.3) (Tan et al. 2003).

In *12 Storeys*, Khoo further takes up the theme of urban isolation and alienation in modern Singapore. He develops associated motifs, fleshing out more "minute, hidden tragedies of daily life in the orderly apartments of HDB [estates where] . . . stories of thwarted desire, love, hate, and conflict are played out."[15] He restricts the narrative to a twenty-four-hour period on one Sunday; the setting to one apartment block in an anonymous HDB estate and its immediate surrounding; and the storyline to four Chinese households residing in this block. The film opens quietly to the light sounds of a violin-and-piano ensemble, with the credit titles intermittently cut by a montage of short and still takes. Long shots of HBD apartment blocks, close-ups of household objects, and portrait-like shots of HDB-dwellers in their homes compose the montage. They characterize HDB locations and living spaces as panoptical (in the Foucauldian sense of the term)[16] when the individually framed shots here break down and compartmentalize the HDB environs, with HDB-dwellers (Chinese, Malay, Indian, and Eurasian) appearing to be boxed within isolated cell-like cubicles. In their midst is a half-naked Chinese man (Ritz Lim); he mills about in his own apartment alone, by turns chain-smoking, drinking, and vomitting. In another apartment is a bespectacled Chinese man; he stands in the shadows (close-up), glaring angrily (at the camera). A quick cut reveals a clock. The time is 1:25 A.M. and the bespectacled man—as viewers soon find out—is Meng (Koh Boon Pin), a PAP-like school teacher figure who chats in government slogans and who lords over his younger siblings, Trixie (Lum May Yee) and Tee (Roderick Lim). Separated by thick walls, the cramped spaces within the apartment analogize atomized living conditions, while the deficiency of contact between "holed-up" HDB-dwellers amplifies the theme of segregation and isolation. From their cells, the outside world may be a phone call away, but as Ritz Lim's character shows, one can disconnect from that world by lifting the phone off the hook.

At daybreak, Meng jogs alone in the deserted HDB estate as the radio announcer cheerfully greets the new day (extradiegetic sound). A large depressed-looking woman, San San (Lucilla Teoh), who turns out to be Meng's neighbor, soon turns up in this HDB-scape, as does Ritz Lim's character; he now dons an Astroboy tee shirt and a pair of ripped jeans. Moments later, he takes the same elevator with San San to the eleventh floor of the apartment block where they live. They then climb up two flights of steps to the next floor, one after another. As San San heads for her apartment on the twelfth floor, he turns in the other direction. Suddenly he leaps over a railing and jumps to his death. (His ghost, identified as Spirit in the closing credits, later returns) The introductory scenes here, like the above montage, highlight the lack of friendly interaction among HDB-dwellers. When they do meet, they maintain a "healthy" distance: San San thus remains at a distance from Meng (Figure 15.4), and on seeing her neighbor (Ritz Lim's character) enter the same lift, she reacts by turning away (Figure 15.5). That montage and these scenes resist official clichés for HDB housing (for example, as constituting a friendly neighborhood), and for film critic Derek Elley, kick in "a darker reality" that stands in sharp contrast to "the official image of Singapore."[17] The film, in this sense, amounts to a "deeply political creation":[18] it portrays the HDB estates as a community of strangers.

The particular turning away also occurs even in supposedly social and friendly environments. For instance, after marriage, Ah Gu (Jack Neo) minimizes contact with his drinking buddies, who usually congregate at the neighborhood coffee shop. When he and his wife, Lili (Chuan Yi Fong), happen to run into them, his first reaction is to keep up the false pretense of a happy marriage. Furthermore, in other scenes at this coffee shop where anonymous taxi-drivers, including Ah Gu's buddies, gather to exchange gossip and to make idle conversation about topical state affairs, the gathering does not show a strong sense of communicative communalism either (Tan et al. 2003).

Gatherings as such—whether seen here or elsewhere in Khoo's trilogy—are part of Singapore's street cultures. They represent the potential coming together of different peoples, languages, foods, ethnicities, and classes, and are seen everywhere in coffee shops, hawker's stalls, and food courts. In Singapore, eating and drinking places as such are always within easy reach: they are found at almost every street corner. Here customers can bet on the lottery, drink alcohol, make idle chit-chat, even speak their minds. That is to say, this open space—although surrounded by panopticon-like urban architecture—offers its temporary occupiers a break from their atomized dwellings, and lets them enjoy a brief moment of open-air fun with friends and associates, even family members. It is also a hangout for pimps, ruffians, and drug-peddlers.

*Mee Pok Man*, *12 Storeys*, and *Be With Me* all portray the breakdown in family communication as severe, ingrained and persistent. Bunny lives with but apart from her family in the same HDB apartment. Ah Gu, a Chinese Singaporean tofu hawker, and his Beijing-born wife, Lili, fight like cats and dogs at home, while in *Be With Me*, Jackie (Ezann Lee) and her mother (Lim Poey Huang) have a quiet standoff. Family members may gather for meals at home regularly, but they appear to do so out of a sense of duty rather than anything else. In *Be With Me*, Sam (Samathan Tan), her parents (John Cheong as Pa; Sherry Lim as Ma), and her younger brother (Shaun Koh) have breakfast together in their semi-detached house: they all eat in silence and seem to be lost in their own world of thought. Trixie and Tee of *12 Storeys*, on the other hand, have to endure Meng's condescending lectures at the breakfast table. When Fatty Koh runs into his father (Ng Sway Ah) and brother (Lim Poh Huat) at home, he suffers in silence their delight in hurling derogatory and hurtful remarks at him. Haunted and taunted by memories of her late mother's endless sneering snipes, San San

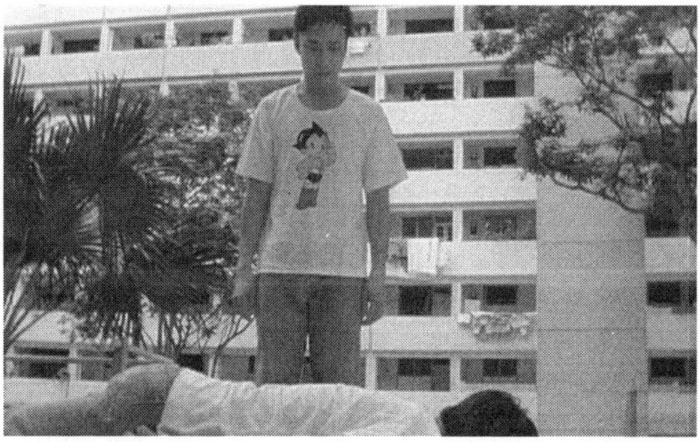

Figure 15.6 San San's neighbor (presently a ghost) stares at his dead body—no contact, for sure. *12 Storeys*. Dir. Eric Khoo. Zhao Wei Films, 1997. Courtesy of Zhao Wei Films.

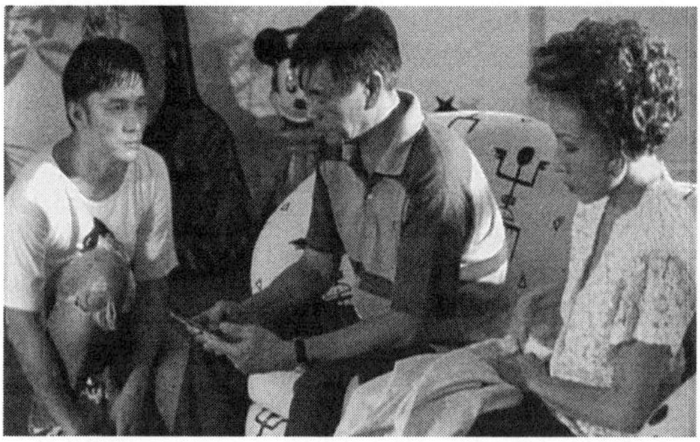

Figure 15.7 A picture of physical and psychological estrangement: the ghost looks at his living parents quietly, as they grieve over their son's suicide. *12 Storeys*. Dir. Eric Khoo. Zhao Wei Films, 1997. Courtesy of Zhao Wei Films.

contemplates suicide. Finally, this same theme of intrafamily communicational difficulties extends to the supernatural dimension. Spirit appears next to his grieving parents. The family—father, mother, and ghost son—occupy the same frame, yet physical and psychological estrangement prevails (Figure 15.7). Here, the parents (Tan Kheng Hua as Mother; Ng Sway Ah as Father) cannot establish eye contact; they speak in monologues (in Teochew) and are clearly unable to offer each other comfort. Meanwhile Spirit watches quietly; his very presence serves as an ironic amplification of the humans' inability to connect (Tan et al. 2003). The ghost of an old shopkeeper's late wife, on the other hand, becomes a visual metaphor for unfathomable love, deep guilt and profound grief in *Be With Me* which harbors an implicit theme about euthanasia.

The prevalent existence of family secrets further indexes dysfunctional intrafamily communication, with related storylines expanding to draw in a pervasive mood of urban blight. For example, a secret diary reveals Bunny's life as a prostitute. In *12 Storeys*, the dark deeds and desires behind closed HDB doors are told through the ghostly eyes of Spirit, who "enters" the home of his living neighbors uninvited and unnoticed. The eyes divulge unspeakable secrets about unrequited love, failed marriages, extramarital affairs, and illicit underage sex.[19] They silently disclose abusive and sadistic behavior, and hint at the existence of incest, rape, matricide, and alternative lifestyles such as lesbianism. In *Be with Me*, Spirit makes an unmotivated appearance, as does San San. This occurs in the food-court scene where San San settles into a meal with a man and a baby, with Spirit watching nearby—again quietly and unobtrusively. While providing a narrative interface with *12 Storeys*, that brief scene—in giving privy to a moment of happiness in San San's otherwise sad life—anticipates *Be With Me*'s thematic preoccupation with finding love and fulfillment.

Ghostliness in the trilogy is primarily achieved without generic tricks of horror cinema such as sudden cuts, eerie music, and rapid mood changes that bring in a creepy environment. The ghosts look just like the living (Figures 15.6 and 15.7), and the visual style of Khoo's camerawork generally maintains a certain detached calmness that comes with measured takes, minimal camera movements, and nominal actions from the characters, dead or alive. These shooting and editing strategies make it possible for the appearance of ghosts in Khoo's films to seem unmotivated. They dampen ghostly horror; in the particular context of *Mee Pok Man*, they similarly help nullify the horror associated with necrophilia, surrealistically bringing to fore the sublime beauty of the noodle seller's unconditional love for Bunny instead. In sum, the extraordinary—whether pertaining to necrophilia or apparitions—is rendered somewhat ordinary. It has no drama about it but represents a fantastical extension of the everyday. The coexistence of the dead and the living in the films therefore establishes an analogy about the putrid in everyday life, and about the dea(r)th of everyday moralism in Singapore's rigidly ordered, capitalistic society (Tan et al. 2003). This, together with themes about dysfunctional individuals, families, and communities, and leitmotifs pertaining to unspeakable family secrets, serves a volley at "One-dimensional Singapore", especially the PAP government's "Shared Values" national ideology premised on transcendental ideals of self-sacrifice, family, community, consensus, and harmony. Collectively they point to the deficiency of communication that makes Singapore a society of strangers.

## Hope and Despair in a Society of Strangers

*Be With Me* extends the theme of social dysfunctionalities, chiefly through the metaphor of "social de-voicing." Closely related to the notion that info rmation-and-computer-technology (ICT) has the effect of turning humans into "technomaniacs," social de-voicing is thought to be detrimental to close personal communication between people who actively favor the use of "coolly efficient 'info-speech'" over "warm personal chats" and "intimate talking" as a means of interpersonal communication.[20]

In this film, info-speech (ICT-related mediated communication) is portrayed as pervasive to the extent that human speech (chatting and talking) becomes almost a superfluity. This prevalence defines people's lives in important ways. A nameless social worker (Lawrence Yong) files his reports through a computer, and when not spending time with his perennially quiet shopkeeper-father (Chiew Sung Ching), the filial son periodically calls him with his mobile phone. Youngsters such as Sam and Jackie find each other through the Internet and maintain contact by exchanging text messages. When Sam and Jackie finally meet in person, they become lesbian lovers, doing things couples do like shopping, watching movies, clubbing, hanging out, having sex, the works. Terminating a relationship is only a fingertip away: choose the delete button on the cell phone. In *Be With Me*, the pervasive use of ICT as a means of communication, together with the noticeable lack of warm personal conversations ferret out critical analogies about the "social de-voicing" that concurrently generates social atomization and contributes to dysfunctional relationships within familial and friendship contexts.

*Be With Me* is in fact the least talky of the trilogy. This 86-minute-long feature film has only about three minutes of spoken speech in total. The characters hardly speak or talk to each other; they seem to have nothing to say, and if they do speak, the exchange amounts to a perfunctory word or two—for example, "You're fired!" or "How much?" or "*Chia*!" or "*Pui Eh*!" (the latter two being Hokkien expressions for "Eat!" and "Fatty!" or "The Fatty One!," respectively).

Theresa Chan (b. 1943)—the only real-life person (as opposed to a fictional character) in the film—has the most lines. This 62-year-old woman was born to poor and illiterate parents. She lost her hearing at the age of fourteen, and some time after she lost her eyesight as well. She now lives alone in an HDB apartment, works at the Singapore School for the Visually Handicapped (formerly known as School for the Blind) as a teacher, conducts her classes in English, and reads the *New York Times* in Braille. She still speaks some Cantonese, which is her native tongue, and helps raise funds for charities, from time to time. Theresa learned English, from scratch, at the Perkins School for the Blind in Massachusetts (US) when the Royal Commonwealth Society of London (UK) and the School for the Blind (Singapore) helped her secure a scholarship in 1960. She once planned to get married and raised a family. That fell through after her fiancée died of nose cancer on "Christmas day of 1968": "Till today, at five to five every Christmas morning, my tears [would] flow freely," she recounts in her autobiography, explaining, "[I am] still very much in love with him."

Theresa writes her autobiography on a manual typewriter. When the camera is not trained on the words she is keying on the typewriter, excerpts of her remarkable memoirs appear as English subtitles, sometimes functioning as segues that connect the jumps between situations or locations. Despite her handicaps, Theresa epitomizes, in inspiring ways, the human spirit of perseverance and determination: she clearly has lived an extraordinary life, with more gusto than all the fictional characters in film can ever hope to pull off, singularly or collectively.

*Be With Me* weaves Chan's autobiographical tale with three fictional stories, eschewing easy sentimentality, triviality, and melodrama: "Meant to Be" is about an aging shopkeeper (Chiew Sung Ching) who plunges into deep depression when his wife (Leong Kooi Eng) dies; "Finding Love" is about Fatty Koh, who loves food and desires Ann; and "So in Love" is about two teenage girls, Jackie and Sam, and their tragic love story. The shopkeeper's social-worker son (Lawrence Yong) serves as a thread that connects the film's three plotlines. He is depicted as a friend of Theresa: he regularly calls on her and takes her out grocery shopping. He also translates her autobiography into Chinese, and later gives his father (Pa) a copy, hoping that Theresa's inspiring life-story will lift him out of his depression. With the supernatural intervention of his ghost-wife, Pa starts to read it and becomes engrossed in it. In the meantime, Theresa gets to know about Pa through Son, who brings her food cooked by Pa. Theresa and Pa eventually meet at her apartment towards the end of the film. This occurs when Son asks Pa to deliver the food, on his behalf, as he has an attempted suicide case to attend to. The son thus crosses paths with the suicidal Jackie: the pain of her unrequited love for Sam has driven her to despair. She jumps off a building and kills Fatty Koh when she lands on him, as he walks past that same building to deliver Ann the love letter he has arduously penned.

In the living room of the apartment, Pa unpacks the takeaway container that holds the food he has cooked for Theresa who in the meantime is busy making beverage in the kitchen. A quick flashback takes Pa to the hospital where he visited his sick wife. He looked at her tenderly and lovingly by the bedside, but in silence (closeup). Then the wife reached for his hand, pulled it towards her face, and pressed it over her nose and mouth area, as if pleading to him to help end her misery (closeup). He reacted by kissing her on the forehead (closeup), his hand still in the position where the wife left it. This is followed by a quick cut which shows Pa (back to camera) in another part of the hospital, leaning against a wall and crying by himself (mid-to-long shot). The montage suggests that he might have indeed committed an act of euthanasia. After this, the narrative returns to Theresa's apartment. Pa, now tearful, collapses onto a chair—sobbing quietly at first and then uncontrollably. Sensing something amiss, Theresa puts her arms around Pa and embraces him. This embrace closes the film. The tenderness and affection Theresa shows for Pa here, in emphasizing the possibility of a meaningful human connection in a society of strangers, offers a glimpse of hope and optimism that makes the film stand apart from *Mee Pok Man* and *12 Storeys*. Khoo's message in *Be With Me* is therefore quite simple: What the society of strangers needs is the human touch.

## Notes

This chapter both extracts from and extends the paper I co-wrote with Michael Lee and Annette Aw, "Contemporary Singapore Filmmaking: History, Policies and Eric Khoo," published in *Jump Cut: A Review of Contemporary Media* 46 (Summer 2003): http://www.ejumpcut.org.

1. Gina Marchetti, *From Tian'anmen to Times Square: Transnational China and the Chinese Diaspora on Global Screens*, 1989–1997 (Philadelphia: Temple University Press, 2006), 148–149.

2. n.d., "Mediacorp Raintree Pictures: Corporate Profile": http://www.mediacorpraintree.com/about_us/corp_profile.htm; accessed May 1, 2007.

3. Tom O'Regan, "A National Cinema," Graeme Turner, ed., *The Film Cultures Reader* (London: Routledge, 2002), 155–56.

4. Kenneth Paul Tan, *Cinema and Television in Singapore: Resistance in One Dimension* (Leiden/Boston: Brill, 2008), 188.

5. Cherian George, *Singapore: The Air-conditioned Nation: Essays on the Politics of Comfort and Control 199–2000* (Singapore: Landmark Books, 2000), 147.

6. Gina Marchetti, *From Tian'anmen to Times Square*, 124.

7. Ibid., 126, 153.

8. Esha Niyogi De, "Masculinity, Community, and Time in Singaporean Cinema," *Emergences* 12.2 (2002): 201.

9. The Housing Development Board is a state body that oversees the provision of affordable public housing to Singapore nationals and permanent residents.

10. Chua Beng Huat, *Life Is not Complete Without Shopping: Consumption Culture in Singapore* (Singapore: Singapore University Press, 2003), 181–82.

11. Gina Marchetti, *From Tian'anmen to Times Square*, 125, 126. See also Tan, *Cinema and Television in Singapore*, 213.

12. Lee Kuan Yew, *Memoirs of Lee Kuan Yew: The Singapore Story* (Singapore: Times Publishing, 1998), 130.

13. Chua Beng Huat, *Life Is not Complete Without Shopping*, 179.

14. n.d., "Housing Development Board: Ethnic Group Eligibility": http://www.hdb.gov.sg; accessed May 1, 2007.

15. Audrey Wong, "Considering the 'Singapore Film,'" *Arts* 7 (1999), 12. See also Nazir Keshvani, *12 Storeys*, *Cinemaya* 35 (1997), 26–28.

16. Michel Foucault, *Discipline and Punish: The Birth of the Prison*, trans. Alan Seridan (New York: Vintage, 1979).

17. Derek Elly, "*12 Storeys*," *Variety* (June 9–15, 1997): 71.

18. Cherian George, "Not All Can Be Under One Roof," "Life!" in *Straits Times* (1997, June 27): L4.

19. Michael Lee, "Dead Man Gazing: Posthumous Voyeurism in *12 Storeys*, or 'Splacing' Singapore's Official and Unofficial Discourse," *Asian Cinema* (Fall/Winter 2000): 107–24.

20. John Locke, *Why We Don't Talk to Each Other Anymore: The De-voicing of Society/How E-Mail, Voice Mail, the Internet and Technomania Are Making Us into a Society of Strangers* (New York, Touchstone, 1998), 17–21.

# 16
# Chinese Cinema Revisits the City

## *Beijing Trilogy and Global Urbanism of the 1990s*

JENNY KWOK-WAH LAU

> *The failure of the systematic thinker constitutes the true triumph of the master of hermeneutics who, in "reading" the things of the world as if they were sacred texts, suddenly decodes the overwhelming forces of human history.*
>
> —PETER DEMETZ ON WALTER BENJAMIN[1]

The cinema of the People's Republic of China of the 1980s was called by some the "cinema of the Western," pointing to an outpouring of quality films at the time primarily set in the remote areas of China. Films such as *Yellow Earth* (1984, Shanbei), *On the Hunting Ground* (1985, Inner Mongolia), *Sacrifice Youth* (1985, Yunan), and *King of Children* (1987, Yunan) bear similar geographic features to the western United States. But by the mid-1980s and early 1990s a sharp turn had taken place in which "the city" replaced the "remote" and became center stage. When so-called Sixth Generation cinema gained recognition worldwide in the 1990s, almost all of its films were "city centered."

Several reasons contributed to the ups and downs of "the city" on the screen in Chinese cinema. During the golden period of the 1930s and 1940s, classics such as *Twin Sisters* (1933), *Three Modern Girls* (1933), *New Women* (1934), *Street Angel* (1936), *Money Tree* (1937), *Lights of Ten Thousand Homes* (1948), and *Crows and Sparrows* (1948) were well remembered for their urban settings and narratives. What one sees in these films is a reflection and criticism of the national project of modernization conducted under the late Qing Dynasty and the early Republic. This project followed an ambitious modernist agenda of establishing municipal (versus familial or tribal) governments, spatially rearranging the urban landscape for commerce, setting up health standards and enforcing public hygiene, allowing female participation in social and political life, and so forth. City symbols in these films include banks, neon lights, automobiles, streets that are clean and wide, men dressed in Western style, women dressed in urban Shanghai "Chang sam," jammed living quarters for the poor, and modern high-rises for business offices and the rich. For instance, in the beginning credits of *Street Angel*, flickering neon lights pop up all over the screen. A tilt-down shot from the top of a stylized modern high-rise to the ground shows a large puddle of water reflecting the building's splendor, as well as bits and pieces of floating garbage. This conveniently forms a visual metaphor for the city—a place filled with disparity between the rich and the poor, the powerful and the powerless.

But during the 1950s and 1960s, criticism of the city gave way to the "socialist- realist" interest in peasant life, prerevolutionary heroes, minorities, and past proletarian nobilities.[2] In addition, as is pointed out by Paul Clark and Paul Pickowicz, there were intrinsic potential problems in depicting the city itself. In the postrevolutionary period, films were expected to celebrate a new China where social ills were not supposed to exist. The theme of the city, which was inevitably related to contemporary social conditions, risked being critical. Thus, most of the city films made during this period adopted the comedy genre as a means of avoiding any serious eyebrow raising.[3] This practice resulted in a serious reduction in city films. Not until decades later, after China's open-door policy in the 1980s, did Chinese cinema revisit the city.

Close reading of this new round of city films (of the late 1980s and early 1990s) shows a paradigmatic shift, which could be one of the most interesting phenomena in contemporary Chinese cinema. In the classic films of the 1930s and 1940s, the urban was seen as a source of greed and vanity, a place of excess (mostly violence and sex), an arena for outlaw activities, a struggle between the rich and the poor, and a war zone of the revolutionary and the reactionary. But after the mid-1980s, a different perspective took hold. The city was now seen not as a place of evil materialism but as one of economic opportunity (albeit a difficult or even problematic place) that could offer a reprieve from desperation, and as an environment of openness and connections that promised freedom and liberty. Films that explore this relationship include *Yamaha Fish Stall* (1984), *Sunshine Rain* (1987), *Coffee Add Sugar* (1987), *Black Snow* (1989), and some of the highly popular "Wang Sho" films, such as *The Trouble Shooters* (or *The Masters of Mischief*, 1988) and *Samsara* (1988). This group of films examines the operation of free markets in different contexts (family, government bureaucracy, general public culture) and exposes or satirizes the consequences of market practices. In focusing on the central role of the market, these films question capitalism while simultaneously endorsing it.

But this nascent notion of the city in the 1980s reflected only tentative thinking on the issue. In later films of the 1990s, especially in the films of the Sixth Generation, more sophisticated ideas taking into account the economic, social, and cultural implications of the city began to emerge.

Many of these films focused on the city of Beijing, which had undergone extraordinary urbanization during the same period, including widespread demolition of almost all of its "old" areas and replacement with "modern" high-rises. This drastic change was addressed in many films of the 1990s, such as Zhang Yuan's *Seventeen Years*, Ning Ying's *Police Story,* and the highly popular film *Shower* by Zhang Yang, which questioned the purpose and meaning of such a massive reconstruction. As the process of "modernization" accelerated throughout the 1990s, Beijing was increasingly caught in a struggle between its role as a city of culture, history, community, governmental power, national symbolism, and revolutionary idealism, and its new role as a city of modernization and materialism. Many films of the 1990s reflected the anxiety caused by such a drastic change.

To investigate examples of this new urban cinema of the 1990s, I will analyze three films written by the young scriptwriter Tang Danian: *Good Morning Beijing* (1990, directed by Zhang Nuanxing), *Beijing Bastards* (1993, directed by Zhang Yuan), and *City Paradise* (1999, directed by Tang Danian himself). These films are interesting because in some ways they continue the discourse of the city of the previous classical era but in other ways offer a definitive break from the past by looking at the new situation from a modern perspective.

I call these three films a "Beijing Trilogy" since it is apparent that the writer has expressed a consistency in theme and form. Although the visual styles of the three films are different, as they are directed by three different directors, the form of storytelling—details of ordinary life portrayed in loosely connected narratives—remains quite consistent. As a freelance scriptwriter, Tang, who wrote three consecutive scripts about the same city spanning the decade of the 1990s, shows a strong sense of engagement, if not obsession, with this particular space. His interpretation of the city can be observed both in the narratives and the *mise-en-scène* of the films.

In the analysis of *Good Morning Beijing*, Chinese scholar Tang Xiaobing uses the term "crudeness" to portray the "premodern" living condition of the city before the 1990s, which he also considers to be "third-world" in a negative sense. He contrasts the "third-world" part of Beijing with the newly developed commercial business areas and sees the latter as a symbol of the "utopian" desire of the filmmaker.[4] Although this interpretative scheme of modern versus premodern, native crudeness versus Western sophistication, and desirable versus undesirable has the merit of clearly pointing out the differences that modernization has brought to the city, this framework presupposes a mutual exclusivity of these dichotomies as well as the superiority—and therefore the desirability—of a commerce-based, modern city. More importantly, it misses the opportunity to ask what exactly is the culture or the ideology that underlies such modern or premodern settings and what exactly is desirable for human life.

History shows us that the form of a city itself defines, and is defined by, a certain way of life, value, and power system. For example, the so-called modern city, a phenomenon developed after European industrialization, typified by what became known as the "downtown business district (DBD)," functions not only as a physical landmark for most modern cities but also reflects the central position of trade and consumerism in contemporary life. On the other hand, early Greek cities such as Athens were well known for the "agora" located at the city center, where the exchange of ideas through debate and dialogue took place, while marketplaces were relegated to the edge of or outside the city. This distinction is not simply a matter of modern versus premodern but also a matter of ideas and values.

The nature of the city of Beijing approximates a combination of a European medieval and a European baroque city. It is "medieval" in its community-oriented, multicentered layout.[5] Before the 1980s, the east and the west of the Forbidden City were two neighborhood commercial areas (Dongdan and Xidan). The east of Beijing was the residential area mostly for foreigners, the west contained the university campus communities (Tsinghua and Peking Universities), and the south was composed of the "old Beijing" neighborhoods with their own schools, shops, markets, and so forth. Each of these districts had unique characteristics and subcultures recognizable by most of the city natives. This spatial arrangement of old Beijing created a unique ambience and reflected the value of tradition and community. In the following analysis of the Beijing Trilogy, one can see that under the encroachment of a new (DBD) city model human relationships begin to change among various city districts.

Beijing is also a baroque city in which grand landmarks of royalty define its unique national and historical significance. For instance, the Forbidden City, which has always been the center of the cultural and political life of the country, is often visually centered in films. But this baroque notion of authority is challenged in the film *Beijing Bastards*, which uses unconventional off-center and off-foreground framing to question its relevance to modern life.

In the three films—*Good Morning Beijing*, *Beijing Bastards*, and *City Paradise*—a discourse of modernity is espoused through the city life of three very different groups of people: the ordinary Beijing natives, the artists, and the outsider immigrants. By examining the spatial and physical arrangement of the city and the activities that such an arrangement dictates, one can delineate a culture that both seduces and coerces its protagonists into a certain value system, a certain way of life.

Starting with admiration for a city, the protagonists of the trilogy move through a range of circumstances and emotions. Tang's detailed analysis of the protagonists' response reveals the connection and contradiction between global commercialism and personal love, the politics of mass culture and creative freedom, and the exploitative and yet seemingly emancipative nature of the new urbanism. His insights on the new urban environment transcend the pure moralistic approach of his predecessors.

## Beijing Trilogy

*Good Morning Beijing* has a simple plot of a romance gone sour. A city bus driver falls in love with his colleague (Hon), the ticket salesperson. After a lengthy courtship with the bus driver, Hon is attracted to another young man who boards her bus every day. A new relationship develops, and the girl finally decides to leave her old boyfriend. In the end Hon changes her job and finds work in a private retail garment business. This film was well received in China and won the National Government Award, a special prize for the best upcoming filmmaker of the year. Tang's second film, *Beijing Bastards*, was not shown in China but was well distributed in Europe. It involves a very loose narrative about a young rock-band member who is searching for his pregnant girlfriend. The film consists of segments intercut between city roaming, rock band performances, and documentary-like street scenes of Beijing.

*City Paradise*, a film directed by the scriptwriter himself, is the least known to date. Although it was screened at different film festivals—such as the San Sebastián Film Festival (1999), the UCLA New Chinese Cinema Screening (2000), and the Boston Film Festival (2001)—and although it won the Gold Award for foreign-language films in Worldfest Houston (2001), it has not attracted further attention.[6] It is an interesting film that forges a new direction in the writer's long discourse on contemporary urbanization. The story is about a young man who leaves his wife and aged mother in his village for job opportunities in the city. His new life in the city turns out to be unpleasant and he finds relief with a girlfriend. In the end he divorces his wife, leaves his mother, settles in a ghetto area, and starts a new and precarious life with his new love. The story is deceptively simple, but what is significant is the characters' fierce struggle with their environment.

These three films, which so emphatically represent the reverberations of a changing city, manifest both the fascination and the anxiety of its residents toward modern urban life. The urban is not simply a place of corrupt or greedy commerce, as was portrayed in classic cinema, nor does it simply represent a new opportunity, albeit a challenging one, as was reflected in the films of the 1980s. The films of the 1990s are instead concerned with the immense tension created by the fundamental spatial and temporal rearrangement brought about by urbanization. In studying the three films, one finds that life in the modern city involves incessant movement, boundary crossing, an accelerated pace of making and breaking social associations, creation of contrasting spaces, and the rearrangement of priorities. In other words, the modernized city sets up new paradigms, alters the time and space that define fundamental human experiences, and in the end, restructures life itself.

## *Good Morning Beijing*

Taking mobility as a sign of the urban, the romance in *Good Morning Beijing* actually takes place on a city bus. The bus, a symbol of the new city, transits on a modern thoroughfare lined with high-rises, stores, and restaurants. In contrast, the sea of bicycles, the once ubiquitous Chinese socialist mode of locomotion, has disappeared. Scenes of the bus coming to a stop and starting off again, passengers getting on and off, people chasing after the bus, and the occasional skirmishes all remind one of the ceaseless jostling that creates opportunities for some and anxiety and boredom for others. The driver and his ticket salesperson are brought together by their mundane jobs, but they each succeed in adding some excitement to the other's life.

The story begins with an early morning scene. A high-angle shot shows the traditional Chinese-style tile roofs of the houses of "old Beijing" waking up to a misty morning. People get up and rush to work. A few of them are riding bikes, most are walking. Some people buy steamed buns from the peddlers and eat as they go. The mood reminds one of the morning scene in the film *Berlin: The Symphony of a Great City*, directed by Walter Ruttman. But as the bus roars past this residential area and turns onto a boulevard, things change drastically. A city of businesses and high-rises suddenly appears as if the bus has been transported into a different world. This contrasting landscape between two blocks indicates a sharp spatial split, a sudden departure from the previous resident–market continuum.

This spatial split, which so dominates the rest of the film, also coincides with the cultural split between the driver and the new boyfriend. The two romances of Hon take place in two distinct spaces. Hon and the bus driver accidentally run into each other in an elaborate modern department store. But subsequent courtship takes place in both of their homes, which are located in the old part of town. The interiors of these homes are full of "common" Chinese touches: the parents' bed is set in the living room; paper butterfly kites, cheap traditional paintings, and family photos decorate the walls. A quick tour of the kitchen shows a semiopen courtyard, where neighbors meet each other while doing house chores. Hanging fabrics separate the "bedrooms" of the younger generation (the driver or the saleswoman) from the "living room." In the bus driver's "room" there are signs of "modern" life, such as a poster of the rock star Cui Jian and a poster of a stylish racecar.

The activities within the houses also reflect strong Chinese customs. For example, the bus driver, in the midst of his dinner, serves his father's foot-washing habit, a sign of filial piety and compliance. Later, he offers to do the same for Hon's father (traditional Chinese normally would extend piety to their in-laws). After dinner he entertains himself with a classical musical instrument—the erhu. But he shifts to a Western instrument—a guitar—when he starts dating. Similarly, Hon helps in family chores and serves her sick father in her own home. Here the native identity, as seen in the small habits of daily life, survives in the "primitive" domestic spaces and the "shabby" alleys. While the courtship portrayed here may be traditional, it brings not only two people together but also their families and to some extent their neighbors. Underneath the humble material living conditions lies simple love, which allows them to relate to every aspect of each other's life—work and leisure, family and neighbor—in the most unpretentious way.

The narrow alleys contrast sharply with the streets outside. An accidental reunion with Hon's old classmate on the bus leads to a trip to the latter's office. The mazelike high-rise office and the geometrically balanced office space with its clean environment impress her. In the midst of this modern commercial area Hon meets another young man. A new round of dating takes place in nightclubs, karaoke bars, fancy Western restaurants, and an orientalized tourist site (mostly for Westerners). Hon is attracted and at the same time disoriented in this new setting. She cannot read the restaurant menu and does not know the songs sung in the karaoke bars. Nevertheless, she pretends to understand and later begins to enjoy the adventure. The romance that happens in the modern space is also highly individualistic, one that does not connect to families or friends. Hon's friend never meets her family. Nor do we see Hon meeting his. In fact, Hon does not even know that her friend is not mainland Chinese or that his family does not live in China. Thus, while this modern kind of love is adventurous and seductive, it is also individualistic and shallow.

The two spaces of the two romances clearly divide the city into a "dual" character, namely modern and Western versus Chinese (native) and traditional. The division of the physical space also overlaps with a division of the social space—the "old, cultural, working class" versus the "modern, commercial, upper class." The spatial arrangements of the film are not simply "locales." When structured through the narratives of two romances, the space reveals a discourse on urbanization itself: that the old native Beijing is not as attractive as the capitalistic cosmopolitan. The two are spatially divided and they fracture the culture of the neighborhoods.

Hon's new boyfriend turns out to be the son of a Singaporean business family. Global commerce has brought him to China for a brief period. At the end of the film Hon chooses to stay with him and joins the international endeavor to advance her material life, whereas the bus driver is content with his (socialist) service vocation. Thus, the reorganization of space, which is obviously an urban agenda, is also a reorganization of culture. What comes with the new spatial order is a new social and cultural order of transnational capitalism, individualism, and materialism. While some people (for example, the driver) may choose to value a traditional lifestyle, others venture out. Instead of taking a moralistic stand and condemning materialism, this film does not pass judgment on Hon or her boyfriends. Rather, it is left to the audience members to decide which structure of life they would choose.

## *Beijing Bastards*

While the story of *Good Morning Beijing* takes place on a vehicle shuttling back and forth in the city, *Beijing Bastards*, with its very loose narrative, has its protagonist roaming all over the city. This freedom of mobility, which many outside of China may take for granted, was actually uncommon in China before the mid-1970s. Historical research shows that during the Qing dynasty Beijing was one of the most policed cities in the world.[7] Although some relaxation was found during the Republican era, the post-1949 period was marked by the establishment of a neighborhood surveillance system, which considered idling on the streets a suspect activity.

However, after the mid-1970s, when the students who were sent to the rural areas during the Cultural Revolution came back to the city, Beijing had its share of "educated youngsters" roaming around. They formed a group called "luilang renkou" (wandering population). Among them were artists who made their names through street-art sales, mostly to foreigners. This openness generated a new kind of freedom, namely that of mobility and anonymity, which is now enjoyed by the wandering protagonists in *Beijing Bastards*. On the other hand, even though street life is inextricably associated with contemporary urbanism, the street life portrayed by the characters in the film is not precisely "liulang" since they are not exactly homeless. They are actually residents of the city. Neither is this excessive amount of "leisure" time a surplus gained through industrialization, since no one of them seems to have a job to begin with. In this sense, their lack of anchor in the city prompts one to wonder why this cultural metropolis has so few opportunities for its artists.

Sociologist Marshall Berman has pointed out that modernity is "a condition that at once empowers people and constrains them."[8] The openness that the film conveys, for example, by frequent gatherings of street-side singers seems to empower the people. But ultimately this power is highly limited by a variety of factors. For example, in one scene, a rock band is preparing the stage for a performance, but the police come and dismantle the stage for no obvious reason. Even though rock music may convey a sense of liberal openness, the lyrics of these songs reflect the frustration of the artists' lack of control over their own destiny. This theme of "citizen without citizenship" can also be found in *City Paradise* and *East Palace,*

*West Palace*, where government control (through the police) is frequently exercised in the life of regular people.

The inability to negotiate with government authorities is only one among many issues that constrain the artists. The landlord kicks them out of their apartment during a band practice because of unpaid rent; friends get drunk in a restaurant and get into fights; and a loose sex life results in an unwanted pregnancy. It seems that the city's promise of freedom and opportunities does not always deliver.

Modernity generates linkages to the outside world. The English-language television news is present in almost every domestic scene in the film. And interconnectivity is not limited to the airways. A well-connected worldwide market threatens the artists in Beijing. In one scene, a number of artists express their dismay about the withdrawal of state support for their arts and the compromises that they have to make to appease the Hong Kong art connoisseurs. Thus, the global culture that opens up the society also exposes its people to the consequences of the marketplace. Neither the new "market economy with Chinese characteristics" nor the new global capitalism favor Max Weber's "iron-cage" bureaucratized stability. The reality of globalization is that capital is mobile and location has little importance. Under such a condition, the artists in Beijing may or may not be able to do their job or serve their city or even their own country.

The other side of connectivity is boundary crossing. Chinese rock music, which is central to the film, is obviously crossing into the cultural territory of the West. This fusion of cultures results in hybridized identities. As Jonathan Friedman says, "Hybridity should be seen as the cultural corollary to economic globalization."[9] A double hybridization takes place in the film when the Chinese musicians consider themselves to be "more rock" than a group of San Francisco (Western) Chinese American musicians. Since the Chinese musicians see rock music more as a "world" rather than as a Western form of music, a Chinese rock band can be more "authentic" than one coming from the United States.[10] But while hybridity provides a broader world for the artists, it also creates a dilemma. The very nature of hybridity, which calls into question the notion of the "original," the "center," and the "authentic" (and empowers the Chinese to "co-own" rock music with the rest of the world), contradicts the Beijing artists' pride in being at "the center" of an "authentic" national culture.

It is not only culture that gives way in this new Beijing. Even politics cannot be center staged. Although the Forbidden City and Tiananmen Square are seen in the film, they are not shot from any angle that will give them the significance or the weight that these symbols used to carry. Bicycle-driven carts that carry outsized goods are seen crossing the screen with the Forbidden City far in the background. One side shot of Tiananmen Square in the rain shows a crowd busy with daily life. A new discourse of commercial globalization is taking place right in front of the Square.

While the Beijing artists are roaming and moaning, the film is matching the changing skyline of the city with its changing notion of culture and life.

## *City Paradise*

Of the three films, *City Paradise* is the one that actually addresses the city as a place of economic opportunity. It reframes the issue of urbanism and moves it from the city center, as in the previous two films, to its periphery, both geographically and culturally. It focuses on migrant workers coming to Beijing from the rural areas. *Paradise* deals with a process that literally and metaphorically moves the rural and the marginal toward the center.[11] The story of *Paradise* almost sounds like a traditional "Chen Shimei rejects-his-wife"[12] story except, contrary to the traditional novel, the protagonist in the film divorces his rural wife even before he can ever get rich and famous. A migrant worker (Dasheng) from a nearby village works as a high-rise window washer. As previously mentioned, the high-rise has always been one of the most fascinating images of modernism and urbanism. As early as the turn of the century, writers such as Kang Youwei remarked on this Western architectural innovation with great amazement.[13] Dasheng's daily "trips" up and down the outside of the building provide him with an overview of the city, which he sees both as spectacles of real life and as images reflected from the mirrored wall. As he is cleaning windows he also satisfies his voyeuristic urge by peeping into the building, whose extravagant world is off limits to him. The opportunity to broaden his view also stimulates his desire.

Dasheng has a number of jobs. After he finishes window washing he works as a domestic cleaner for his uncle. While the uncle's family is eating and watching television in the living room, he is scrubbing the stove and mopping the floor in the kitchen. He gets some leftover dinner as a tip from the wife and is happy that he can go back to his den afterward. He shares a room with a few other fellow migrant workers in a dilapidated house at the outskirts of the city. The rich metropolitan cultural life does not belong to them. Rather, their entertainment is to cramp together in a small space to watch television or read pornographic magazines.

According to sociological research, most migrant workers remain outsiders even after long years of working in the city. They tend to group together and hardly consider themselves to be part of the urban community.[14] This is painful spatial separation is seen in *City Paradise*. The spaces of the former are kitchens (versus living rooms), the outside (versus inside) of fancy high-rises, and unattractive places where they spend their leisure time. For instance, in one scene, Dasheng's housemates, a group of migrant workers, gather under a bridge during a late evening to commiserate in their depression. Apparently, no locals are spending their after-hours there.

It is only during work that they may be closer to the locals, who are usually their bosses. The few times that Dasheng shares the same space with the locals (inside an apartment, inside a taxi, inside a McDonalds) occur when he is dating his girlfriend, who is also a migrant worker doing housekeeping for her city relatives. But later one will see that he is forced to leave this house exactly because he has transgressed into a local's space.

Dasheng's dating takes place in the girl's "workplace," which is a modern condominium. A slow-pan camera shows "gadgets" of technology such as a modern table lamp, a decorative crystal bowl, and a bronze statuette. All these unfamiliar objects signal the material abundance a city can provide. But this space, which does not really belong to the two youngsters, soon turns against them. They are driven out by the owners because they are caught performing unwelcome (sexual) activity. Here one sees the transformation of a relationship because of a transposition of space. On the one hand, the distance separating Dasheng and his rural family loosens the restraints of family tradition and enables him to conduct a different social life. On the other hand, the loosening of family relationships also works against him. Since the culture of a commercial city privileges "workplace affiliation" over old "kinship relations," the relative-boss has no hesitation in firing her relative-housekeeper. The former has no concern in helping or protecting family members. They even report her sexual (mis)conduct to the police, causing her immense embarrassment. Consequently, the liberation from tradition is coupled with the uncertainty that comes with destabilized family relationships. Again, the apparent freedom that the new city provides comes with a loss of stability. At the same time, the locals have an enforcement system that gives them the upper hand. In a subsequent scene we see the police, who are the street-level bureaucrats, interfere with the workers' private lives. They confiscate Dasheng's pornographic magazines and arrest some of the other migrant workers.

Scenes intercut between the workers' city life and the life of the rural family emphasize disharmony. The countryside, which is presented with lovely idyllic shots, does not indicate a lovely family relationship. There is constant anger and fighting between the rural wife and her mother-in-law. They obviously resent Dasheng's absence. The centrifugal force toward the city has created tremendous tension. Even twenty years after China's open-door policy, people's intense desire to advance their material condition has not abated.

But the lower-class life in the city is not very attractive either. Dasheng and his girlfriend frequent cheap fast-food restaurants and cannot afford anything more. They admire material goods, and because of that have a strong commitment to stay in the city. An overly traumatic divorce at the end of the film completely breaks up the three-member rural family. Yet, the migrant worker grasps onto his newly found freedom and will not stop seeking economic opportunities. Both he and his girlfriend, now wife, will take any jobs, including those in which the girlfriend suffers sexual harassment and discrimination. This determined effort of the characters to succeed sharply contrasts with the city films of the 1980s, where pessimism about the new market system abounds at the conclusion of the stories.

## Conclusion

The urban as a universal symbol of modernization (Westernization) is a prime site for the investigation of the current culture in China. The Beijing Trilogy looks at the city not merely in economic terms, as do earlier films, but also in terms of the drastic spatial and temporal change that alters the citizens' feeling, experience, and interpretation of the world. This new cityscape witnesses not simply new architecture but also a new system of values, significations, and meanings.

In *Good Morning Beijing*, the protagonist's feelings toward friends and family change as her bus brings her to a wider global environment. Similarly, in *City Paradise* Dasheng's experience of the urban alters his feelings about and understanding of his rural past. His bird's-eye view of the city in the beginning of the film releases him, probably for the first time in his life, from the ground-level perspective of the world. This transformation of spatial position is the beginning of his new approach to life. In *Beijing Bastards*, the new globally connected city provides empowerment, opportunities for border crossing, and new identities. But none of these comes without problems. The artists suffer from a lack of true citizen-power and a loss of their role in the modern city. Hon, in *Good Morning Beijing,* loses her first love and her innocent simple life. By connecting to and marrying a Singaporean, she loses some of her strong Beijing identity. At the end of the film she is no longer a shy person, but a shrewd trader, assertive and unsentimental. Dasheng in *City Paradise* continues to be exploited because of his obsession with the city. He sees a paradise from the mirror reflection of Beijing, but it is doubtful he can ever break from the ghetto.

Modernity entails temporal movement, crossing social and physical space, linkage to the outside world, and redefining relationships and priorities. But at the same time it cannot guarantee the freedom and the plentitude it promises. It creates instability in identity, life, and human relationships, which is signified in the films by the lost (architectural) center of Beijing city. In the trilogy, the filmmaker examines how modern urbanization brings about fundamental changes in the perception of selfhood, society, and the world. As Chinese cities move toward globalization and a market economy, the scriptwriter, while not endorsing the old way of life, asks: What exactly is this new human condition? What exactly is the human cost?

## Postscript

It is interesting to see that, soon after this writing, the film *Beijing Bicycle* appeared in many U.S. theaters. This new film by Wang Xiaoshuai was again coscripted by Tang Danian. Similar to *City Paradise*, the film is about a rural migrant worker who comes to the city and encounters waves of adversity, ranging from the harsh demands of the Chinese nouveaux riches to harassment by city schoolboys. The film addresses many of the concerns surrounding urbanization mentioned earlier. At the end of the film, Tang reiterates his respect for the tenacity of these migrant workers. As in *City Paradise*, the protagonist presses on, despite many traumatic setbacks.

## Notes

1. Walter Benjamin, *Reflections: Essays, Aphorisms, Autobiographical Writings*, Peter Demetz, ed., trans. Edmund Jephcott (New York: Schocken Books, 1986), xvi.

2. For details, read Paul Clark, *Chinese Cinema: Culture and Politics since 1949* (Cambridge: Cambridge University Press, 1987).

3. Paul Clark, "Chinese Cinema," and Paul Pickowicz, "Melodramatic Representation and the "May Forth" Tradition of Chinese Cinema," Ellen Widmer and David Der-Wei Wang, eds., *From May Fourth to June Fourth: Fiction and Film in Twentieth Century China*. (Cambridge: Harvard University Press, 1993), 295–326.

4. Tang Xiaobing, "Configuring the Modern Space: Cinematic Representation of Beijing and Its Politics," *East-West Journal of Film* 8:2 (1994): 47–69.

5. The communities referred to here are neighborhood-based, not church-based, as were the communities in medieval Europe.

6. Biographical information on Tang was provided by Professor Wang Xinshin, Senior Professor at the Beijing Film Academy.

7. Alison Dray-Novey, "Spatial Order and Police in Imperial Beijing," *Journal of Asian Studies* 52.4 (November, 1993): 885–992.

8. Marshall Berman, "Why Modernism Still Matters," Michael Lerner, ed., *Tikkun . . . to Heal, Repair and Transform the World: An Anthology* (Oakland, California: Tikkun Books, 1992), 35.

9. Mike Featherstone and Scott Lash, eds. *Spaces of Culture: City, Nation, World* (London: Sage Publication, 1999), 11.

10. For a well-researched discussion of Chinese rock music, see Jeroen de Kloet, "Marx or Market: Chinese Rock and the Sound of Fury," Jenny Kwok Wah Lau, *Multiple Modernities: Cinemas and Popular Media in Transcultural East Asia* (Philadelphia: Temple University Press, 2003).

11. This situation caused so much attention that a number of documentary films have been made on migrant workers. Among them, *Return to the Bridge of Phoenix* (dir. Li Hong, 1998), was shot by cinematographer Meng Fen while he was also shooting *Paradise. Beijing Bicycle* (2002), a Sixth Generation film popular in the United States, is also about migrant workers. Young director Jai ZhangKe is well known for making films on similar themes.

12. Chen Shimei is a villainous figure in Chinese folk stories. He is a poor man whose wife works very hard to support his education. When he finally excels in the government examination and is rewarded with a high official position, he marries a rich woman and refuses to acknowledge his wife.

13. Jung-Pang Lo, ed., *K'ang Yu-wei: A Biography and a Symposium* (Tucson: University of Arizona Press, 1967), 36.

14. "Globalization and the Urban System in China,"by Anthony Gar-on Yeh and Xueqiang Xu in *Emerging World Cities in Pacific Asia* edited by Fu-Chou Lo and Yue-man Yueng., (New York: United Nations University Press, 1996). Pp. 219–267.

# 17

# Taiwan Fever?

## *Tsai Ming-Liang and the Everyday Postnation*

PETER HITCHCOCK

For those locations for which national identity is set as a task rather than as a commentary on what "is" in an extant state, national cinema traces the logic of nation formation. It is not that national cinemas of established nations are excluded from this logic, but that their assumptions of identity tend to mask the inner workings of their imaginary schema (and this often gives rise to a misplaced elitism and self-righteousness). To that extent, nations are always in formation, but newer nations, and especially postcolonial nations, accentuate this logic of formation in provocative and complex ways. Countercolonial insurgency and the struggle over postcolonial statehood affect every level of political and cultural interaction, although not in any simply deterministic or predictive manner. Cinema may serve a key ideological function in postcolonial identity, but it is just as likely to question statehood as it is to confirm the tenets that made independence possible. Rather than develop a laundry list of attributes for postcolonial national expression, I am more interested in exploring cinema's capacity to create and rearticulate cultural logics of nation through a form of political and aesthetic unconscious. These are produced in different intensities and are highly context specific; indeed, they confound most regulatory aesthetic categories, allegories, epics, and the like by imaging the presence and absence of a formulaic ideal. Postcolonial cinema at this level not only highlights a logic of nation formation but can simultaneously indicate the possibilities of reformulating nation or of superadequating nation formation altogether. We are so used to seeing this as a function of economic logic, particularly the logic of globalization, that cultural criticism elides the creative contribution of particular locations. The empire does not only "write back" in the form of a forthright postcolonial revenge of history; it also doubts the very form of statehood that putatively corresponds to its postcolonial status.[1]

Although cinema in Taiwan began in 1901, the first all-Taiwanese production was not made until 1925 with *Whose Fault Is It?* (One answer to this question is Japanese colonialism.)[2] The industry picked up quickly after the arrival of the Nationalist Party (Guomindang, or KMT), in part because of an acknowledgment of film's strong ideological potential in nation building, and also because key figures from the mainland—from the Shanghai film studio, for instance—followed Chiang Kai-shek to the island. It should be noted that the Guomindang's support of Chinese film generally came at the expense of indigenous Taiwanese production, with Mandarin films becoming predominant by the end of the 1950s. (In part, this can be read as an ideological extension of the horrendous February 28 Incident of 1947 when anti-government protesters were massacred by the KMT). One-party rule and martial law do not provide a friendly atmosphere for art, but even during the time of KMT repression, films and filmmakers were not simply reflections of Guomindang desire. True, the so-called "health realism" emitted more than a faint whiff of authoritarian didacticism, and the Qong Yao romantic melodrama that succeeded it was not much better, but there was also a sense that the main tension in artistic creativity was not so much between the filmmaker and the State as between tradition and modernity in nation narration. We should not be surprised that under authoritarianism the dominant genre had been escapist, but how to visualize an alternative modernity increasingly became the substance of narrative style. Not all of the influences behind the Taiwan New Cinema or New Wave were aesthetic—for instance, Taiwanese cinema in the early 1980s was trying to fend off Hong Kong film and the emergence of the bootleg videotape—but it is clear that wherever production money was coming from (the government, the booming economy, the United States), Taiwanese film broke from its own prescriptions. (The collaborative effort of 1982, *In Our Time*, is generally accepted as the turning point).

The New Wave of the 1980s is tremendously important in world cinema history, a movement in which key directors, including Hou Hsiao-hsien and Edward Yang, altered the landscape of film in general by imaging modernity's contradictions as a politics of the local. From his quasi-autobiographical films like *A Time to Live and a Time to Die* (1985) to the award-winning *City of Sadness* (1989), Hou Hsiao-hsien offered a wrenching panoply of everyday Taiwanese life and its relationship to history. Stylistically, the long takes, deep-focus nonlinear narrative, and documentary feel transformed Taiwanese cinema in ways that have influenced both second-wave directors like Tsai Ming-liang and the more recent stirring of a third wave. (Obviously, this wave analysis comes from French and Italian cinema, but it also has a more general generational implication.)

Rather than focus on the history that has overdetermined Taiwan New Cinema, I want to offer a critique on the work of Tsai Ming-liang as a way to pose questions about the relative status of Taiwanese film to Taiwanese national identity and the problems that nationalism and globalization represent within this context.[3] This also involves invoking the question of "what is Chinese," which is controversial not only because of the stark difference in nationalist agendas that inform the People's Republic of China and the Republic of China, but also because the mainland nationalists in Taiwan can be read, like the Japanese in the first half of the twentieth century, as an occupying force. Rey Chow notes that to emphasize "Chinese" often does not just overstep the realm of difference in "Chineseness" across the globe, but also normalizes specific notions of "Chinese" that in their own way may be as debilitating as the orientalist conceptions from which they would otherwise wish to diverge.[4] It is partly because of this that Taiwanese identity in film is both critical and salutary, especially when globalization in its sweep tends to circulate Chineseness as a monolithic trait of cinema from Taiwan (although Chineseness itself is contestable in a Taiwanese context). Tsai's films simultaneously question both their own status as correctly representing Taiwanese identity and those transnational narratives that would render Chinese modernity in a single key, as something that naturally aspires to or is in accord with "nation." The time of this teleology is significantly treated as a problem by Tsai, just as the space of Chineseness in Taiwan is radically recalibrated according to the complexities of postcolonial statehood. If Tsai's films are marked by a profound angst, their ennui picks away at formulas of identity that oscillate within the binaries of nation and transnation, Taiwan and Greater China, and modernity and postmodernity (even as each second term insistently calls into question the first). Orientalism continues to produce a burden of Chineseness (sometimes shouldered by different Chinese themselves), an identity girded by both a traditional mythology and globalization's ideological reflexes. Tsai answers both this and the truisms of modernity that make his contribution amenable to the international art-house circuit on one level (with its own ideological reflexes) and deeply troubling on another level (because Tsai eschews the particular logic of its transnational "I"). Taiwan thus becomes less modernity's triumph in globalization and more its *mise en abyme*.[5]

Tsai made his debut feature in 1992 with *Rebels of the Neon God*, a study of disaffected Taipei (Taibei) teenagers set against a backdrop of urban decay and empty development. In his second production, *Vive L' Amour* (1994), three vacant souls play out an almost wordless narrative of interaction in a vacant apartment. *The River* (1997) takes up many of the same themes of urban estrangement as its predecessors, although on this occasion Tsai revisits family dysfunction in order to question the norms of modernity. *The Hole* (1998) deepens Tsai's idiosyncratic and radical vision by troping on contemporary existence through the experiences of two loners living one above the other in a Taipei apartment block. *What Time Is It There?* (2000) expands his palette in important ways by including Paris in his existential gaze. Tsai notes, "I have always wanted to probe deeper into the roots of humanity. While shooting *The River*, I kept reminding myself to probe into the deeper, the darker half of ourselves."[6] Born in 1957 in Malaysia, Tsai wrote and directed stage plays and television dramas before he established his film credentials in 1992. He is not best described as an optimist when it comes to modern existence, although there are glimpses of a kind of humanist redemption in his work. What time is it there? What time is it here? Changing the question emphasizes a certain transnationalism in Tsai's work that defies or stands askew to the nationalist agenda of Taiwan itself and reconstitutes the scale, as well as the time and space, of location. This is more explicit at some moments in his oeuvre than others, but I would not put it down to the simple aesthetic choice of elite modernism over populist melodrama, over and above the politics of difference implied. For some Taiwanese critics, filmmakers like Hou, Yang, and Tsai are just not explicit enough and their marginal box-office success in Taiwan is used as evidence that they seek only an art-house or international audience and do not identify with the people they film. Because of the astounding international success of *Crouching Tiger, Hidden Dragon* (Ang Lee, 2000), the furor over Taiwanese New Cinema obscurantism has abated somewhat, but a pertinent question remains: is it Tsai's arty idiosyncrasy that grates, or is it what he says about being Taiwanese in the contemporary era that disturbs the components of nationalist identity as a cinematic problem? (I should say that the question can also be posed of first-wave directors like Yang, particularly in his film *The Terrorizer* and even in the more populist *Yi-Yi* [*A One and a Two*].) Tsai bears some comparison to Yang, but he is definitely the anti-Lee, the raucous id of Ang Lee's aesthetics, one whose interiority doubts the slick surfaces of Lee's oeuvre.

Let us frame the issue in a somewhat more theoretical way. If we can say that Tsai explores a certain hollowness in Taiwanese existence, a hole in the whole of being, as it were, or a vacillation in the dyad of nation and belonging, it follows that his art is driven not just by a conscious self-identification as outsider (as a diasporic Chinese Malaysian who came to Taiwan in his late teens) but by a logic of ambivalence about identity itself. In part, Tsai evinces some of what Hamid Naficy has usefully explored as "accented cinema," with the obvious qualification that whatever is "situated but universal"[7] in Tsai's art is overdetermined by the Chinese diaspora in Asia rather than by migration to the West. Indeed, Tsai's art demonstrates more of a political unconscious rather than an intentional stance—or it arises from a geopolitical aesthetic, as Fredric Jameson terms it in his reading of Yang's *The Terrorizer.* Jameson opens *The Geopolitical Aesthetic* with a typically laconic yet sweeping gambit: "All thinking, whatever else it is, is also an attempt to think the world system as such."[8] My reading of Tsai may lack the idiosyncrasy of Jameson's dialectical touchstone, but I do think that whatever is Taiwanese about Tsai's films is simultaneously postnational in its logic and image. Jameson's own perspective has been seriously criticized by, for instance, Hu Hsing-chi, who finds in Jameson's remapping of Taipei an orientalist desire to reference the third world in terms of first-world auteurism and the emergence in Taipei's objectified cityscape of all the trappings of Western existence.[9] It is *de rigeur* at this point to criticize Jameson for a lack of reflexivity in his re-representation of the third world, the East, and matters Chinese in particular. While some of this criticism is clearly justified, there are elements of Jameson's work that answer the very argument that Hu Hsing-chi makes. In *The Geopolitical Aesthetic*, for instance, Jameson refigures his controversial reading of allegory to accentuate the unconscious and the unrepresentable in global cinematic space: "On the global scale, allegory allows the most random, minute or isolated landscapes to function as a figurative machinery in which questions about the system and its control over the local ceaselessly rise or fall, with a fluidity that has no equivalent in those older national allegories."[10] Allegory, then, is "beyond the landscape" of the representational zeal of the world system, yet attempts to substitute for its unmappable integration. The hole in the whole of being is an ugly metaphor for any number of reasons (feminist, philosophical, poetic), yet it is not an unusual way to show as metaphor specific shifts in identity. One thinks, for instance, of Slavoj Zizek's Hegelian-Lacanian reading of Romanian nationalism and the fall of Nicolae Ceausescu. Rebels rather literally displayed their displeasure with the old tyrant's national allegory by tearing out the star from the center of the Romanian flag. Imagine Zizek's delight: "The hole in the big Other, the symbolic order, became visible."[11] As Judith Butler has noted, Zizek here is a little too amenable to phallic law,[12] but another contentious issue is that Zizek imagines this space, this hole in the heart of a nation, as the place of the critical intellectual. No one should doubt the political efficacy of positioning oneself askew to national prescriptions, but this does not quite grapple with that geopolitical unconscious invoked by Jameson, which remains for me crucial in understanding the vexed texture of Tsai's films.

While rejecting a Western reflex to read Tsai as "the Rainer Werner Fassbinder of Taiwan," it is hard not to measure Tsai's work within the context of world cinema. How, though, does Tsai build a logic of emptiness without providing a convenient lack or hollowness to be filled by Western desire or recouped and rearticulated within a conventional Taiwanese discourse of nation? Certain stylistic motifs are repeated in Tsai's works:

painfully long takes, a camera that seems set in concrete, a sound track where silence or ambient sound is the key interlocutor, a screenplay with no more than a few pages of dialogue, a failure to communicate in public space (or more accurately, public space denies communication), a failure to communicate in interior space, visual gags delivered with expressionless glee, a small ensemble of actors featuring Lee Kang-sheng (appearing post-modern *avant la lettre*, he lives in an eternal present and therefore does not age), cramped and cropped apartment spaces with an emphasis on lounging and visits to the bathroom (in *What Time Is It There?* Lee does not even make it to the bathroom on several occasions: scared of disturbing the ghostly spirits of his recently departed father, he uses plastic bags and bottles), and finally, and importantly, social relations that challenge all kinds of norms, like compulsory heterosexuality (in *The River*, for instance, in the dim lights of a sauna, a father unwittingly masturbates his son; then, when the lights come up, he slaps the son for *his* transgression). It is not that social and sexual relations are deemed dysfunctional; in fact, Tsai's films are interested precisely in reframing the social beyond the constellation or binary of normal and aberration. But if you put together the elements of Tsai's style, the overwhelming mood of his work conveys the sheer banality and absurdity of modern existence.

Taiwan, of course, has been heralded as a dragon or tiger economy, an NIC (newly industrialized country) that has proved the pudding of capitalist modernity (and, more recently with the DPP, or Democratic Progressive Party, of democratic yearning). Not so, says Tsai's work. The "miracle economy" has indeed seen a spirit of enterprise and working-class toil, but the miracle has simultaneously eviscerated the modes of social interaction. More is less. The drive to attain more goods and more luxuries has meant less time to enjoy them or even care about their function. For Tsai, the urban landscape is shorn of its existential reason, that is, to congregate people in meaningful ways. Instead, we see people make love in empty, unsold, or unrentable apartments (a function of a bloated real estate market in the late 1980s and early 1990s) and witness restaurant conversations where not a syllable is spoken. In *Vive L'Amour*, one cannot forget the final scene in which May Lin (Yang Kuei-mei) sits on a park bench and cries inconsolably against a desolate background of a half-built park (Taipei New Park). She cries and cries (a seven-minute sequence briefly punctuated by the lighting of a cigarette), and this is not some rage against the dying of the light. No, it is the very sound of hollowness in a life that is unsound.

But lest we simply translate such moments as the ultimate metaphors of Taiwan, Tsai's films insistently step back from summary judgments and convenient symbols. Indeed, *Vive L'Amour* proclaims a kind of nonnarrative of nation—or narrative of nonnation—in which the emptiness of the characters' collective existence refuses its status as an effect of nation. At one point the street trader Ah-Jung (Chen Chao-jung) opines, "Our society is all messed up, so we have lots of things to talk about," but none of that dialogue takes place in the film. Instead, the commentary on society is framed by the absence of narrative depth. Hints are offered (May Lin attempts to sell the apartment of an owner who is moving out of the country; meanwhile Hsiao-Kang [Lee Kang-sheng] sells box space for a columbarium that has the slogan "Be with your ancestors"), but death and departure are not viewed as solutions to the ennui the characters live. Ah-Jung goes to Hong Kong, but returns, and with more goods to sell. Hsiao Kang listlessly attempts suicide with a Swiss Army knife and bleeds just enough to inspire him to dress the wound. They are staying put, and it is this emphasis on the persistence of location that actually interrogates the space of the modern, "developing," postcolonial nation. The tendency is to read this as yet one more allegory on postcolonial dysfunction in general, but that kind of narrative is imposed primarily by the West and fails to come to terms with the questions posed by creative notions of collective identity. For instance, what is the "becoming Taiwan" of Tsai's films that registers identity even in conditions that might otherwise seem to thwart it? And how can this interrogation of selfhood be separated both from what Kuan-Hsing Chen suggestively calls "global nativism" (in which intense localism becomes a distribution requirement of transnational cinema marketing) and a form of gestural humanism that short-circuits the specificity of social contradiction by universalizing its claims to identification (the humanist version of "situated but universal")?[13]

Tsai's is not a strategy that offers an essence of being Taiwanese, still less of being Chinese, but it does speak to the absurdities and paradoxes of modernity's malevolence. Tsai is far from being dour, although his visual relief sometimes takes the form of nostalgia. This is one way to read the musical interludes and dance sequences that erupt within *The Hole* using the songs of Grace Chang ("Ge Lan" to the Chinese), Hollywood-style song-and-dance numbers via Hong Kong, bright costumes, and so forth. (The film ends with a statement by Tsai that "in the year two thousand we are grateful that we still have the songs of Grace Chang to comfort us.") Unlike the fixtures of the urban landscape, these songs work because of—as much as in spite of—their kitschy and camp delivery. By contrast, Taipei itself is remarkably broken down despite the smoked glass and shiny surfaces of urban development. Gutters leak, drains flood, garbage flows, and the brand-new subway system is in a permanent state of ruin (a step slightly beyond "creative destruction"). Concrete does not always set, walls are damp, mold is constant—the city is a paradise of instant decay. Mopeds are tossed away when they break—they litter the sidewalks and side streets, along with discarded bicycles and other urban detritus. Taiwan's modernity can be characterized as fast and temporary, in the same sense that, initially at least, the Nationalists believed their stay was but a brief prelude to a triumphant return to the mainland. Obviously, while that desire remains for some, today's Taiwan evinces a much stronger strain of nativism and rootedness in which the Hakka, Min-nan-jen, Wai-she-jen (the mainlanders), and island aborigines struggle over what defines Taiwanese independence. It is not that Tsai has nothing to say about such struggle but that one reaction to the desire for "nation" is a willing suspension of its mandate. At this level, the ennui in Tsai's films bespeak a certain resignation on the nation question, a disavowal that can be read to recuperate self-centeredness and the individual as the bounds of the visual, but that also projects nation as absence, as a location that is bounded but post-nation (a point to which I will return).

If Taipei's spontaneous entropy is a key characteristic of Tsai's oeuvre, it serves several different functions that go beyond the brusque dismissal of life in Taiwan. The omnipresence of water, for instance, has less to do with a dearth of plumbers than with the associative effects that Tsai can generate from water's roles in everyday life. For instance, in Taipei each year there is often a period of rain that defies description. It is a version of this seemingly limitless rain that is the sound track of *The Hole*. Is water the enemy? True, apartments appear to leak at regular intervals (in *Rebels of the Neon God*, in *The Hole*, and in *The River*) and water can seem downright malevolent (in the apocalyptic rain of *The Hole*, in the neck-pain inducing Tanshui of *The River*), but water is also a life-giving and life-affirming force in Tsai's films. His characters drink (and pass) water regularly, water plants, and wash themselves with a passion unmatched in film history. Given the role of water in quotidian existence, Tsai seems intent on exploring the ways in which it facilitates human interaction. Yet, while his attention sometimes reaches spiritual intensity (commentators have drawn links to Buddhism, and Tsai himself has implied it), he tempers belief with an acknowledgment of the absurdity of everyday needs. There is a point in *The Hole* when we see May Lin in her apartment, in the midst of interminable rain and flooded floors, unable to get water out of the faucet! And even when the plumbing does work, the viewer is continually offered the image of a modern city where bottled water is the drinking water of choice, if not of necessity. Again, however, the absurdity of modernity as entropy is not projected as the monopoly of postcolonial or Taiwanese life. Achille Mbembe has examined the aesthetics of vulgarity and banality in the postcolonial condition.[14] To this we may add a critical stance on absurdity as a struggle to articulate differently what counts for living in the postcolony.

What time is it there? What time is it here? There are dozens of questions in Tsai's films that go without answers. People hear them perhaps, or perhaps not, but they do not respond. I relocate the question "What time is it there?" because I believe that it might start a conversation that undoes the pieties and stereotyping that often accompany the typification of Taiwanese Chineseness in a transnational frame. Certainly Tsai enjoins that conversation in the Paris scenes of *What Time Is It There?* But here the idea is to heed to the specificities of Tsai's highly ambivalent "chronotope" of Taiwanese urban existence while keeping the question alive within considerations of transnational cinema in general. As more than one critic has surmised, the hole is not a hole in *The Hole*, but a bizarre umbilical cord that links two lives despite their urban estrangement. To some degree, this is merely a modernist moment, a brief interlude in which the repetition of modernity's angst prepares the way for true postmodern schizo paradise. —but I think, more seriously, Tsai takes film art in its form as interrogative, so that the answer to his questions lies in film's ability to visualize a constructive use for emptiness. Neither an organic whole, nor a humanist wholeheartedness, Tsai's work suggests that the ontological delirium of nation and modernity fail to feed the soul and thus his films question any time and place in which this often nefarious nirvana has been taken up.

"Taiwan fever," then, is less a descriptor for Taiwanese nationalism and more a commentary on the desire for nation itself. Tsai's films do not suggest that the Taiwanese have been duped by nationalism or infected by it, but that the formula for postcolonial nationhood lies within the specific mode of decolonization itself, not in some spurious approximation or mimetic affinity for the West as the immoveable measuring stick of modernity. It is not for nothing that a kind of nonmimetic difference is announced by Tsai at the beginning of *The Hole*, when we are introduced to "Taiwan fever" in a radio broadcast while the screen remains black. With a week to go before the new millennium, the commentary says, Taiwan has been beset by a fever, an epidemic, described as an end-of-the-millennium virus. Tsai is playing with *fin de siècle* catastrophism (in fact, the film was commissioned by the French cable company La Sept Arte as one of ten international films to explore the meanings of the turn of the millennium). One could argue, in fact, that the artifice of the fever is a mere gesture by Tsai to satisfy his backers or is demonstrably superfluous, since so much of Tsai's work does not need this obviousness to convey the entropic mood at its heart. Yet the notion of "Taiwan fever" is of a piece with Tsai's absurdism and ingeniously links this to the feverish obsession with what is otherwise an arbitrary marker of time. To this extent, the time of "Taiwan fever" cannot fill the metaphoric hole of the film, just as Hsiao Kang resetting all of his clocks to Paris time in *What Time is it There?* cannot bring back Shiang-chyi (Chen Shiang-chyi), the object of his affection, or indeed Hsiao Kang's recently departed father. If the gesture is empty, it still confirms emptiness as a governing theme. But why locate the fever at all? In interviews Tsai has suggested that he is increasingly attempting to deemphasize the specificity of his urban locales in order to generalize his commentary on the human condition. "Taiwan fever" thus would be an ironic comment on a certain irrelevance to space, an art that views the politics of place and the trajectories of nation as unremittingly beside the point. But this is, I believe, where Tsai's films may be read against the grain of his prescriptions while not simply recuperating them within a problematic that excludes the intricacies of Tsai's auteurism.

The radio report at the beginning of *The Hole* announces that to contain the virus that has attacked the island, the government is setting up quarantined areas and is encouraging people to move by threatening to turn off water supplies and cease garbage collection. What does "Taiwan fever" do? Infected humans tend to assume cockroach-like attributes by crawling on all fours and seeking dark, damp interiors to hide. Tsai uses this conceit, which is far from being gesture alone, to build tension into his tableau. Will the virus infect the bleak apartment block where "the Man Upstairs" (Lee Kang-sheng) and "the Woman Downstairs (Yang Kuei-mei) live one over the other, or do they learn from the absurdity of their situation? It is true their interaction could proceed without the emergency situation that frames the relationship, and it is also likely Tsai names the fever merely to identify his contribution to an international film collection. Yet if Tsai is indeed attempting to distance his work from the messy coordinates of the time and space that is Taiwan, then it is remarkable how much of what passes for content in his oeuvre requires precisely this integer of location for the films to work as film. The more pared down the *mise en scène*, and the more minimalist the dialogue, the more the location and the question of nation is assigned. In *The Hole*, for instance, the narrative takes great pains to mock the routines of everyday existence, but surely the humor resides in the specificity of the routines, not in some appeal to a more general condition. Both central characters subsist on a diet of cigarettes, instant noodles in Styrofoam bowls, and canned fish (at one point Tsai juxtaposes shots of them eating the same thing simultaneously). Time and again Tsai draws comparisons between the consumption of processed foods and a kind of processed, potted existence. The Man Upstairs feeds a stray cat on canned food (animals, like humans, are taught to survive on fast food), a noble gesture undermined by the fact that he leaves every empty can behind (again, trash as the sign of irredeemable transience). Tsai separates his characters from the paradoxical torpor of fast food by slowing down their actions, as well as the camerawork used to capture them. The television badgers them to live the dream of modernity: "It would be foolish to believe that anyone can live on rainwater," opines one expert while the Man Upstairs consumes peanuts, beer, and cigarettes. Meanwhile, the Woman Downstairs slurps down noodles as a program instructs her in "the fine culinary art of instant noodles—any brand will do." She adopts a siege mentality by stocking up on toilet-paper rolls (dozens of them), while bags of trash tossed from upper floors whiz by the window. Everything that signifies ease of use also implies waste, wasted processes, and wasted time. "Taiwan fever," like the hole itself, is an awkward trope, but it is not an arbitrary term to frame the hole in existence portrayed. If this life is everywhere, it is the "somewhere" that brings it to light.

This is one way to explain the curious musical interludes that pepper the film. Slowed almost to flatliner status by lack of dialogue, action, and camera movement, the film bursts into life via campy and stylized lip-synced renditions of Grace Chang melodies from the late 1950s and early 1960s. Chang, like Tsai, was part of a Chinese diaspora, in her case one that took her from her native Shanghai to Hong Kong at the time of the 1949 revolution. A doyenne of cultural syncretism, Chang made her mark in a series of films that adapted a Hollywood musical structure (Hollywood itself being obsessed with the song and dance of the Caribbean and South America) to local content and glamour. *Mambo Girl* (1957) is a classic of the genre, a frenetic paean to the joys of song and dance that made Chang's name synonymous with mambo, cha-cha, and ja-jambo. Tsai uses five of her songs; their inclusion, like the hole itself, is quite precise, as the lead-up to the first song suggests. The Woman Downstairs has a leak in her ceiling, and the film begins with a plumber visiting the Man Upstairs, who is asleep after a heavy session of Taiwan beer, to investigate. The camera is also asleep: this medium shot alone lasts over a minute. Finally awakened, the Man Upstairs lounges around in his underwear (another trademark of Lee Kangsheng's performances in Tsai's films) while the plumber taps away at the concrete floor (the camera moves to include the front door, and this shot is held for another four minutes). In the next scene we see the Woman Downstairs cleaning up the leak as best she can (she even reattaches the wallpaper). She prepares her instant noodles, tosses the trash out of the window, then plants herself in front of the television to catch up on the progress of the virus (and instant noodle recipes!). It is at this point that she notices the hole in her ceiling (the work of the plumber) in a close-up punctuated by a cockroach crawling through it. How can one answer this plight? The Chang song begins and now we are in the building's lobby with a medium-to-long shot of the elevator. Inside, the Woman Upstairs has been transformed into Mambo Girl, replete with sequined *chongsan* and an ostrich feather headdress, while the walls of the elevator itself have been covered with "starlight." As she dances and sings "Calypso," the camera tracks slowly toward her, as if to emphasize her kinetic pleasure. Again, this stark contrast is both a moment of nostalgic fantasy and a mode of locating its source. For the woman, eating instant noodles in a Taipei apartment that is rapidly flooding, Grace Chang is a wonderful distraction and a revelation of the Downstairs Woman's inner world of desire. Tsai ends the sequence with closing elevator doors and a neatly executed iris shot—but the song is not just an interlude: it is a segue. No sooner have the doors shut than they open again, but now we see the Man Upstairs once more, drunk and barely conscious. The delirium of Grace Chang's songs is the correlative of a desire that will bring the characters closer together. If

Chang's songs brighten the film considerably, it is because they broaden our understanding beyond the often wordless encounters in the rest of the film and provide a second language of connection and communication. The juxtaposition of song-and-dance sequences with comparatively slow-motion slapstick is deliberately alienating, but less so for an audience who understands well some of the costs of living in Taiwan.

The hole itself challenges the emptiness of its associations. Like the Chang sequences, it facilitates the intimacy of the apartment dwellers while straining under the weight of its ripe metaphorical weight. If the Woman Downstairs first experiences the hole through its dripping (and the entryway it provides for cockroaches), the Man Upstairs initially views it as a waste disposal unit and vomits into his neighbor's apartment. The slapstick continues. To dull her neighbor's noise, the Woman Downstairs stuffs a mop into the hole. Next, to quell the roaches now associated with the virus, she sprays insecticide around her apartment and through the hole. The Man Upstairs responds by placing a wok lid over the hole. Later he will open his doors and windows to ventilate his living space. The Woman Downstairs uses duct tape to close the hole, but then the Man Upstairs pours bottled water down it and the tape falls off. From this comic interaction via the hole, other communication emerges (the frequency of incidents, like the Chang songs, provide, if not standard narrative content, a rhythm to the film). The Woman Downstairs writes a note to her neighbor to let him know that when he uses his toilet it leaks into her bathroom (he then uses the sink instead). From this point, Lee Kang-sheng's character begins to view the hole as a practical design element in his social life (like living with the hole in nation). He cleans up the hole, removes the rubble, and widens it to better view his neighbor and her apartment below. Here laughs are garnered by the sheer obviousness of the connotations available (including the position of the spectator, as viewer, of this scene). Thus, the Man Upstairs exercises by pushing his leg through the hole (exercise punctuated by smoking and attenuated by a cramp). He removes his leg just as his neighbor emerges from the bathroom, thereby underlining that even in a film of slow or little action, timing is still everything. Finally, just when it looks as if the Woman Downstairs has succumbed to "Taiwan fever" (she builds a nest of toilet-paper packages and crawls into it on all fours), the hole is transformed from a symbol of dysfunction to one of hope. The Woman Downstairs is awakened from her fever by light shining down the hole. As she looks up, an outstretched arm through the hole delivers a glass of water (water, like the hole, has a double resonance). She drinks the water and then the arm returns again to lift her to the apartment above. The film ends with another Grace Chang song. While the neighbors dance in formal wear in the upstairs apartment, the lyrics declare, "I don't care who you are, but darling hold me close / Alone together in the dark, come the days of carefree spring."

Is the hole not just a conduit to love but a site of possibility that breaks from the soporific and mordant emptiness of Taiwanese urban life? Hardly. If the romantic reverie Tsai ascribes to the hole verges on the platitudinous, this is no less true of a reading that would render the hole only a sign of inveterate Taiwanese being. My point here is to argue for a politics of location that is symptomatic (that is, the extent to which the narrative elements are themselves articulations that cannot be made as if elsewhere) rather than emblematic. Far from being an alibi in an international film collection, the invocation of Taiwan in *The Hole* refracts specific layers of being in Taiwan. It is certainly not a catalogue of all that Taiwan is or could be, but neither can it frame space as if its referent did not exist. Absence as presence? Postcolonial narrativity confounds even the neat reversal of colonial enlightenment.

It would be relatively easy to present Tsai's films as nonconformist exercises in a Western modernist vein. (To the Fassbinder label we could add the Francois Truffaut link, particularly since *What Time Is It There?* shows snippets of *The Four Hundred Blows* on Hsiao-Kang's television and Jean-Pierre Leaud makes a guest appearance in the film). Yet Tsai's idiosyncrasy and his focus on the intensely personal (or what makes up personality) follow much more closely in the tradition of Taiwan New Cinema itself. The main difference is that the experience of the "becoming of Taiwan" is explicit in, say, Yang or Hsiao's films of the 1980s, whereas Tsai's work doubts even the nature of his predecessors' doubt about nation. It is as if the weakening of the KMT on quotidian Taiwanese existence has enervated Tsai's sense of nation as paradigm even as Chen Shui-bian and the DPP proffered a more thorough-going decolonization and independence. The geopolitical implications of Taiwanese nationalism are immense: caught between China's rhetoric of Motherland and the United States' withering definition of regional interest (where, exactly, would that end?), Taiwan simultaneously confirms the spatial coordinates of "nation" and empties out its formula for postcolonial being. In philosophy one can ascribe a certain non-Being to Being in the full range of its meanings. The same is true for "nation," in part because of the philosophical Geist in which it originally emerged. Precisely because of Taiwan's tenuous nature as a barely recognized nation, it challenges the cognition that the nation idea bequeaths. Here the invocation of "postnation" does not mean that Tsai deems Taiwan irrelevant to his art. Far from it. If Tsai's style remains consistent with his Taiwanese cinematic forebears, he yet finds the content of existence more problematic in the context of such affiliation. Indeed, the narrative of "postnation" must pivot on the question of affiliation, a narrative for which the world struggles to find appropriate content. Again, this is a political unconscious and is a symptom, not a program. The reductions in scale in Tsai's films, as well as the reductions in space, dialogue, and movement, certainly indicate a yearning for more basic human interaction (the "comfort" symbolized by the songs of Grace Chang), but only by suppressing the content that would give that desire force. This is why at the end of *The Hole* the neighbors' new-found love is a troubling cure for "Taiwan fever." If the question remains open, it is because the solutions themselves are still forming. What of the others "alone together in the dark"? What time is it there? How long will it take? And are there enough park benches in the meantime?

## Notes

1. Texts on cinema and questions of nationalism abound. Two particularly useful texts are Mette Hjort and Scott Mackenzie, eds., *Cinema and Nation* (New York: Routledge, 2000), and Alan Williams, ed., *Film and Nationalism* (New Brunswick: Rutgers University Press, 2002).

2. For an analysis of the poltical, cultural, and economic impact of Japanese colonialism on Taiwan, see Leo T. S. Ching, *Becoming "Japanese": Colonial Taiwan and the Politics of Identity* (Berkeley, Los Angeles, and London: University of California Press, 2001).

3. There is a fast-developing corpus of criticism on the work of Tsai Ming-liang. A good collection is Olivier Joyard, Jean-Pierre Rehm, and Danièle Revière, *Editions Dis Voir: Tsai Ming Liang* (Paris: Dis Voir, 1999). For a comprehensive critique in English that also considers Tsai in terms of postcoloniality, see Fran Martin, "The European Undead: Tsai Ming-liang's Temporal Dysphoria": http://www.sensesofcinema.com/contents/03/27/tsai_european_undead.html. (Accessed 1/10/04).

4. Rey Chow, "Introduction: On Chineseness as a Theoretical Problem," in Rey Chow, ed., *Modern Chinese Literary and Cultural Studies in the Age of Theory* (Durham: Duke University Press, 2000), 1–25. The issue of Chineseness is far too complex to be engaged sufficiently here, but it should be noted that it does not just divide China from Taiwan—it also divides China from itself. The history of nations shows time and again that ethnic and linguistic homogeneity fail to suture nations together into one, and that this failure itself constitutes the logic of "nation," if not the historical conditions for its demise. For more on the connection between Chineseness and cinema, see Chris Berry's essay in the same volume, "If China Can Say No, Can China Make Movies?," 159–180.

5. This is a different reading of the transnational than that provided by Sheldon Hsiao-peng Lu in his otherwise excellent collection, *Transnational Chinese Cinemas*. Generally, transnationalism is used as an alibi for deploying Chineseness as a common denominator for China, Hong Kong, and Taiwan, but this assumption is transnational in another way; namely, it transects the concept of identity at stake and the national space to which it is supposed to refer. In the term "transnational Chinese cinemas," the "trans" serves to place the rest of the term under erasure. See Sheldon Hsiao-peng Lu, ed., *Transnational Chinese Cinemas* (Honolulu: University of Hawaii Press, 1997): 1–34.

6. Online interview with Tsai Ming-Liang, by Rachel Chen, translated by Jean Yeh: www.peripherfilm.de/derfluss/interview.htm (Accessed 01/10/04).

7. Hamid Naficy, *An Accented Cinema: Exilic and Diasporic Filmmaking* (Princeton: Princeton University Press, 2001), 10.

8. Fredric Jameson, *The Geopolitical Aesthetic* (Bloomington, IN: Indiana University Press, 1995), 4.

9. Hu Hsing-chi, "Review of *New Chinese Cinemas*," *Cultural Studies from Birmingham*, 2.1(1998): http://www-staff.lboro.ac.uk/~ssghz/articles/foreign32.htm (01/10/04).

10. Fredric Jameson, *The Geopolitical Aesthetic*, 5.

11. Slavoj Zizek, *Tarrying with the Negative* (Durham, NC: Duke University Press), 1993), 1.

12. Judith Butler, *Bodies that Matter* (New York, Routledge, 1993): 196.

13. Kuan-Hsing Chen, "Introduction," in Kuan-Hsing Chen, ed., *Trajectories* (New York: Routledge, 1998), 1–52.

14. Achille Mbembe, *On the Postcolony* (Berkeley: University of California Press, 2001): 102–141.

# 18

# The Spirits of Capital and Haunting Sounds

## *Translocal Historicism in* Victim *(1999)*

ESTHER C. M. YAU

## Dragons and Movies on World-City Screens

In May 2001, the Brussels Museum of Fine Arts held its second Hong Kong Film Festival, with twelve movies featuring Chow Yun-fat, Maggie Cheung, Michelle Yeoh, Jackie Chan, and other spirited stars. Not unlike what happens in a French cinema retrospective run in Tokyo or an International Film Festival organized in Shanghai, moving images form a vital presence in a world city's visual art environment that is increasingly intertwined with the entrepreneurial use of culture. A publicity cliché has it that the movies' kinetic energy represents a vital city. Described as "over-the-top," "rollercoaster ride," and "offbeat," would the movies' emotions reveal something of value in Hong Kong cinema besides offering a sensational feast?

The Belgium-Hong Kong Film Festival is the place where the new city emblem for the Hong Kong Special Administrative Region (SAR) was put on publicity banners and movie posters. This emblem, a digitally generated flying dragon, has a wavy form in red and orange. The dragon's head resembles the snout of a fox, and its body has flamelike slashes made up of the letters "H" and "K". The words "Hong Kong" and "Asia's World City" are written under it. Resembling neither the Dragon King in Chen Kaige's Fifth-Generation classic *Yellow Earth* (1984), nor the animated dragon sidekick in Disney's *Mulan* (1999), this new city emblem joins a series of imperial-Orientalist clichés of a "mysterious and ancient" China.

In creating this emblem, three research firms—Burston-Marsteller, Landor Associates, and Wirthlin Worldwide, Inc.—were hired by the SAR government as part of a well-budgeted "Brand Hong Kong" campaign to run a design contest and focus-group tests in Hong Kong, North America, and Western Europe. These firms chose the flying dragon design from among contestants' entries without consulting local artist groups, thus continuing past colonial-government procedures. Officials endorsed the selected prize-winning design as a "historical and cultural icon," embracing the designer's intention to "impart a sense of movement and speed" and to "mirror Chinese calligraphy."[1] If Manuel Castells was optimistic about statism becoming powerless in the face of new information-embodying technology,[2] the state-entrepreneur alliance has complicated this conclusion. Not unimportantly, the process is a sign of urban governance by a new (trans)local alliance of state, multinational corporations, and entrepreneurs in world cities.

Asia's financial crisis at the time of Hong Kong's transfer from Great Britain to the People's Republic of China brought to economics as much attention as politics in renationalization. Savvy entrepreneurs promoted Hong Kong as the business "gateway to China", and the Chinese government created policies to favor flows between the city's businesses and the mainland's resources. Notably, creative industries and culture zoning became projects of state-entrepreneurial partnership. In a critical study of cultural geography titled *Spaces of Capital* (2001), David Harvey incisively analyzes various claims to uniqueness and authenticity to show that these are articulated as distinctive, nonreplicable cultural claims so that their monopolistic powers can be asserted either translocally or globally in the capitalist market. Accepting capital's relentless moves to "co-opt, subsume, commodify and monetize such differences just enough to be able to appropriate monopoly rents therefrom," Harvey's analysis leads him to coin the phrase "the art of [monopoly] rent"[3] to illustrate, among other things, the symbolic capital value of distinctive architecture. Citizens, Harvey notes, must beware of eye-catching constructions and they must ask: "Whose collective memory?" "Whose aesthetics?", and "Who benefits?" Indeed, citizens have taken action to preserve their cultural memory by contesting demolition projects. [4]

The "art of monopoly rent" concept can illuminate the cultural production strategies of national cinemas trying to reach global screens. Zhang Yimou's well-known features throughout the 1990s, criticized for their exhibitions of faux ethnographic practices and backward rural landscapes (from *Raise the Red Lantern* to *Not One Less*), can be understood as extracting "monopolistic powers" from these aspects, because he perceived art-cinema festivals as arenas already well occupied and mined by American and European movies. The success of his films, moreover, spurred other art-house movies to elaborate on cultural differences. The popular reception of director Ang Lee's swordplay-and-martial-arts film *Crouching Tiger, Hidden Dragon* (*Wohu changlong*, 2000) is another instance to see in a similar light. Thus, American films have incorporated martial-arts choreography in titles such as *The Matrix*(1999), and the makers of Chinese blockbusters, building on the success of television imperial melodramas, turned to imperial China for legends. Subsequently, *Hero* (*Yingxiong*, 2002), *House of Flying Daggers* (*Shimian Maifu*, 2004), and *Curse of the Golden Flower* (*Mencheng jin dai huangjinjia*, 2006) used stars and talent who already had worldwide reputations. The box-office profits of Zhang's strategies prompted Hong Kong filmmakers to bank their claims on traditional China to compete on the blockbuster market, eyeing the success of *Lord of the Rings*-type productions.

A monopoly analysis situates cinema productions within a global screen culture economy that departs from the old cultural exhibitionism debate. In that debate, film directors either were accused of being disloyal to their ethnic culture to appease a biased audience or were defended for their less discernible critical visions of that culture, and their audiences were unwittingly implicated in this critique. The shift places the productions, the cultural resources, and the talents within the dynamics of the global screen culture, and it recognizes genre reinventions that achieve unusual resonances with local audiences in a particular context. Rapid proliferation within the movie-genre business can lead to a faster exhaustion of "monopoly rent" in the genre, as in the instance of Dreamworks producing *Kung Fu Panda* (2008) that raises other issues.

## Bleak Emotions and The Value of Affect

> *"The entertainment industry and the various culture industries are . . . focused on the creation and manipulation of affects."*
>
> —MICHAEL HARDT[5]

It is worth mentioning the overseas ethnic Chinese networks that fueled a family-business-centered ethos and helped finance director Ang Lee's early films. Lee's "Father Trilogy"—*Pushing Hands* (*Tuishou*, 1992), *The Wedding Banquet* (*Xiyen*, 1993), and *Eat, Drink, Man, Woman* (*Yinshi nan nu*, 1994)—contain intergenerational reconciliation motifs and old-fashioned virtues alongside mutual respect, resilience, and tolerance among a range of family formations that include singles, homosexual unions, and senior marriages. The experienced father does what he knows best in response to his grown-up children, and his intimate emotions are given fine elaborations while they are also about immigrant life, bodily experience of aging, and letting go of traditional roles and expectations. Raymond Williams once noted that "tradition is never an inactive fragment from the past" but is "the most powerful practical means of incorporation . . .

operative in the process of social and cultural identification."[6] As an elderly man who has surprisingly open-minded decisions, the father powerfully exerts an impact on the family members' wrestling with their own identities. The settings in Lee's films correlate to the inner realm, such as the images of kitchen knives hanging on the wall reflecting muted tensions, and cuisines with appealing looks but a wrong taste betraying secret despair. These and many other material and aesthetic features carry the undertones and overtones of a range of emotions.

These three films stand out among Chinese-language films for not having women do the affective work for men. They also do not displace male anxieties onto women to make them go through suffering. Instead of making spectacles of feudal practices that victimize women and eroticize female suffering as in some notable China's Fifth-Generation films of the 1980s and the early 1990s, Lee's films open the narrative space to visualizing the father's inner realm and necessary emotional adjustments.

How refreshing is the attentive representation of the father's expressive hesitations in these films? For one, it relinquishes masculinity's "scandalous" all-powerful performance. The stories weave themselves around reaching difficult decisions and the crisis moments of reaching across that make or break deep bonds. Rather than spectacular action, intimate and complex emotions have a structuring role in the filmic narration, resonating with the attentiveness given to feelings in a postmodern cultural economy. Michael Hardt writes about "the affective human contact and interaction" as immaterial labor in advanced capitalist nations that entails service work, knowledge making, and communication. Caring work in feminist writing, Hardt recognizes, is the affective "living labor constituting a form of life,"[7] and one basis to produce communities that will contest biopower from above and sustain biopolitical productions from below. His focus on the "bios" of power and politics and references to feminist writings on maternal work, however, is still sketchy and it has not included fraternal relationships or its critical reconsideration.

Aihwa Ong raises a different though not unrelated set of questions about male melodrama. Using John Woo's *A Better Tomorrow* (1986) and *A Better Tomorrow III* (1988) as examples to discuss "soap operas without borders," Ong is wary of a fraternity-centered nostalgia. Woo's male melodramas, Ong poses, have transposed onto an ethnic Chinese culture the themes of American westerns, including male bonding for survival in a lawless world, men defending a safe domestic space, and making a last stand against the authorities. The gangster mode of honorable self-destruction through the last and blasting acts of brotherly love in *A Better Tomorrow* and in *The Killer* can be read as a nostalgic attempt to resist the temporality of capitalism exerting a toll on the body and the psyche—an aging gangster in *The Killer* admits the times are moving beyond him. If the films' overall message is that "the Chinese values of fraternal solidarity and justice are both vulnerable and vital in the chaotic world of Asian capitalism," this ambivalence about Asian modernity that motivates fraternal support also sets the latter apart from families of women and children.[8] Instead of setting part the maternal "immaterial labor" as Hardt has, Ong's analysis astutely critiques the absence of solution to capitalism's search for remedy of what it destroys and marginalizes.

Like Woo's 1980s productions, many Hong Kong crime and police thrillers commonly stage crises to put fraternal relationships through trials that bring to the foreground male hysteria, sacrificial death wishes, murderous rage, fear, courage, cynicism, and other similarly strong and naked emotions. In the years approaching 1997, more films ventured into such states as jealousy, self-deprecation, depression, and split personalities. The creation of "nonnormal men" in action films, according to one critic, gives psychological depth to these films as actors like Francis Ng, Anthony Wong, and Lau Ching-Wan interpret the dark side of men.[9] The popular reception they have received from audiences has prompted more directors to put efforts in building more complex topographical features in the intersecting emotional terrain of multiple characters that is still exclusively male-defined, competitive, and claustrophobic.

A new value in the "dark-emotions" realm has appeared, evidenced by a growing corpus of films engaging states of loneliness and abnormality, ranging from those of Wong Kar-wai to Herman Yau's. As in scenes with Tony Chiu-Wai Leung talking to his psychiatrist in *Infernal Affairs II* (*Wu Jian dou 2*, 2003), digging into the male psyche gives screenwriters an idea for a sequel. Without making a full-length study of this corpus, my discussion focuses on a film that exemplifies some of the problems experienced action directors face as they rework the action genre to address bleak emotional expressions in a world city. Ringo Lam's *Victim* (*Mu lu xiong guang*, 1999) is a hybrid genre films of the "bleak emotions" variety. The story makes an overt parallel to the financial crisis that plagued Hong Kong around the time of its writing and production. In 1999, murders of whole families by desperate fathers and mothers in dire distress were reported in alarming numbers,[10] and the label "negative asset" was used to refer to middle-class property owners who had huge mortgage debts when the real estate market crashed. Except for *Victim*, Hong Kong cinema as a whole was almost completely silent on these disturbing phenomena of family murders and negative assets. [11] *Victim* tried to combine both in a genre film. Critic Wong Ain-ling notes that the movie "began with some deceitful genre film tricks, but ended up in (rare) humanistic strides."[12] In the midst of this trajectory is, arguably, every Hong Kong action directors' renegotiation with genre limits to raise the stakes in the realm of complex and intricate emotions within a largely masculine and fraternal context, as is evidenced by action films made by Johnnie To and Andrew Lau/Alan Mak in the 2000s. Looking into the components of generic idioms, time, family photographs, and old music, my reading will discuss the critical implications beyond the film's own limits. By referencing Stanley Kubrick's *The Shining* (1980), one can say that *Victim* is a film open to an historicist reading through Tony Williams and Fredric Jameson, such that Kubrick's film can be viewed as a kind of global prophetic statement, and Lam's film a depiction of the loss of the city's myth.

## Victim's Secrets and Family Exposures

> *Without that which secretly unhinges [the living present], without this responsibility for justice concerning those who are not there, of those who are no longer there or who are not yet present and living, what sense would there be to ask the question "where?" "where tomorrow?" "whither?"*
>
> Jacques Derrida[13]

### *The Order of Action and the Order of Horror*

The film *Victim* portrays a victim-turned-criminal and a workaholic police investigator playing hide-and-seek and becoming each other's double. Manson is a well-groomed computer programmer who has lost his job and is on the verge of losing his house. He has killed the go-between who gambled away the little money he could salvage to repay a loan shark. Pit, a stressed-out, workaholic police detective who is hypersensitive and always anxious to prove his superior abilities, finds the hostage story of Manson and begins finding suspicious threads that lead to exposing his connection with some gangsters planning to turn the Monetary Authority's money-printing factory into their own get-rich device. In the course of investigation, Pit finds Manson alive but hung upside down in an abandoned hotel room in which a family murder had taken place in 1967. Manson is released from police interrogation and refuses to discuss anything with his domestic partner Fu. As Pit elicits the support of Fu, Manson is alarmed by her readiness to cooperate while hiding this fact from him. Pit turns into an anger-prone workaholic while Manson, deeply mired in debts and negative property asset, succumbs to the loan shark's gangsters to print forged money. Becoming a ruthless killer, Manson eliminates several gangsters and escapes the police with bags of newly minted thousand-dollar notes. Fu refuses to leave with him in his half-crazed state, prompting his attempt to kill first her, and them himself, while Pit, stopped short of falling off the edge by his colleagues, pursues the criminal. The film ends in a gunfight near a cemetery with massive police presence to witness Manson's death.

Depression and stress, secret despair and overt tension, together with loss, give this action-suspense-horror movie its emotional overtones and undertones. Several action-film protagonists in his earlier films (*City on Fire*, *Lenghu fengyun*, 1987) and *Full Alert* (*Gao du jie bei*, 1997) suffer from identity crisis and psychological disturbance, and a police station visitation scene from *Full Alert* shows the criminal muttering words on the difficulties of killing and the cop listening in lonesome terror while they face each other across a glass panel. Francis Ng, an impressing performer of crazed criminal types, says to the stoic Lau Ching-wan, "We are both non-normal people." In *Victim*, Lau Ching-wan occupies that state when he uses a woman's comb to smooth his hair in front of a mirror after turning himself into a ruthless gangster-killer. The juxtaposing of action and horror idioms take place throughout the film in two alternating "orders" of genre idioms; action cinema giving kinetic expressivity to fast-moving sequences, and horror-suspense cinema drawing attention to disturbed emotional states. Hit-and-run accidents, violent outbursts, car chases, and fights with weapons alternate with images of peaceful domestic settings imbued with violent and horrific implications, and both converge in the site of death.

The city in *Victim* is an "un-homelike" place of sudden deaths. The parking lot and the Monetary Authority's printing site are horror settings where senseless killing occurs, and deaths are traceable to money troubles. The frequent appearance of close-circuit television monitors and black-and-white photographs emphasizes technologically-mediated looking, with impersonal screens as silent witnesses in a city with too many incidents to monitor. The city's historical riot-ridden year of 1967 becomes the time a family massacre took place in a mountain-view hotel, a hint at the confluence of political, social, and economic elements behind most incidents. A large cemetery appears to be in walking distance from an affluent suburban district, alluding to the proximity of death despite oblivion among busy and stressed citizens.

Besides a dense juxtaposition of multiple elements in space, the city is a hybrid temporal entity. The trope of haunting disrupts the presumably linear, empty time of a world city, and the haunted house is a locus of the "fantastic" in anachronistic temporality. In the writings of Walter Benjamin and Jacques Derrida, anachronistic time provokes a sense of accountability for the injustices and unfulfilled expectations of the past, and a respect for justice toward humans already dead or not yet alive.[14] Anachronistic time in the haunted scenes in *Victim*, besides a metaphorical *déjà vu* of the city's crisis culture, has a prophetic quality regarding masculinity's deadly dealings. Not accidentally, the investigator Pit holds his gun at a mirror in the haunted hotel and the criminal Manson has himself hung upside down, and both face a similar family-killing decision later in the plot. Pit enters anachronistic time when, during his investigation, he reads the Chinese characters scrawled in blood on the bedroom walls of the couple in the 1967 murder, and the words "May this moment stay forever (*yuan cike yongliu*)" seem to have leapt out of the past towards him while his reflection appears trapped within the bedroom mirror frame. The moment of anachronism unleashes a hidden past to disturb the characters who have no time for history and cultural memory, not to say the social margins, in the property-accumulation, upward-social mobility game. The murder story's off-screen reference to the stories of despair which ended in family killings in 1999, however, prompts the inclusion of stories in the social margins that are a bleak contrast to the city's dragon emblem flying on its banner with delusive connotations.

Keenly aware of there being no assurance in the "living present," director Ringo Lam points to a treacherous flip that brings about tragedies. In an interview, critic Ye Nianchen notes that Lam, in a seminar, "alluded to a murder case that happened thirty years ago in the Mountain View Hotel and . . . impart[ed] a sense of prophecy." Lam noted that "tragedy sometimes occurs on a whim" (or "tragedy births in one fleeting thought").[15] Certainly, a flip is the intersection of many factors rather than a real whim that one remains passive about. Going further, the haunted hotel is an example to remind us of the value of cultural memory at the margins and during hard times, such that the world cities are indeed places where substantive cultural memory has as much to do with the dynamic presence of migrant workers, service workers, and marginal populations as the architecture and the movies.

## *Family Romance in Picture Frames*

Old family portraits, in Freudian terms, are phantasmic entities that arouse the longing for the "*heimlich*" as the vanished originary relationship for the subject. Writing on some landscape photographs, Roland Barthes evokes the desire for a maternal body that "carri[ies] me back to somewhere within myself", and a virtual mother to "bear me forward to a utopian time."[16] In film, photographs of togetherness may evoke nostalgia (the "homely") or horror ("the unhomely"), or both when they hail the audience through the protagonist who inexplicably gets in touch with what has been long forgotten or suppressed in memory. In Stanley Kubrick's *The Shining*, for example, a group photo of employees on the wall of the hotel's main lobby brings a retroactive recognition at the vaguely vicious look of the head attendant standing among hotel staff and guests before this man, in a murderous rampage, killed his family and others. Through a scene in spectral time in which the head-attendant hails the writer about a violent resolution to domestic trouble (both characters played by Jack Nicholson), nostalgic notions of the swinging 1920s are intertwined with the near-forgotten horror that are no longer safely locked up in the past but ready to erupt in the 1970s.

The phantasmic quality of the family portrait is a useful starting point to read the critical potential in the photographs. Appearing in an abandoned hotel room filled with shadowy sounds, an old family portrait evokes middle-class comfort and happiness while standing as a remnant in the sudden collapse of a normative social order unable to sustain itself. In the film, the gruesome reference enacts a foreboding sense of the thin divide between family romance and murderous passion even in a technological age. Reflections on the film's cautionary tale, furthermore, must take note of the unquestioning acceptance of the problematic view of family as private-property and emotional enterprise. A decent male citizen (or a female one, for that matter) killing the whole family in rage and despair flips from responsibility to destruction, revealing an absence of boundary and community support that plague family murders off-screen. The film's Chinese title, *Mu Lu Xiong Guang*, translated literally as "eyes with glimmers of brutality" or "a murderous shine of the eyes," can be read as referencing one man's rage and jealousy, but perhaps also implicating a broad sense of frustration and despair.

Family photos make happy exposures, but as the saying goes, looks are deceptive, even if they seem secured by capital and male privilege. *Victim* includes a scene with colleagues telling the overworked investigator Pit that his wife is seeing a man somewhere, and Pit rushes to the restaurant and draws his gun on the dining pair. His killing impulse is stopped by colleagues, who suddenly gather around them and bring out a birthday cake, explaining that this is a deliberate setup to give Pit a surprise birthday party at the restaurant. They bring along his wife and daughter, and tell them to sit close and appear happy as they take a picture of the family celebration. The family photo-taking scene exposes the facile security of a "happy family" in a still image. It comments on the rhetorical untruth in putting dad, mom, and child in perfect roles and positions to signify intimacy and happiness. In a visual setting where black-and-white photographs in the police office are records of death, the scene once again registers the thin divide between family romance and domestic horror.

## *Mothers and Nostalgic Songs*

In many American horror films, the suppressed past finds an analogy in the maternal body. From a feminist perspective, Barbara Creed notes the "fragility of the symbolic order in the domain of the body which never ceases to signal the repressed world of the mother."[17] Informed by Julia Kristeva, who writes that the maternal body is made to carry the child's struggles as the latter breaks away and rejects the (m)other, Creed's discussion of horror images of blood and gore pertain to the order of abjection. She further notes that as women are being made to scream when they see horrific sights, and are subjected to murderous assaults in horror films, the maternal body projects a sonic presence that has never been fully suppressed.

In response to a critic's questions about his film, Ringo Lam reminisces about the time when he loved to "listen to Bai Guang's songs by myself in the still of the night as I wrote my scripts."[18] Shanghai oldies fueled his imagined nostalgia as he says, "I would look out the window and through the skyscrapers, I could see the lights of Victoria Harbour. Each time I think about the beautiful scene, I felt like I was in Shanghai." In the course of making *Victim*, Lam admits, "My state of mind was really up and down" and "I put in Bai Guang's songs as a nostalgic allusion to bygone days."[19] In the place of the conventional scream, Bai Guang's songs as sensuous, tender vocal work evokes a coziness which, through the music records of a nostalgic-culture industry, provides a home for the writer-director. In old-time Shanghai songs, then, Lam finds a virtual maternal presence to bear him to a utopian time-space that is the very contrast of the time-pressed characters in a world city that he portrays. The Lau Ching-wan character also plays nostalgic compact discs (CDs) of Bai Guang's songs in his depressed state of mind.

Genres ranging from action to melodrama to hybrid films have featured the wearied, tender, and sensuous sounds of Chinese women singers. In Hong Kong films of the last three decades, Anita Mui (*Homecoming, Sishui liunian*, 1984), Teresa Tang (*Comrades, Almost a Love Story*, *Tan mi mi,* 1996) and Tsai Chin (*Infernal Affairs*, *Wu jian dao*, 2002) have created a rich sonic dimension to resonate with the films' motifs of memory, conflicting relationship with the Chinese homeland, migration, alienation, nostalgia, unresolved identity crisis, and death in the city. The imagined plenitude of women's tender singing voices, nevertheless, is kept in a utopian space. In *Victim*, Bai Guang's is a disembodied singing voice coming through amplifiers. The Cantonese mother shows up only briefly, with a Filipino houseworker, at her daughter Fu's request to come to Manson's house. Her only line of conversation to Fu is to eat well. The time that these women shared, presumably to talk about how to carry through trying circumstances, is compressed into one shot of arrival and one of departure that last for a few screen seconds altogether. What shuts Fu out of Manson's emotional struggle is operative on the level of the film's design, and not just on the level of the story. A film about men struggling with their own affective barriers and the crisis of having negative assets has replicated a male-centered, and action-effects prone narration. It has an axiomatic lack that points to the negative asset of sexism. Failure to integrate women's affective work in the filmic narration shows that Lam and his team have not left behind the trappings of a "market-sense of male citizenship" elaborated by Aihwa Ong, even as Lam is one of the few directors still attentive to the urban nightmares in Hong Kong.

## *Historicism in a Translocal Context*

Ringo Lam has established his name with the action-filled "On Fire" films: *City on Fire* (*Long hu feng yun* 1987), *Prison on Fire 1* (*Jian yu feng yun*

1987), *Prison on Fire 2* (*Jian yu feng yun: tao fan,* 1991), and *School on Fire* (*Xue xiao feng yun*, 1988). These films are relentless with hard-hitting urban realism, and their male protagonists are shown to be torn between a collapsing moral world and disintegrating social institutions. Lam's crisis cinema caught the attention of critics Lisa Stokes and Michael Hoover, who titled their study of Hong Kong cinema *City on Fire*[20], giving recognition to Lam's vision of the city that is as much about dreams as about nightmares. If in director John Woo's movie-world honor constitutes the basis for nostalgia, in Lam's postnostalgic, crisis-ridden world there is no vanishing cause to save, only repetitions of destructive incidents that make ruins out of myths. The allegorical city on fire had the year 1997 to face as marking the unknown beginning of its handover to the People's Republic of China. Returning from a short stint directing for Hollywood, Lam made *The Suspect* (1998), a crime thriller produced by Hong Kong's Sil-Metropole Company and shot in the Philippines with the Asian film market in mind. Making *Victim* allegorize the city's crisis by enjoining the failure of family romance and the middle-class economic-miracle myth, Lam's mixed genre approach has clear limitations, and director Fruit Chan's haunted figures in a realist setting, or Andrew Lau and Allen Mak's psychologically intricate *Infernal Affairs* trilogy are two different approaches in telling complex stories in the city.

Critic Wong Ain-ling commented that *Victim* was an awaited work that responded to the social reality of Hong Kong. She juxtaposed Lam and Kubrick, whom she thinks both make films about middle-class vulnerability and manhood's corrosion. Besides the obvious parallel, *Victim*'s story of closed roads and diminished future prospects for Hong Kong's residents contains a historicist reading of the success myth. In retrospect, the years from the 1960s to the 1990s were a golden time for upward social mobility. Having weathered the riots of the late 1960s, Hong Kong remade itself through regional and global capitalism, turning into a world city by serving transnational and translocal businesses and investments. For many young men, the rags-to-riches story of tycoon Li Ka-shing is a living myth and Li is the central figure of this grand narrative of Asian capitalism. The propagation of this myth in the 1990s continues even when the road to that kind of opportunity-filled accumulation of wealth is no longer available in Hong Kong. It is in this respect that a future without prospect in Ringo Lam's *Victim* connects to the historicist readings of Stanley Kubrick's *The Shining* that Tony Williams and Fredric Jameson have made. Jameson noted that "Kubrick's hero is already a reflective commentary . . . [he] is not a writer, but rather someone who . . . lives a fantasy about what the American writer is, along the lines of James Jones or Jack Kerouac."[21] More tellingly, "that fantasy is anachronistic and nostalgic," because "all those unexplored interstices of the system, which allowed the lumpens of the fifties to become, in their turn, figures of the 'Great American Writer' have long since been absorbed into the sealed and achieved space of consumer society." As *Victim* references this American film in telling a story of the closing of paths to miraculous success in the city, the ruins in the film connect translocally to other ruins of capital. Besides, as horror and suspense have global purchase, a translocal historicist reading of *Victim* as a sequel to *The Shining* is also about the Americanization of popular culture in this part of the world.

## Away from the Affective Culture of Female Ghosts

In 1987, Stanley Kwan's ghost film *Rouge* conjured the return of a love-obsessed female spirit. Its local acclaim overlapped with the rise of a local nostalgia industry that lasted for about a decade. Moving away from *Rouge*'s alluring brothel and leisurely erotic practices, the urban ruins of passion in *Victim* show the faint chalk marks that outline a decapitated female body in a gloomy house where the family lived. This departure from the golden hues of *Rouge*'s spectral passions that Rey Chow has written about calls attention to its difference from Hong Kong cinema's compendium of female love idealized as obsessive and fearless. As it turns out, the ghost genre that appeared in the early 2000s mines the fears and fantasies of unemployment in other ways, often taking up the idioms of Japanese horror films and Hollywood movies. Another New Wave director, Ann Hui, revived her career with the titles *Visible Secret* (*Youling renjian*, 2000) and *Visible Secret* 2 (*Youling Renjian zhi guiwei rejian*, 2002). In these films, the female ghost is no longer a romanticized giver of selfless love in the deprived, traditional, male scholar's fantasies. Nor is she a form of sensuous resistance to modernity's cold, linear temporality. The 1980s ghost imaginations are gone, and the disappearance of a ghost doing the work of affection prompts the question of whether the postmodern market of affective labor is now the business of transnational domestic workers. These women workers have taken on a spectral motherhood for middle-class Hong Kong families, as in the Filipino mother-surrogate in Fruit Chan's *Little Cheung* (*xilu xiang* 1999).

As Hong Kong's economy is entwined with Chinese capitalism, it is illustrative to read the comments of a visiting Chinese scholar published in *Hong Kong's Economic Journal Monthly.* Writing in 2000, Yi Xiao-rong characterizes globalization as "a competition in which the weak [are] devoured by the strong, and we must try to become the strong one in the equal competition of financial globalization."[22] Yi speaks of the survival of the fittest but uses "we" to refer to financial citizens of the Chinese nation, which is a symptom of a self-defeating discourse in either the class or community context. Habitual reference to an abstract community of "us" in essays like Yi's reiterates the contradictions that can be compared to adopting traditional symbols to stage continuity with tradition while in fact it is monopolistic power that people are after. The city that produces the looks of capital makes their nostalgic songs and tender ghost figures in cultural productions. And these have been staged for years to pass for passionate work.

## Notes

1. For "Brand Hong Kong" campaign details see: htto://www.brandhk.gov.hk/brandhk/eview.htm. Tung Chee-Hwa, HKSAR's first Chief Executive, told guests at the 2001 Fortune 500 Global Forum in May 2001, "Our vision is to make Hong Kong playing the same role [for China?] as London plays for Europe and New York plays for North and South America."

2. Manuel Castells, *The Information Age: Economy, Society and Culture, Volume III: End of Millennium* (1998), 67. The basis of this reference is the presence of old-fashioned paternalism in the SAR government that retained Chinese statism while being savvy about modern information technology.

3. David Harvey, *Spaces of Capital: Towards a Critical Geography* (New York: Routledge, 2001), 394–411. The notion of "world city" is informed by Saskia Sassen's *Globalization and Its Discontents* (New York: The New Press, 2001), among other studies.

4. See Helen Grace, "Monuments and the Face of Time: Distortions of Scale and Asynchrony in Postcolonial Hong Kong," *Postcolonial Studies*, Vol.10, No.4 (2007), 467–483.

5. Michael Hardt, "Affective Labor," *Boundary 2* (Summer, 1999), 95. My use of "affective work" also refers to Antony Negri's "Value and Affect" in the same issue, in which Negri argues against macroeconomics by theorizing the value of affect as "beyond measure." Negri also notes that globalization involves "the absorption of all of social life within capitalist production" (82–83).

6. Raymond Williams, *Marxism and Literature* (Oxford: Oxford University Press, 1986), 115.

7. Michael Hardt, "Affective Labor," 89–100, and Ibid., 99.

8. Aihwa Ong, *Flexible Citizenship: The Cultural Logics of Transnationality* (Durham: Duke University Press, 1999), 118–119. Also, Aihwa Ong and Donald Nonini, eds., *Ungrounded Empires: The Cultural Politics of Modern Chinese Transnationalism* (New York: Routledge, 1997), 164–166.

9. Bryan Chang, "We Are Not Normal People," in *The 24th Hong Kong International Film Festival: Hong Kong Panorama 1999–2000* (Hong Kong: Leisure and Cultural Services Department, 2000), 90–91.

10. The tragic killing and suicide committed by a father of three children shocked the whole city in early June, 1999. Hong Kong newspapers continue to report on tragic incidents like this one in the 2000s.

11. One film that deals with unemployment appearing in the same year was Joe Ma's comedy, *Afraid of Nothing: The Jobless King* (1999), about a chief executive officer who is fired from his job. Joe Ma produced Ringo Lam's *Victim* (1999).

12. Wong Ain-ling, "Men Can't Fail," *Hong Kong Economic Journal*, October 22, 1999, reprinted in *The 24th Hong Kong International Film Festival: Hong Kong Panorama 1999-2000*, 57.

13. Jacques Derrida, *Specters of Marx: The State of the Debt, the Work of Mourning, and the New International*, trans. Peggy Kamuf (New York and London: Routledge, 1994), xix.

14. Bliss qua Lim links the critical implications of time and the "fantastic" Asian films in "Spectral Times: The Ghost Film as Allegory," *positions: east asian cultural critique*, Vol.9, no.2, fall 2001, 287–299.

15. Ye Nianchen, "The Sense of Suspense and Horror: Ringo Lam's *Victim*," *The 24th Hong Kong International Film Festival: Hong Kong Paranorma 1999–2000*, 55–56.

16. Roland Barthes, *Camera Lucida: Reflections on Photography* (New York: Hill and Wang, 1981), 40.

17. Barbara Creed, "Horror and the Monstrous-Feminine: An Imaginary Abjection," Barry Keith Grant, ed., *The Dread of Difference: Gender and the Horror Film* (Austin, TX: University of Texas Press, 1996), 44.

18. Ye Nianchen, "The Sense of Suspense and Horror: Ringo Lam's *Victim*," 56.

19. Ibid., 56.

20. Lisa Odham Stokes and Michael Hoover, *City on Fire: Hong Kong Cinema* (London, New York: Verso, 1999).

21. Fredric Jameson, *Signatures of the Visible* (New York and London: Routledge, 1992), 82–98. Also, Tony Williams, *Hearths of Darkness: The Family in the American Horror Film* (New Jersey: Associated University Press, 1996), 247–248.

22. Yi Xian-rong, "Financial Globalization: Phenomena, Causes, and Prospects," *Hong Kong Economic Journal Monthly* 276 (March 2000): 3–9.

# 19

# Zhang Yimou's *Hero*

## *The Temptations of Fascism*

Evans Chan

> *The "privatization" of art is a necessary part of the peaceful aftermath of the Stalinist campaigns of centralization, but this does not mean a resurgence of individualism. Rather, it is a sign of the permanent assimilation of the individual. The post-Stalinist artist is a model of the new individual. The state points to him to illustrate how expertise and talent must be utilized.*
>
> —Miklos Haraszti[1]

> *Of course, I still first consider whether or not a film will be approved—this is a question that's always existed. When you make a film in China, you will definitely confront it. It's about survival, and only next is artistic value. If you can't survive, then where does this value come from? If you can't shoot, then isn't it a waste of time to talk about it? It's useless.*
>
> —Zhang Yimou, from a 1999 interview[2]

## Dancing with the Censors

No other People's Republic of China (PRC) filmmaker has performed a more complex dance with the official censors in the last twenty years than Zhang Yimou, who, along with Gong Li, the actress whose career he launched, is almost synonymous with Chinese cinema internationally. Zhang is a master at finding a simple story as a vehicle for his cinematic art. As the cinematographer for *The Yellow Earth* (*Huang tu di*, 1984), his first film project, he definitely displayed his share of the Fifth Generation filmmakers' critical, inquiring spirit, which emerged from the ruins of the Cultural Revolution to participate in China's rocky reintegration into the global system. But mixed in with his corpus of penetrating critiques of power is a no-less-glaring streak of pernicious apology for a (post)totalitarian regime, of which *Hero* (2002), his biggest-budget and seemingly most commercial film to date, might be the stupendous summation.[3]

Zhang's *To Live* (*Huozhe*, 1994) will remain an eminent example of his presentation of Chinese history on an epic canvas. In this film you can also find Zhang's subtlest dismissal of the Communist-Socialist regime. The film is scripted with a comic tone, meaning that the ups and downs of the protagonist's fortunes always hinge on something fortuitous. Originally a landlord's son, the ne'er-do-well protagonist Fu Gui loses his inherited wealth by gambling; as it turns out, Fu has also blessedly pawned off his undesirable (feudalist) class background when the Communists arrive. Underneath its comic veneer, the tragedy of the Great Leap Forward and the Cultural Revolution campaigns unfolds. (Another comic mishap ends up costing the life of Fu's daughter.) *To Live* is a piece of "humanist cinema," as indicated by its title, which suggests the Chinese people's obdurate will to survive. The caveat we have with certain humanist cinema may be that almost every character is delineated as essentially a "good" person. People misbehave only because of the force of circumstances. Thus, in *To Live*, even the notorious Red Guards are glimpsed as frightened kids who botch, tragically, a birthing process.

There is a scene in the middle of the film, in which Fu Gui tells a story to his son: A small chick will grow up into a goose; a goose will turn into a sheep; a sheep into an ox; oxen into . . . Communism, which will bring meat and dumplings every day. The scene is reprised at the end when an elderly Fu Gui, after losing both his children to the Great Leap Forward and the Cultural Revolution, repeats the story to his grandson: a chick turns into a goose, a goose into a sheep, a sheep into an ox. Yet instead of saying oxen will turn into Communism, Fu Gui tells his grandson that he will ride first the oxen, then trains and airplanes. So Communism has been quietly dropped from the fairy tale of fulfillment and development in *To Live*, maybe the most daring and masterly film among the Zhang corpus.

As an internationally successful Chinese filmmaker with a "bad class" background (his father a Nationalist officer and his mother a medical doctor), Zhang has always been a target. His early films repeatedly ran into censorship problems. And China's Film Bureau decided that the only way of saving the Chinese film industry from total collapse would be by roping in filmmakers like Zhang to work for it. *To Live*, which was Zhang's fourth feature financed by overseas producers, quickly became a scapegoat of unspecified disapproval. Zhang was intimidated enough to cancel an intended visit to Cannes. His next film, *Shanghai Triad*, originally intended to be a French production, was instead taken over by the Shanghai Film Studio at the Film Bureau's prodding. (That could be the reason *Shanghai Triad* seems a lesser work of his.) From then on, Zhang would make films only for China's studios, and the Film Bureau had full censorship over his films.[4]

## Exploiting the Anti-Art Bias—The Story of Qiu Ju and Not One Less

In her book *Regarding the Pain of Others*, Susan Sontag observed that photography is one field of the arts that suffers from a prejudice against training and professionalism—an amateur's photo at times appears to be as good as those taken by established artists—because of "the bias toward the spontaneous, the rough, the imperfect." She maintains that there is no "comparable level playing field" in literature, the performing arts, or "in filmmaking, which is not guided to any significant degree by the anti-art prejudices of contemporary art photography."[5] However, the rough-and-spontaneous look does have an appeal in the film arts. For some filmmakers, an anti-art stance doesn't necessarily spring from a cultural bias, but can be an aesthetic and political decision. One prominent recent example is the Dogme Group, who, in their 1995 Manifesto, declared their objective of achieving "the ultimate democratization of the cinema" by riding the crest of the digital revolution.

In two of his most famous films—*The Story of Qiu Ju* (*Qui Ju da guan si*, 1992) and *Not One Less* (*Yi ge duo bu neng shao*, 1999)—Zhang has carefully introduced the anti-art bias in order to create an aura of "the spontaneous, the rough, the imperfect." But his goal has nothing to do with democratizing cinema. Zhang is not a Sixth Generation filmmaker who has been forced to go the route of guerrilla-filmmaking because of inadequate funding. Choosing a rough look is a deliberate and conscious move. In short, he wants the films to pass as *documentaries* by enshrining his style in a presumable modesty that is on a par with his heroines—those salt-of-the-earth heroines from peasant stock. Hence, *The Story of Qiu Ju* was shot in super-16mm with a lot of handheld movement to give it a gritty feel. *Not One Less* used hidden cameras to capture the most natural performances. And *Not One Less* went even further than *The Story of Qiu Ju* in using an entirely nonprofessional cast. These films have been acclaimed abroad. Zhang was hailed as an authentic successor to Italian neorealism. And the *New York Times* film critic A. O. Scott, echoing the French, saw in Zhang's films a single theme: "the heroic obstinacy of women who, with almost comical determination, succeed in bending the world to their own will."[6]

However, certain Chinese audiences do not feel exactly easy with the "realism" exhibited in these two films under discussion. Reportedly, it was no less than Li Ruihan, then head of the Propaganda Ministry, who personally viewed *The Story of Qiu Ju* and praised it as a film worthy of promulgating through the official propagandist channels.[7] Was China's foremost propaganda official so gullible, so tone-deaf to art, that he saw something entirely different from film academics and foreign critics? After *To Live*, Zhang's boldest put-down of the Communist system, and the mangled production situation of *Shanghai Triad*, *The Story of Qiu Ju* is Zhang's skillful attempt to reconcile with the party leadership. That it paid off not only politically at home—after *Qiu Ju*, two of Zhang's previously banned film were released in China—but critically abroad reveals Zhang's enormous talent in picking his subject, creating shades and shadows around his position, or simply covering his tracks, if you will.

After all, these two films are *not* documentaries, but fictional features adapted from novels and short stories, as the credits clearly show. Additionally, a more immediate question of realism concerns the validity of Zhang's women of the Qiu Ju variety, as well as the presumable readiness of the world—which is nothing less than a China that still fits the totalitarian mold—to bend to their wills. Both films are "social issues" films: *The Story of Qiu Ju* deals with redressing injustice, and *Not One Less* with rural China's education crisis. Writing for the *New York Review of Books*, Jonathan D. Spence sensed a "major false note" in *The Story of Qiu Ju* that concerns the film's presentation of the law enforcers and bureau personnel who, one by one in ascending levels of the government, lend an ear to Qiu Ju's complaint that her husband had been kicked in the testicles by the village chief, who has refused to apologize. Spence observed:

> These men—for they are all men—are presented without exception as being courteous and kindly, ever receptive to a simple peasant woman's right to complain. They are clean and neat and gentle. They never take bribes or even accept presents. . . . Surely to most Chinese in the PRC, and to any Westerners who have had business there, this presentation appears absurd, a mocking echo of all those legions of selfless "model cadres" who have filled Communist plays, films, and fiction since the 1930s.[8]

Undoubtedly Qiu's search for an official apology, three years after the Tiananmen crackdown, resonated with the Chinese public. Qiu Ju is both humility and persistence incarnate, the face of every Chinese person who has felt wronged by the government. Qiu Ju wants justice, but only in a "reasonable" way.[9] Through the plot's twist and turns, she finally gets what she wants, but the wheels of justice also seems to have spun out of control. If the film does its utmost to look "realistic," its tone, finally, is that of a certain kind of fairy tale—one in which the answered prayer is to be avoided. And *The Story of Qiu Ju* is indeed a fairy tale at heart. No wonder Spence was left wondering: "In this film there is not a single selfish official—except for Chief Wang [the testicle kicker] himself, and even he is redeemed at last by grace—to set off against the *sugary* state [my italics]. I left the film unsure whether this group portrayal was 'part of the joke' to Zhang Yimou, intended to be seen through at once, or whether it was"—Spence was onto something, just as some Chinese audiences at the time strongly suspected— "a peace offering to the powers-that-be in order to be left alone to pursue more important matters."

How "realistic" could this film be when the democratic uprising in Tiananmen only three years before was prompted most directly by abysmal corruption among the state sector? (Now look at all these selfless officials populating the bureaucracy!) Didn't the real-life drama in Tiananmen begin with some students on their knees begging simply for "dialogue" with the state officials? (And now Qiu Ju is met and addressed deferentially by officials all the way up the ladder. Compare fictional Qiu Ju with the real case of Li Guirong as reported by Nicholas Kristof in his June 7, 2007 op-ed column in the *New York Times*: Because of her protest and pursuit for justice when her husband was fired by a coal-mining company after a work-related injury, Li Guirong made many petitioning trips to Beijing, with the result that she was tortured, sexually humiliated, imprisoned in a mental asylum, and had her younger daughter taken away from her.) If Zhang's vision were, as Spence concluded, that of a China of "colossal—yet sugary?—indifference," then justice would not finally be carried out at all. (In *The Story of Qiu Ju*, when the system responds, it responds to a technicality: medical reports show that Chief Wang had also cracked a rib of Qiu Ju's husband. Even though the husband has totally recovered, Chief Wang is still guilty of assault—of the rib, not the testicles. Subsequently, Wang receives fifteen days' detention at the county center.) Or conversely, a system so embroiled in details and technicality would not have resorted to a *blatantly* exhibitionistic crackdown to begin with. The Tiananmen massacre is not a scene likely to occur in, say, a Kafka novel, which some critics are tempted to compare with Qiu Ju's experience with the PRC bureaucracy.

*The Story of Qiu Ju* is no doubt a slippery film to discuss. However, we can go back to Roland Barthes to look at some of the tools he left for analyzing myths. Barthes said that "myth is experienced as innocent speech: Not because its intentions are hidden— if they were hidden, they could not be efficacious—but because they are naturalized."[10] *The Story of Qiu Ju*'s intention is up front—dissecting the possibility of justice in post-Tiananmen China. What has been subtly "naturalized" is a benign bureaucracy's interaction with its citizens, achieved through Zhang's "anti-art, documentary" approach. The authoritarian state is ultimately humanized by its gentle servants and its final concern for justice, which brings us to the precise moment when its citizens feel chagrined by their insistence on justice. (When informed of Chief Wang's arrest, a stunned Qiu Ju blurts out, "I only want an apology, why an arrest?" Then she runs out of her house through the snow-covered country, following the blaring siren, presumably from the police car that is carrying Chief Wang away. She acts as though she is trying to stop the car, to repair the wrong she has done Wang. The film ends with a close-up of her pained, bewildered expression in freeze frame.)

Among the language of myths, Qiu Ju's ending is what Barthes would have described as "neither-norism," which consists of "stating two opposites and balancing the one by the other so as to reject both . . . a final equilibrium [that] immobilizes values, life, destiny, etc.: one no longer needs to choose, but only to endorse."[11] If the myths that Barthes discussed reinforce the bourgeois state, Zhang's subtle and dexterous film blends in with the totalitarian statecraft: Yes, it is not a matter of choosing, only endorsing the world as it is (or as it is surreptitiously altered in his film)—that is, a China that is not at all repressive, where the search for justice becomes a misguided utopian quest because the arrival of justice carries harmful, excessive force. With such a message, does it come as a surprise that a special video compact disc–digital video disc (VCD-DVD) edition of *The Story of Qiu Ju* was released by, among other government entities, the departments of Propaganda, Culture, and Information, to commemorate the fiftieth anniversary of the founding of the PRC? One doubts it is simply because *Qiu Ju* is an award-winning film.

## Creation Myths—Red Sorghum and The Road Home

In her perceptive discussion of *Red Sorghum*, Zhang Yimou's first film, Chinese critic Dai Jinhua observed that the film is set in the time of the narrator's grandparents, in an ahistorical, pastoral setting. The passionate illicit sexual union of Grandpa and Grandma, played by Jian Wen and Gong Li, in the red sorghum field actually "represents the Chinese Adam and Eve in the act of reconstructing the national myth . . . . it is a story about the grandeur of heroism and the power of a national, primitive life force."[12] This ahistorical community, which centers on a distillery, enters the stream of history by confronting the Japanese invasion. A member of this ur-society wanders outside Acadia and returns in the second half of the film as what Dai called "the transcendent father." He was a manager of the distillery; now he is a member of the Communist Party who, later, fearlessly curses the Japanese while being skinned alive by these horrendous invaders. And the grandparents who take over the distillery follow the lead of the dead to continue their sacrificial fight.

So from the very beginning, Zhang Yimou is a self-elected national-myth-maker— the nation being the new China under Communism. Remember, it was the Communists, rather than the Nationalists, who engaged in fighting off the Japanese, giving the Communists one of their strongest claims to running the nation (hence, "the transcendent father" Dai Jinhua hinted at in *Red Sorghum*). Apparently, Zhang's unquestioning ode to the bloody, heroic origin of the nation was shaken by the Tiananmen Massacre of 1989. *Ju Dou*, his second film, came out the following year. From this film on—through *Raise the Red Lantern*, *To Live*, and *Shanghai Triad*— Zhang became the most engaging, fiercely critical storyteller about the throttling hold of gerontocracy until, alas, the tightening grip of the state finally caught up with him.

The year 1987, when Zhang Yimou kicked off his filmmaking career with *Red Sorghum*, according to Dai Jinhua, is "a crucial moment in the history of New China, a moment rich with historical events and rare opportunity."[13] She was referring to the rehabilitation of Deng Xiao Ping ten years earlier, the onset of the four modernization programs, and the first taste of economic advancement among the Chinese. Such optimism would come tumbling down two years later when widespread graft and corruption set off political unrest and the subsequent crackdown at Tiananmen. However, the tragedy hardly hindered China's speedy economic growth. Barely two decades later, China's ascendancy on the international stage is an undisputed fact. China has joined the World Trade Organization, and it was none other than Zhang Yimou who directed the promotional movie for China's successful bid to host the 2008 Olympics. There is a newly gained confidence and probably still a deep-seated insecurity. Today's China is haunted by memories of its glorious past, its humiliation at foreign hands, and recently, self-inflicted acts of barbarism. After all, 1989 Tiananmen, as Paul Virilio reminds us, was the first democratic "uprising in a Communist regime played out, for the first time in real time, before the eyes of the entire world."[14]

## Recreating the Founding Myth—Fascist Hero

In *Hero*, Zhang Yimou harks back two millennia to reinvent the founding myth of China— not China as an ethnic, cultural entity, but China as an *empire*. And the impulse behind the film can be called fascist— it promotes a personality cult that claims oneness with the progression of the national destiny, and which inspires willful, bloody sacrifices. Zhang surely has examined sacrifices before—in *Red Sorghum*, heroic sacrifices are lauded for battling off alien invasion. Dai Jinhua points out that the first half of *Red Sorghum* is about a symbolic patricide and the establishment of a new order by the son. In *Hero,* we have a narrative moving in the opposite direction. Instead of patricide, we have Saturn devouring his children. The film is reinscribing an authoritarian old order, mythologized and naturalized through a perfect vehicle—the martial-arts film, the genre film *par excellence* to aestheticize combat and death.

*Hero* reappraises the place of Qin Shihuang (First Emperor of Qin) in Chinese history. The sudden fascination shown by both Zhang and his peer Chen Kaige, whose historical saga *The Emperor and the Assassin* (1998) covers the same subject, toward a figure whom the Chinese have always considered the ultimate autocrat is itself an interesting phenomenon. One surmises that this is a resonant moment for the resuscitation of Emperor Qin for the Chinese psyche: with China still being an authoritarian state, the Communist party seems eager to fan Nationalist sentiments to make up for the decline of the Socialist ideology in rallying unity. An immensely popular book, *China Can Say No* (*Zhong Guo Ke Yi Shuo Bu*), published in Beijing in 1994, is a polemic against America, against its demonization of the PRC in the post-Cold War era. So this is a moment of assertion. China seems ready to take on the United States in the coming duel between empires. Not surprisingly, during the recent Iraqi war, an American commentator prophesied the eventual showdown between the United States and China over access to global energy sources.

Chen Kaige's *The Emperor and the Assassin* is not exactly a piece of felicitous filmmaking. Yet it is an ambitious attempt at vivifying history by reaching into the dark recesses of a power-hungry tyrant's mind. The film does not deviate much from China's traditional understanding of Qin Shihuang, builder of the Chinese Great Wall, except by filling in the no-longer-familiar details—his queen mother's adultery, his bastardly origin, which he tries to hide by performing, in effect, a patricide, and his disowning of the woman he loves because of his ambition to quash the six other warring states to build a unified empire. To spice up history, Chen has Gong Li play the beauty that becomes a pawn between the Emperor and his defeated assassin; this facet of the story constitutes the less successful part of his film.

Unquestionably a sumptuous spectacle, Zhang Yimou's *Hero*, however, is the coldest, most calculating film he has ever made. The pseudo-Rashomonesque structure is not meant to examine motivations, rationalizations, or the unreliability of human perception. It is an unfolding plot device to lead us to the final epiphany— the assassin(s) must die. Jet Li, who plays the assassin, Nameless, gets an audience with the Emperor to tell stories about how he kills off other assassins; this enables him to gain the emperor's confidence. In this *danse macabre*, Nameless's tales are debunked one by one to reveal that all the other assassins are in fact sacrificing themselves for Nameless's final attempt at the emperor's life. (Fascism is of course interested in hierarchy—the propping up of Nameless as the top assassin to confront the emperor enacts a stylized succession of action spectacles. And ultimately the greatest swordsman submits himself to the emperor's messianic "Idea" by seeking death.)

The Chinese saying "the dagger at the end of the unrolled scroll" (*tu qiong bi xian*) actually originates from this famous historical episode, in which the assassin, disguising himself as a peace-offering consular officer, placates the emperor by showing him the map of his future conquests in a scroll. According to plan, as the assassin unrolls the scroll, he will arrive at his hidden dagger to stab the emperor. What happened, historically, was that the assassin missed and got killed instead. But in Zhang Yimou's stylized, radically revised, scroll-less retelling of this ancient tale, the dagger is in fact always hidden in the Emperor's hand. It is the dagger of empire-building and all the concurrent sacrifices that it demands.

It is hard not to see *Hero* as a full-length conceit—obviously the assassin recognizes, way ahead of "the moment of truth," the *necessity* of the empire-building machinery embodied by Qin Shihuang. It has been suggested that one way to read the film concerns what made Nameless's stories possible. Is he telling only the stories that are pleasing to Qin Shihuang's ears? I do not think this is a convincing reading, unless Nameless is a captive from the beginning; whereas the *raison d'être* for his action, thus *Hero*'s narrative, is to gain Emperor Qin's confidence in order to slay him. So it is just the director's manipulated suspense that leads the audience to the crucial moment when Nameless gives up his carefully conceived plan to assassinate the emperor—sacrificing his own life, as well as those of other assassins.

The cruel joke, at least on this writer, is that Nameless is seeking, from the beginning, a suicidal ritual to exalt the emperor's mission. And Tony Leung's character, Broken Sword, another assassin, is the primary inspiration that reinforces Nameless's conviction, because Broken Sword embraces the emperor's imperialist ambitions, even though his own home state, already a victim of horrific atrocities, will be totally vanquished. (Are we on war propaganda terrain?) To plead his case with Nameless, Broken Sword uses his sword to scrape two Chinese characters in the desert sand: Heaven (*Tian*) and Earth (*Xia*). They are translated as "All Under Heaven" in the English subtitles. Yes, *Tian Xia* refers to the world, or in this context the Chinese's known world. If *Tian Xia*, torn among the warring states, could submit itself to the unifying might of Qin, ponders Nameless, then peace can be established and individual sacrifices would not have been made in vain. The question is, we may ask—are Nameless and Broken Sword talking about "individual" sacrifices? How individual could it be when their sacrifices involve hundreds of thousands of civilians in the would-be subjugated states? Zhang Yimou has finally portrayed Qin Shihuan as a misunderstood philosopher-king, whose weepy self trembles under the false disguise of being a tyrant when his real intention is to bring universal peace to *Tian Xia* through war and conquests, that is, building an empire. With tears in his eyes, Zhang's sentimentalized Qin Shihuang realizes that Broken Sword, the wanted assassin, is the one radiant intelligence that sheds light on the deepest secret of his peace-loving heart. (Among the many Chinese postings about *Hero* that bounced through the Internet, one gave a tongue-in-cheek homoerotic reading of the film. While the posting was an intentional joke, homoeroticism is of course compatible with fascist aesthetics, which always strive to fashion a leader with a charisma that is exceptional enough to summon total surrender of body and mind.)

By allowing Qin Shihuang to "mumble-jumble" about the spirituality of the sword, Zhang elevates him to a mystical plane. Here's a leader who submits himself to a mystical mandate to attain peace; and in recognition of that spirituality, Nameless chooses to let the emperor live at the very cost of his own life. If such glorification of capitulation to a powerful leader is not fascist enough, wait for the final twist of Zhang Yimou's dagger—the emperor could have spared Nameless's life, but he does not, as he recognizes the sanity of the surrounding crowd's pleading that unless the assassin is executed, *the rule of law* in his kingdom will be compromised. Hence the emperor's assertion of mind over emotion is complemented by the assassin's emotion over mind, both an expression of a squeamish aversion to, hence ruthless suppression of, division, differences, and heterogeneity. Zhang Yimou's archeological finding is truly breathtaking.

## Debating Qin Shihuang's Legacy

In *Not One Less*, Zhang has recycled the Lei Fung myth from the ruins of the Cultural Revolution. And in *Hero*, he has recycled yet one more mythologized figure from the Cultural Revolution's insidious personality cult—Mao Zedong was the one who, unleashing a ferocious attack on Confucius, praised the virtues of Qin Shihuang. So what is Emperor Qin's most pronounced legacy today? First, the Great Wall: we know that its remnants do bring in quite a few tourist dollars. Second, his standardization of the written Chinese language: it has supposedly facilitated the absorption of subgroups with different dialects into the larger cultural and national unit that is China. But that is a simplification of the tension between language and speech, language and dialect. For example, in today's Taiwan, the Fujian dialect speakers are pushing for a nativist independence movement, thus displaying a marked hostility toward the Mandarin speakers. And we know that the island's people all read Chinese. Another example: north of the United States is Canada, an English-speaking neighboring country. Why are the United States and Canada not one country yet? And should they be? Are these not immediate examples that undercut the myth of language being the agent of cohesion?

Most importantly, the Qin regime did not bring millennial prosperity for the Chinese race, as is implied in *Hero*. The problem that plagued the Qin dynasty is the same as the one that threatened the political system of Communist China—the thorny issue of the succession of leadership. Emperor Qin had accomplished extraordinary engineering feats, including the building of the Great Wall, the Great Canal, and an extensive national road network, to shore up his kingdom. However, his empire collapsed three years after his death because his inept son quickly spurred widespread rebellions. And Qin Shihuang's decisions to burn dissenting books and massacre Confucian scholars are rightly remembered as infamous episodes of autocratic rule.

## The Temptations of Empire

So what does *Hero* leave us with? Why revise the Emperor Qin myth at this moment in Chinese history? Tony Leung's pro-Tiananmen crackdown statement, issued in response to queries about *Hero*, might have given us some clues.[15] However, *Hero* goes beyond being a merely rearguard defense of the 1989 government action. The film resonates with the awakened ambitions of Empire within contemporary China. Here is what Slavoj Zizek, a philosopher from a former Eastern block country, Slovenia, recently wrote:

> The key news from China 2002 was the emergence of a large-scale workers movement, protesting against the work conditions which are the price for China rapidly becoming the world's foremost manufacturing place, and the brutal way the authorities cracked down on it— a new proof . . . that China is today the ideal capitalist state: freedom for the capital, with the state doing the "dirty job" of controlling the workers. China as the emerging superpower of the twenty-first century thus seems to embody a new kind of ruthless capitalism: disregard for ecological consequences, disregard for workers' rights, everything subordinated to the ruthless drive to develop and become the new superpower.[16]

What Zizek alludes to is the new kind of post-Deng Xiaoping Socialism "with Chinese characteristics," in which the state becomes an active organizer of the painful process called "primitive capitalist accumulation" by Marxian economists. The fact that this troublingly compressed, or delayed, transformation is taking place in this era of postmodernity makes it a unique threat to global labor in general—by setting up a new low in wage levels that has created a race toward the bottom—and to Chinese labor in particular.[17] Yet it also gives the collective Chinese psyche an unusual headiness. Maybe there is a degree of historical parallel between the present moment and the times of Qin Shihuang. According to at least one Marxian reading, it was during the end of the Zhou period and the beginning of the Qin Empire in the second century B.C. that despotism emerged thanks to the rise of commercial capitalism and a commodity economy, which undermined the power of the feudal lords. The monarch could now concentrate power, protect the nobility and merchants, suppress peasant revolts, and create an encompassing state as the intermediary to reconcile conflicting forces and interests. Yet Chinese despotism, flanked by bureaucracy and mercenary armies, also perpetuated feudalist exploitation down through the centuries. And despite two millennia of periodic rebellions among the peasantry, China was never able to break out of a despotic, dynastic, precapitalist circularity.[18]

Is the current Chinese government picking up what the Qin Shihuang era left unfinished in terms of pushing China from a precapitalist into a capitalist economy— but to be accomplished through the distinct form of contemporary Chinese despotism still known as Socialism? This is where *Hero* seems so potent and insidious—it subliminally extols the current leadership, endowing it with a new messianic mission. It is also a rallying cry in order to mute dissent among the populace and to help them accept the ruthless flogging of the authoritarian, post-Socialist capitalist machine that is spinning in full force, with Zhang himself as one of its most valuable export items. The beast of superpowerdom is growing, salivating for sacrificial offerings. (One also should not forget that today's Xinjiang and Tibet provinces continue to be hotbeds of racial and ethnic unrest, requiring constant vigilance from the central government. Moreover, the intrepid Fa Lun Kung sect poses a strong psychological threat to the authorities; throughout China's dynastic cycles, such sects have been mobilizing forces among peasant revolts.) In this context, *Hero* has given China's dream of, and striving for, superpowerdom its most seductive and escapist face so far.

We can see *Hero* going beyond mere entertainment to work on at least two psychological levels for the Chinese audience. First, *Hero*'s production glamour, supposedly rivaling that of a Hollywood blockbuster, gave the public another pride-booster—one of having arrived on the international arena. Second, parts of the film were able to channel xenophobic, gung-ho anger toward the United States, China's archrival in global domination.

Often, superpowerdom and expansionism go hand-in-hand with an opportunistic leadership's cultivating among the public a sense, real or imaginary, of being victimized. I do not mean that China is now embarking on a seriously imperialistic military buildup. But a psychological war has been waged domestically, inflaming Nationalist sentiments and superpower fantasies, diverting the public from China's tough internal problems as it marches bloodily—for the first nine months of 2003, the official figure of industrial deaths at work stood at 11,500—into the global capitalist system.[19]

With the recent films of Zhang Yimou and Chen Kaige, one can readily see the menacing collusion between state censorship and commerce: only officially approved films can be released to China's huge domestic market. State disciplinary tactics use both sticks and carrots, but the Chinese carrots can now be studded, potentially, with diamonds. Hungarian poet and critic Miklos Haraszti once commented bitterly on the plight of artists working under Socialism, when the ethics of state Socialism seem indistinguishable from the ethics of a large company. He asked,

> Is it censorship that guarantees that the employees of Twentieth Century Fox will create movies that serve the interests of the entire company? Do relationships within the film studio require censoring? Is the unavoidable process of creative compromise and self-correction

> properly to be called censorship? Voluntary discipline, identification, and devotion are essential elements in the professional's acceptance of the company as his own. Is this not freedom? After all, didn't someone once observe that freedom is simply the recognition of necessity?[20]

Haraszti was writing then in Hungary, under a kind of what he termed "post-Stalin," "soft," and "civilian" Communist rule—as distinguished from its "hard," "military," "Stalinist" variant. It was 1987, and he sarcastically remarked on Gorbachev's attempts "to wrap more velvet on the bars of his prison in order to create a less primitive and more manageable order in the heart of his empire."[21] Haraszti's prescient statement fits only too well in today's China, a country practicing a hybrid Socialist state capitalism, or capitalist state Socialism, which has been celebrated, secretly or overtly, by the government and even the people themselves in reaction to what is understood as a cautionary tale of the 1989 Soviet disintegration. Today's filmmakers who can function well within the state directives in China will be cheered on by domestic and global capital. Alas, the kind of plush comfort awaiting them! Forget the velvet prison (which is also the title of Haraszti's book); it is virtually a velvet paradise. Hence the great divide yawning between approved films and underground films in the PRC today—the latter enterprise is essentially the domain of the Sixth Generation directors.

*Hero* is a powerful summation of the apologist streak in Zhang's work. However, look at that streak's humble beginning in dramatic terms: Qiu Ju seeks justice, but is finally appalled by the sight of justice in action. In *Hero*, the assassins also are looking for justice—presumably to save the world from a tyrant's devastation. But they end up finding justice on the side of power and determinedly pay with their lives to honor it. Zhang Yimou is now the closest thing to being the Leni Riefenstahl of China. Still one can't help wondering: since *Hero* is essentially a film about self-laceration—each assassin readily allows him or herself to be lashed, stabbed, pierced, or killed for some questionable greater good— is there a parallel act of self-laceration, artistic, psychological, spiritual, going on for the filmmaker of *Ju Dou* and *Raise the Red Lanterns*? Is Zhang—arguably China's leading filmmaker of the last two decades—the ultimate beneficiary or the victim of the Chinese censors? Yet, Zhang's dance with the state is a complex exercise of servitude, survival, and surging forth. After all, *To Live*, his most artful, politically audacious film, was made after *The Story of Qiu Ju*, his first conciliatory bow to the authorities.

There are of course other important filmmakers at work in the Chinese-speaking world today. (Some scholars and critics, including this writer, might have voted Hou Hsiao-Hsien as, artistically, the most outstanding contemporary Chinese filmmaker.) But none compares with

Zhang's unique positioning in the intricate tapestry of power and art woven by China, a driven economic giant, and by an evolving brand of global entertainment, niche-produced by Chinese cinema. After the seemingly purely commercial *House of Flying Daggers* (2004), Zhang's *Curse of the Golden Flower* (2006) is yet another interesting entry in the unfolding saga that is Zhang's intriguing and disturbing career, one worthy of not only the attention of the film community, but of observers of China's resurgence in the new millennium.

## Notes

This paper was previously published, in a longer version, in *Film International* # 8 (March 2004), a "film and dictatorship" special issue, guest-edited by Charlotte Sjöholm. A portion of the piece was first presented at the *From the Book to the Internet* conference organized by Arif Dirlik at the University of Oregon in mid-October 2003. I appreciate the Chinese gay *Hero* joke that Mirana Szeto sent me, and I benefited from the critiques of Chris Berry, Chris Connery, Shih Shumei, Zhang Xudong, Rob Wilson, and Dirlik himself, whose book *Marxism and Revolution* enabled me to look at Qin Shihuang from the perspective of Marxist historiography. My special thanks to the close readings of Marina Heung, and Russell Freedman, and to Gina Marchetti and Tan See-Kam, editors of this volume, for their invitation to include the essay in this abridged form.

1. Miklos Haraszti, *The Velvet Prison: Artists Under State Socialism* (New York: Basic Books. 1987), 97.

2. Yeung Wai-lan, "Zhang Yimou: No Going Back," in Frances Gateward, ed., *Zhang Yimou: Interviews* (Jackson: University Press of Mississippi, 2001), 150.

3. I understand that the term "totalitarian" can be problematic, as Slavoj Zizek has so valiantly argued in *Did Somebody Say Totalitarianism?* (2001). However, I cannot discard this term completely in describing today's China, even though over there it may already be a form of totalitarianism in transition. Today's China seems to operate in what Haraszti describes as a post-Stalinist stage regarding its censorship control.

4. See Tony Rayns, "China: Censors, Scapegoats and Bargaining Chips," in Ruth Petrie, ed., *Film and Censorship: The Index on Censorship Reader* (London: Cassell, 1997) p. 161–168.

5. Susan Sontag, *Regarding the Pain of Others* (New York: Farrar, Straus and Giroux, 2003), 28–29.

6. A. O. Scott, "Women of China, Chasing Their Impossible Dreams," *New York Times* (27 May 2001). This is a review of Zhang Yimou's *The Road Home.*

7. Xiao Wei, "Mainland Art and Literature World Turns Against the Left on the Eve of the Fourteenth Party Congress," *China Times Weekly* 35 (30 August 1992): 14–15.

8. Jonathan D. Spence, "Unjust Desserts," *New York Review of Books* (24 June 1993).

9. This involves a scene in *The Story of Qiu Ju*, in which Qui Ju asks the professional letter-writer in the district town to write a complaint. After finding out that a "merciless" complaint can lead to a death sentence, a horrified Qiu Ju pays to have a "reasonable" complaint written for her.

10. Roland Barthes, *Mythologies*, trans. Annette Lavers (New York: Hill and Wang, 1972), 131.

11. Ibid., 153.

12. Dai Jinhua, *Cinema and Desire* (London and New York: Verso, 2002), 36.

13. Ibid., 32.

14. Paul Virilio, *Desert Screen: War at the Speed of Light* (London and New York: Continuum 2002), 59.

15. In response to the controversy over *Hero*'s political message, Tony Leung told a Hong Kong magazine that he thought that the Chinese government did the right thing by clamping down on the Tiananmen demonstrators in 1989 in order to maintain stability. Leung later claimed that his comment was taken out of context and that he was only interested in acting, not politics. See Joseph Kahn, "Film on Ruthless Dynasty Delights China's Leaders," (*The New York Times*, January 2, 2003)

16. Slavoj Zizek, *Welcome to the Desert of the Real* (London and New York: Verso, 2002), 146–147.

17. The *New York Times* has published a series of articles about the occupational hazards of industrial workers in China, posted online (http://www.nytimes.com/interactive/2007/08/26/world/asia/choking_on_growth.html). Another useful Web site for understanding labor conditions in China is *China Labour Bulletin* (www.china-labour.org.hk/en ), founded in 1994 in Hong Kong by independent trade unionist Han Dongfang, who was once jailed for being a "black hand" behind the 1989 Tiananmen uprising.

18. Arif Dirlik, *Revolution and History: Origin of Marxist Historiography in China, 1919–1937* (Berkeley: University of California Press, 1978), 209–210.

19. Joseph Kahn, "Foul Water and Air Part of Cost of the Boom in China's Exports," *New York Times* (4 November 2003). After reporting a case of two deaths caused by a pharmaceutical plant's sending unprotected workers to handle poisonous chemical waste, Kahn noted: "[The] case suggested that the enormous human and environmental toll of China's rapid development is not just an unintended side effect but also an explicit choice of business executives and officials who tolerate deaths and degradation as the inevitable price of progress."

20. Miklos Haraszti, *The Velvet Prison*, 68.

21. Ibid., 161.

# Appendix A

## *On Chinese Names*

In the People's Republic of China (PRC), *pin yin* is the official romanization system for transcribing Chinese names, words, and phrases. Primarily based on Mandarin phonemes, it is also presently the most widely used system in the world. It is therefore our preferred choice for this anthology.

However, we also recognize that unlike PRC nationals, a good majority of people of Chinese origin living in the Chinese diasporic world do not always have a *pin yin* name—for example, Ng Yue Sam. Please replace "The phonemic basis for the two . . . is Wu Yusen" with "The phonemic basis for this romanized name is Cantonese, which is the *lingua franca* of Hong Kong, where Ng Yue Sam made his name as a premier film director. Its *pin yin* equivalent is Wu Yusen." To distinguish between romanized dialect names and *pin yin* (Mandarin) names, we give the following cues at the first occurrence of any Chinese personal name: (1) In the case of a PRC national, we will give the name only once and in *pin yin* only—for instance, Zhang Yuan and Zhang Yimou. (2) In the case of a non-PRC national, we will present the romanized dialect name first, followed by its *pin yin* equivalent in parenthesis—for example, Ng Yue-Sam (Wu Yusen); if such persons have no known Romanized dialect name, we will use *pin yin* to transcribe their Chinese name. The hyphen in "Yue-Sam" serves as a further indicator that this "double-barrel" given name is a dialect moniker, whereas Chinese given names rendered in *pin yin*, as a rule of thumb, would be conflated as one; hence Yusen, as in the case of Yimou.

The nomination sequence given in the above three examples closely abides to the Chinese practice of placing a person's surname before his or her given name, which in turn may consist of one or two words, as in Yuan, Yimou, or Yue-Sam (Yusen). Some people of Chinese origin, such as Khoo Kim-hai (Qiu Jinhai), have adopted a Western name: this Singaporean filmmaker is better known as Eric

Khoo. Some may adopt a Western name for religious reasons—for example, Yue-Sam also goes by the name of John, this being his Christian name. In such instances, the Western or Christian name of the person concerned would also be given at the first reference as well, using the Western nomination style—hence Eric Khoo, or John Ng Yue-Sam (Wu Yusen). Since the latter is most famously known as John Woo, we would use "John Woo" as the primary name for Ng Yue-Sam. In Hong Kong, the romanized surnames "Ng" and "Woo" are sometimes used interchangeably—they are the respective "English" homophones for the same Chinese surname, in both Cantonese and Mandarin. Finally, for people of Chinese descent who, for whatever reasons, have adopted the Western nomination sequence, such as Ang Lee, we reference them in accordance to their preferred choice.

# Appendix B

## *Chinese Names, Words, and Phrases*

COMPILED BY ELISABELA LARREA AND TAN SEE-KAM

| **Names/Words/ Phrases** | **Complex Script** (*fantizi*) | **Simplified Script** (*jiantizi*) |
|---|---|---|
| A Lan | 阿蘭 | 阿兰 |
| A-Cow (Huang Di)/ANiu | 阿牛 (黄弟) | 阿牛 (黄弟) |
| Ah Di/A Di | 阿娣 | 阿娣 |
| Ah Jung/A Rong | 阿榮 | 阿荣 |
| Ai Nu | 愛奴 | 爱奴 |
| A-Sheng/A Sheng | 阿勝 | 阿胜 |
| *baise kongbu* (*White Terror*) | 白色恐怖 | 白色恐怖 |
| *biaojie* (older female cousin) | 表姐 | 表姐 |
| Cai Yuanpei | 蔡元培 | 蔡元培 |
| Chan Ka-Seung, Gordon/ Chen Jiashang | 陳嘉上 | 陈嘉上 |
| Chan, Evans/Chen Yaocheng | 陳耀成 | 陈耀成 |
| Chan, Fruit/Chen Guo | 陳果 | 陈果 |
| Chan, Jackie/Cheng Long | 成龍 | 成龙 |
| Chan, Jordan/Chen Xiaochun | 陳小春 | 陈小春 |
| Chan, Peter/Chen Kexin | 陳可辛 | 陈可辛 |
| Chang Cheh/Zhang Che | 張徹 | 张彻 |
| Chang, Eileen/Zhang Ailing | 張愛玲 | 张爱玲 |
| Chang, Grace/Ge Lan | 葛蘭 | 葛兰 |
| Chang, Sylvia/Zhang Aijia | 張艾嘉 | 张艾嘉 |

| Names/Words/ Phrases | Complex Script (*fantizi*) | Simplified Script (*jiantizi*) |
|---|---|---|
| Chen Duxiu | 陳獨秀 | 陈独秀 |
| Chen Huaikai | 陳懷愷 | 陈怀恺 |
| Chen Kaige | 陳凱歌 | 陈凯歌 |
| Chen Shimei | 陳世美 | 陈世美 |
| Chen Shiang-Chyi/Chen Xiangqi | 陳湘琦 | 陈湘琦 |
| Chen Shui-bian | 陳水扁 | 陈水扁 |
| Chen, Joan | 陳冲= | 陈冲 |
| Cheng, Carol "Do Do"/ Zheng Yuling | 鄭裕玲 | 郑裕玲 |
| Cheung Kin-Ting, Alfred/ Zhang Jianting | 張堅庭 | 张坚庭 |
| Cheung Man-yuk, Maggie/ Zhang Manyü | 張曼玉 | 张曼玉 |
| Cheung, Jacob/Zhang Zhiliang | 張之亮 | 张之亮 |
| Cheung, Leslie/Zhang Guorong | 張國榮 | 张国荣 |
| *chi/qi* (energy) | 氣 | 气 |
| Chor Yuan/Chu Yuan | 楚原 | 楚原 |
| Chow Yun Fat/Zhou Runfa | 周潤發 | 周润发 |
| Chu Tien-wen/Zhu Tianwen | 朱天文 | 朱天文 |
| *ch'uan fa/quan fa* (Chinese boxing-art) | 拳法 | 拳法 |
| Chun Li | 春麗 | 春丽 |
| Chung, Christy/Zhong Liti | 鍾麗緹 | 钟丽缇 |
| Comrade Wang | 王同志 | 王同志 |
| Comrade Yang | 楊同志 | 杨同志 |
| Cui Jian | 崔建 | 崔建 |
| Cui Wei | 崔巍 | 崔巍 |
| *dang daibiao* (Party's representative) | 黨代表 | 党代表 |
| Deng Xiaoping | 鄧小平 | 邓小平 |
| Dongdan | 東單 | 东单 |
| Dr. Wong/HuangYisheng | 黃醫生 | 黄医生 |

| **Names/Words/ Phrases** | **Complex Script (*fantizi*)** | **Simplified Script (*jiantizi*)** |
|---|---|---|
| *Fangong kang E* (Oppose Communism, Resist the Soviet Union) | 反共抗俄 | 反共抗俄 |
| *fantizi* (complex Chinese characters) | 繁體字 | 繁体字 |
| Fish Man/Yu Fu | 漁夫 | 渔夫 |
| Fong/Fang Yanmei | 方艷梅 | 方艳梅 |
| Forbidden Palace/Zi Jin Cheng/Qu Gong | 紫禁城/故宮 | 紫禁城/故宫 |
| Fu Jie | 傅傑 | 傅杰 |
| Golden Harvest/Jia He | 嘉禾 | 嘉禾 |
| Gong Li | 鞏俐 | 巩俐 |
| *gongfupian* (kung fu films) | 功夫片 | 功夫片 |
| Guangzhou (formerly Canton) | 廣州 | 广州 |
| Hakka/*kejia* | 客家 | 客家 |
| Hou Hsiao-Hsien/Hou Xiaoxian | 侯孝賢 | 侯孝贤 |
| Hsiao Kang/Xiao Kang | 小康 | 小康 |
| Hu Jun | 胡軍 | 胡军 |
| *hu nan hu nü* | 忽男忽女 | 忽男忽女 |
| Hu Shi | 胡適 | 胡适 |
| *hua* (flowers) | 花 | 花 |
| *hua qiao* (overseas Chinese) | 華僑 | 华侨 |
| Huang Jianxin | 黃建新 | 黄建新 |
| Huang Shuqin | 黃蜀芹 | 黄蜀芹 |
| Hui On-Wah, Ann/Xu Anhua | 許鞍華 | 许鞍华 |
| Hung, Sammo/Hong Jinbao | 洪金寶 | 洪金宝 |
| *jianghu* (rivers and lakes) | 江湖 | 江湖 |
| *jiantizi* (simplified Chinese characters) | 簡體字 | 简体字 |
| Jin Xing | 金星 | 金星 |
| King Hu/Hu Jinquan | 胡金銓 | 胡金铨 |
| KMT/Guomindang | 國民黨 | 国民党 |

| **Names/Words/ Phrases** | **Complex Script** (*fantizi*) | **Simplified Script** (*jiantizi*) |
|---|---|---|
| Koo, Sam/Gu Jiaming | 顧家明 | 顾家明 |
| *kung fu/gong fu* | 功夫 | 功夫 |
| Kwan Kam-pang, Stanley/ Guan Jinpeng | 關錦鵬 | 关锦鹏 |
| Kwok, Crystal/Guo Jinen | 郭錦恩 | 郭锦恩 |
| Lai, Ivan/Li Jiming | 黎繼明 | 黎继明 |
| Lam Ling-Tung, Ringo/Lin Lingdong | 林嶺東 | 林岭东 |
| Lau Wai-Keung, Andrew/Liu Weiqiang | 劉偉強 | 刘伟强 |
| Lau, Carina/Liu Jialing | 劉嘉玲 | 刘嘉玲 |
| Law Kar-Ying/Luo Jiaying | 羅家英 | 罗家英 |
| Law, Clara/Luo Zhuoyao | 羅卓瑤 | 罗卓瑶 |
| Lee Wen-Ho/Li Wenhe | 李文和 | 李文和 |
| Lee, Ang/Li An | 李安 | 李安 |
| Lee, Bruce/Li Xiaolong | 李小龍 | 李小龙 |
| Lee, Theresa/Li Qihong | 李綺紅 | 李绮红 |
| Leung Ka-Fai, Tony/Liang Jiahui | 梁家輝 | 梁家辉 |
| Leung, Tony/Liang Chaowei | 梁朝偉 | 梁朝伟 |
| Li Cheuk-to/Li Zhuotao | 李焯桃 | 李焯桃 |
| Li, Jet/Li Lianjie | 李連杰 | 李连杰 |
| Lin Ching-hsia, Brigitte/Lin Qingxia | 林青霞 | 林青霞 |
| Lin Nong | 林農 | 林农 |
| Liu Haisu | 劉海粟 | 刘海粟 |
| Lu Xuechang | 路學長 | 路学长 |
| Lu Xun | 魯迅 | 鲁迅 |
| *luilang renkou* (mobile population) | 流浪人口 | 流浪人口 |
| Macao/Macau/Ao Men | 澳門 | 澳门 |
| *mah-jong/mahjong* | 麻將 | 麻将 |
| Maid Foon/Huan Gu | 歡姑 | 欢姑 |
| Mao Zedong/MaoTse-Tong | 毛澤東 | 毛泽东 |

| Names/Words/ Phrases | Complex Script (*fantizi*) | Simplified Script (*jiantizi*) |
|---|---|---|
| May Fourth Movement/Wusi Yundong | 五四運動 | 五四运动 |
| Mi Jiashan | 米家山 | 米家山 |
| min-nan-jen/*minnanren* | 閩南人 | 闽南人 |
| *Minzhu qiang* (Democracy Wall) | 民主牆 | 民主墙 |
| Mui, Anita/Mei Yanfang | 梅艷芳 | 梅艳芳 |
| Nan Hai | 南海 | 南海 |
| Nanking Massacre/Nanjing Datusha | 南京大屠殺 | 南京大屠杀 |
| Nanyang | 南洋 | 南洋 |
| Neo, Jack/Liang Zhiqiang | 梁智強 | 梁智强 |
| Ng Chun-yu, Francis/Wu Zhenyu | 吳鎮宇 | 吴镇宇 |
| Ning Dai | 寧岱 | 宁岱 |
| Ning Ying | 寧瀛 | 宁瀛 |
| Pan Wenzhan | 潘文展 | 潘文展 |
| Peking University/Beijing Daxue | 北京大學 | 北京大学 |
| *qikung/qigong* (shadow boxing) | 氣功 | 气功 |
| Qin | 秦 | 秦 |
| Qin Shi Huang | 秦始皇 | 秦始皇 |
| Qing Dynasty/Qing Chao | 清朝 | 清朝 |
| *qing gong* (weightless martial-arts skills) | 輕功 | 轻功 |
| *qingmei zhuma* (childhood sweethearts) | 青梅竹馬 | 青梅竹马 |
| Qiong Yao/Qong Yao | 瓊瑤 | 琼瑶 |
| Qiu Ju | 秋菊 | 秋菊 |
| Red Guards/*Hongweibing* | 紅衛兵 | 红卫兵 |
| Revoluntaroy Model Performances (Geming yangbanxi) | 革命樣板戲 | 革命样板戏 |
| Rose/Mei Gui | 玫瑰 | 玫瑰 |

| **Names/Words/ Phrases** | **Complex Script** (*fantizi*) | **Simplified Script** (*jiantizi*) |
|---|---|---|
| Ruan Lingyu | 阮玲玉 | 阮玲玉 |
| Sang Hu | 桑弧 | 桑弧 |
| Sek Kei/Shi Qi | 石琪 | 石琪 |
| Shanbei | 陝北 | 陕北 |
| Shandong | 山東 | 山东 |
| Shanghai | 上海 | 上海 |
| Shanghai Art School (Shanghai Meishu Zhuanke Xuexiao) | 上海美術專科學校 | 上海美术专科学校 |
| Shanghai Film Studio (Shanghai Dianying Zhipian Chang) | 上海電影製片廠 | 上海电影制片厂 |
| Shaolin Temple | 少林寺 | 少林寺 |
| Shenzhen | 深圳 | 深圳 |
| Shi Xiaohua (Xiao Shi) | 史小華 (小史) | 史小华 |
| Shu Lea Cheang/Zheng Shuli | 鄭淑麗 | 郑淑丽 |
| Shu Qi | 舒淇 | 舒淇 |
| Si Han | 司汗 | 司汗 |
| Street Fighter (video game)/ *jietou bawang* | 街頭霸王 | 街头霸王 |
| *su jiu* (talking about the past) | 訴舊 | 诉旧 |
| Sun Yat-Sen/Sun Zhongshan | 孫中山/孫逸仙/孫文 | 孙中山/孙逸仙/孙文 |
| Taibei New Park (Taipei Xin Gong Yuan) | 台北新公園 | 台北新公园 |
| Taipei (Taibei) | 台北 | 台北 |
| Taiwan | 台灣 | 台湾 |
| *Taiyu pian* (Taiwanese films) | 台語片 | 台语片 |
| Tang Danian | 唐大年 | 唐大年 |
| Tang Xiaobing | 唐小兵 | 唐小兵 |
| Tao Jin | 陶金 | 陶金 |
| Three Kingdom/San Guo | 三國 | 三国 |
| *tian xia* (under the heavens; the Chinese world) | 天下 | 天下 |
| Tian Zhuangzhuang | 田壯壯 | 田壮壮 |

| **Names/Words/ Phrases** | **Complex Script** (*fantizi*) | **Simplified Script** (*jiantizi*) |
|---|---|---|
| Tiananman Square | 天安門廣場 | 天安门广场 |
| To Kei-fung, Johnnie/Du Qifeng | 杜琪峰 | 杜琪峰 |
| Tong Shu Shuen/Tang Shuxuan | 唐書璇 | 唐书璇 |
| *tongzhi* (comrades; slang for sexual minorities) | 同志 | 同志 |
| Tsai Ming-Liang/Cai Mingliang | 蔡明亮 | 蔡明亮 |
| Tsang, Eric/Zeng Zhiwei | 曾志偉 | 曾志伟 |
| Tsinghua University/Qinghua Daxue | 清華大學 | 清华大学 |
| Tsui Hark/Xu Ke | 徐克 | 徐克 |
| Wan Hua | 萬華 | 万华 |
| Wan Yanhai | 萬延海 | 万延海 |
| Wang Jiayi | 王家乙 | 王家乙 |
| Wang Jin | 王進 | 王进 |
| Wang Xiaoshuai | 王小帥 | 王小帅 |
| Wenhua da geming (Cultural Revolution) | 文化大革命 | 文化大革命 |
| *wenjian* (document) | 文件 | 文件 |
| Wong Kar-Wai/Wang Jiawei | 王家衛 | 王家卫 |
| Wong, Faye/Wang Fei | 王菲 | 王菲 |
| Woo, John aka Yue-Sam/Wu Yusen | 吳宇森 | 吴宇森 |
| *wudapian* (*kung fu* or unarmed-combat films) | 武打片 | 武打片 |
| *wushu* (martial arts) | 武術 | 武术 |
| *wuxiapian* (martial arts films) | 武俠片 | 武侠片 |
| *wuxia xiaoshuo* (martial-arts novels) | 武俠小說 | 武侠小说 |
| Xia Gang | 夏鋼 | 夏钢 |
| Xiao Gong Yuan | 小公園 | 小公园 |
| Xidan | 西單 | 西单 |

| Names/Words/ Phrases | Complex Script (*fantizi*) | Simplified Script (*jiantizi*) |
|---|---|---|
| Xie Jin | 謝晉 | 谢晋 |
| Xie Tieli | 謝鐵驪 | 谢铁骊 |
| Xinjiang | 新疆 | 新疆 |
| *xuesheng dianying* (student films) | 學生電影 | 学生电影 |
| *yang* | 陽 | 阳 |
| Yang Kuei-Mei/Yang Guimei | 楊貴媚 | 杨贵媚 |
| Yang, Edward/Yang Dechang | 楊德昌 | 杨德昌 |
| Ye Daying | 葉大鷹 | 叶大鹰 |
| Ye Shaoweng | 葉紹翁 | 叶绍翁 |
| Yeoh, Michelle/Yang Ziqiong | 楊紫瓊 | 杨紫琼 |
| *yin* | 陰 | 阴 |
| *Youhua renti yishu dazhan* (Nude Exhibition) | 油畫人體藝術大展 | 油画人体艺术大展 |
| Yuen Woo-Ping/Yuan Heping | 袁和平 | 袁和平 |
| Yuen, Anita/Yuan Yongyi | 袁詠儀 | 袁咏仪 |
| Yun, Daniel/Yun Huixiang | 雲暉翔 | 云晖翔 |
| Yunnan | 雲南 | 云南 |
| Zhang Nuanxin | 張暖忻 | 张暖忻 |
| Zhang Yimou | 張藝謀 | 张艺谋 |
| Zhang Yuan | 張元 | 张元 |
| Zhang Ziyi | 章子怡 | 章子怡 |
| *zhao le zi* (looking for fun) | 找樂子 | 找乐子 |
| Zhao Wei Films | 昭偉電影公司 | 昭伟电影公司 |
| *Zhongguo keyi shuo bu* (China can say No) | 中國可以說不 | 中国可以说不 |
| Zhongshan tang | 中山堂 | 中山堂 |
| Zhou Xiaowen | 周曉文 | 周晓文 |
| *zuguo* (ancestral country) | 祖國 | 祖国 |

# Appendix C

## *Chinese-Language Filmography*

COMPILED BY ELISABELA LARREA AND TAN SEE-KAM

| English Title (Production Year) | Chinese Title (in *pinyin*) | Complex Script (*fantizi*) | Simplified Script (*jiantizi*) |
|---|---|---|---|
| *12 Storeys* (1997) | *Shi'er lou* | 十二樓 | 十二楼 |
| *15—The Movie* (2003) | *Shiwu* | 十五 | 十五 |
| *2000 AD* (2000) | *Gongyuan 2000* | 公元2000 | 公元2000 |
| *A One and a Two* (2000) | *Yi Yi* | 一一 | 一一 |
| *Amnesty Decree* (1988) | *Renshe* | 人蛇 | 人蛇 |
| *Anti-Corruption* (1975) | *Lianzheng fengbao* | 廉政風暴 | 廉政风暴 |
| *Arch, The* (1970) | *Dong Furen* | 董夫人 | 董夫人 |
| *As Tears Go By* (1988) | *Wangjiao kamen* | 旺角卡門 | 旺角卡门 |
| *Ashes of Time* (1992–1994) | *Dongxie xidu* | 東邪西毒 | 东邪西毒 |
| *Banana Paradise* (1989) | *Xiangjiao tiantang* | 香蕉天堂 | 香蕉天堂 |
| *Bauhinia* (2002) | *Zijing* | 紫荊 | 紫荆 |
| *Beijing Bastards* (1992) | *Beijing zazhong* | 北京雜種 | 北京杂种 |
| *Beijing Bicycle* (2001) | *Shiqi sui de danche* | 十七歲的單車 | 十七岁的单车 |
| *Better Tomorrow, A* (1989) | *Yingxiong bense* | 英雄本色 | 英雄本色 |

| **English Title (Production Year)** | **Chinese Title (in *pinyin*)** | **Complex Script (*fantizi*)** | **Simplified Script (*jiantizi*)** |
|---|---|---|---|
| *Black Mask* (1996) | *Hei xia* | 黑俠 | 黑侠 |
| *Black Snow* (1989) | *Hei xue* | 黑雪 | 黑雪 |
| *Bodyguard from Beijing* (1994) | *Zhongnanhai baobiao* | 中南海保鏢 | 中南海保镖 |
| *Brighter Summer Day, A* (1991) | *Gulingjie shaonian sharen shijian* | 牯嶺街少年殺人事件 | 牯岭街少年杀人事件 |
| *Bullet in the Head* (1990) | *Die xue jietou* | 喋血街頭 | 喋血街头 |
| *Chungking Express* (1994) | *Chongqing xenlin* | 重慶森林 | 重庆森林 |
| *City of Sadness* (1989) | *Beiching chengshi* | 悲情城市 | 悲情城市 |
| *City on Fire* (1987) | *Longhu fengyun* | 龍虎風雲 | 龙虎风云 |
| *City Paradise* (1999) | *Doushi tiantang* | 都市天堂 | 都市天堂 |
| *Confucian Confusion, A* (1994) | *Duli shidai* | 獨立時代 | 独立时代 |
| *Conjugal Affairs* (1994) | *Xin tongju shidai* | 新同居时代 | 新同居时代 |
| *Crouching Tiger, Hidden Dragon* (2000) | *Wohu canglong* | 臥虎藏龍 | 卧虎藏龙 |
| *Crows and Sparrows* (1948) | *Wuya yu maque* | 烏鴉與麻雀 | 乌鸦与麻雀 |
| *Daughter of the Nile* (1987) | *Niluohe de nüer* | 尼羅河的女兒 | 尼罗河的女儿 |
| *Days of Being Wild* (1991) | *A fei zhengzhuan* | 阿飛正傳 | 阿飞正传 |
| *Days, The* (1993) | *Dongchun de rizi* | 冬春的日子 | 冬春的日子 |
| *Daughter of the Party* | *Dang de nüer* | 黨的女兒 | 党的女儿 |
| *Desperation*, aka *The Last Frenzy* (1987) | *Zuihou de fengkuang* | 最後的瘋狂 | 最后的疯狂 |

| English Title (Production Year) | Chinese Title (in *pinyin*) | Complex Script (*fantizi*) | Simplified Script (*jiantizi*) |
|---|---|---|---|
| *East Palace, West Palace* (1996) | *Donggong xigong* | 東宮西宮 | 东宫西宫 |
| *Eat Drink Man Woman* (1995) | *Yin shi nannü* | 飲食男女 | 饮食男女 |
| *Emperor and the Assassin, The* (1998) | *Xichu bawang* | 西楚霸王 | 西楚霸王 |
| *Emperor and the Assassin, The* (1999) | *Jingke ci qinwang* | 荊軻刺秦王 | 荆轲刺秦王 |
| *Fake Pretty Woman, A* (1995) | *Zhengrong* | 整容 | 整容 |
| *Farewell My Concubine* (1993) | *Bawang bie ji* | 霸王別姬 | 霸王别姬 |
| *Fist of Legend* (1994) | *Jing wu yingxiong* | 精武英雄 | 精武英雄 |
| *Fresh Kill* (1994) | *Huo sha* | 活殺 | 活杀 |
| *Frozen* (1994) | *Jinri li qiu* | 今日立秋 | 今日立秋 |
| *Girl Basketball Player No. 5* (1957) | *Nü lan wu hao* | 女藍五號 | 女蓝五号 |
| *Good Morning Beijing* (1990) | *Beijing ni zao* | 北京你早 | 北京你早 |
| *Great Wall, A* (1985) | *Beijing gushi* | 北京故事 | 北京故事 |
| *Half Flame, Half Brine* (1988) | *Yiban shi huoyan, yiban shi haishui* | 一半是火焰, 一半是海水 | 一半是火焰, 一半是海水 |
| *Happy Together* (1997) | *Chunguang zha xie* | 春光乍泄 | 春光乍泄 |
| *Hard Boiled* (1992) | *La shou shentan* | 辣手神探 | 辣手神探 |
| *Hearty Response* (1988) | *Yi gai yun tian* | 義蓋雲天 | 义盖云天 |
| *Her Fatal Ways* (1990) | *Biaojie ni hao ye* | 表姊你好嘢 | 表姐你好嘢 |
| *Heroic Trio, The* (1993) | *Dongfang san xia* | 東方三俠 | 东方三侠 |

| **English Title (Production Year)** | **Chinese Title (in *pinyin*)** | **Complex Script (*fantizi*)** | **Simplified Script (*jiantizi*)** |
|---|---|---|---|
| *He's a Woman, She's a Man* (1996) | *Jinzhi yüye* | 金枝玉葉 | 金枝玉叶 |
| *His Fatal Ways* (1991) | *Biaoge ni hao ye* | 表哥你好嘢 | 表哥你好嘢 |
| *Hole, The* (1998) | *Dong* | 洞 | 洞 |
| *Homecoming* (1984) | *Si shui liu nian* | 似水流年 | 似水流年 |
| *Hong Kong, Hong Kong* (1983) | *Nan yu nü* | 男與女 | 男与女 |
| *Horse Thief, The* (1985) | *Dao ma zei* | 盜馬賊 | 盗马贼 |
| *Hulk* (2003) | *Lü se juren* | 綠色巨人 | 绿色巨人 |
| *In Our Time:* (1982) | *Guangyin de gushi* | 光陰的故事 | 光阴的故事 |
| *Infernal Affairs* (2002) | *Wu jian dao* | 無間道 | 无间道 |
| *Infernal Affairs 2* (2003) | *Wu jian dao 2* | 無間道 2 | 无间道 2 |
| *Intimate Confessions of a Chinese Courtesan* (1972) | *Ai Nu* | 愛奴 | 爱奴 |
| *Intimates* (1997) | *Zi shu* | 自梳 | 自梳 |
| *Irma Vep* (1996) | Nüfeizei zai xian jianghu | 女飛賊再現江湖 | 女飞贼再现江湖 |
| *Journey to Beijing* (1997) | *Bei zheng* | 北征 | 北征 |
| *Judou* (1990) | *Judou* | 菊豆 | 菊豆 |
| *Keep Cool* (1997) | *You hua hao hao shuo* | 有話好好說 | 有话好好说 |
| *King of Children* (1987) | *Haizi wang* | 孩子王 | 孩子王 |
| *Kiss of Death, The* (1973) | *Du nü* | 毒女 | 毒女 |
| *Kuei Mei, A Woman* (1985) | *Wo zheyang guo le yisheng* | 我這樣過了一生 | 我这样过了一生 |

| **English Title (Production Year)** | **Chinese Title (in *pinyin*)** | **Complex Script (*fantizi*)** | **Simplified Script (*jiantizi*)** |
|---|---|---|---|
| *Life and Times of Wu Zhong Xian, The* (2003) | *Wu Zhongxian de gushi* | 吳仲賢的故事 | 吴仲贤的故事 |
| *Lights of Ten Thousand Homes* (1948) | *Wan jia deng huo* | 萬家燈火 | 万家灯火 |
| *Little Cheung* (2000) | *Xi Lu Xiang* | 細路祥 | 细路祥 |
| *Long Arm of the Law* (1984) | *Sheng gang qi bing* | 省港奇兵 | 省港奇兵 |
| *Long Arm of the Law III* (1989) | *Sheng gang qi bing III* | 省港奇兵 III | 省港奇兵 III |
| *Made in Hong Kong* (1997) | *Xianggang zhi zao* | 香港製造 | 香港制造 |
| *Mahjong* (1996) | *Majiang* | 麻將 | 麻将 |
| *Mama* (1990) | *Mama* | 媽媽 | 妈妈 |
| *Map of Sex and Love, The* (2001) | *Qing se ditu* | 情色地圖 | 情色地图 |
| *Mary from Beijing* (1992) | *Meng xing shifen* | 夢醒時分 | 梦醒时分 |
| *Masters of Mischief* | *Wanzhu* | 頑主 | 顽主 |
| *Mission, The* (2000) | *Qiang huo* | 槍火 | 枪火 |
| *Mistress, The* (1999) | *Mishi senlin* | 迷失森林 | 迷失森林 |
| *My Father is a Hero* (1995) | *Xie gei baba de xin* | 寫给爸爸的信 | 写给爸爸的信 |
| *Naked Killer* (1992) | *Chiluo gaoyang* | 赤裸羔羊 | 赤裸羔羊 |
| *New Women* (1934) | *Xin nüxing* | 新女性 | 新女性 |
| *Not One Less* (1999) | *Yi ge dou bu neng shao* | 一個都不能少 | 一个都不能少 |
| *Nurse's Diary, A* (1957) | *Hushi riji* | 護士日記 | 护士日记 |
| *Obsession*, aka *The Price of Frenzy* (1988) | *Fengkuang de daijia* | 瘋狂的代價 | 疯狂的代价 |

| English Title (Production Year) | Chinese Title (in *pinyin*) | Complex Script (*fantizi*) | Simplified Script (*jiantizi*) |
|---|---|---|---|
| *On the Hunting Ground* (1985) | *Liechang zha che* | 獵場札撤 | 猎场札撤 |
| *Oriental Moment* (1992, China Central Television [CCTV], People's Republic of China) | *Dongfang shikong* | 東方時空 | 东方时空 |
| *Out of Breath* | *Dachuanqi* | 大喘氣 | 大喘气 |
| *Peking Opera Blues* (1986) | *Dao ma dan* | 刀馬旦 | 刀马旦 |
| *Police Story* (1995) | *Minjing gushi* | 民警故事 | 民警故事 |
| *Postman, The* (1995) | *Youchai* | 郵差 | 邮差 |
| *Price of Frenzy, The* aka *Obsession* (1988) | *Fengkuang de dai jia* | 瘋狂的代價 | 疯狂的代价 |
| *Puppetmaster, The* (1993) | *Xi meng rensheng* | 戲夢人生 | 戏梦人生 |
| *Pushing Hands* (1992) | *Tui shou* | 推手 | 推手 |
| *Queer Story, A* (1996) | *Ji lao sishi* | 基佬四十 | 基佬四十 |
| *Raise the Red Lantern* (1992) | *Da hong denglong gao gao gua* | 大紅燈籠高高掛 | 大红灯笼高高挂 |
| *Rebels of the Neon God* (1992) | *Qingshaonian Ne Zha* | 青少年哪吒 | 青少年哪吒 |
| *Red Beads* (1993) | *Xuan lian* | 懸戀 | 悬恋 |
| *Red Detachment of Women* (1960; ballet 1970) | *Hongse niangzijun* | 红色娘子军 | 红色娘子军 |
| *Red Firecracker, Green Firecracker* (1994) | *Pao da shuang deng* | 炮打雙燈 | 炮打双灯 |
| *Red Sorghum* (1987) | *Honggaoliang* | 紅高粱 | 红高粱 |
| *Reincarnation of Golden Lotus, The* (1989) | *Pan Jinlian zhi giansheng jinshi* | 潘金蓮之前世今生 | 潘金莲之前世今生 |

| English Title (Production Year) | Chinese Title (in *pinyin*) | Complex Script (*fantizi*) | Simplified Script (*jiantizi*) |
|---|---|---|---|
| *River, The* (1997) | *Heliu* | 河流 | 河流 |
| *Road Home, The* (2001) | *Wo de fuqin muqin* | 我的父親母親 | 我的父亲母亲 |
| *Rock Kids* (1988) | *Yao gun Qingnian* | 摇滚青年 | 摇滚青年 |
| *Rouge* (1987) | *Yan zhi kou* | 胭脂扣 | 胭脂扣 |
| *Rush Hour* (1998) | *Huo pin shi su/ Jianfeng shike* | 火拼時速/尖峰時刻 | 火拼时速/尖峰时刻 |
| *Samsara* (1988) | *Lun hui* | 輪回 | 轮回 |
| *Sense and Sensibility* (1995) | *Lixing yu ganxing* | 理性與感性 | 理性与感性 |
| *Seventeen Years* (2000) | *Guo nian hui jia* | 過年回家 | 过年回家 |
| *Shanghai Triad* (1995) | *Yao a yao! Yao dao waipo qiao* | 搖啊搖! 搖到外婆橋 | 摇啊摇! 摇到外婆桥 |
| *Shaolin Temple* (1982) | *Shaolin si* | 少林寺 | 少林寺 |
| *Shower* (1999) | *Xi zao* | 洗澡 | 洗澡 |
| *Song of the Dragon River* (1972) | *Longjiang song* | 龍江頌 | 龙江颂 |
| *Song of Youth* | *Qingchun zhi ge* | 青春之歌 | 青春之歌 |
| *Sons* (1995) | *Erzi* | 兒子 | 儿子 |
| *Square, The* (1994) | *Guangchang* | 廣場 | 广场 |
| *Starry is the Night* (1988) | *Jinye xingguang canlan* | 今夜星光燦爛 | 今夜星光灿烂 |
| *Story of Qiu Ju,The* (1993) | *Qiu Ju da guansi* | 秋菊打官司 | 秋菊打官司 |
| *Street Angel, The* (1937) | *Malu tianshi* | 馬路天使 | 马路天使 |
| *Taipei Story* (1984) | *Qing mei zhu ma* | 青梅竹馬 | 青梅竹马 |
| *Teenage Mutant Ninja Turtles* (1987) | *Ren zhe gui* | 忍者龜 | 忍者龟 |
| *Terrorizer*, The (1986) | *Kongbu fenzi* | 恐怖份子 | 恐怖份子 |

| **English Title (Production Year)** | **Chinese Title (in *pinyin*)** | **Complex Script (*fantizi*)** | **Simplified Script (*jiantizi*)** |
|---|---|---|---|
| *That Day, On the Beach* (1983) | *Haitan de yi tian* | 海灘的一天 | 海滩的一天 |
| *This is How Steel is Made* (1997) | *Gangtie shi zenyang liancheng de* | 鋼鐵是怎樣煉成的 | 钢铁是怎样炼成的 |
| *Time to Live and a Time to Die, A* (1985) | *Tongnian wangshi* | 童年往事 | 童年往事 |
| *To Liv(e)* (1992) | *Fushi lianqu* | 浮世戀曲 | 浮世恋曲 |
| *To Live* (1994) | *Huo zhe* | 活著 | 活著 |
| *Touch of Zen, A* (1968–1970) | *Xianü* | 俠女 | 侠女 |
| *Twin Bracelets, The* (1992) | *Shuang zhuo* | 雙鐲 | 双镯 |
| *Victim* (1999) | *Mu lu xiong guang* | 目露兇光 | 目露凶光 |
| *Vietnam Girl* (1996) | *Yuenan guniang/ Bian dan guniang* | 越南姑娘/扁擔姑娘 | 越南姑娘/扁担姑娘 |
| *Village of Widows* (1989) | *Guafu cun* | 寡婦村 | 寡妇村 |
| *Vive L'Amour* (1994) | *Aiqing wansui* | 愛情萬歲 | 爱情万岁 |
| *Wedding Banquet, The* (1993) | *Xi yan* | 喜宴 | 喜宴 |
| *What Time is it There?* (2000) | *Ni na bian ji dian* | 你那邊幾點? | 你那边几点? |
| *White-haired Girl, The* (1950; ballet 1972) | *Bai mao nü* | 白毛女 | 白毛女 |
| *Who's the Woman, Who's the Man* (1996) | *Jinzhi yüye II* | 金枝玉葉 II | 金枝玉叶 II |
| *Women Flowers* (1994) | *Nüren hua* | 女人花 | 女人花 |
| *Xiao Wu* (1999) | *Xiao Wu* | 小武 | 小武 |
| *Xiu Xiu: The Sent-down Girl* (1998) | *Tian yü* | 天浴 | 天浴 |

| English Title (Production Year) | Chinese Title (in *pinyin*) | Complex Script (*fantizi*) | Simplified Script (*jiantizi*) |
|---|---|---|---|
| *Yamaha Fish Stall* (1984) | *Yamaha yu dang* | 雅馬哈魚檔 | 雅马哈鱼档 |
| *Yellow Earth* (1984) | *Huangtudi* | 黃土地 | 黄土地 |
| *Zu: Warriors from the Magic Mountain* (1983) | *Xin shushan jianxia* | 新蜀山劍俠 | 新蜀山剑侠 |

# Contributors

Grace An is Assistant Professor of French and Cinema Studies at Oberlin College and is currently working on a book manuscript titled *A Par-asian Transnational Cinema*. Her articles have appeared in *Contemporary French and Francophone Studies*, *Contemporary French Civilization*, and *Moving Image*.

Aaron D. Anderson is Associate Professor of Theater at Virginia Commonwealth University. He holds an MFA in Acting and Asian Theater from the University of Hawaii at Manoa, an Interdisciplinary PhD in Culture from Northwestern University, and teaching certificates from the Society of American Fight Directors, the British Academy of Stage and Screen Combat, and Dueling Arts International. He has worked as an actor and stuntman and taught at numerous theaters and universities throughout North America and Europe, including the Banff Center for the Performing Arts, London's City Literary Institute, the Denver Center for the Performing Arts, the Italia Conti School of Performing Arts (London), Northwestern University, the University of Illinois, and the University of Hawaii. He is a recognized expert on media violence and on the uses of theatrical training in applied social-science research, and has designed the curricula for several national and international teacher-training organizations. He is a founding member of the Clinical Communication Group, a training and research organization dedicated to improving the quality of doctor-patient interactions. Interviews with him about his research have been featured on television and radio (including National Public Radio and, internationally, on The Voice of America) and in national print media, including the *Washington Post*. His publications can be found in books and journals as diverse as *Jump Cut: A Review of Contemporary Media*, *Theatre*

*Symposium*, *Asian Journal of Communications*, *Fight Master*, and *Journal of General Internal Medicine*.

Chris Berry is Professor of Film and Television Studies in the Department of Media and Communication at Goldsmiths, University of London, where he is the Convenor of the new Screen Studies MA program. His research is focused on Chinese cinema and other Chinese screen-based media, with a particular interest in gender, sexuality, and the postcolonial politics of time and space. His publications include *Cinema and the National: China on Screen*, with Mary Farquhar (New York: Columbia University Press and Hong Kong: Hong Kong University Press, 2006); *Postsocialist Cinema in Post-Mao China: The Cultural Revolution after the Cultural Revolution* (New York: Routledge, 2004); *Island on the Edge: Taiwan New Cinema and After*, edited with Feii Lu (Hong Kong University Press, 2005); *Chinese Films in Focus: 25 New Takes*, editor (London: British Film Institute, 2003); *Mobile Cultures: New Media and Queer Asia*, edited with Fran Martin and Audrey Yue (Durham: Duke University Press, 2003); and, as translator and editor for Ni Zhen, *Memoirs from the Beijing Film Academy: The Origins of China's Fifth Generation Filmmakers* (Duke University Press, 2002). He is coediting an anthology about Chinese television and another on Chinese documentary film.

Evans Chan (website: Evanschan.com), New York-based critic and filmmaker, won a Golden Plaque at the 2005 Chicago International Television Competition for his TV short "Subway, New York." Chan's filmography includes four narrative features, *To Liv(e)* (1991), *Crossings* (1994), *Bauhinia* (2002), and *The Map of Sex and Love* (2001)), and five documentaries, including *Journey to Beijing* (1998), *Adeus Macau* (1999), and *The Life and Times of Wu Zhong Xian* (2003). His latest documentaries, *Sorceress of the New Piano –The Artistry of Margaret Leng Tan* (2004) and *The Maverick Piano* (2007), were released on DVD by Mode Records in 2008. Originally from Hong Kong, Chan has published four books, including two collections of essays, *The Last of the Chinese* (Hong Kong: Su Yeh Publishing, 1998) and *From the New Wave to the Postmodern* (Hong Kong: Hong Kong Film Critics Association, 2001), and is the editor/translator into Chinese of three books by Susan Sontag (*Selected Writings*, *Regarding the Pain of Others* and *Under the Sign of Saturn*, all published by Taiwan's Rye Field Books). Chan has also written a play that was produced Off Broadway in New York: *The Naked Earth*, based on an Eileen Chang novel, was presented at the Bank Street Theatre in 2000. His writings in English can be seen in *Cinemaya*, *Asian Cinema*, *Film International* and *Postmodern Culture*.

Li-Mei Chang graduated from Wayne State University, Detroit. Her doctoral dissertation focused on Hong Kong cinema's response to the city's postcoloniality. Chang was an assistant professor of film studies at Fu-Jen University, Taipei, and has translated *New Vocabularies in Film Semiotics* into Chinese. She is based near London and is working as a creative writer and photographer. She can be contacted at limei828@yahoo.com.

Peter X Feng is Associate Professor of English and Women's Studies at the University of Delaware, where he teaches film history, Asian American Studies, and cultural studies. An expert on Asian Americans and the media, he has authored

*Identities in Motion: Asian American Film & Video* (Durham: Duke University Press, 2002), edited *Screening Asian Americans* (New Brunswick: Rutgers University Press, 2002), and coedited a special issue of *Journal of Asian American Studies* on Asian American Cultural Production. His articles on Asian Americans in film and popular culture have appeared in *Cineaste*, *Jump Cut*, *Amerasia Journal*, and *Cinema Journal*, as well as in *Countervisions: Asian American Film Criticism* (edited by Darrell Hamamoto and Sandra Liu, 2000) and *Aliens R Us: The Other in Science Fiction* (edited by Zia Sardar and Sean Cubitt, 2002).

FRANCES GATEWARD is Assistant Professor of Film Studies in the Department of Media Studies at Ursinus College. Her work has been published in a number of journals and anthologies. She is the editor of *Zhang Yimou: Interviews* (Jackson, MS: University Press of Mississippi, 2001) and *Seoul Searching: Culture and Identity in Contemporary Korean Cinema* (Albany: SUNY, 2007), and coeditor of *Sugar Spice and Everything Nice:Cinemas of Girlhood* (Detroit, Wayne State University, 2002) and *Where the Boys Are: Cinemas of Masculinity and Youth* (Detroit, Wayne State University, 2005). She is currently finishing a book on African American women filmmakers.

ANDREW GROSSMAN is an independent scholar, filmmaker, and the editor of the anthology *Queer Asian Cinema: Shadows in the Shade* (Binghamton: Harrington Park Press, 2001). Specializing in criticism with queer, transgressive, and anticapitalist themes, he is an associate editor of and frequent contributor to the online periodical *Bright Lights Film Journal*. His documentary film *Not That Kind of Christian!!* premiered internationally at the 2007 Montreal World Film Festival. He is currently working on a second documentary about alternative sexuality and leftist politics in post-Sandinista Nicaragua.

PETER HITCHCOCK is Professor of Literary and Cultural Studies at the Graduate Center and Baruch College of the City University of New York. His books include *Imaginary States: Studies in Cultural Transnationalism* (Urbana: University of Illinois, 2003), *Oscillate Wildly: Space, Body, and Spirit of Millennial Materialism* (Minneapolis: University of Minnesota, 1998), and *Dialogics of the Oppressed* (Minneapolis: University of Minnesota,1993).

Coeditor OF *Jump Cut: A Review of Contemporary Media*, CHUCK KLEINHANS teaches in the Radio/Television/Film Department at Northwestern University. His current research centers on the relation of economic and ideological analysis of Hollywood film.

JENNY KWOK-WAH Lau teaches in the Department of Cinema at San Francisco State University. She has published on the subject of globalization and pan-Chinese cinema in various journals, books, and encyclopedia, including her book *Multiple Modernities: Cinemas and Popular Media in Transcultural East Asia* (Philadelphia: Temple University Press, 2003).

HELEN LEUNG, Hok-Sze is Assistant Professor in the Department of Women Studies at Simon Fraser University, Canada. Her research interest includes Hong Kong media culture, Chinese cinema, queer and transgender cultural politics in Asia, and issues of nationalism and postcoloniality. She has published numerous articles on queer cinema and is the author of *Undercurrents: Queer Culture and Postcolonial Hong Kong* (Vancouver: University of British Columbia Press; Hong Kong: Hong Kong University Press, 2008).

GINA MARCHETTI (PhD, Northwestern University) teaches in the Department of Comparative Literature, School of Humanities, at the University of Hong Kong. In 1995, her book *Romance and the "Yellow Peril": Race, Sex and Discursive Strategies in Hollywood Fiction* (Berkeley: University of California, 1993) won the award for best book in the area of cultural studies from the Association for Asian American Studies. Her recent books include *Andrew Lau and Alan Mak's Infernal Affairs (2002–2003)* (Hong Kong: Hong Kong University Press, 2007), *From Tian'anmen to Times Square: Transnational China and the Chinese Diaspora on Global Screens* (Philadelphia: Temple University Press, 2006), and *Hong Kong Film, Hollywood and the New Global Cinema*, coedited with Tan See-Kam (London: Routledge, 2007).

AARON HAN JOON MAGNAN-PARK (Ph.D. University of Iowa) is Assistant Professor of Film in the Department of Film, Television, and Theatre at the University of Notre Dame. He has published on Hong Kong action cinema in *The Politics of Community*, edited by Michael Strysick (Aurora, CO: Davies Group, 2002) and in *Hong Kong Film, Hollywood and the New Global Cinema: No Film is an Island*, edited by Gina Marchetti and Tan See Kam (New York: Routledge, 2007). Publications on contemporary Korean cinema appear in New Korean Cinema, edited by Chi-Yun Shin and Julian Stringer (New York: New York University Press, 2005), *The Korean Herald*, and in *Towards Sustainable Economic and Security Relations in East Asia: U. S. and ROK Policy Issues, edited by James M. Lister* (Washington, DC: Korean Economic Institute, 2007). His areas of expertise include pan-Asian cinema, sound theory, transnational culture, racialism, and the international action cinema. He has taught at Victoria University of Wellington, the University of Iowa, Illinois State University, Illinois Wesleyan University, the American University of Paris, and the Université de Paris IV-Sorbonne.

SEE-KAM TAN (PhD, University of Melbourne, Australia) is Associate Professor of Communication at the University of Macau, Macao SAR, China, and has taught at various tertiary institutions in Australia and Singapore. Tan has been published in *Antithesis, Asian Cinema, Cinemaya, Intermedia, Jump Cut, Media Asia, Screen, Social Semiotic*, and *South East Asian Journal of Social Science*. He also has contributed chapters to *Queer Asian Cinema: Shadows in the Shade* (New York: Harrington Park Press, 2000), *Between Home and World: A Reader in Hong Kong Cinema* (Hong Kong: Oxford University Press, 2004), *Chinese Films in Focus: 25 New Takes* (London: British Film Institute, 2004), and *The Cinema of Small Nations* (Edinburgh: Edinburgh University Press, 2008). Tan is coediter of *Hong Kong Film, Hollywood and the New Global Cinema: No Film Is an Island* (London: Routledge, 2007), as well as a special issue on "Gender in Asian Cinema" for *Asian Journal of Communication* (2001)—both with Gina Marchetti. He is working on a monograph on Tsui Hark's *Peking Opera Blues* for Hong Kong University Press.

GAYLE WALD is Professor of English at George Washington University, where she teaches African American literature and popular culture. Her biography *Shout, Sister, Shout: The Untold Story of Rock-and-Roll Trailblazer Sister Rosetta Tharpe* (Boston: Beacon Press 2007) was a *New York Times* Editor's Choice book. She is also author of *Crossing the Line* (Durham: Duke University Press 2000), about U.S. narratives of racial passing. With You-me Park, she has written about the connections between Asian American and African American women writers in *American Literature* (1998).

ESTHER C. M. YAU teaches in the Department of Comparative Literature, School of Humanities, at the University of Hong Kong. She has published many essays on Chinese cinema. She is the coeditor of *New Chinese Cinemas: Form, Identity, Politics* (Cambridge: Cambridge University Press, 1994) and "Asian Pacific Cinemas: A Spectral Surface" (*positions*, fall, 2001), and the editor of *At Full Speed: Hong Kong Cinema in a Borderless World* (Minneapolis: University of Minnesota Press, 2001).

EMILIE YUEH-YU Yeh is Professor of Film Studies, Director of the Centre for Media and Communication Research, and Associate Director of the David Lam C. Institute for East-West Studies at Hong Kong Baptist University. Her publications include *Taiwan Film Directors: A Treasure Island* (New York: Columbia University Press, 2005, coauthor), *Chinese-Language Film: Historiography, Poetics, Politics* (Honolulu: Hawai'i University Press, 2005, coeditor), and *East Asian Screen Industry* (London: British Film Institute, 2008, coauthor).

XUELIN ZHOU is a senior lecturer in the Department of Film, Television, and Media Studies, University of Auckland, New Zealand. He is the author of *Young Rebels in Contemporary Chinese Cinema* (Hong Kong: Hong Kong University Press, 2007). His current research interest is on youth culture in Chinese-language cinema.

# Index